Further praise for *Exorcising Hitler*:

EXORCISING HITLER

The Occupation and Denazification of Germany

FREDERICK TAYLOR

BLOOMSBURY

LONDON · BERLIN · NEW YORK · SYDNEY

First published in Great Britain 2011

This paperback edition published 2012

Copyright © Frederick Taylor 2011
Maps by John Gilkes

Excerpts from Wladimir Gelfand, *Deutschland-Tagebuch 1945–1946: Aufzeichnungen eines Rotarmisten. A. d. Russischen von Anja Lutter und Hartmut Schröder* © Aufbau Verlag GmbH & Co. KG, Berlin 2005

Excerpts from Noel Annan, *Changing Enemies*, copyright © 1995 Noel Annan. Reproduced by permission of the author c/o Rogers, Coleridge & White Ltd, 20 Powis Mews, London W11 1JN

Excerpt from George Clare, *Berlin Days*, copyright © George Clare 1989, reproduced by kind permission of Pan Macmillan, London

Excerpt from *To the Victors the Spoils* by Colin MacInnes, reproduced by kind permission of the Colin MacInnes Estate and the publishers, Allison and Busby Ltd. Copyright © 1950 by the Colin MacInnes Estate

Excerpt from Diarmuid Jeffreys, *Hell's Cartel*, published by Bloomsbury

Bloomsbury Publishing Plc
36 Soho Square
London W1D 3QY

www.bloomsbury.com

Bloomsbury Publishing, London, New York and Berlin
A CIP catalogue record for this book is available from the British Library

ISBN 978 1 4088 2212 8

10 9 8 7 6 5 4 3 2 1

Typeset by Hewer Text UK Ltd, Edinburgh
Printed in Great Britain by Clays Limited, St Ives plc

To Götz Bergander, Joachim Trenkner and Helmut Schnatz, who were born to a regime founded in war and intolerance but, along with so many others, helped to build something much, much better in its place.

All the time I am asking myself why this misfortune came over me. How have I deserved this? What have I done that one has to treat me like a criminal? That so many people died in Belsen – I could not alter that any more. It is all my fate and maybe I shall even be punished for that.

> – Josef Kramer, commandant of Belsen concentration camp, in a letter to his wife before his execution

Lily the Werwolf is my name.
Hoo, Hoo, Hoo,
I bite, I eat, I am not tame.
Hoo, Hoo, Hoo.
My Werwolf teeth bite the enemy,
And then he's done and then he's gone,
Hoo, Hoo, Hoo.

> – the song 'Werwolf Lily', broadcast to 'German youth' by the radio station of the Nazi *Werwolf* resistance, spring 1945

Your attitude toward women is wrong – in Germany. You'll see a lot of good-looking babes on the make there. German women have been trained to seduce you. Is it worth a knife in the back?

> – booklet for the guidance of GIs in Germany, late 1944

German people, you must know that if the war is lost, you will be annihilated! The Jew with his infinite hatred stands behind this concept of annihilation. And if the German people loses here, then its next ruler will be the Jew! And what a Jew is, this must be known to you. And if anyone doesn't know about the revenge of Juda, let him read about it. This war is not the Second World War, this war is the great racial war.

> – Reichsmarschall Hermann Goering, Harvest Thanksgiving Speech, Berlin Sportpalast, 4 October 1942

God, I hate the Germans.

> – General Dwight D. Eisenhower in a letter to his wife Mamie, September 1944

Contents

Acknowledgements

My profound thanks are due to all who agreed to be interviewed for *Exorcising Hitler* about their experiences during the 1940s, in the process sometimes revisiting traumatic experiences for themselves and their families. Their names are listed at the back of this book.

I am also especially grateful to Steven Simon and Virginia Liberatore, who extended generous hospitality to my wife and me during our working visit to Washington DC. Dr Helmut Schnatz and Frau Ursula Schnatz were extraordinarily kind and attentive hosts in Koblenz, where they further provided me with a number of introductions that led to fascinating conversations about what happened in their beloved city during those grim years of defeat and deprivation.

The staff of the National Archives at Kew, London, and the National Archives and Records Administration at College Park, Maryland, were, as usual, helpful, informative and patient in their dealings.

For their constant – not to say ruthless – encouragement, I should also gratefully acknowledge my agent in Britain, Jane Turnbull, and Dan Conaway at Writers' House in New York. And for all the afore-mentioned, plus a strong dollop of patience, Bill Swainson, my editor at Bloomsbury Publishing in London.

Finally, the warmest of thank-yous to Alice, my wife, who not only provided domestic and editorial support but also tirelessly and skil-fully photographed documents during our archival research trips. As ever, I could have done none of this without her.

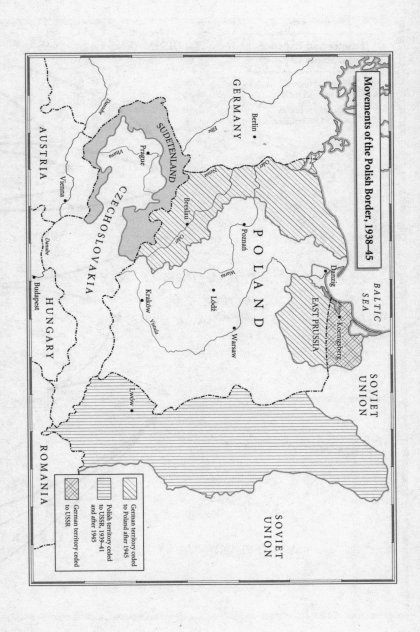

Movements of the Polish Border, 1938–45

German territory ceded
to Poland after 1945

Polish territory ceded
to USSR, 1939–41
and after 1945

German territory ceded
to USSR

GERMANY

Berlin

Elbe

Oder

Neisse

BALTIC
SEA

Danzig

EAST PRUSSIA

Königsberg

SUDETENLAND

Prague

Vltava

Danube

CZECHOSLOVAKIA

Breslau

Oder

Poznań

P O L A N D

Łódź

Kraków

Vistula

Warsaw

Warta

AUSTRIA

Vienna

Danube

Budapest

HUNGARY

ROMANIA

Lwow

SOVIET
UNION

SOVIET
UNION

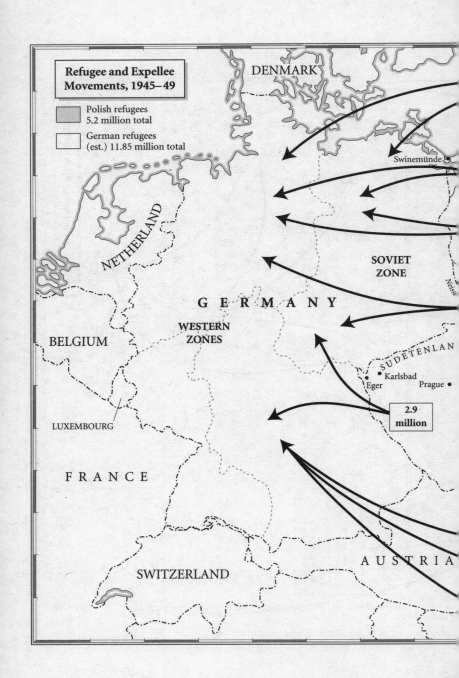

Refugee and Expellee Movements, 1945–49

- Polish refugees 5.2 million total
- German refugees (est.) 11.85 million total

DENMARK

Swinemünde

SOVIET ZONE

Neisse

GERMANY

NETHERLAND

WESTERN ZONES

BELGIUM

SUDETENLAN

Eger • Karlsbad

Prague •

2.9 million

LUXEMBOURG

FRANCE

SWITZERLAND

AUSTRIA

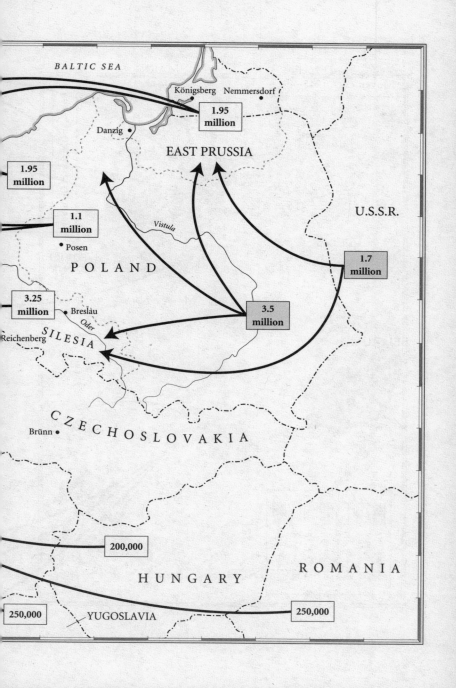

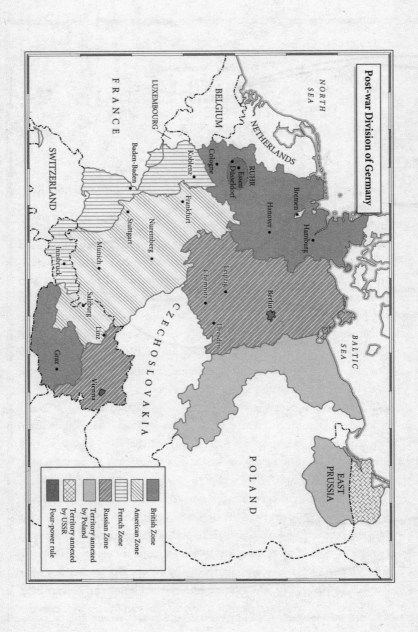

Post-war Division of Germany

NORTH SEA

NETHERLANDS

BELGIUM

LUXEMBOURG

FRANCE

SWITZERLAND

Baden-Baden

Koblenz

Cologne

RUHR
Essen
Düsseldorf

Bremen

Hanover

Hamburg

Frankfurt

Stuttgart

Nuremberg

Munich

Innsbruck

Salzburg

Linz

Graz

Vienna

Chemnitz

Leipzig

Dresden

Berlin

CZECHOSLOVAKIA

BALTIC SEA

POLAND

EAST PRUSSIA

British Zone

American Zone

French Zone

Russian Zone

Territory annexed by Poland

Territory annexed by USSR

Four-power rule

Introduction

In the spring of 1945, the four major powers that had defeated Hitler's armies took an unprecedentedly drastic step: they abolished Germany's sovereign government and took direct control of its territory. A few months later, Allied Military Administration was also imposed on Germany's main co-combatant in the Second World War, the Japanese empire. With these acts, the victorious Allies undertook what most people at the time thought of as an exceptional and final exercise in foreign military occupation of hitherto independent peoples. From now on, with the world cleansed of aggressive war, such measures would no longer be necessary.

Partly due to pressure from America and Russia, the two 'post-colonial' superpowers created by the Second World War, the British, French and Dutch empires soon began to dissolve. India, Burma and Indonesia quickly gained their independence, to be followed, as the 1950s and 1960s progressed, by huge areas of Asia and Africa. The model for the post-war world would, so the largely American-sponsored orthodoxy had it, be one of national sovereignty and self-government. Aggressive wars of choice, campaigns of gratuitous conquest, would no longer be tolerated, and those on the enemy side who had conducted, in the view of the Allies, such a war between 1939 and 1945 would be punished. Hence the Nuremberg and Tokyo war crimes trials that followed the surrenders of Germany and Japan.

There was, of course, a key difference between the occupations of Germany and Japan after 1945. Although in the case of both countries the Allies had demanded unconditional surrender, the Japanese were in the final analysis – for pragmatic reasons –permitted a condition, which was that they could keep their emperor. Only in the case of Germany was all government, from the highest national level to the most parochial, taken, at the moment of surrender, completely into the victors' hands, and the German people thereby entirely delivered up to the mercy of their erstwhile enemies.

Who, more than sixty years ago, would have ever thought that, in the first decade of the twenty-first century, two of those Western powers would be again conducting military occupations of formerly sovereign states? And who would have predicted that those new occupations, after the crucial learning experiences of 1945, would be so halting, so clumsy, so violently problematic?

The invasion of Iraq by America and its coalition allies brought the swift demise of Saddam Hussein's pseudo-fascist Ba'athist state, and the country's occupation by foreign forces. In many respects, the victorious coalition's strategy, such as it was, seemed to resemble that employed by the Western Allies for their occupation of Germany in the wake of Nazism – that is, immediate demilitarisation of the defeated, along with temporary abolition of sovereign government, pending elimination of security threats and political cleansing, in this case 'De-Ba'athification'. Then, finally, punishment of those guilty of political crimes, to be followed by step-by-step introduction of West-ern-style free institutions and representative government.

It is no spoiler to state here and now that after 1945 this recipe for the reconstruction and rehabilitation of the defeated nations was, with hindsight and in the longer term, a success. All we need to do is look at twenty-first-century Germany. There were reasons for this, some obvious and some not. First, to stick to Germany, it was true that the country in May 1945 was absolutely defeated. In November 1918, by contrast, though exhausted and starved and already in the throes of internal revolution, Germany had still been fighting stubbornly on French and Belgian soil when she conceded the truce that eventually brought the First World War to an end.

The German state survived this peace, although authoritarian monarchical rule was abolished. The Reich's government and constitution became democratic, but the official and military classes remained both influential and fervently nationalist, eager to evade the provisions of the harsh Versailles Treaty and secretly longing to avenge what they saw as an unjust defeat – one that they blamed, in great measure, on the revolutionaries who had overthrown the Kaiser.

That pre-war, authoritarian core regained more and more control as the Depression took hold in the 1930s and the democracy set up in 1918 correspondingly lost support to both extreme left and extreme right. It was this elite's representatives, especially the clique surrounding the senile President (and former First World War field marshal) Paul von Hindenburg, who handed over the reins of government to Adolf Hitler and his Nazi Party on 30 January 1933.

Many Germans, even non-Nazis, refused to admit that their armies had been vanquished in 1918. These restless millions also saw the ceasefire and the consequent harsh peace as due to treachery by the democratic government that had supplanted the monarchy after the November revolution. Their stubborn opposition, married with the Weimar Republic's recurrent economic difficulties, had kept the new democracy permanently weak.

In 1918 the Reich had been allowed to retain not just its own government but even its army, which had withdrawn across the country's borders when peace came, marching back through the Brandenburg Gate in Berlin almost like returning victors. True, under the Treaty of Versailles, the size of the army was drastically reduced, but, now called the *Reichswehr*, it nevertheless remained a key state player. The deadly bacillus (as many foreigners saw it) of German authoritarianism and militarism had thus been permitted to survive, then to recover and thrive.

The result, according to this interpretation, was that a little over twenty years after Germany's defeat the infection had begun once more to spread its horrors throughout Europe – this time in an even more virulent National Socialist form, which included the added toxicity of racism, and especially a murderous anti-Semitism.

By the time the Allies approached the borders of Hitler's Germany in the autumn of 1944, they had already prepared for what lay ahead. First, of course, the invasion of Germany itself. Fanatical resistance was expected from many Germans, soldiers and civilians alike, both during the coming battles and even after the fighting within the borders of the Reich concluded. As a consequence, it was even more important that the German nation see itself as comprehensively defeated. The relentless and often indiscriminate bombing of German cities, continuing almost until the very end of the war, although primarily undertaken for military-industrial reasons, was also intended to induce this sense of inevitable and final national collapse and thus help prevent a repeat of what had happened after 1918.

Above all, there were to be no negotiations with the Nazis. Unlike in 1918, Germany must surrender unconditionally, placing its fate and the future shape of its government wholly in the control of the victorious powers. No refuge for the evil bacillus this time.

The unconditional surrender policy seems to have been suggested by a sub-committee within the American State Department and to have been presented by Roosevelt to his initially reluctant British ally during the bilateral conference held in Casablanca, Morocco, between 14 and 24 January 1943.[1]

Roosevelt himself had already put the case succinctly in his New Year message to Congress a week or so earlier, when he told the American people's representatives that he 'shuddered to think what will happen to mankind, ourselves included, if this war ends with incomplete victory'.[2]

In any case, what could the Allies, collectively or individually, have offered, in the case of a negotiated peace agreement? And to whom? If the Nazi regime remained in place, would they have talked terms to Hitler, or to a putative Nazi successor, such as Himmler or Goebbels or Goering? After all the bloodshed and suffering, this was surely unacceptable. Moreover, it would leave an inherently warlike political system intact. And if the Nazi regime had been overthrown, say by the 20 July conspirators? Were these not the men (and a few women) who had for the most part supported Hitler until things started to go wrong? Though personally often decent, did they not represent the same classes of landowners, officers and industrialists who had formed, most Allied thinkers agreed, the root of the 'German problem' even before Hitler vaulted into power in 1933?

From the Allied coalition's point of view, the logic of unconditional surrender was strong, but like all decisions of this kind it caused almost as many problems as it solved. It provided a propaganda bonus for the Nazi regime, whose propagandists could tell the German people, with literal truth, that the Allies planned to dismantle the German nation state. Aware of this drawback, the Allies were keen to emphasise that the policy did not necessarily foreshadow harsh treatment. At the press conference at the end of the Casablanca Conference in January 1943, Roosevelt himself said: 'Unconditional Surrender does not mean the destruction of the German population but does mean the destruction of a philosophy in Germany, Italy and Japan which is based on the conquest and subjugation of other peoples.' 'Peace,' he added, 'can come to the world only by the total elimination of German and Japanese war power.'[3]

Despite his initial misgivings, Churchill publicly supported unconditional surrender, realising that for all its disadvantages it also forestalled possible sources of division among the disparate Allies. All the final, detailed decisions about how to handle post-war Germany could await the Reich's defeat. The British Prime Minister's attempts to minimise the German population's fears were, however, not entirely successful. Speaking in the House of Commons in London, he said:

Unconditional surrender means that the victors have a free hand. It does not mean that they are entitled to behave in a barbarous manner nor that they wish to blot out Germany from among the nations of Europe. If we are bound, we are bound by our own consciences to civilisation. We are not to be bound to the Germans as the result of a bargain struck. That is the meaning of 'unconditional surrender'.[4]

Such clumsy half-assurances were not frequently repeated, perhaps with good reason, for even when couched in ringing Churchillian phrases they were at best useless, at worst counter-productive.

It was no coincidence that the other major strategic agreement that emerged from Casablanca in January 1943 was for the so-called joint air offensive, a coordinated Anglo-American bombing campaign designed to bring Germany to its knees – or at least to persuade a hard-pressed Stalin, in the absence of an immediate Western invasion of continental Europe, that his allies were establishing another 'front', albeit in the air. During the following year, massive, increasingly indiscriminate air raids against German cities cost the lives of around 40,000 civilians in Hamburg and up to 10,000 in Kassel, with 10,000 more deaths caused by the systematic British bombing campaign against Berlin between November 1943 and March 1944. Altogether, in excess of half a million would die in these Anglo-American raids before the campaign was halted towards the end of April 1945. The level of destruction was apocalyptic.

The people of Germany might therefore have been less than fully convinced of the value of the Allied leaders' 'consciences to civilisation'. And, of course, those who knew about the full extent of the Nazi atrocities in occupied Europe and Russia had even less reason to trust in the kindness of the enemy strangers beating at the door of the German homeland.

All the same, after Stalingrad many – perhaps most – Germans had become disillusioned with Hitler. It was the final change of mood among several.

It was true that, even in the half-free elections of March 1933, held soon after the Führer came to power, the majority of the country still didn't vote for him, although with his coalition partner, the conservative-nationalist DNVP, he scraped together a touch under 52 per cent of the total.

Hitler's urgent action programme, immediately tackling unemployment and the industrial crisis, led to a further surge in popularity that increased even more spectacularly when he succeeded in remilitarising the Rhineland and organising the incorporation of Austria and the Sudetenland into the Reich – all without war. Then, when he pushed his luck too far and war came, not just with Poland but with Britain and France, the mood of his people was subdued, even sullen. Most Germans would tolerate dictatorship, were grateful for full employment and a foreign policy that gave the country back its lost self-respect. But they knew enough – in the case of the older generation remembered enough – to fear another European war above all things.

Then, however, Hitler presented his countrymen with a series of victories they had scarcely dared hope for. Poland was subjugated and divided between Germany and the Soviet Union. The Wehrmacht took Denmark and Norway, then crushed France, the old enemy, and the armies of the Low Countries. Under Hitler's leadership, the nation avenged the shame of Versailles, and drove the British into the sea.

By the summer of 1940 Hitler was, for most, the nation's hero; the greatest statesman since Bismarck, the 'greatest military commander of all time'. That last laurel had been awarded to the Führer by his Chief of Staff, General Keitel, after the victory over France.

Cunningly amended, this classic little slice of courtier's flattery would spread itself around in a virus-like fashion after the attack on Russia failed, German troops began to die or surrender in their hundreds of thousands, and the great retreat back into the Reich began. From 1943, Hitler would be referred to sarcastically by ordinary Germans as 'Gröfaz' – a play on the regime's addiction to acronyms – standing for *Grösster Feldherr aller Zeiten* (greatest military commander of all time). Thus began Hitler's final slump in the estimate of his compatriots, the one that ended only with his death on 30 April 1945. So, whatever the reality, before Stalingrad Hitler seemed self-evidently a genius. After Stalingrad, and especially by the beginning of 1945, to all except a tiny, fanatical minority, the Führer looked like a loser.

Another Nazi leader commonly referred to by a nickname at street level was Hermann Goering, the Reich Marshal and Commander of the Luftwaffe. He had famously commented, when the war began, that if the British ever managed to drop bombs on German soil, then 'my name is Mayer'.[5] Sure enough, as the British, later Anglo-American bombing offensive intensified over the next five years, and Germany's cities were reduced to ruins, the plump and deceptively jolly-looking Goering became in popular parlance 'Mayer'.

As with the Führer's Gröfaz soubriquet, Goering's transformation into Mayer represented a serious loss of trust in the regime of which he was a prominent figurehead. After 1943, Hitler was clearly losing the war on land, while the once-admired creator of the Luftwaffe could do nothing to stop the Allied bomber fleets laying waste to the cities of the Reich, killing and injuring hundreds of thousands of ordinary civilians and making many more homeless.

For a regime such as the Nazi one, whose entire ideology embodied the worship of strength and superior force, the one unimaginable, unforgivable fault was failure. In fact, such failure, according to the movement's racist, socially Darwinist precepts, should have been impossible. The German race represented the very pinnacle of humanity and therefore, if led by the perfect leader (Hitler) and organised in the perfect (Nazi) state, they must triumph. It became clear to most in 1943–4 that this would not be the case. Barring a miracle, at least.

And what might this 'miracle' be?

First, there remained the vague hope for some diehards that Germany's armies, supplied by the Reich's efficient war industries – which until late 1944 had survived the Allied bombing onslaught disrupted but still surprisingly productive – might yet find it in themselves to withstand the enemy. This hope diminished to almost nothing after the successful Anglo-American landing in Normandy and the rapid advance that followed.

Second, the regime's talk of 'miracle weapons' that would turn the tables at the last moment remained a straw at which a surprisingly large number of Germans clutched. The V1 flying bomb, and then the V2 rocket, while certainly wonders of German technology, proved disappointingly limited in their effects on Allied morale and industrial and architectural substance alike. Despite Goebbels-inspired propaganda reports of the apocalyptic damage wrought by these new weapons on British cities, ordinary German citizens' hopes quickly faded there, too. The same went for the remarkable Type XXI submarine, the so-called 'Elektroboot' – only a few of which were ready to put to sea before the end of the war – and the revolutionary Messerschmitt jet fighter, which again was produced in numbers too small to make a real difference.

And third, many Germans – from Hitler and Goebbels down – hoped and believed that the unlikely coalition of plutocrats and communists formed by Britain, America and the Soviet Union could not last the distance; that this coalition of convenience would somehow falter and crack in the face of impending Allied victory, reflecting the deep and ultimately irreconcilable ideological and political conflicts that lay beneath its surface. There were, of course, many who recalled the even more bizarre compact between Hitler and Stalin in August 1939, which had endured less than two years and ended in the epic and savage bloodshed of Operation Barbarossa.

What seemed like just such a possible turning point presented itself when President Roosevelt died suddenly in mid-April 1945. Goebbels rushed to Hitler's bunker and excitedly informed the Führer: 'The Tsarina is dead.' To Hitler, a keen student of the career of Prussia's greatest monarch, Frederick the Great, Goebbels' words would have instantly conjured up hope.

The Propaganda Minister's pronouncement referred to the sudden death of Empress Elizabeth of Russia in 1762, at the height of the Seven Years War. With her armies occupying Berlin, and Frederick the Great steeling himself to sue for a humiliating peace (in fact, contemplating suicide as a decent alternative), Elizabeth's demise triggered the succession of the young Tsar Peter III. The new Russian ruler, German-born and a great admirer of Prussia, promptly withdrew from the war, imposing no claims on the kingdom that had just a few weeks earlier seemed on the brink of extinction.

Within six months, Peter had been deposed and murdered, and his successor, Catherine II, had re-entered the war on the Franco-Austrian side, but Frederick had used the breathing space well. The peace treaties that followed in 1763 favoured Prussia and her chief ally, Great Britain.

No such new 'miracle' occurred when Harry S. Truman succeeded FDR. The level-headed former senator from Missouri was a very different man from Roosevelt in many ways, but he had no game-changing plan. The great alliance held, at least for the moment. And the inexorable Allied advance into Germany from East and West continued.

The Wehrmacht conducted a surprisingly determined resistance, even in the west, at least until the beginning of 1945. The initial Anglo-American advance, after the breakout from the beachhead, was surprisingly swift, but it came to an equally surprising and abrupt halt after the falls of Paris and Brussels. In September 1944, attempts to seize a Rhine crossing at Arnhem failed disastrously. Although American troops had a fleeting opportunity to breach that barrier in Alsace, the moment quickly passed and German resistance stiffened noticeably. Thousands of British and American troops died during the autumn and early winter, hammering away at the unexpectedly tough German defences. Twenty-four thousand Americans were killed, wounded or captured between September and December during the fight for the Hürtgen Forest, just inside Germany. More than 2,000 of General Patton's men died taking the eastern French city of Metz in the last week of November.

Then, less than a month later, came the German counter-attack in the Ardennes (the so-called 'Battle of the Bulge'). Some 19,000 American troops were killed, most during the first few days, and many more wounded or taken prisoner, the US Army's worst losses of the entire war in Europe. There were also 100,000 German casualties in this shockingly violent, if ultimately unsuccessful attempt to show that the Wehrmacht still had teeth.

Even after the Rhine was finally crossed at Remagen in early March 1945, Germany's soldiers – many under or over age, or the desperate combings of hitherto exempt employment groups – made the Allies pay dear for every kilometre of the homeland they occupied. For a great deal of the time the Anglo-American (and by now Free French) forces had to fight village to village and house to house against stubborn resistance.

Only after the surrender, in the second week of April, of more than a third of a million German soldiers in the critically important Ruhr industrial area, and the beginning of the Russians' final advance on Berlin, did the Wehrmacht begin to collapse in any meaningful sense. And even then, in the east, where the fear of Russian vengeance was greater than despair, many Germans fought on grimly to the end. They fought for their capital, Berlin – the capture of which cost the Russians some 80,000 men – and so that their comrades, and any civilians who could do so, might manage to surrender to the Western Allies rather than to the Soviet forces.

The brutal fate of German prisoners of war in Soviet hands was already well known (as was the even more savage treatment of Soviet troops by the Germans). As for Soviet behaviour towards civilians, many Red Army units had already gained a deserved reputation for rape, murder and pillage.

Although most of those fighting for Germany had ceased to care about anything much beyond survival and saving what they could of their people and heritage, there were undoubtedly fanatics among the German population right to the end of the war and beyond. There were rumours on the Allied side of minutely organised resistance cells composed largely of brainwashed Nazi youth, of 'stay-behind' terror groups, and of a planned withdrawal by the regime's rabid remnants into the near-impregnable so-called 'Alpine Redoubt', the mountainous region on the German/Austrian border.

Some experience with so-called *Werwolf* resistance units in both east and west – and, most spectacularly, the organised assassination by a Nazi hit squad of the American-appointed High Burgomaster of the western German city of Aachen in March 1945 – caused the Allies, as they advanced inexorably into the heartlands of the Reich, to act with circumspection and not a little resentment of the native population. The Germans, it seemed, just would not admit defeat.

Even though the supposed 'Redoubt' proved a chimera, there was enough evidence in individual acts of resistance – not forgetting the ghastly revelations of concentration camps and prisons captured during the Allied advance – to sour the average GI's or Tommy's view of the defeated. This would make for a nervous, unforgiving and sometimes aggressive relationship with the conquered Germans during those early months, an understandable attitude on the part of the vulnerable individual soldier. More ominously, it would also be reflected in the lobbies and conference rooms of Washington and London, where by this time the hardline attitude had, at least temporarily, gained the upper hand. The word 'revenge' might not be uttered openly, but German collective guilt and an Allied policy of, in effect, collective punishment were soon unspoken assumptions, guiding the actions of the victors in the time shortly before and after the surrender.

Civilian Affairs officers in the American army, trained before embarkation to administer and liaise in the liberated territories, and their rough equivalents in the Russian, British and French forces, became, once the border of the Reich was crossed, officials of the Military Government of Germany. The rules were now different. In the former German-occupied countries, relations with the locals had mostly been friendly and expected to be such. Even in the (fairly frequent) cases of misunderstandings and bad behaviour by Allied troops, enough basic goodwill remained to make the overall picture a happy one. After all, for the vast majority of civilians in all the formerly German-occupied countries, freedom felt better than captivity. And, more importantly, although there were problems and shortages, there was now hope that these would get better with time.

The moment they crossed into Germany, the advancing Allied troops knew they were no longer among friends. This did not mean that the bulk of the German population necessarily hated them, or wanted them dead, or even that it planned to resist. The difference was visible, even in the last border town of a just-liberated country such as France,

Belgium or Holland. The liberated locals' response was to display their own, often long-hidden, national flag, perhaps combined with the flag of the liberators, if they possessed or could quickly make one. Across the line in Germany, mostly there was nothing. Germans shut themselves in their houses. If anything was displayed, it was a white flag, often improvised from a bed sheet hung out of an upstairs window, unreadable beyond its basic message of surrender.

Germany, as it came under Allied control, resembled a blank object, a clean sheet. What government or political life had existed there before was viewed by the conquerors as unremittingly evil. In Belgium or Holland or Norway, even in the more frenetic and complicated conditions of Italy and Greece, the aim was to restore something like the situation that had existed before the fascists took power (the situation in Poland and Eastern Europe was different for a number of reasons, most notably because the Soviet 'liberators' had an aggressive and radical political agenda of their own). In Germany, however, the first aim was unquestionably to get rid of what was presently there, to destroy the fabric of Nazi totalitarian control, not just in the administration but throughout industry, the arts, education and the sciences.

The question of what should, or could, replace these malevolent structures was much less clear and, in the initial stages, largely irrelevant. Germany had first to be secured by and for the occupiers, a task that was not expected to lack danger or difficulty. Aside from the likelihood of fanatical, *Werwolf*-style resistance, there was a vast, defeated German army of five million or so to be disarmed, detained, its surrendered ranks checked for war criminals and politically dangerous individuals. The weeding out and neutralisation of these latter categories was a process that combined the two most pressing tasks of the occupiers – the securing of the occupation from potential enemies and the parallel political cleansing of the country itself.

The situation discussed between the Allies at the Yalta Conference in February 1945, with victory still months away, was not the same as that which, half a brutally eventful year later, formed the basis of the arguments at their post-war meeting in Potsdam, just outside the recently conquered German capital.

By the time the Potsdam proceedings began, Hitler and Mussolini were no more, and one great Allied leader – Roosevelt – was also dead. Yet more terrible, bloody battles and massacres had occurred – the forced expulsion of millions of Germans from eastern Germany, Poland and the Sudetenland, the apocalyptic bombings of Dresden, Pforzheim and Würzburg, the siege of Berlin, the 'death marches' as the prisoner-of-war and concentration camps were emptied. Above all, a vast forced population movement had been set in motion, the greatest in Europe since the fall of the Roman Empire – involving not just Germans but also Poles, Ukrainians, Hungarians, Italians and others. Churchill, finally subjected to the verdict of the British electorate, resigned on 26 July 1945. The leader of the socially radical Labour Party, Clement Attlee, had been swept to power in a landslide that showed the British public moving on from the heroics of war to the hard practicalities of peace, making its resultant political choice clearly and without sentimentality.

So a triumphant but anxious Allied presence met a dazed, disillusioned German populace, amid ruined cities and the general breakdown of communication and supply in what had once been the best-organised state in Europe. The possibility that harsh, or at least stern, treatment of the former Reich during the post-war occupation might somehow conflict with the aim of creating a future Germany fit to take its peaceful place in the family of nations seems to have dawned on most in the Allied camp relatively slowly.

In Britain, all but a handful of critics, led by the Labour MP Richard Rapier Stokes and Bishop Bell of Chichester (both of whom had been prominent wartime critics of the bombing of German cities), plus the passionate, if eccentric left-wing publisher Victor Gollancz, considered the Germans had brought their miserable fate upon themselves. The publication of press accounts of the liberation of the concentration camps forced this forgiving minority even further into their corner.

Likewise, in America, many in high places – most prominently

Secretary of the Treasury Morgenthau – promoted rigorous post-war treatment of Germany, dismantling of all war-related industries, total decentralisation, and even the country's forced downgrading into a purely agrarian state. It was a radical, in its way idealistic solution to the perceived problem, presuming continuing good relations between the wartime Allies, thereby allowing for a post-war condition of peace which only a militarily resurgent Germany could possibly disturb. The main, even only, aim was to prevent that resurgence, most crucially by removing the heavy industrial capacity that would permit it.

Most of the US State Department and the Department of War – including Secretary Stimson – were, on the other hand, in favour of firm but flexible policies that would neutralise the Nazi danger but allow Germany to get back on her feet. The initial aim was to save her from being an undue burden to the victors, but politico-military reasons quickly started to play a role. Soon after the end of the war (in fact, arguably even before it, given the inter-Allied conflicts over the future of Poland that arose in the final wartime months), it became clear that a smoothly functioning Anglo-Russian-American-French-controlled Germany, run from a single coalition HQ in Berlin, was unlikely. The French were especially keen to sabotage this. However, ruthless Soviet behaviour in Eastern and Central Europe, and clear indications of communist ambitions elsewhere, combined with an awareness in the new Truman administration that fifty million hungry and unemployed Germans in the Western-ruled zones did not represent the raw material out of which a recovering Western Europe could be communism-proofed, also served to send the star of the Morgenthau group into inexorable decline.

It would take some time to elapse after the end of the war, and some bitter clashes within the occupation administration, before the pragmatists gained a clear upper hand over the idealists. After they did, however, policies towards the German population, Nazi or not, became much more pragmatic, and, to some, disappointing. The Morgenthau Plan to divide Germany and make it new gave way to a three-quarter Germany, rebuilt within a democratic framework, but with its industrial potential intact and with the country's structure including old, suspect materials the occupiers had initially, in the flush of victory, never planned to use. Germany would, of course, in the end be made new – but it would take almost fifty years.

In the case of the Russians, any post-war status quo would be an imposed one, in their occupied parts of Germany as much as elsewhere in the rest of Eastern and Central Europe 'liberated' by the Red Army. Any such considerations therefore inspired mostly tactical, as opposed to strategic, reactions.

Certainly, the creation of a communist-totalitarian satellite state in East Germany was Moscow's achievement. There is very little likelihood that without Russian direction and control, not to mention its cohorts of tame German communists, such a state would have evolved spontaneously out of the ruins of Nazism. The form of statehood achieved in the Western-occupied parts in the late 1940s was, perhaps, more complicated in its origins and took a lot longer for its final shape to become clear. In particular, the Western-oriented 'Federal Republic', created almost exactly four years after the end of the war out of the British, American and French zones, would, at least initially, remain much more like pre-war Germany than its rival, the Soviet-controlled 'Democratic Republic'.

The consensus on the success or failure of the occupation(s) of Germany has wavered and changed in the years since 1945. At the height of the Cold War, when West Germany was a valued ally and bulwark against communism, the story ran that the Germans had embraced democracy pretty quickly after 1945 – at least where they were given the chance, i.e. in the West. The Western Allies, so this version of the story went, had provided the Germans in their zones with the framework and the education for this successful transformation. Within a few years, West Germans were firm friends of America, France and Britain, fellow members of NATO. This was the natural consequence of the wise occupation policies pursued. The Western victors had embraced a much less harsh attitude than had been apparent after the First World War, and more especially a less punitive economic policy.

Certainly, by and large, the positive story was the one that the elites of the countries involved, including West Germany itself, France (which by the 1960s was locked in a positively romantic embrace with its former hereditary enemy), America (whose own free and easy popular culture and decentralised politics had also influenced the new Germany) and Britain (which prided itself on giving the West Germans a liberal education system and efficient trade unions) had agreed upon.

The Soviets, with their mass expulsions, rapes and pillage, had made an even worse start than the Western Allies. Their belated and often clumsy attempts to curry, if not favour with the natives, then at least a little less unpopularity, failed to conceal the fact that the East German government was essentially an imposed puppet regime. The discontent of the population compelled the building of a fortified border, first (1952) in the German–German interface that ran down the middle of the former country from Lübeck to Hof and then (1961) in that last refuge of inter-Allied rule, Berlin. In 1953 the population of the Soviet Zone rose up in an open rebellion that could only be suppressed by massive use of force and a range of repressive measures that included hundreds of executions and thousands of long prison sentences. The seventeen million Germans unfortunate enough to find themselves in the Soviet Zone after twelve years of Nazi dictatorship were then seamlessly subjected to more than forty years of a competing brand of totalitarianism, marginally less brutal and at least not racist, but no less disappointingly oppressive for that. Even worse, the new communist bosses went around claiming that, unlike the West German elite, they represented a clean break with the Nazi past and were therefore morally superior.

Both Cold War versions were somewhat true, or at least not gross distortions. West Germany was not quite the rapidly resuscitated bastion of freedom and tolerance that many presented her as. The framework for some such existed, just as it had been between 1918 and 1933. However, as we shall see, at the time of the foundation of this part-state in 1949, 60 per cent of those polled among its fifty-something-million population still thought that Nazism was a good idea gone wrong – a figure that was actually substantially worse than in earlier, post-war opinion polls. When asked if, were the necessity to arise, they would choose security over freedom of expression, a majority saw security as the greater good. Many also continued to espouse various forms of anti-Semitism.

Large numbers of Nazis, many of them guilty of crimes against their own people as well as against innocent enemy nationals, went unpunished at the hands of the West German state. Even when proceedings against such malefactors were initiated, they often found protectors within sections of the post-war establishment. The social and cultural focus of West Germany for the first fifteen years or so of its existence was deeply, at times oppressively, conservative.

The political and cultural revolution of the 1960s, driven mostly by young people who had been barely old enough for kindergarten at the end of the war, affected West Germany more intensely than any other Western country, up to and including America. Suddenly, after twenty years of restoration and reconstruction but relatively little re-evaluation, there were ageing war criminals on trial before West German courts, there was talk of the Holocaust (largely ignored in the 1950s), there was a national debate about the country's past and where it should be heading. In effect, the debate that might have been had in the years immediately following the German defeat (which many among the occupiers and the fairly small numbers of passionate German anti-Nazis had wanted to have) finally began to take place more than twenty years later. It has continued, and continues to shape the varied, vibrant and tolerant Germany we see in the twenty-first century.

Not that forms of fascism, many directly based on the Nazi model, have been entirely banished from the new Germany. Denazification, even the self-directed, subtle and long-term kind that ultimately triumphed in Germany, could never be and has never been complete. A substantial minority support exists in the reunited Republic – as it does, to be fair, elsewhere in Europe – for dark, xenophobic fantasies of racial purity and perfect 'order'. The difference from the 1930s is that the numbers are relatively small, and there is no support for such ideologies within the cultural, political or for that matter the economic elite.

As for East Germany, for all its pretence of ideological purity, and its claims to have been the only post-war German state to properly cleanse itself of the Nazi infection, there is in fact strong evidence that the Marxist-Leninist spell under which its people were forcibly placed, while outwardly different, was every bit as subtly damaging as West Germany's hyper-capitalist orgy of forgetting. Perhaps it was worse, because there was no 1960s, no younger generation asking awkward, often unfair questions of their elders, as there was in West Germany. East Germany claimed to have solved the national problem through communism, but in fact, after 1989, the bacillus of Nazism was found to have survived in far more virulent forms in the so-called 'German Democratic Republic' than in its capitalist-democratic competitor state. It is in the East that the neo-Nazis have most of their electoral strongholds, and where, in certain vulnerable towns and cities, they can seriously affect their fellow citizens' quality of life.

In modern Germany, there is much talk about what was bad in the past, but at the same time there is also increasing debate about the suffering of Germans in the twentieth century, whether in the bombing of the country's cities during the Second World War, or in the forced expulsion of millions from ancestral German territories, or under the sometimes harsh, vengeful and often plain incompetent interregnum of the Allied victors that followed defeat. So Jörg Friedrich's passionate, tendentious 2003 account of wartime bombing, *Der Brand* (The Fire), for all its flaws, unleashed a cleansing national debate about German victimhood. So, likewise, bestselling works about the brutal 'population transfer' from the eastern provinces, most prominently Andreas Kossert's *Kalte Heimat* (Cold Homeland, 2008), have made this other facet of German suffering the subject for rational debate rather than simple accusation.

So far as this book's core subject matter is concerned, post-war and denazification history have become quite fashionable – particularly since reunification opened the East German archives – enabling scholars to take a more variegated and nuanced view of what was achieved (or not achieved) in freeing Germany from the shadow of Nazism.

Writers in the former Allied countries, especially Britain and America, have also – in part encouraged by a new flourishing of 'occupation studies' in the wake of the Afghan and Iraq wars – taken a long, hard look at what the Allied occupation of Germany actually involved. Books such as Giles MacDonogh's *After the Reich* have taken an aggressively forensic line, rightly detailing the failures and brutalities, but often failing to explore the unspeakable Nazi occupation policies during the previous six years that helped cause the Allied powers and their individual representatives (down to the most humble, frightened, sometimes angry soldier) to behave as vengefully as they did. More balanced treatments, such as Perry Biddiscombe's indispensable *The Denazification of Germany* (interestingly informed by his earlier work on the Nazi *Werwolf* resistance movement and its offshoots), have, inevitably, also been able to devote limited space to examining the roots and the consequences of the process.

What is clear from important work such as Biddiscombe's is that Germany's experience between 1944 and 1949, roughly the period of post-war denazification, was neither straightforward nor complete. The beginnings of Germany's journey back to international respectability and prosperity, and eventually even to moral wellbeing – in short, to what passes among the community of nations for normality – were halting, compromised, sometimes brave and noble, sometimes forced or self-serving, and mostly no more than just that: beginnings.

Like all such human progressions, Germany's was both aided and hindered by external and chance forces. History was still working away in the background, enigmatic and almost inconceivably complex, even while victors and vanquished alike struggled to find some way of making sense of what had happened and was continuing to happen. These had been truly terrible years and, even with the advent of peace, the misery was by no means over. Many of the things that subsequently happened to all involved were much worse than they had hoped, while others were, especially in the end, much better than expected.

The story of Germany's enforced transformation begins, as it must, in the thick of war, when a still defiant German heartland was bracing itself for the now inevitable enemy invasion. Although the Allies had broad ideas about what they needed to do once they controlled the enemy's country, much policy was as yet only sketchily defined, and would be made on the hoof according to the exigencies and anxieties of the moment.

So we join the advancing Allied troops at the point when they took their first modest and cautious steps on to the soil of the Third Reich.

The day was, as it happened, 11 September – or as Americans usually express it, September 11 – 1944.

Into the Reich

Ninety-six days after the Allies' first landings on the Normandy beaches, a seven-man patrol of the 2nd Platoon, Troop B, 85th Cavalry Reconnaissance Squadron, attached to the 5th Armoured Division, 1st United States Army, crossed the River Our from Luxembourg into the pre-war territory of the Third Reich.

The bridge that normally straddled the border had been demolished by the retreating Wehrmacht, but the waters of the Our were shallow enough for Sergeant Warner W. Holzinger and his men to wade across and cautiously make their way on to the far bank. Encountering no enemy troops, they proceeded up the slope on the German side.

Soon the Americans observed a German farmer at work in the field. Sergeant Holzinger – a German-American who spoke his parents' language – addressed the man, who offered to show them the enemy bunker system. Led by this disarmingly friendly native, they walked a mile or more into Reich territory and, sure enough, found themselves gazing at a set of German fortifications – in this case, consisting of nineteen or twenty concrete pillboxes. Adjoining one of these, incongruously, locals had constructed a chicken shed. There was no sign of enemy forces.[1]

Deciding not to push their luck, the American soldiers quickly retraced their steps and returned to the Allied-held side of the river. They reported at about 18:15 hours on 11 September to their platoon commander, Lt Loren L. Vipond.

The news of their incursion into Germany was quickly radioed to the Headquarters of Lieutenant General Courtney Hodges, Commander of the First Army, from where the long-awaited message flashed around the world: the Allies had finally pierced the Reich.[2]

The 2nd Platoon's dart across the border was the first of several undertaken by American units. In early evening, a company of the 109th Infantry, 28th Division, crossed the Our on a bridge between Weiswampach, in the northern tip of Luxembourg, and the German village of Sevenig. Near St Vith, Belgium, a patrol from the 22nd Infantry, 4th Division, likewise went over the border near the village of Hemmeres and roamed around the countryside for a while. The GIs rounded up and talked to some civilians. Many had been evacuated by the SS. Those of the German population who remained had largely taken to the nearby woods, though for these country people the exigencies of peace proved unsuited to the imperatives of war. A local woman from the small farming community of Heckuscheid reported a little melodramatically: 'Suddenly we realised that the people who had gone back into the village to feed the livestock had not returned: they had been arrested by the Americans who had in the meantime advanced into the village.'[3] To provide proof of their success, the border-crossers brought back a German cap, some currency and a sample of earth.

A more determined incursion in force had to wait until the following day, 12 September, and it took place a hundred kilometres or so north of the previous day's efforts. Shortly before 3 p.m., the Sherman tanks of Colonel William B. Lovelady's armoured task force, an elite outfit that had carved a path to here all the way from Omaha Beach, rumbled in battalion strength past a last farmhouse flying the Belgian flag in anticipation of liberation. Beyond that house, over the railway tracks, clustered more dwellings, but if they flew any banners they were white ones of surrender. Beyond the railway lay enemy territory.

Task Force Lovelady entered the small, picturesque German border town of Roetgen, and occupied it without encountering resistance. In fact, of the locals who risked leaving their houses to take a look at their conquerors, some offered flowers and even, in one case, coffee. They seemed relieved rather than anxious to find themselves under American control.[4] The signals team radioed the task force's immediate superior, Major General Boudinot, of Combat Command 'B', 3rd Armoured Division. The hot-blooded, Iowa-born general – a renowned cavalryman and former balloon racer – radioed back: 'Tell Lovelady he's famous! Congratulate him and tell him to keep on going!'[5]

In fact, the newly minted celebrity was forced to pause. On the eastern outskirts of the town, barring advance towards the Reich's interior, lay the formidable 'dragon's teeth' defences of the famous Siegfried Line, constructed in the 1930s at Hitler's order and substantially strengthened since. When Lt Burroughs, who had led the reconnaissance group that cleared the way into Roetgen, dismounted from his vehicle to check a crater on the outskirts of town, he was shot dead by a German sniper. Lovelady took the hint. He decided to settle down and wait.

Nonetheless, the US Army was established on German soil. It was a sensation. Unlike the earlier patrols, Task Force Lovelady was accompanied by a small but eager flock of journalists. The *New York Times* trumpeted the 'first German town to fall'. Elsewhere it was noted that 'the Germans welcomed their invaders'.[6]

Before long, a Burgomaster, Herr Schleicher, was appointed, to communicate the orders of the American commander to Roetgen's people.[7] Thus the town moved from the process of being conquered to the condition of being occupied, the first of many hundreds to do so over the following weeks and months.

Not a moment too soon, several hundred miles away the would-be victors were finally agreeing on how that occupation should be conducted.

Lancaster House, a grand late Georgian pile built of tawny Bath stone, lay (and still lies) in the heart of the Establishment village that is

London's Mayfair, just opposite St James's Palace and a very short
walk from Buckingham Palace. Its construction was, as might be
expected, the work of a consummate insider – Queen Victoria's uncle,
the Duke of York and Albany, second son of King George III and
heir presumptive to the British throne. He ordered it built in 1825.

The Duke, however, would die, childless, less than two years later
at the age of sixty-three – allegedly of various diseases induced by a
life of dissipation – leaving his house still little more than a shell. It
was nevertheless known for a few years as York House, before passing
into the possession of the Marquis of Stafford. For nearly ninety years
the place was known as Stafford House, and then – after being bought
by the public-spirited Lancastrian soap magnate Lord Leverhulme,
and in short order presented to the nation – Lancaster House.

Back in 1799, the house's original builder had been put in charge
of a British expeditionary force charged with invading France via the
Dutch wetlands. Not helped by his inexperience or by the sorry state
of the kingdom's land forces at that time, the young Duke there
presided over an unreserved military disaster. Ironically, 145 years after
this legendary British defeat, his former residence had now become
the headquarters of the European Advisory Commission, a body
whose work had quite specifically to do with the apportioning of the
fruits of one of history's greatest victories.

The EAC took up residence at Lancaster House in January 1944.
At the Tehran Conference in November 1943, Roosevelt, Churchill
and Stalin had arrived at certain key decisions regarding Germany's
fate once the war was over: first, that large parts of its eastern provinces
would be assigned to Poland; and second, that the German government would be abolished and the once mighty Reich partitioned.

It was the EAC's job to work out the details of this arrangement,
along with the mechanisms of the enemy's surrender. To that end,
each Allied power appointed a delegate – in Britain's case a powerful
Foreign Office official of ambassadorial rank, fifty-two-year-old Sir
William Strang, who acted as full-time secretary general of the organisation. In the case of the United States and the Soviet Union, the

delegations were led by their respective ambassadors, the affable John G. Winant and the altogether less so Feodor T. Gusev. Not yet forty years old when appointed by Stalin to replace the sociable, cosmopolitan Ivan Maisky the previous autumn, Gusev was by most accounts a charmless and narrow-minded Stalinist bureaucrat.[8] Both he and Winant were, however, very much part-time in their commitment. Military, economic and political advisers naturally did most of the day-by-day donkey work.

The EAC having laboured for the appropriate nine months, on 12 September, as American patrols ducked tentatively into western Germany, it gave birth to a protocol on the surrender and occupation of Germany. This was signed by the delegates amidst the faux Louis XIV splendour of Lancaster House.

In outline, the protocol limited Germany's territory to its 1937 borders, that is, to its borders prior to the annexation of Austria and the Sudetenland – and of course before the absorption of huge areas of Poland in 1939–40.

The document stipulated the establishment of three occupation zones, which were to be administered separately. These were to follow existing administrative boundaries and to take population size into account. Moreover, the Allies agreed on the joint administration of the capital, Berlin, by an inter-Allied military body to be known as the *Kommandatura*.

While the occupation of both the 'Eastern Zone' and the eastern part of Berlin by Soviet forces had already been finalised, the exact allocation of the 'North-Western (British) Zone', the 'South-Western (American) Zone', and the British and American sectors of Berlin itself still remained formally open.

The agreement ignored rather more than it acknowledged – above all there was still no real agreement concerning the eventual fate of Germany as a unitary state – but at least the boundaries of the various Allies' areas of control in post-war Germany as a whole were formally laid down. The fortunes of war would, of course, dictate where the armies would stand at the time of the German surrender. However, as soon as possible after the hour of victory the powers would be bound to withdraw to their apportioned zones and commence the distinctly problematic business of ruling over (and feeding and housing) the population of the defeated Reich.

So much for the theoretical map of post-war Germany. In the autumn of 1944 the war was clearly not yet over. While it seemed the Allies' war to win, the real facts that mattered were facts on the ground, and they were still being established. As for the actual map of post-war Germany, it was being drawn not in ink, but in blood.

It is not quite true to say that American patrols were the first Allied units to penetrate German territory. In the east, building on its destruction of the Wehrmacht's Army Group Centre, by July 1944 the Red Army had fought its way almost to the pre-war German border. Marshal Zhukov proposed to Stalin that he press home his advantage by advancing into East Prussia before the Germans had the chance to regroup and organise their defences. However, the Soviet dictator insisted on giving priority to the Polish and Balkan fronts. All the same, on 17 August 1944, a Soviet patrol briefly crossed the border into German territory near the East Prussian border settlement of Stallupönen, a town with a substantial Lithuanian minority. The place had been renamed 'Erbenrode' by the Nazis in 1938 because of sensitivities that the original sounded too 'un-German' (which, of course, it did).

The revenge-hungry men of the Red Army were forced nevertheless to wait two months before mounting anything that could be called an invasion of Germany proper. On 16 October, General Cherniakhovskii's 3rd Belorussian Army Group finally crossed the Niemen River near Goldap and moved in strength into East Prussia. The commander's orders were to annihilate the German formations around the major towns of Insterburg and Tilsit and clear the way for an advance on the provincial capital (and second city of Prussia), Königsberg.

After some initial successes, with several small towns falling to the ruthless Soviet assault, the German 4th Army, showing real courage and tenacity, managed to halt Cherniakhovskii and even drive him back. The thirty-eight-year-old Red Army high-flyer, the youngest commanding general in the entire war, had lost 17,000 men in the so-called 'Goldap–Gumbinnen' operation. He was fortunate not to be demoted like the commander of the neighbouring 2nd Belorussian Army Group, Zakharov, who had been punished for his bloody failure to establish two bridgeheads on the Narew River north-east of Warsaw.[9]

Not until early in the new year would Soviet troops re-enter Germany in appreciable numbers. Meanwhile, they had given Germany and the world a terrifying foretaste of what, at least in the east, occupation would mean.

Early on the morning of 21 October 1944, an autumn mist still hung over the rolling East Prussian landscape. Heavy armoured vehicles of the 2nd Battalion of the 25th Soviet Tank Brigade rattled forward along the main highway, heading west into East Prussia towards the major town of Gumbinnen. They had fought their way around fifty kilometres into Germany since the launch of the offensive five days earlier. Most of the native population had already fled, along with (for the moment) the defending Wehrmacht units. Nonetheless, that morning the Russians found horses and carts queuing in front of the bridge over the River Angerapp. They drove their T-34s forward over the bridge, crushing the carts, animals and humans in their path, and pushed on into the apparently deserted – and defenceless – village beyond.

Nemmersdorf.

Of Nemmersdorf's 637 recorded inhabitants, most had been evacuated. But, as the Russians discovered, not all of them. The fate of those who remained was undoubtedly a terrible one, but the historical record remains so confused, the issue so besmirched by wartime political expediency, that it is hard to be sure of all the details. What seems certain is that the German forces quickly returned and made attempts to retake the village and the bridge, which were repelled.

During German air strikes that accompanied the enemy counter-attacks, Soviet troops took cover in an improvised bunker in Nemmersdorf. This, it transpired, was already occupied by fourteen or so German civilians. After the danger from the air seemed past, a Soviet officer ordered everyone out of the bunker. It was, apparently, shortly after this that a massacre of civilians began. Some – certainly the civilians from the bunker – were shot at close range, others attacked and battered to death with gun butts or entrenching tools.

Later in the day, the Soviet armoured units were ordered to retreat to a more easily defensible position on the eastern bank of the river. The Germans reoccupied the village and found the scene of the massacre, plus – so it was said – a sign painted by a Russian soldier and placed next to a burnt-out building: 'Here it is now, Accursed Germany'.

The reoccupation of Nemmersdorf – followed by a Russian withdrawal that left East Prussia in German hands for some two and a half months more – unleashed one of the great propaganda battles of the Second World War. There can be no question that the Russians committed an atrocity in Nemmersdorf (and also in neighbouring districts, though these were not concentrated upon to the same extent), and that dozens of civilians died at their hands. The furious men of the Red Army, after more than three years of seeing their own country ravaged, felt entitled, in many cases, to a terrible and ultimately unjustifiable revenge. However, the decision by Hitler's propaganda chief, Josef Goebbels, to use the Nemmersdorf outrage as a weapon in his battle to stiffen German resistance and denigrate the Allies in the eyes of the neutral world led to severe distortions of what actually happened.

Within days, the 'bestial bloody deed' was splashed over all the Nazi-controlled press and newsreels, complete with graphic pictures of the bodies. Goebbels was heavily involved in the creation of a last-ditch home guard force, composed of those previously too young, too unfit or too old to fight, to be known as the *Volkssturm*, and he had decided to change tactics in the propaganda war. So desperate was the situation as 1944 drew to a close that it would clearly no longer work simply to crow over victories and deny defeats. Goebbels' new method would be to systematically terrify the German population and thereby strengthen their resolve to resist. They would perforce fight on not in confidence of final victory but in terror of defeat and massacre by Slavic 'sub-humans'. The Propaganda Minister consequently did not shrink from showing the very worst.

When the news of the outrages reached Berlin, Goebbels immediately decided that he would 'make them the occasion for a major agitational effort in the press'.[10] An 'international' war crimes commission (in fact composed almost entirely of foreign collaborators) was hastily assembled by Eberhard Taubert, one of the minister's senior aides, and the East Prussian horror was massively publicised in Germany and the remaining occupied countries. Neutral newspapers also picked up the story.

The corpses of the women and girls were shown in leaflets and newspapers with their dresses pulled up, as if left there after being raped (rape of all females having been established by a medical commission headed by SS leader Himmler's personal surgeon, Karl Gebhardt). There is evidence that the women's clothing was, in fact, rearranged by the photographic teams to establish this impression, and it seems that sequential pictures of the victims with clothing undisturbed and then disturbed exist as part of the same batch of images.[11]

That a massacre took place in Nemmersdorf is undeniable. That the women captured by the Soviets were all raped seems less certain. The sole surviving eyewitness, shot and left for dead, could only confirm the murderous intent of the Russian occupiers.

Suffering from partial disability, Gerda Meczulat lived with her seventy-one-year-old father on the western side of the river. Herr Meczulat having refused to leave along with the other villagers, he had taken refuge with his daughter in the communal bunker. Her account bore witness to the dangerous volatility that became typical of the behaviour of Russian soldiers in Germany. Initially, inside the bunker, the Russian conscripts had appeared friendly enough in their dealings with the anxious Germans – though they had, it is true, rifled through the civilians' bags as they awaited the all-clear. It was only after an officer arrived that the atmosphere changed. Drastically and, as it turned out, fatally. The officer began barking orders in a harsh tone. The German civilians were ordered from the bunker.

'When we came out,' Fräulein Meczulat told the German authorities after Nemmersdorf was retaken, 'soldiers were standing on both sides of the entrance with guns at the ready. I fell down, because I have been disabled since birth, was wrenched to my feet and was so overcome that I lost all awareness. When I came to my senses, I heard children screaming and shots. Then everything went quiet.'[12]

Gerda Meczulat's would-be killer's aim was faulty. That was why she survived and up to couple of dozen others did not.

Within days of the massacre, fuelled by Goebbels' press campaign, stories spread of women nailed naked to barn doors, of mass rapes and killings. Nemmersdorf became a symbol of 'Bolshevik' barbarism (never, of course, connected back to the routinely appalling behaviour of the worst of the German forces in occupied Russia).

In fact, it seems that there is an element of truth in all these tales, but that – apparently like the photographs shown in the Nazi press – they were in fact collected from various atrocity sites and collated to suit the Nemmersdorf story upon which the regime had decided to concentrate. Five days later, a probably more reliable report by a Wehrmacht staff major, who led an official army investigation into all the atrocities committed on the Gumbinnen highway that day, noted that twenty-six corpses (thirteen women, eight men, five children) had been found at Nemmersdorf. Cause of death was mostly shots to the head and chest. Some of the small children had had their heads stove in with rifle butts. One woman's breasts, it said, had been cut off after death (a detail mentioned nowhere else). There is no mention of rape in the report. However, in his description of thirteen more bodies (three men, four women, six children) found two kilometres further along the highway, where a small group of unlucky refugees had clearly been overtaken by Soviet troops, the major notes that 'the nether parts of all the female corpses were exposed. In the case of three women, rape must be assumed.'[13]

Whatever the full truth about Nemmersdorf – and even respectable sources continue to print wild exaggerations[14] – there can be no doubt that it was an inexcusable war crime, the first of many to be perpetrated by Soviet troops on German soil as the war 'came home to the Reich'. It was certainly very different from the occupation of Roetgen the previous month.

The martyrdom of Germany's eastern provinces had begun.

By the end of October 1944, harried by successful German counterattacks, the Soviets had pulled back out of East Prussia. While Goebbels' highlighting of the Nemmersdorf massacre had undoubtedly helped recruitment for the *Volkssturm*, it had unleashed something close to panic among civilians in the province itself. Even during the ensuing two months' uneasy stalemate, and despite official discouragement, a steady stream of refugees began to head west, away from the Russians.

Hitler himself headed west. On 21 November 1944, he left his long-time headquarters in East Prussia, the *Wolfsschanze*,* from which he had directed much of the war against Russia, never to return. With the front line less than 100 kilometres away, the *Wolfsschanze* had become just too risky.

All the same, the rapid collapse of the Eastern Front in the summer of 1944 had given way, at least temporarily, to a more stable situation. As the final winter of the war closed in, Russian advances became more piecemeal. The Red Army faced the task of consolidating its lines of reinforcement, supply and communication before the next big push.

A similar standoff had been reached in the west. After the breakout from the beachhead in July 1944, the Anglo-American forces appeared to carry all before them. The initial crossing of the German border occurred a little over three months after D-Day. Paris and then Brussels fell. After 15 August, a second landing, Operation Dragoon, on the French Mediterranean coast, rapidly pushed the Germans out of

* Usually translated as Wolf's Lair, in fact more accurately wolf's redoubt or rampart.

southern and south-eastern France. The Germans lost many thousands of experienced troops killed, wounded and captured. They began to fall back in a state of some disorder. There was much talk of the war being over before the end of 1944, of the Anglo-Americans' sweeping on into the heart of Germany before Hitler had a chance to organise his resistance.

However, in the west the Germans also rallied. Allied forces, weary after a three-month war of movement, operating at the end of long and vulnerable supply lines, came up against the natural barriers of the Rhine and the Vosges and Ardennes forests. They began once more to pay a high price for every kilometre of ground gained. When the British attempted an airborne attack across the lower Rhine at Arnhem during the third week of September, it was a heroic – and bloody – failure, the Allies' first major setback since D-Day.

Advances elsewhere were modest. The first major German population centre to fall was the landmark city of Aachen (Aix-la-Chapelle). Here Charlemagne, the first Holy Roman Emperor, had been crowned eleven and a half centuries earlier, and here he and his successor were buried. Aachen lay a mere twenty kilometres north-west of Roetgen.

General Courtney Hodges' First Army began its efforts to surround Aachen on 1 October. In September the city's commander, Lieutenant General von Schwerin – a sophisticated, humane officer with close connections to the 20 July plot against Hitler – had privately expressed his desire to give up this cultural jewel without a fight. He hoped thereby to preserve both Aachen and precious men and military resources that would be better employed elsewhere – but in the event, as the Americans drew near, he was replaced by the more pliable Colonel Gerhard Wilck.

Although he later claimed to have shared many of von Schwerin's doubts, Wilck showed little sign of this at the time. He rapidly organised a ruthless defence and called on his troops in a series of radio messages to show 'unshakeable belief in our right and our victory' and fight to the very end.[15] As a result, it would take the Americans almost three weeks of savage house-to-house fighting, until 21 October, and around 5,000 casualties on either side, to overcome the garrison's bitter resistance. By this time the ancient cathedral city lay in ruins, scarcely recognisable, with up to 85 per cent of its buildings destroyed.[16]

Hodges had rejected advice to simply push on past Aachen, preferring instead the symbolically powerful but militarily less significant gesture of siege and conquest (the fierceness of the German defence, with a hardbitten SS group at its heart, also related to Aachen's position as the first major city threatened by the Allied advance).

Hodges' decision cost the Allies dear in casualties and time.[17] The final fall of Aachen, moreover, provided them with a challenge – that of administering at short notice a large (if at first mostly depopulated) German town – one that would invite disaster and opportunity almost in equal measure.

If taking Aachen had been hard, being an occupying presence in the city and its surrounding area was fairly painless.

As in Roetgen, the locals proved remarkably accepting of their conquered status. They were even quite friendly. This was not entirely unpredictable. Before the destruction of Weimar democracy in 1933, the left bank of the Rhine had been one of the least pro-Nazi areas of the Reich, giving most of its votes to the Catholic Centre Party and only around 20 per cent to the Nazis. Moreover, as an intelligence report for the G-5 of the US First Army noted, civilians in Aachen had good reason to hate the Nazis, who had carried out the forced evacuation of the city in brutal fashion.[18] Not until the spring, when the Allies reached the key Rhineland military and administrative centre of Koblenz, Prussian since 1815 and long a major fortified town, with a substantial population of Prussianised 'soldiers and bureaucrats', would they encounter something approaching a Nazi stronghold in western Germany.[19]

What would not prove so easy, as Aachen's new masters discovered almost immediately, was finding a solution to the problem that would dog the victors throughout their occupation of Germany:

which Germans were the 'good' Germans, unsullied by involvement in the Nazi movement, and even if that could be established, was it possible to run the conquered country through the agency of such people alone?

Though in October the Allies could not know it, they had most of the coming winter to explore this formidable challenge in this single locality. Until March they would be stuck on the left bank of the Rhine, and what territory they did manage to take during the rest of the winter would be appallingly hard won. The US First Army lost 21,000 men between 16 November and 16 December in the ferociously bitter battle for the Hürtgen Forest, south of Düren.[20]

During October and November, with costly fighting still raging a score or two kilometres to the east, Aachen settled down, if that is the word, under American occupation.

From the outset, all the difficulties that were later to darken the record of the Allies in the post-war period were foreshadowed here. Keen to ensure that the small number of remaining civilians in the city be checked for political reliability, the occupation authorities gathered up most of the surviving population and shipped them off over the nearby border into Belgium, where they were housed in evacuation centres at a former Belgian army camp, the Homburg Barracks. Specially trained American army teams were detailed to interview each newly subjugated civilian individually to ascertain his or her political history.

Much useful intelligence was, in fact, gathered. However, to undertake mass transfers of civilians to such 'concentration camps', as Goebbels' propaganda machine did not hesitate to dub them (to be fair, a not entirely erroneous description in the original, literal meaning of the words), was to inflict a strain on transportation and human resources that could not be repeated ad infinitum as the Allies advanced further into Germany and captured more major towns.

It seems that one useful piece of future good practice, learned in interrogating the Aachen civilians, was to ask a subject not *if* he or she was a member of the Nazi Party but whether he/she 'had felt compelled' to join the party. A change to this mode of questioning immediately got a much more ready response and a significant rise in the number of admissions of political guilt.[21]

Within a short period, as Aacheners, innocent and guilty alike, began returning to their city, the Americans were forced to set up some kind of civilian administration for the place. Searching around for a suitable Burgomaster, the American Military Government (AMG) officer charged with this task, Leo Svoboda, took advice from the Catholic Bishop of Aachen. Catholic clergy and their flocks were significantly, though not invariably, less likely to have been pro-Nazi than their Protestant counterparts. The bishop helpfully directed Svoboda to one Franz Oppenhoff, a forty-two-year-old lawyer and businessman, who before 1933 had been a stalwart member of the Catholic Centre Party. Oppenhoff had resisted joining the Nazi Party after Hitler's seizure of power, and by all accounts was a competent organiser. What was there to disapprove of?

The *New York Times* described how a 'slight, bald anti-Nazi lawyer of about 40 years' (his name was withheld for security reasons) was sworn in in front of an American flag, the oath being administered by Lieut Col. A. A. Carmichael of Montgomery, Alabama. 'Have you a house?' someone is reported to have asked the new Lord Mayor. '*Ja*, but a house not standing,' Oppenhoff answered dryly before heading for his new official quarters in a city-centre cellar.[22]

As Oppenhoff took charge, however, it became clear that things were not quite as simple as the AMG training guidelines, and the bishop's advice, had implied. Centre Party = Democracy was not quite such a clear equation. In fact, the Centre – although a pillar of the Weimar parliament and supplier of four Reich chancellors out of twelve during the pre-Hitler period – had always contained a strongly conservative, authoritarian faction.

One of the most notable members of this essentially reactionary group was Heinrich Brüning, who had been chancellor from 1930 to 1932. Ruling by presidential decree and bypassing or dismantling many of the safeguards of Weimar democracy, Brüning had thus set precedents that prepared the ground, in many significant aspects, for the advent of Hitler.

The majority of Centre deputies had, indeed, voted for the 'enabling act' that granted Hitler dictatorial powers in March 1933. Oppenhoff belonged to this faction too. He avoided the Nazi Party itself for various reasons, mostly religious ones, but distrusted democracy and, even when it was clear that the Nazis were finished, saw no reason for a return to anything resembling the Weimar system. Like others on the non-Nazi right, he favoured instead a Christian corporate state founded not on parliamentary representation but on appointed delegates from the country's major social and economic groupings – something similar to the governments of Mussolini, Franco or the so-called 'Austro-Fascists' who had ruled in Vienna before the *Anschluss*.

Oppenhoff soon made his views apparent, attacking any criticism of his actions as the work of 'Reds' and demanding arrests of 'trouble-makers'. He also appointed similar conservative, authoritarian-minded officials, mostly fellow businessmen, to head departments in the city administration (including a total of twenty-two Nazis in second-tier but nevertheless key positions).[23] Many of these individuals, who became known as the 'Veltrup Clique', had worked, like Oppenhoff himself, for the Johann Veltrup company, a leading local munitions manufacturer, which had made parts for tanks and for the V1s and V2s. During the winter of 1944–5, however, Oppenhoff proved himself a competent administrator – a fact that silenced many, though not all, doubters in the occupying force.

The chief American thorn in Oppenhoff's flesh was Major John Bradford, deputy chief of Aachen AMG, and his ally Major Saul K. Padover, an Austrian-born intelligence officer and psychology gradu-ate. Both were keen New Dealers (in civilian life, the left-leaning Padover had worked for FDR's Secretary of the Interior) and grimly determined that all Nazis be flushed from positions of power in the new post-war Germany. In their way stood Major Hugh Jones, a former car salesman from Wisconsin with a hard-headed, socially conservative attitude to things.

To Major Jones, what worked was what mattered. To him, Oppenhoff worked. He seemed efficient and was neither a Nazi nor a communist. Moreover, the Burgomaster and his aides remained loyal throughout the few desperate days in December when it seemed that Aachen might need to be evacuated as a result of German advances during the Battle of the Bulge. It was said that during those days Oppenhoff and his officials carried rifles and steel helmets to work. There was grim talk among those at risk of the Gestapo nooses that awaited captured 'collaborationist' German officials. After tense negotiations, the American authorities agreed to take such individuals with them if forced to withdraw.

While Padover continued to exploit his press contacts to raise the Oppenhoff issue back in the States, Jones, for his part, stood firm and refused to dismiss the Burgomaster.

'Where,' the major from Wisconsin asked Padover, putting a question that would be repeated endlessly in the months and years to come, 'would you find competent people who are not Nazis?'

Nevertheless, though Oppenhoff remained in office, Padover's efforts to influence the press did begin to get results. Jones tried to counter this by organising a mild purge of Nazi officials, but in the end the Allied headquarters, SHAEF, felt sufficiently hard pressed to issue formal denials that the Americans had installed a post-Nazi German administration in Aachen that was shockingly anti-democratic.

The appointment of Oppenhoff nevertheless continued to be seen by many as a 'Darlan Deal' – as one AMG official had apparently called it. He was referring to a notorious collaborationist French admiral who, to the outrage of de Gaulle and the Free French, had been permitted to rule Allied-occupied Algeria after the 'Torch' landings in November 1942. François Darlan had lasted in office for a few weeks until his assassination, apparently by a Gaullist sympathiser, on Christmas Eve 1942.

And violent death would play a role in Aachen, too.

Since the early autumn of 1944, his confidence buoyed by the failure of the British attempt to seize the right bank of the Rhine at Arnhem and the consequent pause in the Allied advance into Germany, Hitler had been planning a devastating counter-attack. Despite the Reich's dwindling resources, this offensive would, so he hoped, cut the Allies' fragile supply lines and hurl the invaders back, first into the lowlands and then into the sea.

After an American offensive east of Aachen – preceded by the largest tactical artillery bombardment of the Second World War[24] – failed to gain substantial ground, the Führer must have felt confirmed in his belief that, in defence of their own soil, Germany's soldiers would prove unbeatable.

The fantastic scale of Hitler's ambition even at this late stage was shown in Goebbels' diary entry of 2 December 1944. The Propaganda Minister described Hitler's distress at the renewed Allied bombing attacks on German cities (between May and September the German civilian population had been granted a respite while the British and American bomber fleets turned to supporting the Allies' successful land invasion). At the same time, Goebbels expressed his and the Führer's conviction that the planned counter-offensive would reopen the Channel ports to Germany, enabling the Reich to 'bombard southern England and London ceaselessly from the newly-gained bases on the channel and Atlantic coasts' with its 'miracle weapons', the new V2 rockets and V1 flying bombs.[25]

In the early planning stages, Field Marshals Rundstedt and Model both pushed for the proposed thrust through the Ardennes on the Belgium–Luxembourg border to be combined with a counter-attack more than 100 kilometres to the north that would encircle the Allied-occupied region around and including Aachen. By November, this key area was filling up with British and American units preparing for the coming thrust across the Rhine. However, the field marshals were overruled by Hitler and his aides, who saw this as a distraction from their aim of retaking the key Belgian port of Antwerp.[26] So, when the operation named 'Watch on the Rhine' (*Wacht am Rhein*) commenced early in the morning of 16 December, fighting was confined to Belgium and Luxembourg, and there was consequently no direct test of German civilian attitudes in the areas of the country already occupied by the Allies.

The Ardennes Forest had been the route by which Hitler's forces had successfully invaded France and the Low Countries in May 1940. Nevertheless, in December 1944 this was a weakly defended area, in many places manned by inexperienced and 'resting' American forces. No one expected an attack there. As Paul Fussell recollected almost sixty years later: 'Christmas packages for the boys were arriving from home, and that old, warm American optimism was comforting all ranks.'[27]

Attacking on a 100-kilometre front under successful conditions of secrecy, a total of around a quarter of a million heavily mechanised German troops, well armed and supplied with scarce fuel scraped together at the cost of the Wehrmacht's forces elsewhere, punched their way through the difficult terrain. Fully exploiting the element of surprise, locally superior in numbers to the unsuspecting enemy, and helped by heavy cloud, which initially protected their advance from the vastly superior Allied air forces, the Germans seemed once again invincible.

Even by the grimly exacting standards of front-line infantry life, American casualties were appallingly high, the worst of the European war. For a few heady days, it seemed the Wehrmacht might repeat the success it had achieved four and a half years earlier.

On Christmas Eve, the leading German Panzer spearheads came within nine kilometres of the Meuse at Dinant, halfway to Brussels. There they halted. The German motorised units were already running out of fuel, and insufficient quantities had been captured from the Allies to keep the offensive going.

In the Wehrmacht's rear, the US 101st Airborne famously held out in the besieged town of Bastogne, tying down substantial numbers of German troops, while to the south, even more ominously, General George S. Patton's Third Army, previously targeting the Saar industrial area, had now turned north to head off the resurgent threat. Perhaps worst of all for the Germans, on Christmas Eve, the same day that their vanguard reached the Meuse, the skies cleared over western

Germany, eastern Belgium and Luxembourg. Now the Allied air forces could launch massive attacks against the German spearheads and their supply routes.

By Christmas, it was clear that Hitler's Ardennes offensive, though it had cost the lives of 19,000 GIs, almost 50,000 wounded and 21,000 missing and taken prisoner, was doomed. From now on the best war Germany could expect to fight was a defensive one.

It was also true, however, that the Allies (mostly the American First Army) had not succeeded in advancing more than thirty kilometres into Reich territory. In fact, between September 1944 and the following February, the total area of Germany under Allied occupation did not exceed 900 square kilometres – roughly the size of Greater Berlin – with a total population of only around 60,000.[28]

The war was not over yet. All the country's major industrial areas remained for now in German hands. The Reich's armaments factories were still operating at something close to capacity, producing sufficient quantities of weapons to supply the existing armies and also to fit out and arm fifty new relatively lightly armed and less mobile divisions of 'people's grenadiers' (*Volksgrenadiere*), which for all their relative weakness appreciably reinforced the German capacity for resistance. At year's end the regime's propagandists could (and did) boast loudly of a 'miracle in the West'.

In the Reich's cities, the sixth Christmas of the war was celebrated by many with a kind of tight-lipped optimism. Saxony's Gauleiter Mutschmann, still strutting in full pomp around his undamaged capital, Dresden, could make a speech claiming that 'This Christmas will be beautified for us by the fact that we can see our people back on the offensive' – and Gestapo reports confirmed that a lot of ordinary civilians were naive or desperate enough to believe him.[29] Nevertheless, those in the most westerly as well as the most easterly provinces already knew enough to understand that the coming months would be terrible.

In occupied Aachen, the American commanders and their men remained highly suspicious of the locals. Leaflets and brochures encouraged the troops to see potential enemies everywhere. This was not unreasonable, with the war still raging an hour's drive to the east, and rumours spreading of 'stay-behind' Nazi resistance forces waiting to fall on the occupiers once they relaxed their vigilance. To most Allied soldiers, the Germans remained inhuman, 'not like us'. In American intelligence circles, Germany was sometimes referred to as 'Transylvania'.[30]

As it happens, the Nazi leadership had already created an embryonic resistance organisation, dubbed *Werwolf*. That the drawn-out end of the Second World War had long since turned into a horror movie cannot, with our hindsight, be denied, but that contemporaries on both sides acknowledged the fact at the time is, in its macabre way, remarkably interesting.

2

Hoo-Hoo-Hoo

The idea of organising guerrilla resistance to Allied advances into core German territory appears to have originated, tentatively at first, in 1943, around the time the situation on the Eastern Front showed serious signs of deterioration. By the spring of the following year, the chief of the SS Main Office (RSHA) and Reichsführer SS Heinrich Himmler's main liaison man with the Eastern Front, forty-eight-year-old Obergruppenführer Gottlob Berger, began to take an interest in these matters. Once Berger became involved, research and discussion broadened and deepened.

This was a sensitive area of thinking and therefore top secret. After all, even considering the possibility that German forces could be driven back into the Reich – as a result of military defeat – could be interpreted as, well, defeatist. So, at first the emphasis was on historical parallels such as the Prussian *Landsturm* law of 1813, which had made legal provision for a partisan force to aid the army by guerrilla actions should the enemy encroach on Prussian soil. Studies were made of the resistance movements in German-occupied Europe, especially the Polish 'Home Army', whose role in the Warsaw Rising during the summer of 1944 attracted attention and even reluctant admiration in senior Nazi circles.[1]

The name *Werwolf* for such a force seems to have been adopted in the autumn of 1944, exactly at whose behest remains unclear. The word itself may have been based on a nationalistically flavoured popular novel, *Der Wehrwolf*, by Hermann Löns. First published in

1910, after its author's martyr-like death in the opening weeks of the First World War the book went on to sell almost a million copies. It recounted the romantically imagined exploits of a group of guerrillas operating during the Thirty Years War against foreign occupation forces in the rugged heathland around Lüneburg. This was a theme peculiarly well suited to the National Socialist era, during which it achieved enormous sales.

The changing of the spelling to *Werwolf* (the word *Wehr* with an 'h' means to protect or defend) may have arisen from some Nazi boss's desire to add a lycanthropic chill, or simply been due to political expediency. An organisation called the 'Wehrwolf League' – *Bund Wehrwolf* – had competed with the fledgling Nazi Party for nationalist support in the 1920s, so the SS planners may have wanted to avoid stirring up old memories.

The official foundation on 25 September 1944 of the so-called *Volkssturm* militia, drawing on all German males between sixteen and sixty not yet serving in the regular Wehrmacht, was a crucial step by the regime in universalising and radicalising the war as it approached German soil. The Wehrmacht had been attempting to set up a kind of fallback militia for some time, but the regime's political leadership had consistently refused to consider any such thing. Crucially, when the *Volkssturm* was actually founded – ominously late in the day – Hitler stipulated that the organisation of this militia was to be a Party, not a Wehrmacht matter, reporting to local Kreisleiters (District Leaders) and Gauleiters.

Military training was, of course, provided to these often hapless recruits, but the main emphasis was on morale, on tapping into the alleged fanaticism of the population. Certainly, by this point the *Werwolf* idea was circulating in high SS circles. In his speech of 18 October 1944 to the hurriedly formed East Prussian *Volkssturm*, a rambling oration broadcast on the radio, Reichsführer Himmler himself referred to the fact that the German people, having fought over every town, every village and farm, would proceed to fall upon the enemy's rear 'like werewolves' should their land be conquered.

An announcement in Munich by the Gauleiter of Upper Bavaria, Paul Giesler, caught the drastic flavour of the Nazis' appeal to the population:

We shall not succumb to the spell cast by the momentary material superiority of the enemy, but shall destroy all the enemy's hopes through the long-desired escalation in our power provided by the German *Volkssturm*. In this we see the great, never to be repeated opportunity to transform our racial spirit into martial spirit, to defend the National Socialist people's state with all fanaticism.[2]

This kind of appeal – half deluded, fantastic 'you-can-have-anything-if-you-want-it-enough' motivational rant, half desperate call to arms – became more and more common during the final phase of the war as the Nazi state, frantically aware that it was both outgunned and outmanned, abandoned all but the barest shreds of distinctions between combatants and non-combatants. It thereby revealed its essentially nihilistic nature. The notion that such an ill-armed and ill-trained ragbag army of children and old men, thus inspired, could prove decisive against the enemies that Germany faced at this time was mad enough, but the *Werwolf* enterprise stumbled further still into the dark and treacherous forest of unreason on whose fringes the National Socialist movement had long dwelt.

If the *Volkssturm* project was hindered by the problematic nature of its human material and shortages of arms and equipment, then its *Werwolf* counterpart was even more deeply flawed. Although the idea had originated inside the offices of the RSHA, the proposed *Werwolf* structure was designed to bypass the normal military and SS chains of command. It was, instead, made directly subordinate to Himmler via the regional police commands organised in the form of HSSPF (*Höhere SS- und Polizeiführer* = Higher SS and police leaders). A classic example of the almost anarchically decentralised power structure of Nazi Germany, the HSSPF was an extra network that the Reichsführer had established deliberately in order to bypass the burgeoning, often chaotic SS bureaucracy centred in Berlin, and which he used to progress personal 'special projects'.

Himmler's linkman, named in September 1944 as 'General Inspector of Special Resistance', went by the name of SS General Hans-Adolf Prützmann. At forty-three, the East Prussian-born Prützmann was an experienced SS bureaucrat and a veteran commander of killing squads on the Eastern Front. There he had been deeply and ruthlessly involved in the liquidation of the Jews, in terroristic anti-partisan actions and the 'scorched earth' policy that accompanied the German retreat. He rapidly put together a staff of around two hundred. His entourage included an SS colonel by the name of Karl Tschiersky, who earlier in the Russian campaign had been responsible for Operation Zeppelin, an attempt to infiltrate anti-communist guerrillas behind Soviet lines. The General also assembled propaganda and partisan warfare experts and a certain Frau Maisch, who would recruit female operatives. Prützmann boasted that his efforts would cause 'a rapid improvement in Germany's military situation'.

On the positive side, therefore, the *Werwolf* organisation was effectively run by an expert in the very guerrilla warfare techniques with which it would need to operate. On the negative, the fact that it was deliberately intended to be independent of Ernst Kaltenbrunner's SS empire meant that, despite the desperate situation of the Reich, Kaltenbrunner and his intelligence chief, Walter Schellenberg, did everything they could to block the notoriously ambitious Prützmann's path.[3]

Moreover, like so many leading Nazi bureaucrats, especially towards the end of the war, Prützmann found himself with an almost absurd number of multiple responsibilities – including reinstatement as active head of the HSSPF in his native East Prussia, and from December 1944 an assignment as Himmler's military plenipotentiary in the embattled Nazi satellite state of Croatia.

So, despite Himmler's support and Goebbels' excitement, *Werwolf* began as – and, for all the sound and fury, remained something of – an orphan. Each region had its Commander of Special Resistance,

selected from among the local *Polizeiführer*. Appointees from the
Hitler Youth and the Brownshirts (SA) would provide liaison functions and – theoretically, at least – ensure a flow of recruits for training.
In the event, however, this organisation remained skeletal. The big
reserves of money, power and equipment remained with the conventional SS bureaucracy.

All-powerful as Himmler might appear to be, the new *Werwolf*
organisation, operating apart from this all-embracing network, could
only really be kicked into life in response to specific 'special orders'
from the Reichsführer. It lacked a self-sustaining apparatus that could
assert itself in the relentless and brutal contest for material and political clout within the sprawling power structure of the late-Nazi state.

Nevertheless, the Inspector General managed to set up a substantial
headquarters just outside Berlin, before moving to even grander
surroundings at the moated Schloss Rheinsberg, 100 kilometres to
the north-west of the capital. This was where Frederick the Great had
lived while still Crown Prince of Prussia in the 1730s. Prützmann even
commandeered an official private train to take him on tours of his
nascent resistance empire.

On both the western and eastern borders of the shrinking Reich,
arms and food supply dumps were created. To the west, in the as
yet unoccupied area beyond Aachen, up to thirty bunkers were built
by construction teams co-opted from the Ruhr mining industry. In
these the *Werwolf* teams were to sit out the Allied military tide and,
if and when it had washed over them, emerge and begin their work
of mischief.

And what exactly would this work be? As planned in the latter part
of 1944, it would involve harassment of the enemy's supply lines and
rear, so as to disrupt his operations and to draw vital combat troops
away from the front line. In this way, the *Werwolf* would lighten the
burden of the conventional German forces defending the fatherland.
Small teams of between six and ten guerrillas would form a disciplined
and skilled, not to say fanatical, hardcore around which others,
whether patriotic civilians or Wehrmacht troops who had managed

to evade capture, could coalesce. The kits with which these teams would be provided were to include small arms, grenades and mines, crude bazooka-like *Panzerfäuste* (anti-tank weapons) and various plastic explosives suitable for sabotage operations against bridges, railway lines and parked enemy vehicles.

At this stage, what *Werwolf* seemed not (yet) to be was some kind of post-defeat resistance movement along the lines of the Polish Home Army or the French *Maquis*. Rather, like the *Volkssturm*, it would be part of the glorious, historic *levée en masse* of the German people that would supposedly drive back the enemy. Combined with Hitler's promised wonder weapons and the inevitable (to the Nazis) split between the capitalist Western Allies and their communist Soviet counterparts, such a nationwide uprising would bring for Germany the victorious peace that the Führer still promised his supporters even at this perilously late hour.

The first *Werwolf* unit to undertake clandestine activities against the enemy was not typical. It consisted not of civilians or brainwashed Hitler Youth but of nine regular troops chosen from the 'Hermann Goering' Division, whose duties included guarding the Reich Marshal's hunting preserves at Rominten, East Prussia, now close to the ever-encroaching Eastern Front. Their targets were, in fact, the spearhead units of the Soviet Army that managed to penetrate the Reich in October 1944. Nemmersdorf, where the first major massacre of German civilians occurred, lay around twenty-five kilometres to the north-east.

The unit, led by a Sergeant Bioksdorf, was supplied with explosives, radios and carrier pigeons. Under orders to report on Soviet movements and recruit any Wehrmacht stragglers and willing civilians to the struggle behind the lines, the small band slipped into Russian-held territory in early November. Its operatives transmitted ten messages and failed to blow up two bridges before being captured by the Soviets.

South of this area, in Silesia, the rich industrial province that bordered on Poland and the Czech lands, *Werwolf* bunkers and supply dumps were also built up. In the new year this would prove to be one of the movement's most active theatres of operations. In the west, although some kind of clandestine infrastructure was also coming into being, during the winter there was little actual activity. Perhaps this was because of the massive conventional military confrontation that took place in the Ardennes over the period between mid-December and mid-January (or February, when the Allies actually successfully regained all the territory they had lost). There was, however, a lot of talk on both fronts about the resistance effort that the Allies would encounter as they inevitably advanced.

Although the practical military consequences of Prützmann's plans might turn out, in the scheme of things, to be minimal, their psychological effect on the occupiers was not. In fact, fears of fanatical Nazis lurking round every corner and behind every dark thicket of pines, ready to launch treacherous attacks on 'our boys', were widespread. They would seriously affect Allied attitudes and, consequently, plans for the occupation of the Reich.

At around the time when the first *Volkssturm* units were going into action and the first guerrilla infiltrations were in preparation, in London *The Times* noted Himmler's announcement that the German people would fall upon the invaders' rear 'like werewolves'. *The Times* noted dryly and, in its internationally assumed role as mouthpiece of the British establishment, a little menacingly:

A werewolf is a human being who transforms himself temporarily into a wolf. There is no Hague Convention for the protection of werewolves.[4]

There was sense in this. Prussia-Germany's retaliation against those who resisted its armies' occupations, be it the French *francs-tireurs* of 1870–71 or the recalcitrant Franco-Belgian population during the First World War, had traditionally been harsh. The same went for the Wehrmacht's dealings with the resistance movements in Western Europe, Poland and the Balkans, and especially after June 1941 the large-scale partisan activity behind the German lines in the Soviet

Union. Hitler's notorious 1942 'Commando Order' had mandated the execution of enemy combatants operating in German-occupied Europe or behind German lines, even if uniformed, in direct contravention of Germany's continuing obligations under the 1929 Geneva Convention.

So, for the *Volkssturm*, with their civilian outfits and armbands, or home-made Ruritanian uniforms, the omens were doubtful. For the *Werwolf* recruits, they were ominous in the extreme.

Despite the brief false hope of the Ardennes offensive, there seems little doubt that by the end of 1944 most Germans were war-weary and disillusioned. Their once-proud army was in full retreat on every front, the Reich's all but defenceless cities were being continually devastated by the Allied bomber fleets, and now enemy armies had set foot on German soil. Only the most fanatical or the most gullible Germans (groups which perhaps overlapped) still really believed in the 'final victory' that the Nazi leadership continued to promise.

The most bizarre aspect of the German people's descent into hell was, nonetheless, that so many continued to fight and work for victory right up to the end. There were almost no strikes, no mutinies, no stirrings of popular revolution as there had been at the end of the First World War. This was partly because, unlike during the First War, no Germans starved – though many in the occupied countries did, so that Germans might eat – and partly because Hitler's Germany, especially towards the end of the war, was a far more tightly run and ruthlessly policed country than the Kaiser's had been. In 1944–5, executions were routine and even mildly defeatist talk incurred the severest of punishments.

The early experiences of Russian incursions into East Prussia reinforced this apocalyptic view of Germany's fate, should she be defeated. Widespread, if not always precise, knowledge of the horrors that had been perpetrated in the occupied countries and in the concentration camps, within the Reich and abroad, also played a role in the German people's apparent willingness to fight on at all costs. A conversation between two workers in Berlin was reported to the SD (SS intelligence) in the final weeks of the war. In this exchange, one said: 'We have only ourselves to blame for this war because we treated the Jews so badly. We shouldn't be surprised if they now do the same thing to us.'[5]

In fact, along with recognition of the inevitability of defeat, it seems that the majority of the German people felt anger against both the Allies – especially for the relentless bombing of German cities – and their own Nazi masters, in the latter case mingled with disappointment.

Already, self-excusing themes were developing that would dominate the immediate post-war discussion of the German plight. The 'idealistic' people had trusted Hitler and the Nazis to create a powerful, prosperous Germany, had been prepared for any 'sacrifices' necessary, but had been 'lied to' and 'betrayed'.

Even the above conversation between the two Berlin workers, while seemingly acknowledging the German people's responsibility for its own misfortunes, also contained grains of the conspiracy-obsessed anti-Semitism that the regime had fed the population for the past decade or more. The powerful Jews and their Allied friends were now returning, determined to punish the Germans. From now on, this attitude implied, everything would be the fault of these alien people, bent on revenge – the destruction of German towns and cities, the violence, the expulsions from the old German territories in the east, the post-war deprivation.

Meanwhile, in the first days of 1945, the Reich remained in a state of expectant hiatus. And, in absolute numbers, there were still enough fanatics to give the Nazi leadership the semblance of what it wanted.

Among these was Obergruppenführer Karl Gutenberger, the Higher SS and Police Leader West. On 20 September 1944, with the forced evacuation of Aachen all but complete, Gutenberger summoned the city's Gestapo chief to his headquarters at Erkelenz. The thirty-nine-year-old Gutenberger was brutally clear in his orders. 'Plunderers, deserters and assorted riff-raff' found in Aachen were to be shot summarily and without trial.[6]

So many innocent civilians and soldiers paid with their lives for failure to show sufficient enthusiasm for the pointless defence of Aachen, a pattern that was to be repeated in countless towns and cities throughout western Germany as the Allies advanced.

In accordance with the rules laid down by Himmler, it was Gutenberger who automatically became Inspector of the *Werwolf* movement in northern Rhineland and Westphalia (Defence District VI). Like his colleagues elsewhere, he set up a small staff headed by a *Werwolf* commissioner, the fanatical Standartenführer Karl Raddatz. Because of its closeness to the front, District VI was, of course, a more important and above all potentially active theatre for undercover guerrilla warfare.

As early as the first week of October, while the Americans prepared to lay siege to Aachen, the SS newspaper, *Das Schwarze Korps*, saw fit to issue bloodcurdling threats against any Germans who might accept administrative posts from the Allies:

> In the occupied parts of German territory, there would be no 'German' civil administration, no 'German' authority, no 'German' legal judiciary, because such office holders and administrative organs would scarcely survive their first month. No official would be able to obey enemy orders without experiencing the certainty that he would soon sit cold and sightless behind his desk, no one would carry out the enemy's will without finding himself on the yawning edge of a grave, and no judge would condemn a German in accordance with enemy wishes without ending up dangling prettily from his own window bars one night . . .[7]

At the time, such collaboration remained a merely theoretical possibility. In the event, as transpired weeks later, there did turn out to be Germans prepared to accept such posts. And when this became clear, the big bosses in Berlin began to demand the punishment of Germans who 'collaborated' with the Allies in the still-limited occupied areas of the Reich.

It was in early November that the *Werwolf* supremo Prützmann visited Gutenberger. He came straight to the point. Himmler and Goebbels, Prützmann told the SS and Police Leader, were both furious that Oppenhoff, a collaborator, possibly a Jew (sic), had accepted the post of Lord Mayor of Aachen from the Americans. An example must be made. The traitor must be killed, and Gutenberger must organise this mission.[8] The Obergruppenführer was not enthusiastic. With more important problems on his plate, he simply ignored the instruction and hoped it would lapse. He was, in this case, to be disappointed.

Within a few weeks, a telex arrived from Reichsführer Himmler, demanding an update on progress with mission planning. Shortly after, an emissary from Prützmann appeared, bearing a formal warrant for the Lord Mayor's execution. Following this, phone calls and cables arrived in increasingly insistent profusion. Gutenberger was forced to fall back on a plea of 'personnel difficulties' and to complain about how hard it was to infiltrate teams through the confusion of the front line.

Prützmann, aware of how much of his own status was riding on this matter, now decided to force the pace. At his personal behest, training began. In charge was Untersturmführer (Lieutenant) Wenzel, a mysterious character variously thought to have been co-opted from the notorious Obersturmbannführer Otto Skorzeny's commando group (which had famously rescued the deposed Italian dictator Mussolini from his mountain prison in September 1943) or to have been a former member of the Aachen Gestapo.

The rest of the would-be assassination squad was drawn from *Werwolf* volunteers undergoing training at Schloss Hülchrath on the outskirts of Düsseldorf. It included an Austrian-born SS-trained radio operator by the name of Leitgeb, an eager Hitler Youth leader from the Aachen area, Erich Morgenschweiss – at sixteen little more than a child soldier – and Ilse Hirsch, twenty-two, a League of German Girls organiser. Fräulein Hirsch came from just a little farther away, the border town of Monschau, in the Eifel, which by November 1944 was already in American hands. Morgenschweiss and Hirsch would be responsible for reconnoitring the city and identifying and locating the American-appointed Lord Mayor. Wenzel and Leitgeb would carry out the actual murder. Two former border policemen-turned-Gestapo men, Hennemann and Heidorn, who knew the area around Aachen well and had already been back and forth between the lines several times, would act as guides.[9]

In the new year, the pressure on Gutenberger increased. The Führer himself was said to have taken a personal interest. Moreover, the Luftwaffe had agreed to fly the team to a suitable point west of Aachen. They were given parachute training.

The codename for the operation was *Karneval*, which implied that it had originally been planned for the beginning of Lent in mid-February 1945. However, it was not until mid-March, a time when the German military position had suffered a serious deterioration and the front line had moved many kilometres to the east, that, after a small farewell party sponsored by Gutenberger, the team finally embarked on its 400-kilometre trip to an air base at Hildesheim, near Hanover. From here they would take off on their mission.

On the evening of 19 March 1945, Wenzel and his motley crew boarded a captured American B-17 (with German Luftwaffe markings). Their target was a drop zone in Dutch territory, apparently on the supposition that security would be less tight outside Germany.[10]

In the second half of January, the Anglo-Americans had begun to push the Germans out of the areas they had occupied during the Ardennes battle. By mid-February, the Allied air offensive was achieving new levels of destruction. Central Berlin was devastated on 3 February. Historic Dresden was ravaged on 13–14 February, with upwards of 25,000 civilian dead. The Russians were once more advancing into eastern Germany. The prospect of German underground resistance within the rapidly increasing areas of occupation had now become a serious Allied concern.

One of the Allied planners' chief worries was the extent to which

German youth might have been fanaticised by the Nazi system. Any young German still under military age had known only the Hitler regime. Twelve years of brainwashing in the Nazi Party's youth movements and the Reich's increasingly politicised school system would, it was thought, have turned them into willing tools of last-ditch Nazi bosses such as Himmler and Goebbels.

There was some proof of this. The *New York Times* reported the commutation of the death sentence on a sixteen-year-old Hitler Youth leader, Karl Arno Pünzeler, also of Monschau, the place where the would-be assassins' helper, Ilse Hirsch, had grown up. 'Hitler Youth learns of American Justice' read the headline over a photograph of the blond-haired boy as he learned, in his cell at Aachen prison, that he would not die a martyr's death but be condemned instead to life imprisonment. His crime was 'reporting American troop movements to the enemy'.[11]

An even more widely covered case, found in both the American and British press and guaranteed to make readers' flesh creep and AMG officers lock their billet doors, was that of another painfully youthful enemy of the Allies from picturesque Monschau, seventeen-year-old Maria Bierganz. Fräulein Bierganz was soon dubbed by Anglo-American journalists, with their profession's taste for alliteration at all costs, 'Mary of Monschau'.

This new focus of anxiety was, by all accounts, an attractive, sweet-seeming girl with typical 'Aryan' looks of exactly the kind most GIs quickly developed a soft spot for. She and her family, along with around 1,500 of Monschau's 2,000 permanent residents, had chosen to stay behind when the Allies advanced into the quaint half-timbered town on 14 September 1944. During the Ardennes offensive, the main German thrust passed a few kilometres to the south. For a while there was fighting right on the outskirts of the town. Attempts to retake the town by the Wehrmacht's 326th Grenadier Regiment, and even the dropping of some paratroopers to the west of Monschau, cost much German blood, but in the end failed to deliver the prize. Monschau remained in American hands.[12]

Even after the Wehrmacht had been driven back almost to its starting point, in mid-January 1945, Monschau remained just a few kilometres on the Allied side of the front line. More than four months of such a frustrating situation seems to have piqued those citizens of the little town who had remained Hitler loyalists, and young Maria, a keen member of the *Bund Deutscher Mädel* (BDM)* was one of them.

She was discovered after being spotted by officers of the American army's Counter Intelligence Corps (CIC) talking to a teenage Hitler Youth leader in the street shortly before his arrest for sabotage. He was named in newspaper reports as a suspiciously generic-sounding 'Karl Schmidt' – only Maria's first name was mentioned. In fact, possibly due to some kind of censor-enforced obfuscation, he was the same Karl Arno Puzeler who would be convicted and finally reprieved for similar offences during this period. Despite the girl's protestations of innocence – why shouldn't she talk to a school friend in the street? – the CIC searched her bedroom and found her diary. It told a very different story.

Maria Bierganz was, it seemed, the brainwashed BDM girl from every Allied soldier's nightmares. She had a sweetheart in the SS by the name of Peter, and the diary took the form of unsent letters to him. Her defiant observations showed that she was filled with hate for the Allies, and determined to do what she could to resist them. She and a handful of other young die-hards had founded a clandestine organisation named 'The Homeland Loyalists' Club' (*Klub Heimattreue*) where they expressed outrage at 'collaboration' by other Monschau residents (including BDM leaders rumoured to have been seen dancing with GIs), listened to Goebbels and other Nazi leaders on the radio, angrily watched newsreels of German cities consumed by flames in the Allies' final, apocalyptic air offensive, and longed for a change in the tide of war.

On 29 October, Maria wrote contemptuously in her diary: 'In the

---

* 'League of German Girls' – female equivalent of the Hitler Youth.

distance we hear another V1. The Amis [Americans] just have to hear one of these monsters, and they dive for cover.' She continued:

The American is a comical soldier, he stands guard with an umbrella. When one stared at me so stupidly yesterday, because I grinned at him, I had to laugh out loud . . . they are not soldiers – jitterbugs and tango lovers, but 'fight' and 'advance' are foreign words to them . . . I hate the Americans. One thing they cannot take away from us. We shall start our new life under the old principle that we have been taught – to live is to fight . . .'[13]

Although her secret thoughts were revealed to the press by the CIC in mid-February, Maria had actually been arrested on 6 January 1945. 'At around half past one in the afternoon, heavy steps thudded up the stairs at our house,' she recalled years later. 'Two armed MPs and several CIC people stood before me. "Are you Maria Bierganz?" "Yes!" "*Mitkommen*! Let's go, go on!"' They then searched her room and found her diary. To Maria's mother's anxious questions about what they planned to do with her daughter, the intelligence officers answered curtly 'Court-martial!'

In fact, Maria was never put on trial. The 'thought crimes' of the diaries were just that, and American justice retained sufficient integrity even in wartime to refrain from prosecuting her. She certainly served a propaganda purpose, as the articles in the press showed – details were also widely disseminated among American and other Allied troops to make them wary of German womanhood.

On 4 March 1945 Maria was returned to her home and parents, still clinging to her idealism but increasingly disillusioned with the patent cynicism of the Nazi leadership and decreasingly convinced that Germany's 'final victory' would ever come. At one point, a senior American officer had even offered Maria a job on his staff as an adviser on German youth. She turned it down, though she was also forced to admit that the American military men she came into contact with behaved in a 'fair and friendly' fashion.

Goebbels lost no time in exploiting the story of Maria Bierganz's arrest, embellishing it with mendacious detail to create a youthful martyr figure for the 'resistance'. In a radio speech in late February, he invented a fictitious trial, at which she had 'behaved like a heroine in the shadow of death', defying her American judges, confronting them with their alleged crimes 'in holy anger', and repeating that the German people would bear any suffering and create a new world. 'We all know,' he thundered, 'that this girl spoke in our name, and that this child of our people spoke for the whole *Volk*.' His pronouncements were illustrated with 'artist's impressions' of the Aryan maiden staring down her would-be executioners.

If Goebbels' shameless misrepresentation of the facts about Maria Bierganz's rather mild two-month spell in custody was supposed to rouse the Reich's youth against the wicked Allies, there is little sign that it was widely successful. There were, however, exceptions, and three weeks later, on 19 March, two of them joined their comrades aboard a captured B-17 at Hildesheim air base and took off in the direction of the Dutch border.

It was dark when the team parachuted, successfully, close to the drop zone on the Dutch side of the German border. They hid their parachutes and collected food – canned goods, pumpernickel bread, chocolate and two bottles of water each – from the supply canisters that had also been dropped nearby. Then they settled down within a clump of fir trees to wait out the remainder of the night and the dangerous hours of daylight.[14]

As the light faded the next day, the group set off, on a zigzag path aimed at taking them unobserved, by woodland trails and logging paths, across the border into Germany. Their goal was to be at a prearranged hiding place just outside Aachen by morning.

It was late in the evening when the team rounded a bend in the trail and encountered a uniformed member of the Dutch border police. The guard, a young man called Jost Saive, from a German-speaking village just inside Holland, levelled his rifle and called on them to halt. After a few moments of shocked silence, the frontier guard's challenge was answered with a hail of fire. Some reports maintain that it was Morgenschweiss, the sixteen-year-old Hitler Youth boy, who fired first.[15] Saive collapsed and lay bleeding on the path.

Ilse Hirsch, who was unarmed, had already fled. Suspecting that there would be other police in the vicinity, her male companions did not look for her but quickly plunged into the woods, eager to distance themselves from the scene.

Saive's comrades had heard the shots and rushed to his aid. The grievously wounded young man was carried back to the Dutch border post, where he was able to tell his superior little, other than that the perpetrators had been German. He bled to death at around a quarter to ten that evening. Operation *Karneval* had already cost one life. Jost Saive's would not be the last.

Ilse Hirsch reached the outskirts of Aachen much more quickly than the men. Instead of resting up until morning, she stepped out of the coveralls she had worn for the jump and hid them on the thickly wooded hillside. Now underdressed for the chill of a March dawn, she tramped down into Aachen wearing just a skirt and blouse, with a knapsack slung over her shoulder. Although she had no idea where the rest of the team had got to, Hirsch set about identifying and locating the collaborationist Lord Mayor.

For their part, the men, having evaded capture, duly arrived a little later at the so-called 'Three Country View' (*Dreiländerblick*) outside the city. From there it was possible to gaze out over the frontier areas of Germany, Belgium and Holland.

Heidorn, whose family home was very close to the border, suggested they take refuge in thick forest just on the Belgian side. This was where they spent the risky daylight hours. At nightfall, they moved back into the Aachener Wald, the forest immediately around the city, near the suburb of Köpfchen. Leitgeb, the radio operator, and the boy Morgenschweiss were delegated to go into the city and carry out the reconnaissance work that Ilse Hirsch, whereabouts unknown, had been earmarked to perform.

Hirsch had neither been captured nor lost her nerve, as her comrades had feared. She had spent the previous day and night in the city, sleeping at the apartment of a former BDM acquaintance and then making enquiries about the Lord Mayor's personal details. They had not been hard to discover. The Amis might have avoided publicly naming him, but everyone who had remained in the still sparsely populated city knew Oppenhoff.

Ilse Hirsch would later claim that she had begun, by this time, to assume that her comrades had been arrested. Her next task should therefore be to acquire papers and, if possible, a job in Aachen. This was why, that next afternoon, she found herself in the vicinity of the city labour exchange.

However, any such intentions, if they existed, disappeared when Hirsch heard a voice whispering her name and turned to see Erich Morgenschweiss nearby. Leitgeb was hovering on the street corner not far away, one hand thrust into a pocket and curled around the butt of a revolver.

Hirsch asked Morgenschweiss where the rest of the group were. He answered that they had found a hiding place in Köpfchen. As she knew from her enquiries, this was close to where Lord Mayor Oppenhoff lived. Hirsch followed the men to their hiding place. There was no going back now.

In fact, the next day, Saturday, Wenzel decided to move camp once more, this time back over the border to woods near the small Belgian village of Hauset. The attack on the Lord Mayor would take place on the evening of Palm Sunday, 25 March. They would reassemble at their hiding place here after the operation, and then try to get back to German-held territory. The Allies had recently crossed to the east bank of the Rhine, so this would not be easy.

Herr and Frau Oppenhoff spent Sunday in the vegetable patch at their house, with their children playing in the garden behind. The war was drawing to an end, but this was unlikely to improve the food situation, and, like most Germans who had a little land, they thought it prudent to prepare spring plantings of vegetables. However, they had been invited to a small party that evening just along the street, hosted by a colleague at the city administration (one of the deputy Lord Mayors), Dr Faust.

When Wenzel and Leitgeb, guided by Hennemann, arrived at the door of the Oppenhoff house shortly before 11 p.m., there seemed to be no one at home. The trio were dressed in Luftwaffe coveralls and carrying knapsacks. According to their story, they were German aircrew who had been shot down behind Allied lines.

The two would-be assassins entered by the garden, leaving Hennemann keeping lookout just down the street. Leitgeb cut the telephone wires to the property. They then forced a window that led into the basement, and made their way up into the main part of the house. Searching room by room, when they reached the second floor they found a terrified young woman in bed with the sheets pulled over her head. She was, it turned out, the Oppenhoffs' teenage maid, Elisabeth Gillessen. Having assumed that the intruders were American GIs intent on burglary or possibly rape, when she heard herself being addressed in German the girl relaxed a little. Asked the whereabouts of the Lord Mayor, she answered truthfully that he was out. She would go and get him if they would just withdraw long enough for her to get dressed.

The social event that Oppenhoff was attending with his wife crystallised the situation in which occupied Germany found itself. It was a farewell party for some members of the city hall staff, appointed by Oppenhoff, who had been forced to resign when their Nazi connections were revealed.

Eventually, Oppenhoff appeared, in the company of the maid and of his neighbour and colleague, Dr Faust. They asked the intruders, who by now were standing on the street near the house, what they wanted. Wenzel came out with his prepared story – that they were Luftwaffe fliers who had been forced to land near Brussels. They needed Oppenhoff's help, in the form of guidance and papers, to make their way through the enemy lines to 'safety'.

Oppenhoff said he could not help them with documentation, and advised them to hand themselves over to the Americans. However, after some thought he decided that, as a patriotic German, he should at least give them something to eat. Fräulein Gillessen was instructed to go back to the house and make some sandwiches.

After Faust bade them goodnight, Oppenhoff and the two 'fliers' (Hennemann had been instructed to stay on the street, minding their rucksacks) walked into the garden. They waited while their visibly nervous host went to the cellar to check on the maid's progress with the food preparation.

It was when Oppenhoff began to climb the steps up from the cellar that he found Wenzel and Leitgeb blocking his way. Wenzel held a silenced Walther pistol in his hand. But he did not fire, and nor did he inform the Lord Mayor of his condemnation to death *in absentia*, as he had been ordered to do. The squad leader had lost his nerve at the last moment. As the terrified Oppenhoff opened his mouth to speak, it was Leitgeb who snatched the Walther from his co-conspirator's grasp, levelled it at the Lord Mayor and wordlessly put a bullet through his left temple. Oppenhoff toppled backwards down the steps and crashed to the ground. Leitgeb and Wenzel turned and ran, making for the street, where Hennemann would be waiting with the rucksacks. As they did so, more shots rang out in the night.

Cutting the house's telephone connection had been a mistake. The shots had been fired by an American army signals unit, which had come to investigate the break in the line. The assassins fled, scattering as they did so. Wenzel and Hennemann, the guide, became separated from Leitgeb. The burly radio operator decided to return alone to the hiding place where Ilse Hirsch, the Hitler Youth boy Morgenschweiss and the sickly Heidorn were waiting.

There was a delay before the news was released to the international press. The story appeared in both London and New York four days later, on 29 March. The Associated Press report in the *New York Times* said that the killing of Oppenhoff had been carried out 'gangster fashion'. 'Hitler,' the report continued, 'has often threatened retaliation against Germans who cooperated with the Allies, and some persons believe the killing was the first manifestation of this policy. Military intelligence investigators, however, said they had established no motive yet.'[16]

Meanwhile, the Nazi propaganda machine, still running at full tilt, did all it could to exploit the propaganda value of the Oppenhoff murder. At the beginning of April, there were reports that German planes had been dropping leaflets over the Allied-occupied Rhineland, warning that the Wehrmacht would be back before long and that all 'collaborators' would then be held to account.[17] At the same time, Goebbels' broadcasters set about putting 'Werwolf Radio' on the air.

Despite the assassination of Oppenhoff – which was given great prominence in the written and spoken media throughout the Nazis' shrinking empire – it had for some time been clear, as Goebbels' diary gloomily reported telling the Führer on 22 March, that 'our troops in the west are not putting up a proper fight any more'.[18] Five days later, while the Propaganda Minister wrote in his diary that he was busy 'organising in grand style the so-called "Werwolf Action"', in stark contrast he also noted reports that in some parts of the western theatre of conflict '. . . the population are approaching the Americans bearing white flags; some of the women abase themselves to such an extent that they even greet and embrace the Americans. In the light of these circumstances, the troops don't want to fight any more and either retreat without offering resistance or surrender themselves into enemy hands.'[19]

This was the atmosphere in western Germany as the killers of Burgomaster Oppenhoff went on the run. Ilse Hirsch, Erich Morgenschweiss and the remaining guide, Heidorn, had been preparing to break camp and head for the Rhine when an anxious, panting Leitgeb appeared at their hideaway in the woods. The man who had shot Oppenhoff explained how he had become separated from Wenzel and Hennemann. They might, he said, have been killed or captured, so the group decided quickly to start the march east. Despite his poor state of health, Heidorn led them through the thick Eiffel woodland in the dead of night. By dawn the next day they were many kilometres from the scene of the crime.[20]

In the end it was not the vigilance of Allied patrols that caused the little group's downfall, but the deadly legacy of recent fighting. Hiding for much of the next day in a shooting blind and pressing on again through the next night, at daylight they reached the edge of the village of Rollesbroich. As they crossed an innocuous-looking meadow, there was a powerful explosion and Leitgeb was flung into the air. Morgenschweiss bravely picked his way through the possible minefield, only to find the Austrian dead. Half his face had been blown away.

The Hitler Youth boy took Leitgeb's papers to make identification difficult, covered the body with branches and made his way back to join the other survivors. They pressed on – only to set off a smaller trip mine, which wounded Ilse Hirsch so badly that she could not continue. It was getting dark. The other two survivors, also injured but still able to walk, were forced to leave her, hoping that she would be found next day by locals. In the early hours, she was, in fact, able to attract the attention of a passing farmer, who helped her on to his cart and took her to the town for medical attention.

Morgenschweiss made it through several hours of marching before, weakened by loss of blood, he too had to be left behind. He was also picked up by a local – a woman by the name of Frau Sülz, who prudently disposed of the boy's gun before taking him to a nearby hospital for treatment.

Despite the state of his own health, Heidorn continued alone, following a route that led him across the flooded River Urft. Early on the morning of 1 April 1945, he reached his destination. This was a farmhouse, early twentieth century in origin but built in the style of a medieval manor, hidden in the woods near Mechernich and known as Gut (or Haus) Hombusch. It seems to have been designated as a *Werwolf* safe house (after the war, a substantial arms and weapons dump was found nearby and exploded by British Army engineers).[21] The house itself appeared deserted, but when Heidorn cautiously made his way into the building, he heard familiar voices. In the kitchen, two men were in conversation: it was Wenzel and Hennemann.

The three conspirators, reunited but still far behind enemy lines, set off for the Rhine a short while later. When they reached the big river, Wenzel mysteriously announced that he planned to go no further. After parting from his comrades, he made his way to a remote farm in the area, which seems also to have been recommended during their *Werwolf* training as a safe refuge. He stayed there for another four months, helping out with the work and even conducting a small dalliance with the farm maid, before announcing at the beginning of August that he was going to 'find his uncle in Halberstadt'. Post-war investigations would reveal that he had no such relation. Wenzel was never seen again.

Heidorn and Hennemann swam the Rhine, only to be picked up by an American patrol and shipped back to an internment camp – in Aachen. They managed to convince the Allied authorities there that they were harmless and were soon released. After this they travelled east into what was now the Soviet Zone, to join their wives, who had been evacuated the previous autumn to escape the Allied bombing of western Germany.

And so ended the actions of the most notorious *Werwolf* team, its members either dead, scattered or captured. None was connected to Oppenhoff's death until well after the war, when the British, who now controlled Aachen, reopened the case.

In fact, the Oppenhoff assassination, while it made a splash, did not represent any kind of yardstick by which to judge the Nazi guerrilla movement. The Lord Mayor's murder had been undertaken only because of pressure from Berlin, not as a result of any local anti-collaborator groundswell. For the rest of the war, the Rhineland was as peaceful as could reasonably be expected. There were no more major acts of violence against the Allies or their appointed German officials.

In the Catholic, less pro-Nazi west of the country, the *Werwolf* movement was even feebler than elsewhere, but as the Anglo-American forces pushed further east into the centre and east central part of Germany, they found a more hostile environment in which planned and spontaneous guerrilla activity could thrive.

In another notorious case associated with *Werwolf* agitation, on 21 April two of British Field Marshal Montgomery's liaison officers, Major Earle and Major Poston, were ambushed by a heavily armed Hitler Youth unit while driving their jeep through a rugged part of Lüneburg Heath. Only lightly armed, they were forced to ram their attackers' machine-gun nest as a last resort. Thrown from their vehicle by the impact, they found themselves at the enemy's mercy. Poston was promptly bayoneted, while, mysteriously, the wounded Earle was spared and transported back through enemy lines, first to a farmhouse and then to a German field hospital (where he would be rescued within twenty-four hours by advancing British troops).[22]

Sporadic acts of sabotage and violence would continue to occur in the areas occupied by the Western Allies – the stringing of wires across country roads to decapitate jeep drivers was a favourite, though rarely successful, ploy – but broadly speaking the organised *Werwolf* movement took a serious, lasting form mainly in the Soviet- and Polish-occupied areas of Silesia, East Prussia and the Czech borderlands. Here the continuing guerrilla struggle was symptomatic not just of Nazi fanaticism but of a desperate resistance against rape, massacre and forced resettlement.

East of the Elbe, the greatest population movement since the fall of the Roman Empire was under way, driven by the advance of the Red Army and their vengeful Slavic brothers, who for nearly six years had suffered under a brutal German occupation.

Vengeance is never beautiful. In what was to follow, it was ugly beyond belief.

3

The Great Trek

In early 1945, the Allies began to advance once more on all fronts. The Soviets in particular made spectacular progress. They finally took what was left of Warsaw, once Hitler's executioners and demolition squads had finished with it, pushing through pre-war Poland and into the historic eastern provinces of Germany – lands that had formed an integral part of the Reich since the Middle Ages.

The German population fled or was subjected to rape, pillage and forced expulsion. Among these refugees was sixteen-year-old Katherina Elliger, born in Upper Silesia, a traditionally culturally diverse region close to where Poland, the Czech lands and Germany met. As the fighting came closer, she and her mother fled into a nearby corner of the Czech lands, heading by a roundabout route for the home of Katherina's uncle, which lay in the county of Glatz (Polish Kłosko, Czech Kladsko), a short way back across the German border in Lower Silesia. She later described what they found as they journeyed through the wooded landscape:

One evening, we arrived at a farm, which lay off the beaten track in a hollow . . . We entered the spacious hallway. Lights were burning inside. Around a large, round oak table knelt six or seven people. They were quite still and made no movement. Their heads had slumped forward. When we came closer, we saw that they had been nailed to the table edge by their tongues.[1]

Afterwards, they learned that 'hordes' of Slavic locals had swept through the district, seeking revenge on their German neighbours. Presumably the nailing of their victims' tongues had to do with a symbolic retaliation against the language, as well as the bodies, of the hated former 'master race'. Katherina and her mother were warned on no account to continue towards their planned destination.

However, it was not just old local racial scores that would be settled as the Reich crumbled. After a winter of stalemate in east and west, a great Russian offensive had begun on 12 January along a front extending several hundred kilometres between the Baltic Sea and the same Bohemian forest in which the Silesian woman and her daughter had come upon the grisly banqueting scene. The Soviet forces, totalling more than two million, outnumbered the German defenders of Wehrmacht Army Group A by around five to one, with a superiority of six to one in tanks, the same in artillery and four to one in self-propelled guns.

Shortly after Warsaw fell, the Red Army began pressing forward with tremendous speed, often advancing thirty to forty kilometres a day. The great eastern German cities of Königsberg, ancient capital of East Prussia, and Breslau, capital of Silesia, soon lay encircled and under siege.

Most Germans who could flee did so. Vast columns of refugees – women, children and the old, for most adult men were either dead or away fighting – thronged the roads leading westwards into the heart of the Reich, their pathetic collections of portable belongings crammed on to wagons and handcarts. The winter weather was cruel, reaching more than twenty below zero, and would remain so until the end of March. Cold was the first great contributor to the harvest of death that would prove so rich during the year to come.

It was not just consciousness of the vast superiority of the Soviet forces in arms, equipment and numbers that spurred Stalin's soldiers on into German territory. These troops had seen their own land devastated. There were living witnesses of the fact that at least *twenty-five million* of their compatriots of all ages and both sexes had died in battle, or by massacre, and often by deliberate starvation – all in an aggressive German war of choice executed by Hitler's forces with scant regard for even the most basic, minimally humanising rules of conflict. As a result, the Red Army was also driven by hate, perhaps to a degree comparable to no other army in modern history.

A young Wehrmacht ensign from a prominent Silesian family, undergoing his baptism of fire with a Panzer unit in a part of the Czech lands near his own home region, recalled the horrors he witnessed in a Sudeten German village they had temporarily retaken from the enemy during these last bewildering weeks of the war:

> What we found there cannot easily be described in words. Houses full of dead, hanged men, violated women, wandering half crazed through the streets, children with their bellies slit open. If I am honest, I have to say: This is one of those things of which one has suppressed the memory.[2]

Nonetheless, as the young soldier – himself too young to have served on the Eastern Front in Russia itself – went on to speculate, 'What actually must we have done over there that so many Russian soldiers behaved with such bestial rage?'

The great Nazi justification for the war against the Soviet Union had been the alleged German need for more *Lebensraum* ('living space'), which could be gained only at the expense of the racially inferior Slavic peoples who occupied these great fertile plains to the east. When the men of the Red Army finally crossed the border into Germany in the last months of the war and saw how well the Germans actually lived in the supposedly narrow, impoverishing country that they had so urgently needed to outgrow, it caused even more fury. As one simple soldier said to his commander after examining the neat, to him impossibly prosperous-looking farmhouses of East Prussia:

> How should one treat them, Comrade Captain? Just think of it. They were well off, well fed, and had livestock, vegetable gardens and apple trees. And they invaded us . . . For this, Comrade Captain, we should strangle them.[3]

Another Russian, an officer this time, described being billeted in April 1945 in a block of flats outside Berlin:

Each small flat is comfortably furnished. The larders are stocked with home-cured meat, preserved fruit, strawberry jam. The deeper we penetrate into Germany the more we are disgusted by the plenty we find everywhere . . . I'd just love to smash my fist into all those neat rows of tins and bottles.[4]

Rape may or may not have been the Russian soldiers' main intent at Nemmersdorf. By the time, three months later, that the Red Army moved into German territory finally and definitively, there could be no doubt that a hate-fuelled spoliation of German bodies as well as property had become an obsessive preoccupation of the invaders.

Perhaps Russian soldiers saw enemy women as a form of German property. These were the women who – so their own prejudices and their government's propaganda told them – had sat safe at home while the men of the Wehrmacht ravaged Belarus, the Ukraine, the Caucasus, the plains before Moscow; who had received those parcels of exotic good things from conquered Russia while the wives, sisters and daughters of the men who now entered Germany as victors were starved and massacred – and, yes, raped, too. Although rape by German soldiers was not nearly as systematic (the Nazi regime disapproved of sexual intercourse with Russian women on racial grounds), it – and its marginally more respectable cousin, sexual exploitation – was certainly not unknown.

In fact, millions of by no means pampered German women had already suffered bombing, bereavement and loss of their homes. However, this was not, perhaps understandably, how the bitter and infuriated men of the Red Army saw it.

Not that the Red Army's record in other countries was spotless. In September 1944 the Bulgarian Communist Party was constrained to address a complaint to the Soviet General Staff (the *Stavka*), calling for it to 'take measures to end occurrences of banditry, looting, and rape, strictly punishing guilty persons'.[5]

Bulgaria had unwisely allied itself with the Axis early in the war. The same was true of Hungary, and in February 1945 the fall of Budapest to the Soviets was followed by ghastly scenes of mass rape and sexual violence on a scale unseen since the Thirty Years War. However, even though Czechoslovakia was considered a friendly country with close cultural and linguistic links to Russia, and had suffered grievously under German occupation for more than six years, even there, despite clear orders to avoid actions that could alienate the population, the advancing Soviet troops caused problems.

In March 1945, Stalin himself was forced to warn a Czechoslovak delegation, in his sinister, fake-jocular way:

The fact is that there are now 12 million people in the Red Army. They are far from being angels. They have been coarsened by war. Many of them have gone 2,000 kilometres from Stalingrad to the middle of Czechoslovakia. On their way they have seen much sorrow and many terrible things. So do not be surprised if some of our people do not behave as they should in your country. We know that some of our soldiers with a low level of political consciousness are pestering and abusing girls and women, are behaving badly. Let our Czechoslovakian friends know that now, so that the attraction of our Red Army does not turn into disappointment.[6]

All the same, there can be no doubt that, once in Germany, it all got immeasurably worse. Subjected to crushing, brutalising discipline – initially aimed at stiffening defensive resolve during the calamitous months following the German invasion in June 1941 – the Red Army continued to suffer near-catastrophic losses even as the war turned around and its troops began to advance inexorably towards the heartland of the loathed and despised German empire. They had indeed, as their leader said, seen and undergone terrible things.

At the same time, the drumbeat of official Soviet propaganda became ever louder, more jarring and more menacing. No more 'proletarian internationalism'. Increasingly, its message was one of visceral, xenophobic hatred for Germany and all things German. Soldiers were encouraged to keep a 'book of revenge' that would remind them of the need to repay the Germans for their crimes. Most notoriously, the brilliant journalist Ilya Ehrenburg, read by millions of soldiers and civilians, kept up a litany of highly literate hate-speak:

If you have not killed a German a day, you have wasted that day . . . If you kill one German, kill another – there is nothing funnier for us than a pile of German corpses.[7]

On the eve of the crossing into East Prussia, the army's Main Political Administration told the troops: 'On German soil there is only one master – the Soviet soldier . . . he is both the judge and the punisher for the torments of his fathers and mothers, for the destroyed cities and villages . . .' Road signs put up by the advancing army instructed the following units: 'Soldier: You are in Germany, take revenge on the Hitlerites!'[8]

All these factors combined to turn the advance of the Red Army in early 1945 into a thing of ominous horror. The scale of the mass rape, murder and destruction in Germany's eastern provinces during the first months of 1945 was truly appalling. It is quite clear that from the moment the Red Army reached German soil, everything, living or inanimate, was considered fair game. Many uneducated Russian soldiers saw not just improbably neat, prosperous villages and towns, but also insultingly cosseted women and girls, surrounded by items of finery that may well – as their propagandists encouraged them to believe – have been looted from Russian homes during the occupation, perhaps even torn from the quivering, half-starved backs of their own mothers and sisters.

The Nobel laureate Alexander Solzhenitsyn, an artillery officer with the Red Army in East Prussia in early 1945, chronicled that season of terror and destruction in his epic poem *Prussian Nights*:

Zweiundzwanzig, Höringstrasse
It's not been burned, just looted, rifled.
A moaning by the walls half muffled:
The mother's wounded, still alive.
The little daughter's on the mattress,
Dead. How many have been on it
A platoon, a company perhaps?
A girl's been turned into a woman.
A woman turned into a corpse . . .[9]

Solzhenitsyn was arrested and sent to a labour camp in early 1945 after critical remarks about Stalin's leadership qualities were found in his mail home. Likewise, Captain Lev Kopelev, hitherto an enthusiastic communist and commander of a front-line propaganda unit, unwisely intervened to dissuade a group of soldiers intent on the rape of German women and the looting of their homes. He was sentenced to ten years in the Gulag for crimes dubbed 'bourgeois humanism' and 'compassion towards the enemy'.[10]

So, all over the area that was rapidly falling to the Red Army, women were raped and murdered, houses looted and destroyed. Just as Wehrmacht officers had almost never intervened to prevent the brutalities exercised by the German forces in Russia, so it was fairly rare that fastidious men in positions of authority, such as Solzhenitsyn and Kopelev, became involved.

The accounts of the rapes, each an unspeakable horror for individual German women and families, blur into each other. In one small village in Pomerania, which fell in the first weeks of 1945, there was an added curse that would also repeat itself across the conquered lands. Alcohol. The area concerned made its main living from potato growing, with a sideline in distilling schnapps from the crop surplus. When the Soviets took the village, they ordered all the remaining civilian inhabitants from their homes and locked them in the church. Having discovered the local distillery, the Russian soldiers proceeded to drink heavily, after which they laid waste to the village. Finally, they came back to the church, for the women and girls.

The then fifteen-year-old Wanda Schultz, a local farmer's daughter, described her experience many years later:

> It was the worst night of my life, that one I spent then. In the church we were all raped, over and over. Then they dragged me into the main village, where the same thing happened. I thought, it is all over for me . . . Strangely, I had no fear. As a fifteen-year-old, I just thought: 'Now they'll shoot me, because they can't let me go back to my parents in this condition.' But they took me back to the church.[11]

Astonishingly, the following morning there was a savage domesticity to the scene. The Russians summoned their German prisoners and ordered chickens to be rounded up and cooked for them.

A little later, Wanda Schultz and her father ventured out to the family farm on the edge of the village. There they found more Russian soldiers, attacking the pigs with knives and stealing horses to hitch to their wagons full of loot. As dairy farmers will – indeed, must – father and daughter tried to milk the cows, but this was interrupted by new arrivals, who announced their intention to start violating Wanda all over again. She and her father were lucky that an appeal to the men's officer for protection was successful this time, but they took no further chances and meekly made their way back to join the others in the doubtful sanctuary of the church. A few days later they were transferred to the larger village of Polnow.

All were eventually interrogated by the NKVD (Soviet Commissariat for State Security), and many forced to sign statements, often in Russian with no translation. Wanda was one of those deported to a Russian labour camp, a fate inflicted on almost three-quarters of a million Germans from the occupied areas and which she blamed on her membership of the BDM. Under NKVD Order Number 0016, 'Measures for the purging of areas in the rear of the fighting Red Army of enemy elements', membership not just of the National Socialist Party but also of any Nazi youth organisations could be grounds for deportation.

This was the first, most violent, chaotic and crude beginning in the grand scheme of cleansing the German population of Nazism. Russian-style.

Almost a half of those delivered into the clutches of the NKVD's notorious GUPVI (Main Administration for Prisoners-of-War and Internees' Affairs) were reckoned to have died of mistreatment, disease (most commonly typhus) or overwork. Fortunately Wanda was not among them, though she was transported for many hundreds of miles in appalling conditions and witnessed the deaths of many girls she had known all her life. After more than four years' hard labour, first on a collective farm attached to a mining camp in the Urals, then down a coal mine, in winter working at temperatures as low as minus 40°C, she was finally released.

Shortly before Christmas 1949, Wanda arrived in West Germany, where she was eventually reunited with her family. They had been expelled from Pomerania in 1946 and found a home, albeit a tiny one in a prefabricated barracks, in the town of Rendsburg, in Schleswig-Holstein, on the south bank of the Kiel Canal. When Wanda arrived at the station and saw her parents again for the first time in five years, she cried for two hours, uninterrupted, oblivious of her surroundings.

Altogether it is reckoned that around 1.9 million German women were raped by Soviet soldiers in the final months of the war and those immediately following the peace.[12] For a while, in the early summer of 1945, the instance of rape actually got worse again – a fact blamed on older, more educated men being released back to Russia early in order to assist with post-war reconstruction, leaving behind in Germany mainly younger men, many recruited late in the war from areas such as Belarus and the Ukraine, occupied for years by the Wehrmacht. Men from such regions had been brutalised by their experiences of occupation and imbued with a deep loathing of everything German.[13]

Not all Soviet soldiers behaved in such a wild and undisciplined way, however. Repeatedly there are stories of Russians who behaved kindly, or at least correctly. It was said that the elite front-line troops were not so bad; worse were the second and third wave, who were under less strict discipline, had less fighting to do and thus more time for criminality.

Ruth Irmgard, thirteen years old, was hauled from the cellar of her family's home and raped by a gang of Russian soldiers. When she wept inconsolably, her mother, who had herself been raped and had attempted suicide, told her sternly: 'If you can't take it, then go in the Alle', a reference to the river that ran through the small East Prussian town where they lived.[14] A few hours later, Ruth was saved from further molestation by the appearance of an officer, who sent the would-be rapists away. He took her back to her mother, but warned the family that he could not protect them indefinitely. She should leave town, he said, with Ruth and her four other children, and stick to the countryside, where there was less chance of trouble.

Mother and children took to the road. They lost two of the boys to diphtheria, but neither Ruth nor her mother was raped again. They heard after the war that the rest of the townspeople had subsequently been deported to Russia; many were never seen again. Ruth still tells herself that if she had not been raped she would never have met the kindly officer, her family would never have left the town and they too might have perished in the Gulag.

She feels that thought helps. A little.[15]

If the invasion and conquest were bad, they were no worse than many conquered peoples had suffered over the millennia during which human beings have waged war on each other. The Soviets, while brutal and ruthless, and willing, if not eager, to kill and destroy on a massive scale, were not genocidal in their intention – a distinction worth remembering when their conduct in Germany is compared with that of the Nazi occupation of the Soviet Union after June 1941.

But there was another difference in this conquest, and the consequences for the almost ten million or more people who lived in the ancient German lands of East Prussia, Pomerania and Silesia were both drastic and catastrophic. Not only were these provinces subjected to the imposition of foreign rule, they were also, as soon became clear, to be ethnically cleansed. In future these lands were not to be inhabited by Germans but by Poles and Russians. The German border was to be moved hundreds of kilometres to the west. These millions of settled human beings who survived the Russian onslaught were to be uprooted from their homes, farms and businesses and 'resettled' in what used to be known as western and central Germany.

However, it was not just the Germans who were to be forcibly moved as the Russians advanced to victory.

Six years earlier, under secret clauses in his agreement with Hitler (the so-called 'Nazi–Soviet Pact'), Stalin had claimed the eastern half of the soon-to-be-destroyed Polish state. On 17 September 1939, with Poland already near-prostrate under the German assault that had begun on 1 September, the Red Army, accompanied by the Stalinist state's whole ghastly apparatus of oppression, propaganda and enforcement, moved into the eastern provinces.

Eleven days later, after the Polish surrender in east and west, the Russians and the Germans signed an agreement abolishing Poland – or, as the startlingly mendacious words of the treaty's text put it: 'the Government of the German Reich and the Government of the U.S.S.R. have, by means of the treaty signed today, definitively settled the problems arising from the collapse of the Polish state and have thereby created a sure foundation for a lasting peace in Eastern Europe'.[16]

They had done nothing of the kind, of course. But what did happen in eastern Poland (known thereafter officially as 'the Polish region') was in most ways as radical as what happened in the German-occupied west of the country.

In the west, the Germans immediately dismantled Polish state institutions, absorbed large areas directly into the Reich and established a colonial-style regime known as the 'General Government' in the remaining part of the country, with its capital at Krakow. Polish landowners, industrialists and intellectuals began to be rounded up and systematically liquidated. Jews were persecuted and ghettoised. Almost a million Poles,

Christian and Jewish, were expelled at short notice, without compensation, from the annexed areas and dumped into the General Government. It was a precedent that would not be forgotten five years later.

Meanwhile, in the Soviet-occupied part, a little over half the country's area and containing a third of its population, landholdings and industries were seized by the state, the Polish administration dissolved and a communist police state instituted. The difference from the German-occupied area was that the majority of the inhabitants in the eastern provinces seized by Stalin, though ruled by a Polish elite, were not Polish-speaking but Ukrainian (more than a third), Belorussian (around 15 per cent) and Jews.

In June 1941, the Soviet-controlled 'Polish region' was invaded by the Wehrmacht and subjected to the same Calvary as the rest of German-occupied Russia. The question was, what would happen when the fortunes of war were reversed? Britain and France had intervened in 1939 to preserve the integrity of the Polish Republic (an intention which led to no direct military intervention on the battlefield and should, logically, have also involved a declaration of war against Hitler's Soviet co-conspirators).

As the tide turned on the Eastern Front, and in early 1944 the Soviet Army approached the borders of pre-war Poland, it became obvious that Stalin had no intention of giving up the territory he had acquired under the Nazi–Soviet Pact. This had been privately clear at least since the Tehran Conference between the 'Big Three' Allied nations in November/December 1943.

In fact, as early as March 1943, when British Foreign Secretary Eden met in Washington with Roosevelt and his adviser, Harry Hopkins, they agreed that the Poles should have East Prussia after the war. The Russians were duly informed of this. In return, it was made clear by Soviet Ambassador Litvinov that, while approving the expansion of Poland to the west, Russia would insist on her 'territorial rights' on the eastern frontier. This was a statement accepted by all to mean that the territory seized from Poland in 1939 would remain part of the Soviet Union after victory.[17]

At Tehran, the question of Polish compensation for Stalin's cynical detachment of almost half their country – giving Russia a greater slice of Poland than she had obtained in 1795, when the country had been divided between the three great regional powers of the time, Russia, Prussia and Austria – was seriously addressed. Now, instead of 'just' East Prussia, it was proposed to assuage Polish feelings with the gift of Upper Silesia, Danzig and Pomerania as well. Almost seven million Germans lived in these areas and had done so for centuries.

By January 1945, the Russians had further increased their demands. The grant to Poland was now to include further lands between the two branches of the Neisse River, a rich agricultural area inhabited by an extra 2.8 million Germans.[18] East Prussia would now be divided along north–south lines, with the Poles taking the southern and the Russians the northern half. Altogether, a little under ten million Germans would now find their ancestral lands included within the post-war borders of the Soviet Union and Poland.[19]

The Western Allies protested during the pre-negotiations for the big Yalta Conference in February, and they protested further at the conference itself, but by this time there was not much they could do about it. The realities on the ground included massive Russian occupation forces and also a pro-Soviet Polish puppet government, based since the summer of 1944 in the eastern city of Lublin. The 'Lublin Poles' had begun contesting the legitimacy of the London-based Polish government-in-exile, even raising their own army as an auxiliary force for the Russians. The non-communist Poles inside the country had been severely depleted by the Germans' pitiless suppression of the Warsaw Uprising in the summer of 1944. As Churchill and the ailing Roosevelt were forced to realise, Stalin could do with his brother Slavic country (for centuries Russia's intimate enemy) what he wished.

So, as the Red Army burst over the border into what had been the Greater German Reich in January 1945, it was not just rape and destruction that the German civilian population had to fear, but the longer-term intentions of the Russians (and, it soon became clear, of the Poles and the Czechs). These intentions centred on what at the time was referred to as a 'population transfer' and what a later age would call, more brutally and more honestly, 'ethnic cleansing'.

The mass expulsions of Germans that began shortly before the end of the war were not the first such catastrophe of the twentieth century.

During the First World War and the period of violent dissolution that followed it, the Ottoman Empire, for centuries a patchwork of races and religions living mostly peaceably together, had witnessed massacres and internecine war on a huge scale. Most notorious was the officially sponsored massacre or expulsion of the empire's Christian Armenian population – with a death toll estimated at between 300,000 (Turkish figure) and 1.5 million (Armenian figure). Hitler himself was reputed to have declared, with reference to his intended brutal treatment of the Polish population in 1939, 'Who now remembers the Armenians?'[20] But there was another precedent.

The other large Christian minority in the Turkish sphere of rule was that of the Ottoman Greeks, again totalling around 1.5 million, mostly living near to the west coast of Anatolia, where they had been settled since a millennium before the birth of Christ. Numerous Greeks were to be found also in Istanbul (once, as Constantinople, the capital of the Greek Byzantine Empire), on the Black Sea coast and in the eastern province of Cappadocia, where the long-established but isolated Greek population now spoke a kind of Turkish dialect.

The problem of the Christian Greeks in Anatolia had been simmering away since the turn of the twentieth century, but it reached crisis point after the First World War, when Turkey, its empire rapidly disintegrating, seemed prostrate at the feet of its local rivals. The Greek government – one of the victors of the First World War – seized the opportunity to land troops at Smyrna, the largest city on Turkey's west coast, a glittering cosmopolitan trading centre with a substantial and vocally nationalist Greek population as well as Turkish, Armenian and other-nationality citizens, including thousands of French, British and American business people and their families.

Emboldened, the Greeks began to pursue a long-harboured notion of the *Megali Idea* (Great Idea), a restoration of all the nation's ancient lands, including Constantinople (Istanbul). Soon they began to make incursions deep into the Turkish-dominated interior, terrorising the non-Greek inhabitants.

The resulting war between the Greeks and Turks, the latter led by their great national hero, General Mustafa Kemal (later honoured with the name Kemal Atatürk) ended in a definite and tragically bloody Turkish victory. Many thousands of Greeks were massacred or fled (it should be added that, during their own incursions, Greek army and militia units had also slaughtered innocent Turks and laid waste to entire villages and towns). The Greek forces were forced to evacuate Anatolia. On 9 September 1922, in one of the most terrible events of the early twentieth century, the ancient and proud city of Smyrna was laid to waste by an alliance of Turkish soldiery and free-booters and then destroyed by fire.[21]

George Horton, the American consul, who managed to make it to a waiting boat at the height of this mayhem, saw, as he made his way between the Turkish ranks on the quayside, how terrible had been the slaughter. 'Then they [the Turkish soldiers] cleared our way . . . and we rushed past in safety. Among the many dead bodies, we saw men, women and children shot to death, bodies drawn up in horribly strained postures, with expressions portraying the endurance of excruciating pain.'[22] Describing his feelings as he steamed away from the burning city in the safety of an American naval vessel, Horton recollected:

As the destroyer moved away from the fearful scene and darkness descended, the flames, raging now over a vast area, grew brighter and brighter, presenting a scene of awful and sinister beauty . . . nothing was lacking in the way of atrocity, lust, cruelty and all that fury of human passion which, given their full play, degrade the human race to a level lower than the vilest and cruellest of beasts . . . of the keenest impression which I brought away with me from Smyrna was a feeling of shame that I belonged to the human race.[23]

Unspeakably cruel as much of their behaviour was, like the Russians in Germany in 1945 the intentions of the Turks in Anatolia a little over twenty years earlier were brutal, ruthless – murderous on an individual level – but not technically genocidal. They had decided that the Greeks, too ambitious, too rich, infidel and disloyal, had to be made to leave, and a great part of the violence was not just the conventionally opportunistic, sadistic and vengeful behaviour of undisciplined soldiers but part of a cold-blooded strategy to ensure that this would happen.

Kemal, the Turkish commander, openly admitted to his aides that he saw the destruction of the cosmopolitan (and largely Christian) city as a part of a 'purification' process that would return its shell, at least, to its 'true and noble Turkish inhabitants'.[24]

Thousands of Anatolian Greeks died, but tens and hundreds of thousands more escaped of their own volition to the nearby Greek-held islands. Others, if they survived, waited meekly under unspeakable conditions, subjected to continuing harassment and violence, for their fate to be decided.

The appalling situation in Anatolia was finally regulated by the Treaty of Lausanne in July 1923. This mandated a compulsory population exchange, with the surviving 1.2–1.5 million Greeks in Anatolia deported to Greece, while 400,000 or so Muslims, often Greek-speakers, from northern Greece and the Greek islands (most notably Crete and Lesvos), were forced to leave for Turkey.

The situation in the easternmost provinces of Germany in 1944–5 was not so different, for the process of expulsion was likewise double. Polish-speaking people were forced to leave the area occupied by the Soviets in 1939 and now reoccupied in 1944, and, like the Greek Muslims and Anatolian Greeks, they were expected to move into the villages, towns and farms in which the 'enemy' had once lived.

Anatolian Greeks – who often spoke little Greek or, if they did, spoke it with almost incomprehensible provincial accents – had been offered homes in formerly Muslim areas in Greece, while Greek-speaking Cretan Muslims were moved by the Turkish authorities into formerly Christian Greek homes in Smyrna or Ayvalik. A quarter of a century later, the dispossessed eastern Poles were ordered to settle in formerly German areas. Meanwhile, the expelled Germans, on the heels of the terror and the rape and the violence, were to trek west and be taken in by their compatriots within what was left of Germany.

The truth about the so-called 'population exchange' carried out under the Treaty of Lausanne was, when seen from the ground by those affected, savage and sordid, but it was seen by contemporaries as a 'successful' solution to the problem. And it was sanctioned by the international community.

So, when it came in the last years of the war to similar suggestions regarding the fate of Germany and the population of its easternmost provinces, given Stalin's insistence on holding on to eastern Poland, Lausanne was eagerly seized upon as a 'respectable' example of how the seizure of a quarter of Germany's territory and the rendering of around ten million of the country's pre-war population homeless could be effected while retaining some façade of legitimacy.

By February 1945, the great historic cities of eastern Germany were all in Russian hands, or – in the case of Königsberg (pre-war population 300,000 inhabitants) and Breslau (pre-war 650,000) – under siege. Surviving civilians and soldiers were forced into suicidal defensive fighting by fanatical Gauleiters and last-ditch generals.

In the case of the undoubtedly heroic defence of Königsberg, there was some excuse. Just as the Greeks and other Christians had once been trapped in the port of Smyrna, the quaysides of the besieged East Prussian capital were thronged with Germans waiting for a boat – any boat – to carry them westward across the wintry and treacherous Baltic Sea to territory still under German control.

Tens of thousands of refugees were safely evacuated from the port of Königsberg, in a fleet of over a thousand vessels, merchant and military – no less than an East Prussian Dunkirk. The numbers saved from the shrinking area of the Baltic coast in German hands ran after January 1945 into hundreds of thousands. It was an astonishing achievement, despite the sinking by a Soviet submarine of the heavily overloaded converted cruise liner *Wilhelm Gustloff* (named after a Swiss Nazi leader assassinated in 1936). The *Gustloff* catastrophe resulted in the deaths of 8,000 human beings, mostly refugees – the greatest single mass drowning in maritime history.[25]

By contrast, the stubborn defence of Breslau – historic, landlocked, clearly doomed – tied up a few Soviet regiments but was otherwise entirely pointless. This futile resistance, made worse by the authorities' refusal to allow a proper civilian evacuation until it was too late, was led by the fanatical and overbearing Gauleiter Karl Hanke. Still only forty-two, Hanke was former Under-Secretary at the Reich Ministry of Public Enlightenment and Propaganda, and rumoured lover of Goebbels' wife, Magda.[26]

Since the end of March, boys as young as ten and girls of twelve, and even pregnant women, had been conscripted by the Nazi die-hards into labour gangs that often worked under fire. Bunkers and barricades were constructed from dynamited buildings, whole streets razed to provide free-fire zones. Civilian casualty rates were appalling, especially during the forced construction of a second airfield in March, in the centre of the city, to enable it to be supplied from the air. Entire familiar Breslau streets and landmark buildings were demolished by dynamite and fire to create the space between the Kaiser and Fürsten Bridges from which an air link could be re-established. Figures as high as 13,000 dead have been claimed for just this one project, which in any case resulted in a landing strip which was eventually used by no more than a handful of aircraft.[27]

Despite freezing weather, which in itself caused the deaths of thousands, vicious house-to-house fighting comparable to the horrors of Stalingrad, and heavy bombing by the Soviet air force, some German units in Breslau held out until the last days of the war.

Gauleiter Hanke, meanwhile, had been appointed Reichsführer SS at the end of April in succession to the disgraced Himmler. He disappeared from Breslau in a light aircraft – ironically one of the few planes to lift off from that same, tragically underused second airfield

– three days before the war ended. He may have hoped to evade retribution. If this was true, his hopes were in vain, for he ended his life a little over a month later in Czech captivity, disguised as an ordinary SS soldier, by various accounts shot while trying to escape or beaten to death.[28]

There were fanatics among those who fled before the Russians as well as among those who resisted them, but the vast majority of fugitive Germans, no matter how enthusiastic they may have felt about the Nazi regime in earlier times, were by the spring of 1945 concerned with only one thing: survival.

Not all of those in the doomed provinces of eastern Germany were strong enough, physically or mentally, to undertake the trek west. One young Wehrmacht soldier, home in Breslau on convalescent leave in mid-January, two days before the evacuation of civilians began, found his family in a hopeless state.

Many of the city's civilians had already left, despite the authorities' threats. Others had succumbed to despair. The young soldier, Ulrich Frodien, only eighteen years old, entered the flat of an elderly neighbour in their apartment block to find the bodies of the man and his housekeeper hanging side by side in a grim suicide pact. They would be followed by many others. Towards the end of the coming siege, by one local priest's estimate suicides would be running at 120 per day.[29]

Frodien's mother and sisters had permits to leave, but he and his father, a former First World War military surgeon, had been ordered to stay in the city. The two of them inspected a street barricade being built by the city's would-be defenders and decided that it would take the approaching Soviet tanks fifteen minutes to demolish it – 'fourteen minutes for the tank crew to stop laughing, and one minute to brush it aside'.[30] They also saw roaming patrols of Wehrmacht field police, who had orders to shoot looters and suspected deserters – the latter category one into which Ulrich, as one of the walking wounded, might conceivably, though wrongly, have been placed.

So, Breslau was not a safe place for males between school and pensionable age to be. As a consequence, he and his father hit on a wild escape plan, and carried it out. Ulrich's father wore his old First World War surgeon's uniform, complete with medals, and Ulrich festooned himself with serious-looking, stained bandages. Once they had left the apartment for the main station, the young man was to refer to his father as 'Herr Hauptmann' and to behave accordingly.

Even at eighteen degrees below freezing, Breslau's *Hauptbahnhof* was besieged by would-be refugees and defended by a cordon of armed soldiers. They found that the only journey scheduled was that of a hospital train. Without further ado, Ulrich's father put himself at the head of a line of walking wounded, marched them past the point where his son was standing, and growled at him: 'Private! Take your bag! By the right, quick march!' Ulrich joined the column as his impressively commanding father led them through the military cordon, waving a meaningless 'paper' under the soldiers' noses as he did so, and on to the hospital train.

The train was overcrowded, malodorous, filled with sick and dying men, and it was hours before it actually left, but soon Ulrich and his father were on their way to the relative safety of Prague, which would remain under German control until the very last days of the war.

As they left, Ulrich's father had said to him: 'Take a look: you'll never see your homeland again.' He was wrong. Ulrich would revisit years later as a grown man. But one thing was certainly true. He would never see Breslau again as a German city.

Herr Frodien senior had for a long time been an enthusiastic Nazi. His disillusionment had been a later development, though no less heartfelt for that.

Many citizens of Breslau stayed until the bitter end, which came on 6 May 1945, at six o'clock in the evening, when the last German commandant formally surrendered his forces and what was left of the so-called 'fortress city' to the not-so-tender mercies of the Red Army. Rape and pillage proceeded apace. After 7 May much of the remaining architectural heritage of the city centre was destroyed deliberately by fire (and later wrongly blamed on the siege), with the university library and the city museum among the priceless cultural assets to go up in flames. Units of the victorious Soviet forces fought vicious battles against each other for control of the provisions stores on the Sternstrasse.[31]

By the official end of the war on 8 May, Breslau was a chaotic collection of ruins. But one little-noticed event that took place the next day would turn out to be even more ominous for its remaining German citizens, exhausted, disillusioned and utterly war weary though they might be. A group of thirteen Polish representatives of the as-yet-unrecognised Russian-sponsored government arrived in the city and took possession of one of the undamaged houses in the city centre. They were soon joined by further officials, including representatives of the new Soviet-sponsored secret police force, the Office of Public Security.

At the end of the war, the only Poles in the city had been some forced labourers and servants. This soon began to change. In June the first Polish child was born in Breslau, the first Polish couple married under Polish law and the first Polish newspaper was published. Even before the Allies had met to decide on the city's final fate, the nascent Polish post-war government had begun to assert a control to which, as yet, it had absolutely no right under international law.

So confused was the situation, however, that many Germans actually returned to their native Breslau in the weeks after the peace. After all, the situation, though chaotic and dangerous, with the ever-growing risk of starvation, was no worse than elsewhere in occupied Germany, especially east of the Elbe, where the Soviets held sway. By the early summer of 1945 there were, despite initial voluntary flights and expulsions of Germans, still around 150,000 left in the city.

Most people found it hard to believe that such a major city of the Reich, in which the German language and culture had been dominant since the Middle Ages, and where by the nineteenth century Poles represented a very small minority, could simply be emptied of its people. It was assumed among those who had already fled that at some point soon, when the war was over and things had settled down, they would be able to return and try to pick up the pieces of their former lives. Such had been the case in many wars, however savage, over many centuries. But the Second World War had been a war unlike any other, right from the start – when Germany had held the whip hand and had broken all the usual conventions of conquest – and now that the Reich was on its knees, the Allies would likewise throw away the rule book when it came to the territorial and human consequences of victory.

It was also true that, as the war ended, many of the plans being discussed by the soon-to-be-victorious Allies were framed so as to leave the eastern branch of the Neisse River, which ran through Breslau, as the new border. This meant that much of Silesia, Pomerania and East Prussia would be lost, but historic Breslau would remain German, with only the eastern suburbs in Polish hands.

However, all this changed at the Potsdam Conference in July/August 1945.

The great post-war conference of the Allies might well have taken place in the city of Berlin – such a venue would, after all, have been satisfyingly symbolic – except that, such was the scale of destruction wrought on the German capital, no buildings existed capable of comfortably housing the Allied statesmen, their advisers and entourages.

The officials of the Soviet Commissariat for State Security (NKVD) and of the Soviet Foreign Ministry, jointly charged with organising the congress-cum-victory-jamboree, therefore moved their field of choice into Berlin's relatively undamaged south-western suburbs, and finally settled upon Potsdam. More precisely, they found a collection of luxury villas near the famous UFA film studios at Babelsberg, on the town's outskirts (mostly in the possession of German movie luminaries) that could be requisitioned for the use of the delegations. A former palace of Germany's last crown prince, the Cecilienhof, situated along with several other royal residences in the idyllic 250-acre

Neuer Garten (New Garden), close to the shores of the Jungfernsee, was in fit condition to be used for the conference proceedings.[32]

Potsdam had been the residence of the Prussian kings and later of those Prussian kings who were also German emperors – its relation to Berlin was rather as Versailles is to Paris. It contained many grand and beautiful buildings, including Frederick the Great's pleasure dome, Sans-Souci. However, it had not survived the war totally unscathed. In one of the last major air attacks of the war, on the night of 14–15 April 1945, 500 Lancasters of RAF Bomber Command, supposedly targeting troop concentrations and the railway station, had devastated the previously untouched historic town centre. They also killed, by the most reliable estimates, almost 1,800 civilians.[33]

Less than two weeks later, Potsdam was captured by the Red Army. A further 1,200 deaths and large amounts of artillery damage further wrecked the fabric of the town. Except for the Babelsberg villas, near the film studio, and the Crown Prince's palace. The palace was modern and comfortable – a 176-room mock-Tudor mansion built between 1913 and 1917, supposedly modelled on a large English country house near Liverpool. The Crown Prince and his wife, the former Princess Cecilie of Mecklenburg, after whom the house was named, had lived there until February 1945. The Cecilienhof remained more or less as they had left it.

It was there, on 17 July, that the leaders of the three victorious nations (France was not invited) settled around a large round table supplied by the state-owned Lux furniture concern of Moscow, to dot the i's and cross the t's on the post-war settlement.

President Truman and Prime Minister Churchill had driven to the Cecilienhof through Berlin's ruins, which in the past weeks had been festooned by the Soviets with propaganda hoardings, including huge billboard posters of Marx, Engels, Lenin – and, of course, Stalin. The thoroughfares were swarming with Soviet soldiery. Although detachments of British and American troops had belatedly been permitted to take up their quarters in the capital ten days or so earlier, as had been agreed at Yalta, there could be no doubt who was in charge in Berlin.

What was decided here, over the following sixteen days, was not good news for Germany in general, and it was even worse news for those Germans still clinging on to their homes in the country's eastern provinces. The leaders agreed on the 'Five Ds' (demilitarisation, denazification, democratisation, decentralisation and decartelisation), which would, it was planned, for ever divest Germany of her potential for aggressive war. They agreed on the destruction of German war industries. They agreed, too, on reparations, including, in recognition of Russia's special suffering at German hands, the considerable percentages of plant and production that the Soviet Union was to receive from both its own zone *and* the zones controlled by the Western Allies. But above all, from the point of view of the German expellees, they discussed the formalisation of Germany's loss of around 25 per cent of its territory – from which its millions of long-established inhabitants would be forcibly evicted.

Churchill had begun the negotiations insisting that these ancient German areas should not be given to the Poles. His own British people, he insisted, would be 'shocked' by such a huge movement of population, which was 'more than I could defend':

> Compensation should bear some relation to loss. It would do Poland no good to acquire so much extra territory. If the Germans had run away from it they should be allowed to go back. The Poles had no right to risk a catastrophe in feeding Germany. We did not want to be left with a vast German population who were cut off from their sources of food. The Ruhr was in our zone, and if enough food could not be found for the inhabitants, we would have conditions like the German concentration camps.[34]

Perhaps inevitably, Churchill's words proved empty. Within days, the Conservative Party was officially declared the loser in the British general election and Churchill was forced to break off the conference and fly home to present his resignation. His successor, Labour leader Clement Attlee, and his new Foreign Secretary, Ernest Bevin, took

Churchill's and Eden's places on 28 July, but had little time to make their presence felt.

The Western Allies, and especially America, should perhaps have been able to get more of their way at Potsdam than they did. On 25 July, the day before Churchill left the conference, President Truman had informed Stalin of the USA's possession of a 'new weapon of unusually destructive force' – the atomic bomb. Stalin reacted with cool indifference (he already knew about it from his spies).

The fact was, however, that on the last day of the month the Americans, though at first they had supported Churchill's view, eventually settled for a border on the western Neisse, meaning that Breslau would go to Poland. The British, beset by other pressing concerns, including defending their position in the Ruhr, did not contest this at the time.[35] The expulsion of the Germans who lived in the areas given over to 'Polish administration', like the other 'transfers of population', was to happen, in theory, over a period up to August 1946, 'in a humane and orderly fashion'.[36]

Since vanishingly little about the occupation of what had been eastern Germany had so far been 'humane and orderly', few would have trusted that matters would be any different in future. And they would have been right.

In the end, almost ten million Germans were forced to leave the territories assigned to Poland under the Potsdam Agreement. A huge, seemingly endless wave of terrified refugees – mostly women, children and the elderly – had been on the move along the highways of eastern Germany since midwinter. They carried their bundles of precious heirlooms and belongings in their hands or on their backs. If they were lucky they had a handcart, or, if they were among the most fortunate, a horse-drawn vehicle. At no time were they safe, at least not until they reached the areas of central and western Germany occupied by the Western Allies. They risked being caught up with the advancing Soviet spearheads, wandering into battles, or falling victim to Allied bombing raids.

An unknown number of westbound refugees certainly died in the bombing of Dresden in mid-February. In another notorious but less well-known case, on 12 March 1945, thousands of refugees from eastern Pomerania and East Prussia, queuing in the open for the ferry to cross the river at Swinemünde,* found themselves trapped beneath a rain of American bombs. The raid, requested by the Soviets, had been intended to destroy the German naval ships concentrated in the town's harbour. At one time, civilian casualties were estimated at up to 23,000, causing the attack to be dubbed the 'Dresden of the North'. The true figure is now thought to be between four and five thousand, but it remains a ghastly illustration of how exposed these defenceless refugees were to the vagaries of modern total war.[37]

By the spring, the refugee tide had turned into a vast, uncontrollable torrent of misery – and the coming of peace did nothing to halt it, for now the formerly oppressed peoples of Central Europe had their opportunity for revenge. To many among them peace was not an end to violence but a beginning.

The ethnic cleansing in Breslau had actually begun with the so-called 'wild' expulsions of early July 1945, well before the victors had signed on the line and regularised the Polish administration there.[38]

However, after the formal ceding of the city to Poland, the cleansing began to move apace. As the summer went on, thousands of Poles forced to leave the formerly Polish territories seized by Stalin began arriving in the former German lands. These new arrivals, angry and bewildered, brutalised by a savage interlude of Soviet rule, followed by German occupation, were mostly not city dwellers but farmers and country people. Not only did they not want to be in this German city, but they did not actually know *how* to live in such a place.

There was a period of months when the half-ruined city of Breslau was seriously overcrowded, with Germans often being thrown out of their apartments to make room for newcomers, so that German

* Now the border town of Świnoujście in Poland.

families were often crammed two or three to a formerly single-family dwelling. In conscious emulation of the Nazis' stigmatisation of Jews, it was reported that remaining Germans were seen wearing armbands bearing the letter 'N' (for '*Niemiec*', or 'German' in Polish). Germans were allowed only one-third to one-half of the general ration, and their children were charged 100 zloty (at a punitive rate against the Reich mark) for inoculation shots against typhus, diphtheria and other diseases of overcrowding and deprivation that now became rife (Poles were immunised for free).[39] When asked to show pity, Russians and Poles could, and did, point to the starvation rations and murder-ous neglect practised during the German occupation of their countries earlier in the war.

So, after the first wave of German refugees who fled before the Red Army, there followed, as the first post-war summer progressed, a new wave. This one was made up of those who had stayed behind but were now forced to leave.

At the end of 1945, 33,297 Poles were registered in Breslau (hence-forth Wrocław), against more than 160,000 Germans. By the following autumn, the city contained 152,898 registered Poles, against only 28,274 Germans.[40]

The atrocities in such eastern German cities were bad enough. In the Sudetenland – the border areas of Czechoslovakia settled for hundreds of years by Germans, part of the multinational Austro-Hungarian Empire until 1918, for twenty years part of the Czech and Slovak state, then for seven short years incorporated into the Greater German Reich – they were unspeakable.

Unlike in the case of Breslau, Königsberg or Stettin, the Germans here had been only briefly 'Reich Germans'. Czechs of the western part of the country, where most Germans had always lived, had coexisted side by side with them, sometimes amicably but often uneasily, as linguistic components of a cosmopolitan post-feudal monarchy, for centuries past.

Now, after six years of brutal Nazi oppression, many, perhaps most,

Czechs loathed their German compatriots and wanted merely to be rid of them.

'We hated them,' declared one Czech woman, unrepentant more than half a century later. 'People who had survived the concentration camps were returning and they were describing what happened to them there. The fact is that people hated the Germans, genuinely hated them so much that there was a spontaneous reaction, and the feeling was that if they liked the Third Reich so much, they could go there.'[41]

But first there was revenge to be taken, as one Czech eyewitness – himself a member of one of the makeshift militias that sprang into life along with the liberation – reported:

As I was marching with my unit of the revolutionary guard, I experienced something terrible. In one town, civilians dragged a German out into the middle of a crossroads and set alight to him. I am haunted by this experience to this day. I could do nothing, because if I had said something, I should have been attacked in my turn. The crowd was fanatical. The person burned for a half an hour. Then a soldier of the Red Army came and shot him. He gave him the *coup de grâce*.[42]

Cynics also pointed out that some of the most violent and apparently vengeful 'resistance' fighters who took part in such atrocities had dark pasts to hide. One member of the Czech National Council at the time of the liberation explained, 'Some wanted to hide the fact that they had previously collaborated with the Gestapo. They just pinned red stars on and set the tone of the outrages that followed.'[43]

It also seems to have been true that the majority of the most violent acts against Sudeten Germans were not committed by those Czechs who had lived in the area with them but by outsiders, who had entered the Sudeten areas in the wake of the Soviet and American armies.[44]

Just weeks after the end of the war, an armaments depot in the mainly German industrial town of Aussig (Czech name Usti nad

Labem), one of the many places where Sudeten Germans had been retained as forced labourers preparatory to their planned expulsion, was blown apart by a massive explosion. Twenty-seven workers died. In the aftermath, rumours spread that this was an act of sabotage by a German *Werwolf* gang. Up to a hundred Sudeten Germans – easily identifiable by the white armbands they were reportedly forced to wear – were subsequently killed by an angry Czech mob. Most were beaten and bayoneted, with others being tossed off the bridge in the town centre into the River Elbe or drowned in a fire pond.[45]

After conducting an 'inquiry' into the explosion, Czech Defence Minister Ludvík Svoboda declared:

It is necessary that we deal with the fifth column once and for all, and we can take the Soviet Union as our exemplar, as the only country that dealt with this problem in a secure fashion: As an example I present the case of the German Volga Republic [in the Soviet Union], where one night dozens of German paratroops were dropped. When they were concealed by the Germans there and not handed over when urgently demanded by the Red Army, it came to pass that, 48 hours after the final ultimatum, this German Volga Republic ceased to exist and will never again exist.[46]

Certainly, there was some *Werwolf*-style German guerrilla activity in the Czech borderlands, as there was in Silesia, where inter-communal warfare and expulsions were also rife in the months following the end of the war. However, that these were actually all official *Werwolf* units seems unlikely, and the Aussig disaster seems more likely to have been due to negligence. The aim of such pronouncements as Svoboda's, drawing on hoary lies from the Stalinist propaganda store, was quite clear. Every possible excuse was to be found in order to justify the expulsion of the Sudeten Germans from their homeland – no matter how cynical.

During the previous winter, East Prussian and Silesian refugees had struggled through snow and ice, desperate to keep ahead of the Soviet tank spearheads, knowing full well that if they were overtaken, murder and rape and pillage could be their fate. In the sweltering May of 1945, their cousins in the Sudetenland suffered less from the depredations of the Russians – the western districts were largely occupied by the Americans, in any case – than from the Czech 'revolutionary guards', whose motive was not just to gain momentary pleasure and revenge, but to drive the Germans from their country. There were many cases where the Germans were forced to appeal for help from the Soviets against the Czechs, and the slogan among them was: 'When the Red Army withdraws, it is the end for us!'[47]

Three weeks after the end of the war, on 29 May 1945, the revolutionary guard in the important Moravian city of Brünn (Czech: Brno) ordered its remaining German-speaking citizens to assemble at dawn the next day in the garden of the old Augustinian monastery, carrying only hand luggage. By this time, Germans made up 10 per cent of the town's quarter of a million inhabitants, totalling around 25,000 souls (the previous year, the German population had been around 60,000 but more than half had fled in advance of the war's end).

By 6 a.m. the German civilians had duly assembled to await the Czech militants' pleasure. A little later, with the sun rising on what would become a blazing May day and the church bells ringing for the Feast of Corpus Christi, the long column of Germans began to move off. They were told they were going to the Austrian border. The armed militants' meaning was clear: Brno's German population was leaving, never to return.

Escorted by armed revolutionary guards, the Germans trudged out of the city, heading south on the highway that led to the Austrian border some fifty kilometres distant. As far as the city limits they were watched by people who had once been their Czech fellow citizens, but who now applauded their departure and pelted them with any objects they could lay their hands on. The heat built relentlessly, until by late morning the refugees, without water or food, began to slow, to stagger, eventually to collapse on the open road. They were beaten with rifle butts until they moved on. Those who didn't or couldn't were frequently dispatched with a rifle bullet.

An officer of the Czechoslovak army, Josef Kratochvil, set off that morning with his brother, a doctor, on a motorcycle, and was able to see the full horror of what would become known as the 'death march of Brünn'. They reported 'dead old men, women and children collapsed in the ditches, women who had been raped'. They intervened where they could, but they could not be everywhere at once. Later that afternoon they returned to the city, where the officer told his commander what he had seen. The major, just returned from exile in England, shrugged. 'Are you telling me to conduct a private war against those crazy partisans?' he asked, and did nothing.[48]

Only when the column reached the small town of Pohrlitz (Pohořelice), a little under thirty kilometres from Brünn, were those who could no longer walk allowed to stop. In effect, they were interned here under guard, crowded into an improvised camp set up in a warehouse by the side of the highway. Meanwhile, the young and the relatively fit were forced to continue on their way. Days passed. Sanitary conditions in the warehouse were unspeakable and soon became lethal. There was no food. Typhus broke out. The stench of diarrhoea and death filled the air. Any local Czech who took pity on the Germans was liable to get a beating from the revolutionary guards for his or her pains.

Altogether, some 800 German expellees died of hunger, exhaustion or dysentery at Pohrlitz. According to a then member of the revolutionary guard who was interviewed almost half a century later, 1,700 of the 25,000 or so who had set off for the Austrian border on the day of the Feast of Corpus Christi perished en route, many murdered by their 'escorts'.

Elsewhere, there were especially brutal massacres of German internees at Miröschau (Mirosov) near Pilsen and at Duppau (Doupov) near Carlsbad.

At Duppau, the headmaster of the local secondary school, who had habitually appeared before his pupils dressed in full SS uniform, was, according to a reported deathbed confession by the bricklayer involved, immured alive on the orders of Czech partisans. Other prominent local Germans were shot or beaten to death.[49] One twenty-year-old Sudeten German woman later reported how a group of German men were forced to dig a mass grave. Then they were ordered by Czech soldiers to stand in line on the edge of the pit while the soldiers formed a firing party.

One [soldier] gave the order and the men were shot. I don't know if all the soldiers fired. Afterwards big white sacks filled with a white powder* were dragged there, and the German men who had not yet been shot sprinkled it all over the corpses. It was very bad. When I saw it, I cried very hard. A woman told me I didn't need to cry, because the Germans had done exactly the same thing to the Jews. I stood there as a young woman and didn't know what to say. Probably it was good that I said nothing.[50]

A letter published in the London *Times* in mid-June 1945 from three former Sudeten German deputies to the Prague parliament, now refugees in Britain, protested against the persecution of their German-speaking compatriots. 'Almost one-third of the population of the new Czechoslovakia is thus outlawed by their own Government, the decisive criterion of guilt being merely language or racial origin', they wrote, adding, 'the present position of Czechoslovakia's minorities is worse than that of war criminals, who will be judged on their individual guilt and by fair standards'.[51]

The exiles' appeal fell on deaf ears. Thousands of Sudeten Germans had not supported the Nazis, and many, like the letter writers, had been driven into exile or, like their Czech fellow citizens, suffered from persecution during the occupation years. However, many more had been eager to accept Hitler's solution to the ethnic problem in Czechoslovakia – a solution which formally acknowledged them as the 'master race' and the Czechs as disposable sub-humans.

In August, the Potsdam Agreement finally put the Allies' stamp on

* Presumably quicklime.

the Czechoslovak and Polish governments' already proclaimed goal of ridding themselves of all the Germans within their borders. The Sudetenland would be returned to Czechoslovakia, with the Czech government able to dispose of its population as it would. Prague Radio declared the Potsdam Agreement 'the greatest diplomatic and political victory ever achieved by our nation in its long historical fight for existence against the German nation'.[52] A *New York Times* reporter would later describe its 'solution' to the problem of German refugees, rather more accurately, as 'the most inhumane decision ever made by governments dedicated to the defence of human rights'.[53]

The most widely accepted estimate of the number of Germans who died at the hands of their Czech compatriots is approximately 30,000.[54] Official Czechoslovak figures registered 3,795 suicides by Sudeten Germans from May to October 1945. The 1946 figure, with many Germans forced to serve under terrible conditions as forced labourers before finally being expelled, would be even higher, at 5,558. Even those who escaped often could not summon the strength to go on. A month after the war's end, the Soviet NKVD's senior officer in Germany (and later first head of the KGB), General Ivan Aleksandrovic Serov, told his boss in Moscow, the notorious Lavrentiy Beria, that the death rate among Sudeten German refugees who had fled over the border into the Soviet Zone of Germany was also high:

Every day, up to 5,000 Germans arrive from Czechoslovakia, most of them women, old people and children. Without any future or the hope of anything better, many end their lives by suicide and cut open their veins.[55]

All the same, the surprising thing was, perhaps, not that so many died, by their own hands or those of others, but that they were relatively so few.

4

Zero Hour

When the dark music of the guns and bombs finally died away, on 8 May 1945, there began what became known to the German people as *Stunde Null*: Zero Hour.

The Nazi regime's last-ditch propaganda had incessantly repeated the message that, if Germany lost this war, the country would not just cease to exist, but would be systematically ravaged and dismantled. Most Germans, in the end, believed it, especially after the Red Army began its brutal rampage through the Reich's eastern provinces.

The destruction and loss during the last phase of the war was so tremendous, the chaos so thoroughgoing and the fall from apparent grace so dramatic, that however strong the sense of relief that the fighting was over, there was little hope of a tolerable future. Germans felt anxiety about what the victors would do to them. They also harboured a numb feeling of humiliation and a slow-burning anger, above all against the Nazis who had promised them so much – order, prosperity, first place among the nations of the earth – and failed them. This was especially true of popular attitudes towards the now-dead Hitler, the Führer whom tens of millions had once adored and thought infallible.

The anger against Hitler was sincere and deeply felt, but for many – perhaps the majority – an emotion born of disappointment rather than moral outrage. The Führer had failed his people and then, by his suicide in Berlin, left Germans to face the catastrophe alone.

Ulrich Frodien, the teenage soldier who had escaped Breslau with his father, had come close to being sent back to the near-certain death of the Eastern Front, but then finally, with almost incredible luck, had been packed on a hospital train bound for the west. He had experienced all these feelings all too vividly, even before the war was actually over.

Once, when Frodien's westbound train stopped, as it did so often in the chaos of the final days of the war, on the open railway line, between stations, he and his comrades heard the distant drone of aircraft engines. Soon the drone turned into a mighty roar. They looked up and saw an apparently endless, perfectly disciplined stream of hundreds of American Flying Fortresses, some 15,000 feet above them, flying east. Accustomed to air attacks, those passengers that could, including Frodien, left the train and scattered into the nearby woods. From there they watched the bomber swarm, which showed no interest in them, and marvelled. Frodien, an idealistic Hitler Youth leader who had volunteered at the age of sixteen and experienced the hell of the Eastern Front, but who still believed in the Führer and victory until close to the end, experienced one of the great realisations of his young life:

It was all definitely over for us. Now, at last and far too late, I had really come to understand this. The much-vaunted miracle weapons and the 'military genius' of the Führer were nothing against this casual, relaxed stream of a thousand four-engined bombers passing over our heads. There was no more hope, Germany was finished, it was all over.[1]

Nazi ideology paid little attention to the real practicalities of warfare. At the back of its assurances to the German people lay the idea that, even though the Reich and its European allies totalled at most a hundred and fifty million, and these were up against the military and economic might of two hundred million Americans, plus roughly the same number of Russians − not to mention the

British and their empire – the Third Reich could not lose because Germans were inherently, biologically superior to non-Germans.

This extreme, rigid social Darwinism simply could not cope with losing the war; it had, basically, no fallback position for that eventuality. In other words, in the view of the Nazi ideologues, it was not just that Germany would not lose the war, but that it simply *could* not.

In the second week of April 1945, a pair of convalescing Wehrmacht soldiers, dressed in hospital fatigues, watched open-mouthed from the side of the road as the fit, well-fed men of the American army, with its apparently unlimited complement of shiny new tanks, guns and trucks, drove all but unopposed along the Weender Landstrasse into the university town of Göttingen, south of Hanover. For years these German soldiers had had to fight their war using patched-up weapons and vehicles, outnumbered, subjected to constant fuel shortages and supply problems. Now they saw, really saw, what they had been up against all this time.

Soon the mass of Germans' bewilderment turned to anger against the men who had ruled their country since 1933, and who were responsible for this fiasco. One of the wounded soldiers in Göttingen, a plain-speaking farmer's son from now-lost East Prussia, spoke for a great many ordinary Germans and was recorded for posterity by the young man beside him, Ulrich Frodien:

> When it comes to what our high-ups were thinking, there's only two possibilities. Either they were total idiots, who had no idea what the Ivans and the Yanks were capable of putting into the war. That's bad enough. But the other possibility would be even worse. They knew full well, but they took the risk all the same, at our expense. They gambled our homeland on a hand of blackjack, and we stupid a***holes went along with it![2]

Göttingen is the seat of one of Germany's most famous and prestigious universities. It was founded in 1737 by King George II of Hanover and Great Britain. This British connection lasted exactly a

hundred years, until the throne was divided, because the feudal Salic
Law did not allow Queen Victoria to succeed to the Hanoverian
crown. Meanwhile, the town had welcomed many English-speaking
luminaries, including the English Romantic poet Samuel Taylor
Coleridge, and also, in his pre-Revolutionary days, the great early
American polymath Benjamin Franklin.

As it happened, Göttingen University would be the first German
academic institution to be permitted to reopen, in October 1945, but
in the spring and summer of that year it was the city's closeness to
the border between the designated Russian Zone of Occupation and
the British Zone that was especially significant (although the Americans captured Göttingen in April 1945, two months later it was handed
over to the British, as agreed the previous year). So, thousands of
refugees, military and civilian, fleeing the Red Army and their German
communist puppets, found their way through and spent at least some
time in the place.

Once he had recovered from the worst effects of his wounds, Ulrich
Frodien spent some months using his military map-reading and scout-
ing skills to guide westbound groups of civilians through the hilly,
wooded border area to safety in the west – a pastime which, while
risky, could prove very lucrative.[3]

By a series of fortunate chances, young Frodien found himself
belonging to a very rare category of human being in Germany during
the immediate post-war period: young, male, German, more or less
fully able and not detained in a prison camp. This was a crucial deter-
minant of post-war life in the ruined Reich. With most of the
able-bodied male population between sixteen and sixty-five sucked
into the armed forces, and by 1945 for the most part either dead,
seriously wounded or captured, German civil society, such as it was,
looked overwhelmingly female and/or elderly.

The brutally aggressive masculinism and racism that characterised
the Nazi view of society had, paradoxically, brought about a situation
where the 'ideal' Nazi male, physically powerful, relentlessly aggressive
– 'lean and slim, quick as a greyhound, tough as leather, hard as Krupp

steel', as the Führer had once described his Teutonic paragon in a speech to the Hitler Youth – had been rendered impotent. He had set out to dominate the world, as was supposedly his biological 'right', and had, inexplicably from the Nazi point of view, failed.

The sloppy, materialistic Americans, the arrogant, decadent British and the hopelessly bolshevised and Jew-dominated, 'sub-human' Russians had triumphed in his place. This left the German woman at the mercy of these same allegedly inferior beings, while the German male, dead or injured or imprisoned, was unable to do a thing about it.

A caricature in the Nazi press in the last months of the war showed American GIs as scruffy, feeble-minded juvenile delinquents with tommy guns, possibly addled by drugs and drink, menacing idealised blond German families whose father and protector was absent defend-ing civilisation against the Bolshevik hordes. Of course, this desperately manufactured image of American inferiority and disorganisation was impossible to square with the fact that, when the weather cleared, German soldiers and civilians alike needed only to glance skywards, like Frodien and his comrades, to see a thousand glistening B-17s parading with impunity 15,000 feet above their heads, on their highly disciplined way to rain down fear and destruction on what was left of the Third Reich.

The situation of Germany in the late spring of 1945 was the Nazis' world turned upside down. German women knew it. Whatever their previous loyalties or otherwise to the Nazi Party, many reacted accordingly. Despite finger-wagging official propaganda, they took a look at the conquering enemy, aware that the vast majority of adult German males were either dead or behind barbed wire, and for the sake of themselves and their families they did exactly what they saw fit.

During the occupation of France, censorious patriots had a phrase for the lifestyle of Frenchwomen who embarked on relationships with Germans – *collaboration horizontale*. Now that the Germans were no longer occupiers but the occupied, and the women of the former alleged master race had similar choices to make, the equivalent phrase was in English and it was 'fraternisation'. Soon the invented verb 'to frat' became euphemistic shorthand for sexual relations between the occupiers and hundreds of thousands, even millions, of German women.

In sophisticated cities and centres of culture, even those Germans hitherto most comfortably situated quickly realised that old hierarchies of order and privilege were no longer, at this point, relevant. In Göttingen, after the Americans took the town but before they established full control, mobs composed of women, the elderly and teenagers too young to have been called up ranged around the central area, looting shops and warehouses.

At the town's goods station, which American fighter bombers had seriously damaged in air strikes a few days previously, many heavily laden supply trains had been immobilised and part-destroyed, and soon a crowd of up to a thousand was engaged in unhindered pillaging of army and railway property, breaking into storage depots and, if they had not already been blown open by the earlier bombing, the goods wagons trapped in the yard sidings. Frodien, who witnessed it, wrote:

The most interesting things were the faces of the people. These were not members of the lower classes, the scum of society or the town mob, as one likes to assume. They were there too, of course, but in ruthless competition with middle-class renegades and members of the cream of society. In my entire life, I have never again seen features so contorted in greed as there on that station. Those faces revealed totally undisguised hatred and envy. Hatred of anyone who got in their way, who didn't make space quickly enough, was too slow or even tried to push them back – that was the cardinal sin – and envy of those who had already managed to grab more than themselves, or who had managed to make off with something they had their own eye on . . .[4]

There were different degrees of suffering for different Germans, as became clear within a very short time after the end of the war. Senior Nazis and war criminals, wanted for actual crimes against Allied nationals or for atrocities in the occupied countries, faced immediate and serious punishment. The rest were largely dependent on luck or cunning.

Certain professions put their practitioners in a strong position to survive the transition in relative comfort. Doctors and dentists, for instance – almost half of whom had been members of the Nazi Party – were nevertheless essential to the continuing functioning of society, and could not simply be replaced by untainted amateurs (unlike, say, the legal and teaching professions, which, in the Soviet-occupied areas, were quickly purged and filled with hastily trained 'politically reliable' officials).

In Thuringia, for instance, Joachim Trenkner's father, son of a prosperous doctor and himself a general practitioner – as well as a member of the Nazi Party – found himself sought after by the Americans soon after they captured the small town in early April 1945. The US occupiers' own medic used the facilities in Dr Trenkner's practice. During the Americans' temporary occupation of the town (it was due to be handed over to the Russians at the beginning of July), a friendly and cooperative relationship soon developed, which the doctor's recent political predilections apparently did nothing to mar. Such closeness to the victors generally paid off in terms of privileges and extra rations.[5]

Hundreds of kilometres to the west, in the Rhenish city of Koblenz, Egon Plönissen, the son of a local dentist, had a similar experience. Although again his father was a Nazi, and his uncle even a local precinct or chapter leader (*Ortsgruppenleiter*) of the party in Koblenz, it became clear, pretty soon after first the Americans and then the French occupied the town, that the Plönissen family stood little chance of suffering serious deprivation. Plönissen senior, a highly respected practitioner, rapidly became a favourite of the French occupiers, especially the civilian administrators, and he also fixed the teeth of local farmers. Both categories of patient, in one way or the other, had access to foodstuffs denied to ordinary, unconnected town-dwelling Germans.[6]

The dentist's son was only just into his teens when the Americans attacked Koblenz in March 1945. He watched the battle from the relative comfort and security of the family villa in Ehrenbreitstein, on the right bank of the Rhine. Other boys in the city, a little older than Egon and therefore liable for military service during the insane conditions of the war's final days, faced a stark choice: volunteer for what might well be a suicidal action with the *Volkssturm*, or hide yourself.

Helmut Nassen was just eighteen and, like most boys and girls in the area, had not attended school since the massive bombing of Koblenz by the British on the night of 6–7 November 1944. The attack had more or less razed the old Rhenish-Prussian administrative centre to the ground, destroying an estimated 58 per cent of the city's buildings, including 'nearly all of the historic courts of the ancient nobility, three old churches and the Castle of the Electors'. Fortunately, it had cost relatively few lives (104) out of a population of 90,000, thanks mostly to the city's plentiful and well-constructed air raid shelters.[7]

Like Egon, Helmut also lived on the right bank of the river, in the pleasant resort suburb of Koblenz-Pfaffendorf. As the front line neared the Rhineland, he was engaged, like all German boys of his age, in *Volkssturm* training, running messages between units, ditch-digging and so on. He also undertook various useful but sometimes not altogether legal activities that brought him, like many other enterprising German boys of the time, an income in the only currency by then worth having – cigarettes. Helmut had found time to get himself a girl and, with a couple of friends, to construct his own hideout in a wooded spot above the river. There they often spent nights and days, together or individually. And from there, in relative safety, they, like Egon, watched the ten-day fight for the main city of Koblenz on the other side of the Rhine.

Helmut kept a diary. On 17 March, two days before Koblenz finally fell to the Americans, he reported almost casually: 'Tomorrow I am

supposed to report to the army at Neuhäusel.* Plentiful machine-gun
fire and rifle shots audible up on the Karthause hill and also further
down. Fierce infantry fighting. The enemy infantry is slowly advancing . . .'[8] His casualness was misleading. Helmut knew that when – or,
rather, if – he reported to the Wehrmacht, it meant the end of his
phoney war and the beginning of the real one. Of the next day's events
the teenager wrote:

> I overslept. The other recruits have already left. Now I'll pack and
> also report for duty. Hans has already gone. More strong artillery fire
> on Koblenz . . . infantry fighting begun again. Enemy artillery targets
> the assault boat moored by the Markenbildchenweg. After about
> 12–15 rounds, they hit it. German flak responds only in minimal
> fashion. At 11.00 I receive my marching orders to Höhr-Grenzhausen
> plus rations. The President of Police has disappeared and I have
> decided not to report, but to go into hiding. I move into a cellar
> along with W. and Karl . . .[9]

With this, young Helmut knew he was moving into the precarious,
perilous shadow world of the survivor, now inhabited by so many in
the bombed-out, besieged cities of Germany. Moving from cellar to
cellar, grabbing food and trading goods where possible, he had to
keep constantly on the watch for Wehrmacht police and Nazi officials.
By failing to report for army duty, Helmut had become a deserter, at
a time in the war when this automatically meant summary execution
without trial.

The pattern of the next week for Helmut and his friends, based at
the 'bunker' in the woods above the river for most of this time, is one
of sneaking around, occasionally meeting small groups of German
soldiers (who show no interest in his status and, though he does not
say so, may also have been deserters), cautiously dropping by the
family home to pick up food and clothes, and hunting for anything

---

* A small town in the Westerwald, ten kilometres or so to the east.

else they can find to keep body and soul together. There are hens' eggs to be found in the woods, and on one occasion a fowl is triumphantly caught, cooked and eaten. They keep on the move, hoping no one will check their papers.

During the regime's dying weeks, Helmut and co. have detached themselves from the rigidly hierarchical, militarised Nazi-ruled society in which they grew up and with which they are clearly, by now, disillusioned. That does not stop them from firing a few defiant shots from their bunker entrance across the river at the Americans, who have now occupied the main city of Koblenz. Their dangerous outlaw status does, however, mean that, for all their teenage bravado, they are anxiously counting the hours until, for them, the war is over. Helmut writes: 'Soon the Yanks will come. I'm curious to see how they behave. Soon I'll have made it . . .'

When, on 27 March, the boys see American vehicles parked by the riverside down below them, they feel only relief. Soon they venture back down into Pfaffendorf itself:

On the bypass bridge there are two [American] guards, but we pass unhindered. When we get down in the town, some of their units are carrying out house-searches. They behave very decently, only blowing open doors when these are locked. They have captured a few more of our soldiers. Six maybe. Then I go with Lo [a friend] to the Bienhorntal [a local beauty spot where there seems to have been some kind of storehouse] and fetch a case of canned meat. I take eight for myself, hand over the others. Lo keeps all his. By then, the Yanks are finished with their searches and are assembling in front of our house, around fifty of them in number. Cars arrive, they get into them along with their six prisoners, and off they head to Ehrenbreitstein. The commander's car even has a radio in it. That's what I call going to war![10]

Helmut and the others had coolly disobeyed the Nazi system, going against twelve years of indoctrination. They made their calculations, risked arrest and possible execution, and – like Ulrich Frodien in his escapes from Breslau and Berlin – survived until the Allies arrived, bringing, for them at least, an end to the war.

These survivors were the lucky ones. Many ended up hanging from trees and lamp posts, placards around their necks declaring them traitors. Whether it was fanatical army field police, renegade SS and Gestapo men, or self-styled *Werwolf* units, until the very last day of the war there were plenty of remnants of the disintegrating regime prepared to murder their war-weary fellow countrymen for any acts, or even attitudes, that passed as 'defeatist' or 'disloyal'.

In Penzberg, a largely working-class and anti-Nazi mining town in southern Bavaria, an at first sight almost tragicomic little *coup de théâtre* occurred days before the end of the war. At dawn on 28 April 1945, the town's pre-Hitler Social Democratic mayor, Hans Rummer, alarmed by reports that local army and Nazi Party last-ditchers were preparing to defend the town against the approaching Americans, and if necessary to destroy its mines and waterworks in order to keep them from the enemy, attempted to accelerate the process of liberation by assuming power at the head of a small group of armed supporters. In this, the daring Herr Rummer had been encouraged by a brief uprising in Munich. Anti-Nazis and Bavarian separatists, calling themselves 'Freedom Action Bavaria', had seized control, for a few hours, of a radio station in the Bavarian capital and broadcast calls for resistance, until the Nazi authorities restored 'order'.

Rummer and his associates successfully managed temporarily to shut down the mine and visited a local concentration camp, where they gained the support of the inmates by promising liberation, before marching on the town hall, where a crowd of socialists and communists, eager finally to be rid of the Nazi dictatorship, had gathered. The Nazi mayor, Herr Vonwerden, was dismissed and told to leave town, leaving Rummer's men in charge.[11]

With the Americans a matter of hours away – the rumble of their artillery could clearly be heard in the town – the takeover might have succeeded but for the fact that a Wehrmacht unit led by one

Oberleutnant Ohm happened to be passing through, and stopped in the town square to investigate why such a large crowd had gathered. Discovering the situation, they quickly arrested Rummer and his associates, after which the punctilious Ohm drove to Munich, fifty or so kilometres to the north, for instructions, taking with him the deposed Nazi mayor.

Almost immediately they arrived, they found themselves in a meeting with none other than the Nazi Gauleiter of Upper Bavaria and 'Reich Defence Commissar South', forty-nine-year-old Paul Giesler, notorious for his extravagant pronouncements on the subject of fanatical resistance.[12]

Within less than five minutes, Ohm and Vonwerden had their orders: 'Rummer and his people must be liquidated.' And they were – seven failed rebels were put up against a wall and shot immediately upon the lieutenant's return to Penzberg later that afternoon.

Typically for many Nazi firebrands during these chaotic final days, however, Giesler was not satisfied with proportionate violence, sufficient to restore immediate order. So far as he was concerned, the disease of anti-Nazism must be not merely suppressed but wholly eliminated. Sensing that Ohm, a loyalist but also a stickler for procedure, would be reluctant to do what Giesler considered necessary, the Gauleiter – astonishingly, since his capital, Munich, was also about to fall to the Americans – took the trouble to instruct one of his aides, a Brownshirt leader named Hans Zöberlein, to round up a posse, so to speak, and also head down to Penzberg. The codename for this death squad was 'Group Hans'.

The bizarre and cruel farce that followed was, appropriately enough, staged by an artist, for Zöberlein was no ordinary thug but a radical nationalist novelist with a background in the post-First World War *Freikorps* movement. Zöberlein's violent non-conformism had caused him to fall out of favour until talent shortages in the last months of the war caused him to be appointed as a regional defence leader and *Volkssturm* commander. His units called themselves '*Werwolf* Upper Bavaria' and specialised in brutal reprisals against villages found flying white flags or in any way thought to be interfering with operations against the enemy.

A hundred or so of these desperadoes accordingly arrived, along with their maverick commander, at Penzberg town hall that evening. Zöberlein announced their intention of completing the purge begun by Ohm and Vonwerden. Local Nazis 'assisted' by drawing up a list of political enemies in a noisy discussion that saw more than one personal score settled under the pretext of 'necessity'.

The flamboyant arrival of Group Hans and the ensuing debate about who to kill enabled some of the shrewder local anti-Nazis to make good their escapes, but nevertheless, once the death list had been drawn up, the killers were able to snatch three of their victims. Within a short time, all were dead, with two of them hanged from the balcony of a building next to the Penzberg town hall, the third from a tree in the main street. When a fourth eluded them, despite threats to the caretaker of his building, the group extended their operations into a neighbouring working-class suburb. Here they found themselves exchanging fire with armed residents. One of the latter, a miner, was killed, but the gun battle was enough to drive Group Hans out of the area.

Moreover, the local Wehrmacht commander, when asked to send help, refused to do so. Nonetheless, several more 'enemies' were hanged during the course of the night, including a heavily pregnant woman – although as the night wore on, with the 'enemy' now forewarned, it became harder to find victims. In one case, when a man was being hanged, the rope broke. He was shot, left for dead, but survived. Another captive bolted while under guard at the town hall, and, despite taking a bullet from his pursuers, managed to make good his escape.

Zöberlein had left before midnight. The last of his lieutenants, a fanatical former officer by the name of Bauernfeind (literally 'coun- trymen's enemy'), pulled out of town at around dawn, still issuing bloodcurdling threats to return and finish the job. He left corpses dangling from improvised gallows around the town square in the early morning light.

So the regime that had always boasted of its success as the bringer of 'order', during its last weeks and days finally became what in its black heart it had always been – the agent of violence, random death and chaos.

An institutionalised sadism that had hitherto been systematically concealed, confined to Gestapo cells and the giant barbed-wire torture cages of the concentration camps, now burst into the open, revealing itself as a licence for every uniformed thug in the country to torture and murder at will. It somehow seems appropriate that on 29 April, the day after ordering the tragicomic and totally unnec-essary Penzberg massacre and just hours before being forced to flee Munich ahead of the Americans, Gauleiter Giesler was appointed in Hitler's Testament to be Reich Interior Minister in place of the disgraced Heinrich Himmler.[13]

The Penzberg atrocities showed two things very clearly: first, that by the last weeks of the war, those who had either never supported the Nazis or were gravely disillusioned with them were now prepared openly to rebel; and second, that, in its response, the regime revealed its degeneration into violent, vengeful brigandage.

The Third Reich had clearly forfeited any claim on the respect or loyalty of all but a minority of fanatical adherents. Most Germans shared this realisation. Whether it made them better or worse disposed towards the advancing Allies was another matter entirely. The image of the adolescent Helmut Nassen and his friend, defiantly firing off rounds at the Americans across the river while at the same time hiding from the Wehrmacht field police who would have strung these young men up as deserters provides, perhaps, a suitable illustration of the dualities at the heart of so many Germans' response to the war's end.

With the end of the war, Germany was deemed to have ceased to exist. This had long been agreed among the allies, and was supposedly set out in a proposed instrument of surrender painstakingly negoti-ated by the European Advisory Commission (EAC) in London during the latter part of the winter. However, owing to procedural errors and some last-minute changes, that detailed and binding document was still not quite ready by the time the actual military surrender occurred.

The document of surrender signed by German commanders at Supreme Headquarters Allied Expeditionary Force (SHAEF) in Reims on 7 May 1945, then – amidst much bad grace – the next day at Berlin-Karlshorst with the Soviets, was much more basic. It consisted of only six paragraphs, none of them more than two sentences long. This text had been put together mostly by a British G-3 colonel at SHAEF, John Counsell, in civilian life a theatrical actor-manager. He had taken a great deal of it from a report in the US forces' newspaper, the *Stars and Stripes*, of the German surrender in northern Italy a few days earlier.[14]

A surrender needed to be signed, EAC or no EAC, in order to bring the fighting to an end and save further loss of Allied and German lives. The improvised text achieved that much. The world celebrated VE-Day, but even before the party was over the politicians and the political generals (among whom Eisenhower should be included) had begun to worry that, in fact, only the German armed forces had so far surrendered. Where did this leave the legal status of the German government? In November 1918, at the end of the First World War, only the politicians had signed their country's surrender, leaving the German generals to cry 'betrayal'. Now that the reverse was true, who knew whether the survivors of the Nazi political elite might also exploit this technically still incomplete situation for their own nefarious ends?

The Allies clearly exercised de facto physical control of Germany. Moreover, the improvised text also contained a reference to the EAC document in preparation, binding the Germans to accept this too once it was presented to them. All the same, this was not an entirely satisfactory situation. Any possible loopholes had to be closed as quickly as possible.

The situation was all the more pressing because a body calling itself the Reich government still existed. This was headed by Hitler's designated successor, Grand Admiral Karl Dönitz, and included War

Production Minister Albert Speer and several other veteran ministers appointed by Hitler. This faintly ridiculous entity hung on for more than two weeks after the formal surrender, housed in a former navy torpedo school at Flensburg, a substantial port on the Baltic just a handful of miles from the Danish border. Stubbornly flying the Reich flag on its meagre collection of government buildings, its troops still patrolled the surrounding streets.

Dönitz's government went through the motions. Its ministers and officials held meetings, squabbled over jobs and seniorities, made decisions, issued commands and even attempted to engage in dealings with the forces of General Montgomery's British 21st Army Group, which now controlled the Flensburg area.

Perhaps the only useful thing that Dönitz and his entourage did manage to achieve in the final week of the war, after Hitler's death, was to delay the Wehrmacht's final surrender until millions of German soldiers and refugees had managed to reach the relative safety of the Western Allied lines – an intentional delay benefiting between 2.5 and 3 million desperate souls.[15]

As it happened, the final version of the EAC surrender document, now reframed as the 'Declaration Regarding the Defeat of Germany and the Assumption of Supreme Authority by the Allied Powers' was not accepted by all the Allied governments until 21 May. During this interval, both Churchill and Eisenhower seem to have toyed with the idea of allowing the dubious legal husk of a Reich government to remain in place in some form or another.

In Churchill's case, he considered letting the Flensburg government continue 'for a while', in the hope that allowing its temporary survival would help bring order to the occupied areas. It would also provide a 'fallback' German authority. This could be useful if, as Churchill had begun to fear, war should now suddenly break out between the Western Allies and the Soviets, and the West needed to call on the support of the defeated German armed forces in a new anti-communist crusade.[16]

Eisenhower, more realistically, saw the continuance of some kind of all-German authority as potentially a useful aid in organising,

disciplining and feeding the unexpectedly vast number – five million
or so – of German prisoners of war now in captivity within the areas
controlled by the Anglo-American forces, a problem already threatening to turn into a humanitarian disaster. To this end, on 11 May, three
days after VE-Day, Eisenhower sent a senior American officer, General
Lowell W. Rooks, up to Flensburg to establish a 'Supreme Headquarters Control Party'. Rooks, accompanied by a British deputy, Brigadier
E. J. Foord, and a high-level political adviser, Ambassador Robert
Murphy, had particular instructions to liaise with what was left of the
Wehrmacht High Command there and 'impose the SCAEF's [Supreme
Commander Allied Expeditionary Force's] will'.

For their part, Dönitz and company harboured somewhat pathetic
hopes that this visit represented some kind of recognition of their
authority. During their visits to his quarters aboard the *Patria*, a
requisitioned German passenger ship moored in the Flensburger
Fjord, they made desperate attempts to impress General Rooks with
their indispensability. However, after their first encounters with this
'strange politico-military ménage', the American general and his advisers rapidly came to the conclusion that it was 'a rapidly decaying
concern with little knowledge of present events and practically no
work to do' and therefore pretty much useless for any of the anticipated purposes.[17]

With the press in Allied countries attacking this embarrassing
anomaly, and now, on 21 May, the EAC declaration accepted as policy
by all the Allies, an end to the Flensburg 'government' was inevitable.
On 22 May, having formally consulted the British and the Russians,
the American War Department ordered the arrest of Dönitz, his
government and the surviving members of the Wehrmacht High
Command. This took place punctually the next day.

At a meeting with General Rooks around a long table set up in the
bar aboard the *Patria*, the German officers were given the bad news,
then were marched ashore and into their cars, and driven back to
their quarters to collect their belongings. Army photographers were
present to record the scene. *É finita la commedia*.

One of the Reich's chief negotiators, who had been on board the *Patria* with Dönitz, General Admiral Hans Georg von Friedeburg, shot himself before he could be formally taken into custody. Most former Reich ministers and senior military officers were quickly flown to the American detention centre for high-ranking Nazis near SHAEF at Reims, in France, known as 'the Ashcan'. Many of those who had played leading roles in the regime's final pantomime would face trial as war criminals at Nuremberg.

The EAC's victory declaration now became the crucial document determining the status of surrendered Germany. 'There is,' it proclaimed, 'no central Government or authority in Germany capable of accepting responsibility for the maintenance of order, the administration of the country, and compliance with the requirements of the victorious powers.' The declaration continued: 'The Governments of the United States of America, the Union of Soviet Socialist Republics and the United Kingdom, and the Provisional Government of the French Republic, hereby assume supreme authority with respect to Germany, including all the powers possessed by the German Government, the High Command and any state, municipal or local government or authority. The assumption, for the purposes stated above, of the said authority and powers does not effect the annexation of Germany.'

So, Germany was deemed to have surrendered unconditionally, as planned since the Casablanca Conference in 1943. Its government was declared to have been abolished, and the Allies to have assumed absolute power in the country – although the second sentence allowed that the German state had not been permanently extinguished and might therefore be re-established if the victors so decided at some future point.

For all practical purposes, however, Germany had ceased to exist, and the powers of the occupiers over its population and institutions were unlimited.

Many Germans, like those in Göttingen, exploited the temporary vacuum, after the collapse of their own government institutions but before the occupiers settled into the task of ruling, to steal, loot, settle old scores or make arrangements to secure their futures. Most did not turn from obedient citizens into criminals, but equally, most realised that in the new post-war world the old rules did not apply.

Three of the four occupying powers were representative democracies, but nevertheless exercised total and far from liberal power over the areas of Germany that they had assigned themselves. The final power, the Soviet Union, claimed to be a democracy but was nothing of the kind. It was, however, paradoxically also the only one of the powers to immediately introduce its 'own' German officials, to allow political activity and to set up something resembling a 'normal' administrative network in its zone.

The advantage that the Soviets possessed over the Western Allies during the early days after victory was quite simple. They had their own German communists, many of whom had spent the war years in exile in Russia, and some of whom had survived in Nazi-ruled Germany and therefore could be realistically presented as 'resistance' activists.

When the Red Army appeared in the heart of Germany in the spring of 1945, these German party members, wherever they came from, were biddable, used to discipline, accustomed to conspiratorial political practice, and, overwhelmingly, quite clear that their aim was the same as it had been before 1933: to assist in the construction of a communist-dominated political structure, at first in the Soviet Zone and then, if possible, in the whole of occupied Germany. This gave the Russians a head start.

The situation in the zones assigned to the Western Allies was quite different. It was true that many non-communist anti-Nazis had gone into exile after 1933, and had eventually ended up in America or Britain, but unlike the communist exiles they were not a homogenous, disciplined group. The same went for those who had either survived imprisonment during the Nazi era or somehow managed to lie low. In 1945, they could re-emerge, but they did not form a group with a clearly defined aim. In fact, unlike the German communists, who were from the first favoured by the Soviet occupiers, they were not even given preferential treatment by the Western Allies, who in that same crucial period tended to treat Germans of any kind – Nazi or not – with uniform distrust.

Within weeks of the German surrender, a group of pre-war German communists under the command – this is not too strong a term – of the former (1929–33) Party Secretary for Berlin and Brandenburg, Walter Ulbricht, had established itself in the Soviet Zone. Ulbricht, born the son of a tailor in the Saxon industrial metropolis of Leipzig in 1893, learned the trade of cabinet-maker but, after serving in the German army in the First World War, quickly became a full-time political agitator and official. He counted as an ultra-loyal servant of Stalin who had refined his ruthless skills during twelve years of exile, first in Prague and Paris, and then, from 1938, in the Soviet Union. His cold efficiency, relentless energy and unquestioned loyalty to Moscow (he was also a signed-up member of the Communist Party of the Soviet Union) enabled him to survive Stalin's frequent purges of foreign émigrés. These characteristics also made Ulbricht a natural choice as the head of the elite group of German communists flown in a Soviet military aircraft into the shattered ruins of Berlin at the end of April 1945, during the final days of the battle for the city.

During the first weeks of peace, it was the humourless, goatee-bearded Ulbricht who explained how, in the power vacuum that preceded the final adjustments of the zones and the admission of Western troops to the status of co-occupiers in Berlin, the communists would covertly establish control of the post-war city. The pattern established was one that would become familiar throughout the Soviet Zone: 'It has to look democratic,' Ulbricht told his colleagues with exquisite cynicism, 'but we have to hold everything in our hands.'[18]

In the Western zones, by contrast, nothing looked democratic at this stage – perhaps because the Western Allies, unlike the Russians, could not feel confident that they possessed a viable political base among the German population. Millions of Germans had fled from the Russians in the first months of 1945, increasing the population of the Western-controlled zones by some ten million homeless, bereft souls, and although they were spared the worst of the rape, pillage and political terror visited on the inhabitants of the Soviet Zone, neither the situation they fled to, nor the population among which they found themselves, were especially friendly.

There was another complication. The lines drawn on VE-Day, when the fighting stopped, were dictated by military chance and necessity. Owing to the sudden collapse of the German forces in middle Germany, by May 1945 the Americans had advanced into parts of western Czechoslovakia, and into tracts of Saxony, Saxony-Anhalt and Thuringia, which under the EAC agreements reached the previous winter were destined to be part of the Soviet Zone. The British, likewise, had advanced from Hamburg and Lübeck along the Baltic coast and also, like the Americans, into parts of Thuringia and Saxony-Anhalt, including the area around Aschersleben. In some parts, the 'line of contact' between the Western Allies and the Russians lay as much as two hundred miles east of the designated zonal boundaries.

The question was, given Soviet attitudes – already clear from their behaviour in Poland and elsewhere – as well as in the negotiations for co-administration of Berlin, should the Western Allies withdraw from these areas at the end of June, as agreed, or should they find excuses to hold on to them and use them as bargaining counters with the Russians?

Churchill, his long-harboured anti-communist instincts once more coming to the fore now that the war was won, wrote a lengthy and frank memorandum to his Foreign Secretary, Sir Anthony Eden, arguing that further advance by the Red Army into central Germany would be a disaster. He favoured finding excuses to hold what the Western Allies had, as a bargaining counter against further Russian non-cooperation.

The Russians, meanwhile, were still full of 'technical' reasons as to why the Western powers could not yet put any of their troops in Berlin. There Ulbricht's people were purposefully and with Machiavellian guile attempting to present the world with a communist-controlled fait accompli in the former Reich capital. And in Austria, where Soviet troops also controlled the capital, Vienna, ahead of a planned four-power occupation, Moscow had installed its own selection as Chancellor of the newly 'liberated' country, with – ominously for those who knew how the comrades operated – a communist as Minister of the Interior, in control of security and the police force.[19]

Just the day after the arrest of the Dönitz government, on 24 May, the British Foreign Office once more suggested to the Americans that the Western troops should only evacuate the areas due to Russia once these 'outstanding matters', especially those regarding Germany, Austria and Poland, had been settled.

The Americans replied two days later that the withdrawal could be postponed 'for a short period' but that they would 'not hold up withdrawal into zones indefinitely'.[20] Too much 'fragile china' could be broken in a serious disagreement with the Soviets – and any stand-off over withdrawal into the agreed zones could affect Russia's willingness to join the war against Japan later that summer.

Churchill might rage at the American envoy, Ambassador Joseph E. Davies, about the Soviets' 'Gestapo methods' in their occupied areas,[21] but there was little he could do to push the US government into a more aggressive stance. The British Prime Minister would have been perfectly but helplessly aware that Ambassador Davies, while American representative in Moscow back in 1936, had publicly asserted the fairness of Stalin's show trials.

In the event, the Soviets successfully faced the West down. The four Allies, having abolished the German government, were faced with the duty of ruling, feeding and keeping order among seventy million or more Germans in a country whose infrastructure was largely wrecked, its industry and agriculture severely damaged, and whose towns and villages were flooded with homeless refugees and non-German 'displaced persons'. Clearly, the country (that was no longer technically a country) needed governance.

As early as April, Churchill and Truman had jointly proposed to Stalin that a joint Control Council to run Germany, as provided for in EAC agreements signed during the winter, should be set up as soon as possible, even before troops were redeployed into the final zones. Stalin ignored the proposal, merely responding in curt fashion that a 'temporary tactical demarcation line' was in order. The British, especially, continued to push for an agreement that uncoupled the formal (and by now urgent) establishment of a Control Council from the question of withdrawal into peacetime zones. Again the Russians stonewalled. It was some time before the issue came to a head.

On 29 May, Ambassador Winant, America's man at the EAC, suggested that the Allied commanders-in-chief meet in Berlin on 1 June to ceremonially sign the Victory Declaration, thereby bringing into force its stipulations, including the formation of the Control Council, and allowing the protocols on zonal boundaries and administrative machinery to take effect. When General Eisenhower asked what he should do in case the Soviets brought up the subject of Western withdrawal, he was told by his superiors at the Joint Chiefs of Staff that if they did so, he was to tell them that it was 'one of the items to be worked out by the Control Council'. The first of June, it turned out, was an unrealistic deadline, but when the Soviets finally replied, on 4 June, having kept everyone waiting, they seemed in a hurry. The signing should take place the next day, 5 June.

Not for the first – or the last – time, the Soviets outmanoeuvred their nominal allies. When Eisenhower's party landed at Tempelhof airfield in Berlin, in the late morning of 5 June, the C-in-C of SHAEF was greeted by a battalion-sized honour guard. After completing his inspection, which naturally took a while, Eisenhower was then driven through the shattered streets to the luxury villa that he, like the British and French commanders, had been assigned for the day. The villas were part of a complex requisitioned by the Soviets for their own senior officers, situated in the relatively undamaged lakeside idyll of Wendenschloss, a resort that formed part of the borough of Köpenick.

Eisenhower then had a brief private meeting with Marshal Zhukov at the Soviet commander's nearby villa. He presented the Russian war hero with the Chief Commander grade of the American Legion of

Merit, before returning to his own temporary accommodation. From here, so Eisenhower thought, he would now be conveyed to the signing ceremony at the local yacht club, which had been due at noon and for which they were therefore already somewhat, though not seriously, late.

Eisenhower still planned to be back at his new headquarters in Frankfurt that same evening. Hours passed, however, without a word from their hosts. Only when Eisenhower got together with the British commander, Field Marshal Bernard Montgomery, and threatened to leave if there were further delays in the signature ceremony, did the Russians react. The American, the Briton and their French colleague, General Jean de Lattre de Tassigny, were finally transported to the signing venue.[22]

However, if the Western commanders thought that this was the end of the matter, they were wrong. When they finally came face to face with their Red Army hosts, it was to be told that the signing could not take place. A minor clause of the agreement could, they were told, be interpreted as committing the Russians to arresting any Japanese nationals they found in Germany, which, since they were not (yet) at war with Japan, was unacceptable. Eisenhower agreed that the clause could be taken out. Zhukov then insisted on consulting Moscow.

By the time the Soviet government's assent was received, it was almost 5 p.m., some hours beyond the originally agreed time. Eisenhower had by this time fully realised that the Soviets were playing games with him.

After the signing ceremony, which took place in a blaze of flash bulbs and faux goodwill, the commanders went out on to the club-house terrace for a private chat, taking along their interpreters. Eisenhower took the opportunity to suggest that, since the Control Council was now formally constituted, its staff could begin their work forthwith. Zhukov swiftly disabused him of this assumption. But could not an agenda for this be agreed? No, Zhukov said. How could he make decisions when he did not control his own zone? He continued not to give an inch, even when Montgomery intervened. When told by the British commander that things were complicated and chaotic, and the formation of a Control Council was therefore urgent, the marshal simply answered that the war was over, and how long would it take to redeploy the troops? When told, about three weeks, Zhukov said this was 'very satisfactory'. In the interim they could be organising their Control Council staffs, could they not?

Since neither Eisenhower nor Montgomery was authorised to make any commitments on withdrawal dates, that was the end of the discussion. Except that when they went back into the building, preparations for the habitual elaborate Russian banquet were under way, with vodka glasses being charged for a toast to the day's 'success'. Eisenhower joined in one toast. A photograph catches him glaring none too amiably at Zhukov as the latter pours a drink for Montgomery (exactly what this consisted of remains mysterious – the British commander was a militant teetotaller). Eisenhower left immediately afterwards to catch his flight back to Frankfurt. It had been planned for his deputy, General Clay, and a small staff to stay on in Berlin, but the Russians made no offer of overnight hospitality and so they too returned to Frankfurt.

The bad-tempered (and disappointing) session at Wendenschloss led Eisenhower to write a report to Washington in which he confirmed that the Russians would not agree to any progress on the peacetime administration of Germany until they came into full possession of their zone, a point of view that was echoed in Ambassador Robert Murphy's account to the State Department.[23] Eisenhower added that the yet-to-be-realised Control Council could well 'become only a negotiating agency and in no sense an overall government for Germany'. In anticipation of this, he recommended either operating the American Zone as an independent economic entity, or combining it with the other Western zones to likewise manage the government and feeding of their people, leaving the Russians to their own. It was a prophetic suggestion.[24]

Meanwhile, despite Churchill's continuing objections, Washington took steps to expedite the withdrawal of American forces from the temporary demarcation line to the pre-ordained zone borders. The British had no choice but to follow. The several million Germans affected by these changes included the population of major central German cities such as Magdeburg, Erfurt and Leipzig, all of which had been captured by the Americans during the final weeks of the war.

In their home town in Thuringia, Schlotheim, which had been occupied by the US Army since 8 April, nine-year-old Joachim Trenkner and his family were still, by the standards of the time, living a charmed life. The small town had never been bombed, had fallen to the enemy with scarcely a shot fired, and, highly unusually, none of the family had been forced to serve in the war. Until the Americans arrived, the 4,000 or so citizens of Schlotheim could almost have pretended the war wasn't happening at all. Even when it did come to them, it was in the form not of shells or bombs but of a metallic grinding sound that the young Joachim recalls to this day. He looked out and saw American tanks clanking along the town's main street. The vehicles stopped, the GIs got out and took possession of the town. That was it. 'Nothing else happened,' Joachim recalls. 'They were just nice guys.'[25]

Initially, there was a problem for his parents, however. Dr Trenkner had been advised by retreating Wehrmacht soldiers that he should wear his Red Cross uniform when the Americans arrived. Perhaps they were influenced by the fact that the figurehead leader of the DRK (*Deutsches Rotes Kreuz*) was the Duke of Saxe-Coburg, a grandson of Queen Victoria and therefore a cousin of the King of England. In any case, it was bad advice.

Under the Nazis, the Red Cross had been politicised and militarised, in effect turned into an arm of the Party, and was already on the list of proscribed Nazi organisations that the invaders carried with them into Germany. The DRK uniform itself was disturbingly military in design. Dr Trenkner was therefore arrested almost immediately. He was saved by the arrival of a group of Serb slave workers whom he had treated, and treated well, when such things were discouraged by the Nazis. The Serbs vouched for him. Within a few hours, the Americans released Dr Trenkner and allowed him to return to his surgery.

Despite this unfortunate beginning, in the weeks that followed, Joachim's doctor father quickly achieved a good relationship with the American medical staff, who shared his office and surgery space. When it became clear at the beginning of July, after ten weeks or so of increasingly amicable American presence, that the town would soon be handed over to the Russians, Dr Trenkner's concern for himself and his family was apparent to his guests. He had, after all, been a member of the Nazi Party, if not an especially fanatical one.

So it was that, with the withdrawal deadline fast approaching, the American medical officer suggested that he could supply his new German acquaintance with a permit to accompany the American forces on their westward move, along with his family. Dr Trenkner accepted the offer, and managed to find another practice just the other side of the zone border. The family cart was packed up with their most important belongings, their faithful horse spanned between its shafts (these were the days of petrol shortages) and in the summer sunshine they prepared to head for a new home in the American Zone, whose border lay a mere thirty kilometres away.

Here came the deus ex machina. Or, rather, the man in the upper window. Joachim's grandfather, also a doctor (and still a loyal supporter of the Kaiser rather than the upstart Hitler), had elected to stay in the roomy and comfortable family home rather than uproot himself. Now, with his son, daughter-in-law and three grandchildren all ready to leave, the old man appeared and called down imperiously to his son: 'If you leave, you are disinherited!' Dr Trenkner paused. A few minutes later, they started carrying their belongings back into the house. Even the threat of the Russian hordes was not enough to overcome the threat of losing everything he stood to gain when the old man died.

The Russians arrived a few days later in Schlotheim, and the nine-year-old Joachim was surprised at his reaction:

My memory was, no fear of them. We sort of pitied them because they looked so poor. Compared with the Americans before. And they had nothing to offer. No more chocolate, no more Camel cigarettes, just those rough Russian cigarettes.

It was not only the Russians who inspired a certain visceral fear in German hearts. In the west, the Americans were due to evacuate parts of the territory their troops had occupied and hand these areas over to the French, whose zone, added late in the day and carved in part out of the British Zone, included the southern Rhineland and part of Württemberg. The sense of disappointment and anxiety was especially strong in Koblenz. Here the Americans had been awaited with a certain complacency by the inhabitants in the weeks and days before the fall of the city in March 1945.

Older Koblenzers remembered the Americans fondly from the period after the First World War, when the US Third Army, first under Major General Dickman and then under Lieutenant General Hunter Liggett, was quartered there as a force of occupation for a little over four years (December 1918–January 1923).

Once the 'doughboys' had settled in, relations with the Koblenz natives in the years after the First World War seem to have been friendly. There were the usual romantic liaisons, leading to long-lasting German–American ties (the rakehell American poet Charles Bukowski, best known for the film adaptation of his life, *Barfly*, was born in 1920 near Koblenz to a Polish-American soldier father and a German mother). General Liggett himself was remembered with gratitude for having helped the locals to circumvent the stipulations under the peace treaty by which the Prussian fortress of Ehrenbreitstein, which dominated the right bank of the Rhine at this, its confluence point with the Mosel, was to have been demolished.[26]

The French occupation, which followed the American withdrawal and lasted six years until 1929, was not so pleasant an experience. In particular, the French attempt to set up a separatist Rhenish republic at Koblenz, which led to widespread fighting and looting, was held against them.

The actual capture of Koblenz in March 1945, as witnessed by young

Helmut Nassen, was not nearly as trouble-free as that of Schlotheim. The Americans had to fight their way into the main city, on the left bank of the Rhine, against quite stubborn resistance, and even after the entire left bank was occupied, by 18–19 March, that left the Germans controlling the right bank. Egon Plönissen, then approaching his fourteenth birthday, spent those suspenseful days, like Helmut Nassen, watching the enemy forces increasing across the river in Koblenz and half loathing them, half longing for them to cross and end the war for him and his family.

The Plönissen family's level of anxiety was increased by the fact that their father, the town dentist in Ehrenbreitstein, a First World War veteran now in his mid-forties who had briefly served once more in the Wehrmacht in 1939–40 before being released due to his age, had been recalled to the colours in the autumn of 1944 as part of the *Volkssturm* mobilisation. Fortunately, for the moment, Herr Plönissen was permitted to continue his essential dental work part-time (his surgery had transferred to a room in the castle when the family home/practice was bombed during the previous winter) while acting as a provisions officer in charge of supplies to the fortress garrison.

A temporary and part-time soldier Herr Plönissen might have been, but he was technically in the armed forces and subject to orders. So it was that, with the Americans reportedly already over the Rhine at Remagen and threatening to sweep down from the north on to the eastern suburbs of Koblenz, rumours spread that the fortress garrison was about to be ordered to leave and move east into the Westerwald, where it would join the other fighting units. This was the moment of decision, and the dentist in uniform made it.

Using a night pass he had been granted for carrying out emergency dental work, Herr Plönissen absented himself from the fortress as the troops were mustering and headed home. With the family's collusion, he hid in a garden house in the grounds of their rented villa. A patriotic man who had done his duty in 1914–18 and 1939–40, he nonetheless had no intention of dying pointlessly miles from home. Sure enough, the Gestapo came looking for him. They were fobbed off by stories of night-time emergencies, but shortly after this Plönissen relocated to the house of an old friend, the local doctor, which had an old cellar with a separate entrance. There he was hidden behind some piles of blankets to wait out the end.

As this drama played out, young Egon – who had already himself spent a night in the fortress for a story involving filching chicken feed for the family's hens from a source on military property – watched with anxious interest as boys little older than himself continued to be sacrificed in aid of the Führer's fantasy of driving the enemy back on to the west side of the Rhine.

Egon clearly remembers being out on the road by the fortress during those days and seeing half a dozen young Luftwaffe auxiliaries, no older than sixteen or so, being led by an elderly *Feldwebel*. They passed Egon slowly, hauling a light 2cm anti-aircraft gun. He followed them and saw them take up position in a local beauty spot, the Mühlental. Even at his age, he knew that a gun like that would stand no chance against American tanks. *If* it ever got to confront them.

In fact, a few hours later, an American spotter plane buzzed overhead, checking out the new arrivals. A short time after it returned to the American-occupied bank of the river, the enemy's heavy artillery opened up. Shells crashed into the Mühlental.

Within seconds, boom, one hit the entire defensive position. Wiped out every single one of those boys. And their little gun. And their *Feldwebel*. It was a tragedy.[27]

Although the fighting for the Rhine crossing at Koblenz had been vicious and spread over several weeks, once the front line had moved east and the city settled into the routine of occupation, things ran decently enough.

Of course, there were frictions. When Egon Plönissen's father wanted to retrieve his dental equipment from the room in the Ehrenbreitstein fortress where it had been kept during the last months of the war, he was politely but firmly told that everything in the fortress, now occupied

by the American garrison, was property of the United States by right
of conquest. So, without his equipment, he could not practise. There
was nothing to be done, it seemed, until at the beginning of July news
came from Egon's pretty female cousin, whose employment as a secretary to the Americans at the fortress was not entirely unconnected with
her good looks. The US Army would soon be pulling out from here,
she revealed, as from elsewhere in the districts that had already been
earmarked for the French Zone of Occupation.

The deal arrived at between the French and the Americans regarding the handover arrangements was a very precise one. We are leaving
on the evening of 14–15 July, the Americans told the German dentist,
and the French will be moving into the fortress to take charge of it
at two in the morning. You, Herr Plönissen, have those few hours,
in the middle of the night, to let yourself in and spirit away your
valuable dental equipment, before it passes into the sphere of influence of the French government and therefore, mostly likely, out of
your hands for ever.

On the evening of 14–15 July, Herr Plönissen, his family and friends
were waiting outside the fortress with a large flatbed cart pulled by
two horses. The moment the Americans left, they moved quickly into
the fortress, and the next couple of hours were a storm of activity,
with everyone involved in dismantling the equipment and getting it
on to the cart. Helped by the fact that the French arrived a little late,
they succeeded in stripping it all out and getting it away from the
fortress precincts before the fatal hour struck.

Within days, Herr Plönissen had refurnished his practice room
and was open for business once more – not least when it came to
those senior members of the new French military administration who
were prepared to pay for highly skilled German dental treatment.

Of course, even dentists' and doctors' families would not have things
easy in the occupation years that followed, but overwhelmingly they
would survive. This was more than could be said for those ordinary
Germans who had no contacts with the occupiers, no professions whose
valuable services could be bartered for, and no connections with the

class that had long been sneered at by urban sophisticates, in Germany as elsewhere, but who would for the foreseeable future hold the key to life and death, survival or starvation: the nation's farmers.

All this lay in the future, however. For now, Germans as a whole faced the worst time. The time when they were totally at the conquerors' mercy, and would find that the quality of such mercy was strained very, very thin.

5

Through Conquerors' Eyes

It would not be an exaggeration to say that in 1945, a great many – in some countries most – Allied nationals clearly hated the Germans.

If we are to believe the opinion polls of the time, between spring 1943 and February 1945 (when Dresden and several other major German cities were bombed to near-destruction) the number of British citizens who identified themselves as either hating or having no sympathy for Germans increased from 43 to 54 per cent.

In America, the number of respondents believing the Germans to be inherently warlike rose from 23 per cent in February 1942 to 37 per cent in December 1944. Thirty per cent consulted in a January 1944 poll for *Fortune* magazine were in favour of completely breaking the Reich up into smaller states.[1]

A letter writer to a British newspaper, identifying himself as a Church of England vicar, spoke for many when he proclaimed:

The first step is to recognise the German character is essentially brutal and understands only force. For fifteen hundred years the Hun, to give him his proper title, has been a menace to his neighbours . . . and one is driven to the conclusion that God will Himself intervene and by some natural calamity obliterate such parts of Germany as may render her for ever afterwards impotent to be a menace to the world.[2]

The wartime broadcasts of the vehemently anti-German Foreign Office mandarin Lord Vansittart, and the publication of his book, *Black Record*, had done much to implant such ideas in the consciousness of the British public. However, the continuing V-weapon attacks on London, which killed relatively few but were deeply feared and loathed, and which ended only when the last launch base was overrun by the Allies at the very end of March 1945, also contributed to the growing bitterness and war-weariness of the civilian population.

After all, it had been obvious for a long time that the war was lost for Germany. Seen from across the Channel, the German population as a whole seemed nevertheless to be set on continuing the fight. The British public, naive about the methods that the Nazi dictatorship could and did use to pressure its people to conform, assumed that this continuation implied near-universal assent and even support. Then came the additional shock of stories about concentration camps such as Bergen-Belsen, Buchenwald and Dachau (the news about Auschwitz took somewhat longer to filter through properly), which were discovered by the advancing Anglo-American forces during the spring advance into the German heartland. The now-undeniable horrors of such places were extensively reported in newspapers and shown in grisly detail in newsreels as the war drew to an end.

The diarist Mollie Panter-Downes wrote about this hardening of public attitudes:

Millions of comfortable families, too kind and lazy . . . to make the effort to believe what they had conveniently looked upon as a news-paper propaganda stunt, now believe the horrifying, irrefutable evidence that even blurred printing on poor wartime paper has made all too clear. The shock to the public has been enormous, and lots of hitherto moderate people are wondering uncomfortably whether they will agree, after all, with Lord Vansittart's ruthless views on a hard peace.[3]

The highest-circulation conservative newspaper of the time, the *Daily Express*, showed the concentration camp photographs in

Trafalgar Square on 1 May at an outdoor exhibition entitled *Seeing Is Believing*, as well as (more comprehensively) at the newspaper's reading room in Regent Street. A visitor to the latter told a reporter: 'After seeing the exhibition I feel we ought to shoot every German. There's not a good one amongst them.'

This ruthless and undifferentiated attitude towards the defeated enemy extended from bottom to top. At the Tehran Conference of the 'Big Three' in 1943, Stalin had suggested shooting 50,000 senior German officers out of hand. Churchill was repelled by that perhaps only semi-serious suggestion,[4] but enthusiastically supported the idea of summary execution without trial of major Nazi leaders and war criminals. He dropped the idea only reluctantly in the spring of 1945 under pressure from the Americans, who by then had decided that international war crimes trials were the only decent solution to the problem.[5] As for the Russians, their feelings were extreme and thoroughly understandable, though many of their atrocious actions after they entered Germany could not, and still cannot, be excused.

General Eisenhower, the C-in-C of the Allied Expeditionary Force in the west, though himself of German descent, had, it seems, also come to loathe not just the obvious perpetrators but the German nation as a whole. In fact, he had expressed a degree of distrust even before America entered the war. In a letter to his brother in September 1939, shortly after the German invasion of Poland, he had written:

> It does not seem possible that people who call themselves intelligent could . . . give absolute power to a power-drunk egocentric . . . one of the criminally insane . . . the absolute ruler of eighty-nine million people.[6]

And much later, after the initial swift advance through France, the Allies were all but halted and the struggle settled into a costly war of attrition. It was then that he wrote to his wife, Mamie, the words about the hatred he felt for the Germans that would become much quoted after the war, though usually out of context. The sentences in which his declaration of loathing was embedded were written during the catastrophic Arnhem operation in September 1944 ('A bridge too far') and read, in full:

You have seen in the papers that two days ago we launched a big airborne attack. Every time I have to order another big battle I wonder how the people at home can be so complacent about finishing off the job we have here. There is still a lot of suffering to go through. God, I hate the Germans![7]

It was an expression, in other words, more of angry despair at the enemy's stubborn persistence, and the needless deaths it was causing, than of crude tribal hatred.

As in Britain, the spectrum of feeling about the Germans in the American military and government, and probably also among the general public in the USA, ran from vengeful and downright racist to resentful but fair-minded. Nonetheless, even among the latter group there was scarcely anyone who felt that the Germans should be treated as a 'liberated' people on a level with the French, the Dutch, the Poles or the Yugoslavs.

The same was not – oddly, perhaps – true when it came to the Austrians. German-speaking, enthusiastic citizens of the Third Reich for the most part since the *Anschluss* of March 1938, and – notoriously – counting Adolf Hitler himself among their number, they could and did claim the status of an oppressed people. As the Russians advanced, and the Nazi authorities retreated, numerous armed separatists appeared in the towns and cities of the so-called *Ostmark*, wearing armbands in the horizontal red-white-red of the old Austrian national flag, and claimed to be restoring the country's freedom. Whereas in Germany, all government was legally abolished by the Allies, in Austria, although the country was occupied and divided into four zones (and the capital, Vienna, into four sectors, like Berlin), from the outset it had a government of sorts, with a Chancellor and ministers.

Karl Renner, a veteran Social Democrat in his mid-seventies, who had also been first President of the Austrian Republic (or technically 'German-Austrian Republic') established in 1918 after the fall of the Habsburg monarchy, had come out of retirement in April 1945, at the Russians' behest, to declare a revived Austrian state. He was supported by a coalition drawn from all non-fascist parties, including his own, the People's Party (conservatives), and the communists. This government was recognised on 27 April by the Russians, who had been in control of Vienna since 13 April, and shortly after by the Western Allies.

It was in many ways an odd, and to outside eyes puzzling, business. Hitler's own people 'liberated' from him? The Viennese and other Austrians, so many of whom had ecstatically welcomed the annexation of the country to the Reich in March 1938, now suddenly so patriotic for the Red-and-White, so insistent that they were not actually 'German' at all? Returning to Austria on occupation business shortly after the war, George Clare, an exiled Viennese Jew, well attuned to such subtleties, noticed that even educated Austrians, who usually spoke a soft, Viennese-tinged version of High German, clearly recognisable as the same language spoken in Berlin or Munich or Hamburg, had begun resorting to the rough dialect of the low-rent Vienna suburbs in order to emphasise their Austrian-not-German identity.[8]

The recreation of the Austrian state was, in fact, an Allied war aim and had been so since the Moscow conference early in 1943, when the Allies had declared the annexation, or *Anschluss*, invalid. Austrian members of the Wehrmacht in the custody of the Allies were therefore among the first to be released after the coming of peace. The fact that many of these had been, so far as their German comrades could see, just as keen on the Nazi regime as themselves, if not more so, caused considerable resentment. As Ulrich Frodien, himself a former Hitler Youth leader and still a convinced Nazi at the time, recalled of the Austrians in his prison hospital:

. . . among whom were several 'super-Nazis', compared with whom I was a wilting flower. They suddenly began to distance themselves from us to a noticeable degree. They put their heads together in conspiratorial fashion and finally demanded . . . their immediate release from captivity, because as foreigners they had served in the German Wehrmacht only under compulsion. Even the general hilarity and numerous sarcastic attacks on them from the Berlin characters among us did nothing to change this distancing operation, which in the end was successful. They were all released and allowed to go home. When the war ended, the [Austrian] former National Socialist Leadership Officer at the hospital . . . made a passionate speech against the Nazi government, in which he declared the opposite of everything he had always said previously. If it had not been so sad, one might have made a grotesque comedy out of the thing.[9]

So far as Germans were concerned, however, the matter was quite clear. The instructions put out to the troops by the Allied commands quite specifically stated that the Germans were not to be treated as a liberated nation. Again, attitudes had hardened.

The Handbook to be distributed to American troops entering Germany also contained the text of a proclamation, signed by Eisenhower, addressed to the defeated population and making their status apparent. In early drafts, the word 'liberation' had, in fact, been used in the context of the Allied invasion, but the powers that be had rapidly backtracked. There was to be no doubt (in contrast to 1918) that Germany had been conquered, would now be an occupied country and would forfeit any right to determine its own destiny. Finally, with American troops approaching the German border in the autumn of 1944, and a decision pressing, a formula was agreed. 'Germany,' the Handbook's American readers were told, 'will always be treated as a defeated, and not as a liberated country.' Eisenhower's proclamation to the German population accordingly read, in English:

The Allied Forces serving under my Command have now entered Germany. We come as conquerors, but not as oppressors. In the area of Germany occupied by the forces under my command, we shall obliterate Nazism and German Militarism. We shall overthrow the Nazi rule, dissolve the Nazi Party and abolish the cruel, oppressive and discriminatory laws and institutions which the Party has created. We shall eradicate that German Militarism which has so often disrupted the peace of the world. Military and Party leaders, the Gestapo and others suspected of crimes and atrocities, will be tried, and, if guilty, punished as they deserve.

All well and good, but German-speakers in the Psychological Warfare Division at SHAEF pointed out that the German word for conqueror, *Eroberer*, was a little more direct and brutal in its implications than its English nearest equivalent – in fact, pretty much synonymous with 'oppressor'. It was finally changed, after consultations at the highest level, in the German translation from 'conquerors' to 'a victorious army' (*ein siegreiches Heer*), which was merely stating the obvious but also fudging the reality of what they were actually doing in Germany.[10] So far as the English version was concerned, however, 'conquerors' stayed in. The practical consequence of all this, which was discussed amidst enormous controversy within the military bureaucracy, is somewhat diminished by the comment of a SHAEF high-up that '. . . nobody reads handbooks anyhow, except very junior officers, whose subsequent actions can have very little effect'.[11]

The Handbook was finally released to the mass of fighting men in December 1944, just in time, as it happened, for the Battle of the Bulge. Semantic spats apart, it did express some basic principles which dominated, possibly for better but arguably for worse, attitudes during the initial period of occupation.

Then, in April, with final victory in sight, came the notorious JCS 1067, a putatively comprehensive set of instructions from the Joint Chiefs of Staff in Washington to Eisenhower aimed at closely directing the behaviour of US forces in occupied Germany. The tone was inevitably moralistic, stern, even harsh. So far as the basic behaviour of American forces towards the Germans was concerned, the message was quite crisp and clear but largely divorced from any notion of what was happening on the ground:

a. It should be brought home to the Germans that Germany's ruthless warfare and the fanatical Nazi resistance have destroyed the German economy and made chaos and suffering inevitable and that the Germans cannot escape responsibility for what they have brought upon themselves.

b. Germany will not be occupied for the purpose of liberation but as a defeated enemy nation. Your aim is not oppression but to occupy Germany for the purpose of realizing certain important Allied objectives. In the conduct of your occupation and administration you should be just but firm and aloof. You will strongly discourage fraternization with the German officials and population.

c. The principal Allied objective is to prevent Germany from ever again becoming a threat to the peace of the world. Essential steps in the accomplishment of this objective are the elimination of Nazism and militarism in all their forms, the immediate apprehension of war criminals for punishment, the industrial disarmament and demilitarization of Germany, with continuing control over Germany's capacity to make war, and the preparation for an eventual reconstruction of German political life on a democratic basis.

d. Other Allied objectives are to enforce the program of reparations and restitution, to provide relief for the benefit of countries devastated by Nazi aggression, and to ensure that prisoners of war and displaced persons of the United Nations are cared for and repatriated.[12]

JCS 1067, even more than the Handbook, had been the outcome of savage infighting between the Pentagon, the White House and the Department of the Treasury. This conflict – which was by no means over even with JCS 1067's approval by the President – expressed both the varying attitudes among Roosevelt's officials and aides when it came to the shape post-war Germany should take, and also differences in quite basic political assumptions.

The political struggle was essentially between the idealists, who wished to transform Germany, by radical action, into a new kind of country, peaceful and harmless by design, and the practical types, who weighed up the plight of the country's seventy million people, most of them now reduced to penury and inactivity and menaced by the threat of starvation, and saw the rapid restoration of its capacity to pay its way and feed itself as the main priority.

The chief protagonists of these two conflicting points of view were fifty-four-year-old Treasury Secretary Henry Morgenthau Junior (for the idealists) and Henry J. Stimson, the veteran Secretary for War, who in 1945 was already seventy-seven (for the realists).

A member of the East Coast Republican elite, educated at Yale and Harvard Law School, Stimson had served between 1911 and 1914 as Secretary for War under President Taft, and in the inter-war period had been American proconsul in both occupied Nicaragua and the Philippines. Despite Stimson's republicanism, Roosevelt had offered him the post at the War Office in 1940 because he was unquestionably anti-Nazi. However, he was also a hard-headed realist with considerable administrative experience and a distrust of utopian schemes.

Morgenthau's background was different. His own father had been Ambassador to Turkey after the First World War, and as a young man Henry Jr had witnessed with horror the massacres and expulsions that followed the disintegration of the Ottoman Empire. He was also a (highly assimilated) Jew. Whether that last fact influenced in a decisive way his views on the future of Germany was a matter for discussion at the time, and remains so to this day.

The idea at the heart of Morgenthau's plan for the post-war fate of Germany was that the country should, quite literally, be rendered incapable of ever waging war again. In short, he proposed that Germany become 'a land primarily agricultural and pastoral in its character', and that it be divided into three, a 'north German' state, a 'south German' state, and an international zone including the heavy industrial and coal-mining areas of the North Rhine and Ruhr, along with a swathe of territory running north and east to include Hamburg, Bremen and the strategic Kiel Canal. Of the Ruhr, the proposal insisted:

Within a short period, if possible not longer than six months after the cessation of hostilities, all industrial plants and equipment not destroyed by military action shall either be completely dismantled and removed from the area or completely destroyed. All equipment shall be removed from the mines and the mines shall be thoroughly wrecked.[13]

The standard of living of the German population should, he suggested, 'be held down to a subsistence level'.

Stimson's response, on 5 September, began by stating that the Secretary of War agreed with the 'principles stated therein', which were 'in conformity with the lines upon which we have been proceeding in the War Department in our directives to the armed forces'. It then added: 'with the exception of the last paragraph'. The last paragraph was the all-important one in which Morgenthau made his drastic, not to say draconian, proposals regarding the future shape of the German economy. 'I cannot,' Stimson said firmly, 'treat as realistic the suggestion that such an area in the present economic condition of the world can be turned into a non-productive "ghost territory" when it has become the centre of one of the most industrialised continents in the world, populated by peoples of energy, vigour and progressiveness.' He concluded:

Nor can I agree that it should be one of our purposes to hold the German population 'to a subsistence level' if this means the edge of poverty, condemning the German people to a condition of servitude in which, no matter how hard or how effectively a man worked, he could not materially increase his economic condition in the world. Such a programme would, I believe, create tensions and resentments far outweighing any immediate advantage of security and would tend to obscure the guilt of the Nazis and the viciousness of their doctrines and their acts.

By such economic mistakes I cannot but feel that you would also be poisoning the springs out of which we hope that the future peace of the world can be maintained.

My basic objection to the proposed methods of treating Germany which were discussed this morning was that in addition to a system of preventive and educative punishment they would add the dangerous weapon of complete economic oppression. Such methods, in my opinion, do not prevent war; they tend to breed war.[14]

It was a crushing rejoinder. Cordell Hull, the Secretary of State, was not far behind him, though less aggressively so. Like Stimson, he was happy to see Germany pay reparations in money, kind and even human labour (there were already plans to allow the other Allies to retain German POWs as forced labour far beyond the coming of peace), but could not conceive of de-industrialising the country.[15]

This joint offensive did not immediately affect the President's apparently keen support for Morgenthau's plans. Roosevelt responded to their objections with a jocular reference to Germans' being 'fed three times a day with soup from army soup kitchens . . . [so that] they will remember that experience the rest of their lives'.

FDR took Morgenthau to his summit with the British in the middle of the month. When they met Churchill at Quebec on 16 September, with the British leader looking to renew a much-needed lend-lease deal with the Americans, it was almost certainly the Treasury Secretary's control of the cheque book as well as his eloquence that tipped the balance. That, and the Americans' assertion that, with German industrial power destroyed and prevented from recovering, a near-bankrupt Britain's economy would find it much easier to forge ahead once more after the war. For whatever reason, they managed to impose a slightly watered-down version on an initially reluctant Churchill.

The prompt leaking of the text to the press – and a widespread negative public reaction – caused Roosevelt, who was running against the youthful New York Governor, Thomas E. Dewey, for his third re-election in November, to deny that the 'Morgenthau Plan' was firm Allied policy.

It also quickly became clear that the Morgenthau Plan was a gift to German propagandists. The Nazi Party newspaper, the *Völkischer Beobachter*, ran a screaming headline: 'Roosevelt and Churchill Agree to Jew Murder Plan'. Goebbels eagerly began to promote a new scapegoat, Morgenthau, 'the Jewish angel of hate'. In a speech at the beginning of October he sneered:

Hate and revenge of a truly old-testament character are clear in these plans dreamed up by the American Jew Morgenthau. Industrialised Germany should be literally turned into a huge potato field.[16]

From now on, Goebbels' journalists and propagandists repeatedly rammed home the simple, stark message: with the Morgenthau Plan now official Allied policy, Germans faced either victory or mass death and starvation.

It seems probable that this propaganda campaign helped stiffen resistance in what was left of the Reich during the final months of the war. Roosevelt's son-in-law, Lieutenant Colonel John Boettiger, who visited the front during the bitter fighting for Aachen in October 1944, reported that the troops on the ground had told him the Plan was 'worth thirty divisions to the Germans'.[17]

Between the Quebec Conference in September and Roosevelt's death on 12 April 1945, the momentum behind the Morgenthau Plan slackened. It was the beginning of a painfully slow backtrack that would take up to three years in all.

Churchill may have signed up for the Plan in Quebec, but even before the Prime Minister returned to London, leading figures in his government – especially Foreign Secretary Sir Anthony Eden, who at Quebec had argued angrily with him about it ('You can't do this!

After all, you and I publicly have said quite the opposite!') within full earshot of the Americans – started agitating against the so-called 'Carthaginian Peace' demanded by Morgenthau.[18] Eden wrote in his diary that he was 'irritated by this German Jew's bitter hatred of his own land'*.[19]

Meanwhile, and almost fatally, no alternative policy was developed. There remained strong 'Morgenthau' elements in JCS 1067 – particularly regarding the feeding of the country at a basic level no higher than any of the surrounding nations and the assertion that the US would do nothing to stimulate or 'rehabilitate' German industry – though some of the most extreme suggestions, such as wrecking German mines and factories, were quietly dropped. Nonetheless, the breathtakingly radical elements contained in Morgenthau's proposal would impede the ruling and feeding of occupied Germany and alienate many in Germany and elsewhere from Allied post-war policy.

Nor was the matter of Morgenthau's Jewish identity left out of the picture, even in Washington. Stimson considered Morgenthau 'so biased by his Semitic grievances that he really is a very dangerous adviser to the President',[20] while Secretary Hull referred in coded fashion to 'Morgenthau and his friends', and asserted that the Plan 'might well mean a bitter-end German resistance that could cause the loss of thousands of American lives'.[21]

The other great pillar of the proposed post-war occupation of Germany was the notorious 'non-fraternisation' order contained both in the Handbook and in slightly modified form in JCS 1067.

The non-fraternisation policy had been framed in the early months of 1944 and was incorporated into Eisenhower's order of the day on 3 September 1944, just before the US Army launched itself into Germany proper. Non-fraternisation was defined as 'the avoidance of mingling with Germans upon terms of friendliness, familiarity or intimacy, whether individually or in groups, in official

* Morgenthau's father had been born in Bavaria in 1857 and emigrated to America at the age of ten.

or unofficial dealings'. Specifically prohibited were marriages, integrated seating at religious services, visiting private homes, attending
dances and even shaking hands. To 'protect' their men against such
temptations, officers were encouraged to keep them occupied by,
among other things, intensified training and the promotion of
education and sports. Transgressions were punishable with a $65
fine for a first offence.[22]

The order was transposed into what was supposed to be a
'GI-friendly' form in the forty-eight-page 'Pocket Guide to Germany',
some two million of which were distributed to American soldiers for
the advance into Germany in the autumn of 1944. Prepared by
German-speaking members of the army's Morale Service Division,
and packed with chilling warnings, the Pocket Guide told its readers:
'Trust no one but your own kind. Be on your guard particularly
against young Germans between the ages of 14 and 28. Since 1933,
when Hitler came to power, German youth has been carefully and
thoroughly educated for world conquest, killing, and treachery . . .'

On the subject of relations with Germans, of whatever age, it was
also perfectly clear that 'you are in an enemy country':

There must be no fraternization. This is absolute! [italicised in the origi-
nal] Unless otherwise permitted by higher authority you will not visit
in German homes or associate with Germans on terms of friendly
intimacy, either in public or in private. They must never be taken
into your confidence.

This warning against fraternization doesn't mean that you are to
act like a sourpuss or military automaton. Your aspect should not be
harsh or forbidding. At home you had minor transactions with many
people. You were courteous to them, but never discussed intimate
affairs, told them secrets, or gave them the benefit of your confidence.
Let that behaviour be your model now.

The Germans will be curious. They will be interested. Their interest
will be aroused by observation. They will notice your superb equipment. They will notice your high pay (high compared to the standards

of their own and other European countries). They will observe your morale and the magnificent spirit of cooperation and mutual respect that exists in the American Army and they will ask questions about America and American life.

Within the limits of your instructions against fraternization and intimacy, you can by your conduct give them a glimpse of life in a Democracy where no man is master of another, where the only limit of success is a man's own ability.[23]

Among other useful, though less worrying, information in the booklet was the revelation that 'Germany is not as large as Texas'. And it contained tourist stuff – weights and measures equivalents, currency and so on, and a twenty-page phonetic guide to useful terms and phrases for non-German-speaking conquerors:

Where is a toilet?	VO ist ai-nuh two-LET-tuh?
When does the movie start?	VAHN buh-GINT dahss KEE-no?
Bring help!	HO-len zee HIL-fuh!

And moving from this back into worrying territory again:

Take cover!	DEK-koong!
Take me to a hospital	BRIN-gen zee mish tsoo ai-nem la-tsa-RET

The entire strictness of the affair, supported by frequent exhortations on American Forces' radio, which ran regular, recorded warnings, was somewhat undermined by the evidence, as early as the end of 1944, that almost all the German secretaries and housekeepers employed at American military headquarters were very pretty and very young.[24]

The British also produced a Guide for their troops and a Handbook for officers. It had more history in it, but otherwise took a similar line. However, the British high command quite quickly showed a more relaxed attitude to the actual practicalities. Judging from the sections dealing with the anti-fraternisation order in the American Pocket Guide, any positive effect from interaction between Allied troops and Germans seemed to be expected to come out of some kind of mime performance or silent-movie routine.

The problem was, of course, that once any soldier, but perhaps especially any American soldier, came into contact with the people hitherto known as the enemy and observed that they both looked pretty much like him and his comrades and also behaved pretty much in the same fashion, there was no preventing fraternisation. And it was hard to see where that fraternisation would stop. The fine for forbidden contact with German civilians was $65, and so asking a German girl out on a date became known as the '$65 Question'.²⁵

Since that same soldier was lonely, frightened, frustrated and bored, in that unique combination that only war service can provide, what was he supposed to do? Within a few weeks of the war's end, soldiers were told they could loosen up when it came to talking with German children. Well, kids were kids, same as everywhere; they liked candy and a few games. And then there were their unmarried aunts and their grown-up sisters . . . according to one magazine story of the time, GIs, spotting an attractive young German woman, would wink at her and say 'Good day, child'.²⁶

At the end of July 1945, the non-fraternisation policy was supposedly modified, so that conversations with German civilians were permitted 'in public places'. This was widely interpreted as a de facto abandonment of the policy. As a *Time* magazine correspondent reported from a Bavarian lakeside resort (under the headline 'Ban Lifted'):

One of the first people in this picturesque town to hear about the rescinding of the ban was a 28-year-old blonde, blousy German girl named Helga. She was told about it by the American soldier whose room in one of the local hotels she had been sharing for the past 30 days. Helga's reaction was mixed. She said she was very happy because 'now we don't have to hide it any more'. But the joy was somewhat shadowed, she allowed, because 'it is much better when it is forbidden'.[27]

One Ilse Schmidt, 'a gorgeous 19-year-old brunette with a figure designed to make men drool', sunbathing on a local pier, when asked by the same reporter for her views on fraternisation, answered: 'I never had any trouble. Have you a cigarette, please?'

In fact, it was not until October 1945 that intimate relations with German civilians were actually permitted, but long before that, the order had become a dead letter. The remaining restriction, on marriages with German women, remained until the military authorities finally relented in December 1946. Many thousands of marriages were entered into during the years to come, with around 20,000 German women emigrating to America as 'GI brides' between 1946 and 1949.[28] It should, however, be added that this was less than a third of the number of British brides who went stateside to join their American soldier husbands during the same period after the passing of the 'GI Bride' Act by Congress in December 1945.

There were also thousands of children born as the result of liaisons that did not lead to marriage, many of them never knowing their fathers. GIs in Germany at that point did not need to pay child support unless they were willing to acknowledge paternity, rendering the obligations of fatherhood entirely voluntary. Many of the children, and their single mothers, suffered severe social exclusion, especially if the children were offspring of relationships with black American GIs.

On the British side, although restrictions on relations with Germans at first seemed equally uncompromising, they were on the whole relaxed more quickly than in the American-controlled areas. The British attitude in general was both a little more cynical and a little more pragmatic. The British C-in-C and, after VE-Day, Military Governor of the British Zone, Field Marshal Montgomery, although himself rather puritanical in sexual matters, pointed out in a letter to Churchill at the beginning of July that if one couldn't actually speak to Germans, how was one supposed to change them from Nazis to something better, which was, allegedly, one of the post-war aims? And in any case, the Field Marshal continued, in the manner of a boy suggesting that some schoolyard 'enemy' be re-admitted to the fold after being temporarily sent to Coventry:

> We crossed the Rhine on 23 March and for nearly four months we have not spoken to the German population, except when duty has so demanded. The Germans have been told why we have acted thus; it has been a shock to them and they have learnt their lesson.[29]

In his diaries, the Chief of the British Imperial General Staff, Lord Alanbrooke – hardly known for his levity – announced in jocular fashion after a high-level meeting shortly before the end of the war: 'Amongst other items, we have appointed Monty as Gauleiter for the British Zone.'[30] By late summer 1946 the first Anglo-German marriage had taken place – in the British sector of Berlin – without an act of congress or of parliament being necessary.[31]

This didn't mean that the British necessarily 'liked' the Germans at that point any better than the Americans or the French or the Soviets did. As occupiers, His Majesty's Forces could certainly be arrogant, stubborn, even cruel. Particularly in the early stages of the occupation, many willingly excluded themselves from any 'normal' relations with Germans, were indifferent to German suffering, or even viewed it with satisfaction. After the British took control of their sector in Berlin, a small German boy of ten or so was caught trying to steal from a British Army mess. A young officer who was present at the time reported on the 'interrogation' of the miscreant:

> The point is that none of us could have cared a bit for that little boy. He was probably an orphan, his father dead on the Eastern Front, his mother rotting under rubble of the bombed-out ruins, and here he was – starving and risking his life climbing up drainpipes in the middle of a British tank regiment. So what? We didn't feel any

compassion for him or any of the Germans. They had been public enemy number one. So now we commandeered their horses, commandeered their Mercedes, commandeered their women. I would reckon 60 or 70 percent of young Englishmen in Germany thought that way. Most of us were for having a bloody good time and believed we could get away with anything.[32]

The notion of conquered women as 'fair game' was, naturally enough, far more widespread than any official account of the time would have wanted to admit. In his (strongly autobiographical) first novel, *To the Victors the Spoils* (published in 1950), British writer Colin MacInnes gave a warts-and-all account of the lives of the young men of the British Army's intelligence corps, careening through the newly liberated France and Low Countries and on into Germany in the winter of 1944–5, chasing collaborators, diehard Nazis and war criminals.

MacInnes, who became well known in the 1950s for such works as *Absolute Beginners*, *Mr Love and Justice* and *City of Spades*, had then just turned thirty. The privately educated son of writer Angela Thirkell, closely related through her to British Prime Minister Stanley Baldwin and the writer Rudyard Kipling, in the novel, and in life, he was content to remain a mere sergeant in Field Intelligence. The narrator in the novel is identified only as 'Sergeant Mac'.

Like his later books, which dealt frankly with London's youth culture and the exotic underbelly of 1950s and 1960s Soho, as well as MacInnes' own open bisexuality, *To the Victors the Spoils* pulled no punches and was widely criticised for this at the time it was published. Throughout, the occasional outburst of idealism among his young Nazi-hunters is more than outweighed by their shameless acquisitiveness, their sexual voracity and their amoral quest for cosy 'billets'. One of them begins by appearing to fall head over heels in love with a Dutch girl, promising her marriage, and then after moving over the border rapidly doing the same with a young German woman in the Rhineland. He never does make his mind up.

As was the case with the American forces, young women hired to clean billets or act as translators are usually the most attractive the team can find. And they make their rules up as they go along, for in effect their powers over the local Germans are limitless. A few weeks before the end of the war, a major of a Civilian Administration unit (Military Government in Waiting), a policeman in peacetime, takes a shine to the attractive assistant of a local Burgomaster. The woman, apparently previously in charge of the meagre rations allowed for Polish forced labourers, makes some racist remarks. The major, who spends most of their conversation staring at her legs, later tries to convince a sceptical anti-Nazi lieutenant of her usefulness:

'I must say,' said Lieutenant Adeane, 'that the powers we'll have almost frighten me at times. I've been reading through the military laws, and some of them are terribly vague and comprehensive.'

'Oh, don't get the wrong idea,' the Major told him. 'I won't come down hard on them all, and I might even let some of them off, you never know. But I reckon an old bobby will be able to pick out the hard cases all right.'

'What worries me a bit,' said the Lieutenant, 'is that we've invented the laws we're going to apply.'

'Well, that's natural, isn't it? Thanks, Captain, I don't mind another glass. You know, I liked that woman over at the Town Hall this morning, didn't you. I'm almost sorry we're not staying here, she'd have been just right for the job of Secretary. Quick-witted, practical, and speaks nearly perfect English.'

'From what you told me, she sounds most unsuitable,' the Lieutenant said.

'Oh? And why so, may I ask?'

'Because she's an obvious Nazi.'

'Oh-ho! A Nazi. But so long as she's not in an Arrestable Category, that wouldn't matter.'[33]

In another incident, one of the intelligence sergeants blackmails the attractive female owner of a hotel where they are billeted, using his knowledge of her son's clandestine presence in the building (a deserter from the Wehrmacht, the young man should have handed himself over to British custody) to force her to sleep with him.

Especially once they are in Germany, there is little respect for either propriety or property. Women are chased, offered the lure of scarce food and consumer goods. And there is outright theft. Desirable motor vehicles are 'requisitioned' and furniture, heirlooms and other moveable valuables 'liberated':

> The things the others had stolen varied with each man's nature. Some had chosen useless souvenirs (decorated daggers were a favourite), others things of value. Cornelis had got some watches, Walter had Lugers and sporting guns. Cuthbert . . . said, 'I've only helped myself to things of general use – nothing personal. The Opel, you see, and these radios to replace my own that was defective.'
>
> Looting is irresistible to anyone who had not a real indifference to possessions or a rare sense of duty. The opportunities are enormous, and there is no risk during the first few days of the fall of a town, when the old authority is overthrown and the new one not yet established. Even for those who are not thieves by nature, the attraction of what seems at first a delightful game, is overwhelming. As time goes on, the playful looters either see that game isn't one, and stop, or else go on till it becomes a habit, and their characters change.[34]

An account of this phenomenon from another contemporary source backs up MacInnes' judgement:

> Some soldiers with a sharper eye for business – officers mostly – looted things for the profit they yielded on the black market in Brussels, the biggest in liberated Europe. Some specialised according to demand. One young officer took adding machines and sporting guns. Another had already taken five car loads of ball-bearings from Germany to Brussels, and made several other trips with slaughtered cows in the back of his car. Cars in particular were at a premium. A 50-year-old

British officer explained how to get hold of one. 'It's no use going to garages. Field Security and Military Government usually put a sentry on those. What you do is drive around until you see a house with a garage. Then you get the owner and take the key off him. He's probably hidden the battery and the tyres, but if you show him a little persuasion he'll cough up quickly enough.'[35]

At one point during the British advance into northern Germany, it got so bad that, with all the cars that had been 'requisitioned' from German civilians, one division's column had reached twice its usual length, and traffic jams were threatening to bring progress to a halt. On orders from the divisional commander, all cars found to be unauthorised were seized by the military police, driven off into the fields on either side of the road, and disabled by gunfire or through setting them alight, to ensure that they could not be further used – either by British troops or, ultimately, by their unfortunate German former owners.

MacInnes shrewdly analysed the mentality of the invading British soldier, in a way that could be applied with relatively minor differences to any conqueror. He describes driving his unit's commander, a captain, along a track beside a canal near the front line in northern Belgium. Their truck gets stuck in the winter mud. The 'Sergeant Mac' character goes off to seek help from a nearby farm. As he does so, he turns back, seeing the officer as a lonely figure in the darkening plain:

He looked almost exotic, standing in his military mackintosh beside the broken-down truck in the middle of the lonely Flemish landscape. But holding a cigarette in one gloved hand, swinging his map-case slowly by the straps with the other, he seemed unaware of this. Generations of captains had come this way before him, and in whatever place an English soldier finds himself, he is cloaked about with the confident assurance that where he is, he should be, and that it is the alien land, not he, which was strange and foreign.[36]

When the British took Hamburg at the end of April 1945, plenty of the burghers of this Anglophile city – which as a major North Sea port and a city state with ancient democratic traditions had enjoyed a long and amicable relationship with the United Kingdom – were relieved that they were to be occupied by 'gentlemen' from the latter-day birthplace of democracy. They were quickly disillusioned. In the defeated Germans' eyes, the victors often behaved in a manner both arrogant and officious. To the victor the spoils, indeed.

Mathilde ('Tilli') Wolff-Mönckeberg was an anti-Nazi, though firmly patriotic, German woman, then in her sixties, living in Hamburg. Appalled by what happened to her country after 1933, she poured out her frustrations in a long series of unsent letters to her children, three of whom had gone abroad (one daughter had married a Welshman and lived in Britain through the war years, another married a German Jew and emigrated to the USA, while her son became a communist and went into exile, first in Russia and then in South America).

Born to privilege (her father served as High Burgomaster of the city towards the end of the nineteenth century), Frau Wolff-Mönckeberg was a woman who as a teenager recorded in her notebook on a single day in the 1890s: 'Prince Bismarck to lunch, Herr Johannes Brahms to dinner'. She spoke fluent English and had often visited her daughter in Britain before the war, but she survived the catastrophic bombing of her native city, along with her liberal, Anglophile academic husband – only to find herself bewildered by the attitude of the British occupiers, whose arrival she and her friends had so longed for during the agonising years of the Nazi dictatorship:

People here are already scraping and bowing to the English, trying to find favour. I do understand that W. [her husband] is deeply depressed, has little hope for his own particular world. Now he is disillusioned by the limitless arrogance and dishonesty with which they treat us, proclaiming to the whole world that only Germany could have sunk so low in such abysmal cruelty and bestiality, that they themselves are pure and beyond reproach . . .[37]

Frau Wolff-Mönckeberg wrote this a little over a week after VE-Day. It was an early reaction, doubtless exacerbated by long years of stress and anxiety that now seemed to have ended in bitter disappointment. In fact, her husband would soon be appointed as Acting Provost of Hamburg University, and within a few months the front-line soldiers (some perhaps influenced by experiences such as the liberation of Bergen-Belsen) gave way to administrators and educators who took a less harsh line, as she would later admit.

Of course, not all of the victors exhibited a blanket hatred of the defeated Germans. Not even the Russians. The behaviour of the Red Army had been unspeakable, and 'incidents', particularly in relation to German women, frequent. As one Berlin woman later said of the period after the city fell, 'We got the impression that in those first four weeks the Russians could do what they wanted. We girls and women had no rights.'[38]

A schoolgirl who kept a diary at this time recorded the progression of events during the siege with a chilling matter-of-factness:

22.4. Sleeping in the cellar. The Russians have reached Berlin.

25.4. No water! No gas! No light!

26.4. Artillery fire!

27.4. The enemy has reached Kaiserplatz [in the suburb of Wilmersdorf].

28.4. Our building received its 4th artillery hit.

29.4. Our building has approximately 20 hits. Cooking is made very difficult by the ongoing threat to life and limb if you leave the cellar.

30.4. When the bomb hit, I was at the top of the cellar steps with Frau B. The Russians have arrived. Rapes at night. I not; mother, yes. Some, 5–20 times.

1.5. Russians are going in and out. All the watches are gone. Horses are lying on our beds in the courtyard. The cellars have been broken into.

2.5. The first night of calm. We have come from hell into heaven. We cried when discovered the blooming lilacs in the courtyard. All radios must be turned in.

6.5. Our building has 21 hits. Cleaned up and packed the whole day. At night, storm. Hid under the bed out of fear that the Russians would come. But the building just rattled from the shelling.

7.5. Swept the street clear. Went to get ration coupons for bread, picked up, cleaned.

8.5. Swept the street. Stood in line for bread. Report that Papa is still alive.

9.5. Ceasefire. There is milk for Margit.[39]

All the same, reflecting the unpredictable mix of brutality and humanity that so many observers have noted of the Russian character, there were plenty of instances where compassion could be and was shown, and even a kind of odd respect for things German that was not necessarily present among the other Allied troops.

So, for instance, during the last days of the war, when the bombed-out city of Dresden finally fell to the Russians, a teenage inhabitant of Löschwitz, a pleasant and historic suburb of the city, found himself, to his terror, surprised by two Soviet officers in what he took to be NKVD uniforms. Expecting to be arrested, or worse, he was instead greeted by a polite request, in near-perfect German, for directions to the little summer house overlooking the Elbe where the great German poet Friedrich Schiller had written his famous *Ode to Joy* a century and a half earlier. The officer and his colleagues were under orders to secure it, as an important cultural monument, from damage during the Red Army's occupation of the area.[40]

On the other side of the city, the fortunes of eighteen-year-old Götz Bergander's family were favoured by two factors: first that the two Russian maids who worked for the household spoke well to the first Red Army soldiers of the Berganders' kindness to them; and second – more enduringly – that the family lived in a flat on the premises of the distillery where Bergander senior, a chemist, was technical director. With so much alcohol available, the Russian commander was fearful that his men would get totally out of control. He put a twenty-four-hour guard on the entire production facility, which had the additional effect of protecting the family's residence as well during the critical, chaotic days when most of the rapes and robberies occurred elsewhere.[41]

Although as a Hitler Youth leader he had been pressed into forced labour for a while by the victors, Lothar Löwe, sixteen at the end of the war, recalled that, once the mayhem accompanying the fall of Berlin was over, many ordinary Russians 'were . . . nice people on a personal level'. The French were worse, in his experience.[42] A woman in Berlin noted that 'the Russians always gave children something to eat, the kids could get anything they wanted from them. They were always very nice to kids, never cruel.'[43]

There were other surprises, some quite bizarre or surreal. Some women who had been hiding in a leafy apartment block near what is now the Stresemannstrasse, not far from the Potsdamer Platz in the city centre of Berlin, were concerned when the horse-drawn baggage train of a Soviet tank regiment set up its carts in the gardens surrounding the flats. Their horses could be hobbled and grazed among the lawns. Within a short time, the German women and the Russians – who included some female soldiers as well as men – came into conversation. The area was peaceful now, with the fighting finally over. One of the German women, who knew a little Russian, screwed up her courage and approached them. They had some food but nothing to cook it with. The German woman offered to help, and duly cooked the Soviet sergeant major and his band a meal, which the 'enemy' happily shared with her and her two female companions.

Within a short time, 'we few Germans were moving freely through the area. The Russians showed us pictures of their families, we laughed together. It was incredible, that something like this could happen, after all those terrible days.' When the baggage train moved on, the sergeant major gave the woman a scribbled note in Russian, a kind

of rough-and-ready letter of safe conduct, which declared: 'This apartment is occupied by tank troops. Guard-Sergeant-Major Abdulguyzn,
Boris N., field post nr. 39907.'

During this same period, perhaps in some kind of recompense
for the behaviour of Soviet troops during the fall of the city – or at
least in awareness of the bad feeling this had caused – the new
Russian commandant in Berlin, Colonel-General Berzarin, provided
for Russian army rations to be diverted to feeding the German
civilians eking out an existence among the ruins. He also quickly
organised, a little more than a week after the capitulation, an exhibition of major possessions of Berlin's bomb-shattered museums in
temporary quarters and, on 26 May, facilitated the first post-war
concert by the Berlin Philharmonic.[44]

None of these expressions of basic decency did, or could, mitigate
the results of the mass rape that had occurred throughout the Soviet
area of advance and, most terribly, in Berlin at the time of the city's
downfall. The violation of the bodies of tens, even hundreds of thousands of German women would have both short- and long-term
consequences. Short, in terms of a huge rise in venereal disease and
unwanted pregnancies (the so-called *Russenkinder*, or 'Russian-
children'), and long in the sense of permanent damage to
Russian–German relations. It effected the alienation of most Germans
in the Soviet-occupied areas of the country from the occupying power,
and reinforced their resistance to attempts on the part of the Russians
and their German communist allies to install, by persuasion if possible, but if not by force, their chosen political system.

During this interval – say, the twelve to eighteen months following
the end of the war – the bizarre difference between the Germany
policy of the Western Allies and that of the Soviets was, in effect, that
the Russians were quite clear about what they wanted (that is, quite
logically, to encourage socialist/communist developments in
Germany), while for their part the Western powers seemed bent on
radical post-war plans that were not in any way patterned on their
own social and political systems.

So, the Morgenthau Plan for Germany was much more radical than the strip-and-socialise Soviet proposals, involving as it did the putative dismantling of two hundred years of German history and the country's forced transformation into some sort of harmless pre-industrial community of self-reliant yeoman farmers – totally unlike the modern United States, although arguably owing something to romantic notions of the American Midwest's rural virtues.

An article in *Time* magazine appraising the Anglo-American preparations to withdraw from their forward positions and back into their agreed zones, at the beginning of July 1945, showed a surprisingly critical point of view on this issue, and even more surprisingly was headlined with the title of a famous essay by Lenin ('What Is to Be Done?'):

With complicated move and counter-move, the four occupying powers settled down last week to the task of ruling conquered Germany . . .

. . . the British and Americans were still united by a common lack of policy: long-range policies were still either undecided or secret. Ordinary soldiers of the occupation armies were beginning to ask: what's going to be done with Germany? Will it be permanently divided into small states? With political activity banned, how can a democratic Germany develop?

Beyond the movement of Russian prisoners from west to east, there was still no apparent coordination of policy between the western allies and Russia. While the Russians were winning friends and influencing Germans in the east, Germans in the west were beginning to show open hostility to the occupying armies.[45]

The reference to the Russians' 'winning friends' in the east was perhaps a little over-indulgent – maybe Western reporters were not yet fully aware of the savagery of the Soviet excesses there. However, there was an element of truth in it. For all the Red Army's disastrous bad behaviour, and, in the microcosm, the touch-and-go nature of personal relations between Germans and their Russian occupiers, the defeated Germans quickly discerned the fairly brutal straight-forwardness of Russian policy in the macrocosm. For some this was more attractive or at least more bearable than Western ambiguity and confusion.

Nor was there, at the beginning, any anti-fraternisation policy in the Soviet Zone (another reason why, perhaps naively, the *Time* journalist thought that the Russians must be increasing their popularity among the locals). Soviet officers were routinely billeted with German families, and this not infrequently led to friendly personal relations with their hosts. One German observer wrote that 'in many German families, single Russians have acclimatised well and act like sons in the house'.

And of course this initial lack of restrictions facilitated relationships between Soviet troops and the local girls and women. Initially, during the 'wild' period following the fall of Berlin, many German women, desperate to avoid repeated rape, realised that their best chance lay in finding themselves a Red Army officer and embarking on an exclusive sexual relationship with him, in the often-fulfilled hope that this would protect them from the mass of the soldiery.

Marta Hillers, a widely travelled journalist in her thirties, kept a diary between April and June 1945, coolly detailing her experiences and those of her friends as the Russians fought for and captured Berlin (it was later published, first in English and only later in German, when it caused a considerable scandal). She suffered the rapes stoically. 'I laugh right in the middle of all this awfulness,' she wrote. 'What should I do? After all, I am alive, everything will pass!' All the same, she saw no reason not to protect herself, and made the hard-headed decision to find a tolerable Russian, as senior in rank as possible, and make him the 'special one'.

Hillers was lucky enough to find, first a rather mercurial, bull-like lieutenant, succeeded when he was posted on by a cultured and intelligent army major, whom she actually found quite pleasant company. 'I like the major,' she wrote, 'and the less he wants from me as a man, the more I like him as a person' –

And he won't be wanting much, I can tell. His face is pale. His knee wound is causing him trouble. He's probably not so much after sexual contact as human companionship, female company – and I'm more than willing to give him that. For out of all the male beasts I've seen these past few days, he's the most bearable, the best of the lot.[46]

After a few more weeks had passed, more natural relationships developed – or at least as natural as was possible in the state of inequality that existed between conquerors and conquered, where considerations of access to food, fuel and cigarettes always lurked in the background of the simple man–woman attraction.

Lieutenant Wladimir Gelfand was a Russian of Jewish extraction, commander of a mortar platoon that accompanied the infantry all the way from Stalingrad to Warsaw and then to Berlin. Born in 1923, he had been brought up in modest circumstances as the son of a factory foreman and a kindergarten teacher in the industrial eastern Ukraine. From childhood, he had been a studious boy, interested in literature, philosophy and poetry, and, despite his studies being interrupted by the outbreak of war and his conscription into the army, retained a certain intellectual bent. He would spend his life wanting, in vain, to make a career as a writer.

So, Lieutenant Gelfand, though he had served courageously for three years at the front by the time he reached Berlin, was hardly the caricature of the crude, lustful peasant. He did, however, like young women very much, and – perhaps influenced by the fact that he had been blessed with dark, almost matinee idol-quality good looks – they liked him too. Even, or especially, the German ones.

Gelfand kept a diary. It is a very frank one, in sexual matters as in others. He could be pushy, and not above using his position to gain favours, but there is, quite credibly, never any suggestion of compulsion, let alone force, in his relations with the girls he meets during his time in Germany (January 1945–autumn 1946). That does not mean he is unaware of what is going on. And he is appalled by the brutal attitude of some of his comrades. On the outskirts of Berlin towards the end of April, he too found himself subjected to pleas from an attractive young woman – supported by her mother – to take him as her exclusive sexual property in order to save her from worse. The girl had already been raped in the cellar of her family's house by a gang of Red Army soldiers:

... 'Stay here!' The girl pleaded suddenly. 'You can sleep with me. You can do what you want with me, but only you, alone! I am prepared to do fuck-fuck, ready to do anything you want, just save me from all those men with their ... you know ...'

She showed me everything, told me everything, and not because she was vulgar. Her fear and her suffering were stronger than her shame and her shyness, and now she was ready to strip in front of all the other people [in the cellar], just to stop her tormented body from being abused, a body that should have remained undefiled for some years still, but had been so suddenly and crudely –

And then her mother pleaded with me too.

'Don't you want to sleep with my daughter? Your Russian comrades who were here wanted to, they all wanted to! They could come back, or there'll be twenty new ones, and then my suffering will be limitless!'

The girl embraced me, pleaded with me, smiled at me through her tears. It was hard for her to beg like this, but she brought to bear a woman's entire repertoire of tricks, and she did it well. It was easy for her to win me over with her shining eyes – I am so vulnerable to female beauty – but in the end my duty as a soldier won out ...[47]

Gelfand was well aware of the horrors awaiting so many German women at the hands of his fellow soldiers. He heard a story from a comrade, Sergeant Major Andropov, whose unit had been attacked by a group of German soldiers, some of when were female. Many were killed and some captured. The group also included two unexplained Russian women in German uniforms, who were interrogated and then shot out of hand.* The younger girls, however, were considered "'booty", to be distributed throughout the various billets and beds, where for some days experiments were conducted upon them that cannot be repeated in writing'.⁴⁸ As if to rehabilitate the image of his comrades slightly, Gelfand adds that after raping at gunpoint one of these girls, who turned out to be a virgin, Sergeant Major Andropov then 'gave her civilian clothes, a dress, to wear' so that she might not be identified as an enemy combatant.

Gelfand himself seems to have had several girlfriends in the months that followed. He was appointed to various administrative jobs and finally assisted in the management of German factories seized by the Soviet government, a job that meant a great deal of travel and many erotic opportunities. He seems to have been bothered neither by the marital status of his conquests nor by the appallingly anti-Semitic and racist opinions – typical of many young people educated in Nazi Germany – that at least one of them openly expressed.

Nonetheless, and despite everything, Gelfand remained at heart a romantic: 'This girl truly deserves love and respect . . .' he wrote of one young German woman with whom he had a casual affair. 'She is really a human being in the truest sense of the word, although she is a woman and a German, and although she works in the theatre, where it is hard for a person of her sex to retain her moral purity.'

---

* It is impossible to confirm this unusual assertion that female soldiers fought in the defence of Berlin on an equal footing with men. Such a thing certainly remained against the Wehrmacht High Command's regulations even at this later, desperate stage in the war. Since anti-aircraft guns were often used as ground artillery during the later stages of the war, it is possible that these women were teenage female flak auxiliaries, who would have had some weapons training. From February 1945, these young women were allowed weapons for self-defence, and they may have resorted to arms in desperation at the Russians' approach. This assumption is strengthened by the report that some of the young women are reported to have been 'as young as 17' and by the presence of the two Russian women. In this it bears a very strong resemblance to the equally violent French encounter at Sindelfingen with a team of female flak auxiliaries, which also included female Russian forced labourers (see later in this chapter). The latter were assigned menial tasks such as transporting ammunition. Sadly, their fellow Russians saw them only as 'collaborators', for whom the penalty was death.

The effect is slightly spoiled by the fact that, in the same diary entry, Gelfand records another intimate encounter, this time with another girl entirely, which seems to have taken place later the same night.[49]

The last few months of Gelfand's stay in Germany were also somewhat darkened by the necessity of treatment for gonorrhoea. Even romantics can't avoid epidemics, and venereal disease reached epidemic proportions in occupied Germany as 1945 wore on.

If Lieutenant Gelfand's account is anything to go by, within a relatively short while after the fall of Berlin, he and other young Russians – especially officers – were enjoying a vigorous, even strenuous social life that included not just the available local women, but also their families, and occasionally involved tourist visits to cultural destinations such as Weimar. In this sense, despite the problems and tensions, the relations that developed, and the basic style of life, were not so different from those experienced by the Western occupiers.

However, whereas in the Western zones anti-fraternisation policies were relaxed as the months passed, in the Soviet Zone they were gradually *introduced* over the same period. This was in part because, once the war was over, the Stalinist authorities were keen to re-establish tight controls over their troops, especially when it came to potentially subversive contact with foreigners. And then there was the continuing military-based crime wave even after the occupation regime had settled down.

The police chief of Halle-Merseburg, an industrial area in Saxony-Anhalt, noted the crimes committed within his jurisdiction by 'persons in Soviet uniform' between 1 January and 31 May 1946 and counted: 34 murders, 345 robberies involving breaking and entering, 328 robberies on the street, 60 train robberies, 123 stolen cows, 212 assaults and injuries (10 ending in death) and 162 rapes. As usual with all occupation troops, but especially the Russians, rampant alcohol use made the situation a great deal worse. The situation was particularly bad on and around the 1 May celebrations, when among loyal supporters of the Dictatorship of the Proletariat a great deal of drink was customarily taken.[50]

The Soviet authorities' attitude towards this kind of violent rowdyism on the part of their soldiers soon ceased to be as indulgent as it had been during the last months of the war. It remained inconsistent, but after the summer of 1945 there were quite frequent prosecutions, with punishments carried out in front of their comrades. Penalties could be light to non-existent, though crimes involving murder as well as rape, for instance, could be punished with death, and those involving insubordination could lead to substantial terms in a labour camp.

The other category of malfeasance – crimes of property – was pursued on a genuinely massive scale, befitting the vast hoard of treasure that the Russians found almost everywhere they looked as they marched, wide-eyed, into rich, sophisticated Germany. This routine theft was, moreover, tolerated and even facilitated by the authorities. The demand for 'Uri, Uri!' (watches, watches!) became as well known to German civilians as the dreaded order, 'Frau, komm!' Bicycles, clocks, radios and alcohol of all kinds (this last responsible for much of the sexual crime wave) were also in great demand by the rank and file as well as the officers, and they were simply taken at will. Rare books, paintings, antique and hunting rifles, bedding, clothes and musical instruments were also popular among the officer classes. The monthly total of parcels passing through the railhead at Kursk, in southern Russia, increased from 300 in January 1945 to 50,000 in April. By mid-May, around 20,000 railway wagons were awaiting unloading or redirection.[51]

As for the fourth occupying power, the French, they came closest to the Soviets in terms of bad behaviour during the final weeks of the war and the immediate aftermath of peace.

Like the Soviets, the French ranks contained many who had suffered – or been forced to bear their families' suffering – under German occupation. Few French troops saw any need to be civil to the Germans, though their officers generally liked to think they were 'correct' within certain narrow military boundaries. And, as with the

Russians, alcohol was in great part responsible for the worst excesses. That, and the presence of colonial troops who, brave as they undoubtedly were in combat, had a poor record when it came to the mistreatment of civilians.

The small town of Magstadt, twenty kilometres west of Stuttgart, fell to the French army on 20 April 1945, and the troops, many of them so-called 'Goumiers' from North Africa, bivouacked there overnight, preparing for their advance on the industrial town of Sindelfingen. The village's pastor reported later:

No pen can do justice to what happened during that night. Our women and girls, especially, had much to endure and much to suffer. The Moroccans had previously got into a distillery . . . and some of them were worse than animals. Around 260 rapes – medically confirmed – starting with girls of confirmation age and extending to the oldest women – will always make this day the most terrible that the people of this parish have ever had to suffer, physically and spiritually. Even in the vicarage I was not able, despite interposing my body and using my every power, to prevent many of those who desperately sought protection and sought refuge in my cellar from having to endure that terrible experience.[52]

When, a few days later, the French advanced on Sindelfingen (home of Daimler-Benz motors), they came under fire from some Luftwaffe flak units based in the Goldberg Housing Estate overlooking the town. Furious at this, the French unit commanders appear to have tolerated physical and sexual violence against the women auxiliaries serving in these units, who also included Russian forced labourers. Again, mass rapes occurred. No exception was made for the unfortunate Russian women, who had already suffered years of near-slavery and semi-starvation at German hands.

Similar excesses occurred elsewhere as the French either fought their way into districts of south-west Germany or took over the areas previously taken by the Americans before the reassignment of zones began. Looting and robbery was common. The colonial troops – particularly Moroccan troops – seem to have been closely involved, as were units made up from the Maquis, the French resistance fighters during the occupation, who after the liberation the previous summer had been turned into regular army units.

The Goumiers had already distinguished themselves in the Italian campaign for their fierceness and bravery, but also, especially following the fall of Monte Cassino, become notorious for the rape of Italian women and the killing of any menfolk who tried to intervene – so much so that in post-war Italy the term '*marocchinate*' was dubbed to describe such an orgy of violence. It was also the theme of Alberto Moravia's novel *La Ciociara* (The Woman of Ciociara), based on his experiences while living in this area during 1943–4, later filmed by Vittorio de Sica with Sophia Loren and Jean-Paul Belmondo and distributed for English-speaking audiences under the title *Two Women*.

It was, however, also true that French officers could and did prevent such outrages. At the small ski resort of Hofsgrund Schauinsland, near Freiburg in the Black Forest, the pastor reported with some relief:

The first enemy troops who passed through the village (25 April) were Moroccans under the command of French officers. They descended the routes leading into Schauinsland in somewhat ragged order. Their bearing showed that they had expected resistance . . . the attitude of the men was in general correct, since the officers kept them under the strictest discipline. When, at several points during the evening, it was reported to the pastor that certain excesses were in danger of being committed, he was accompanied by the French to the houses concerned and in all these instances the worst was prevented.[53]

Once the fighting was past, the French authorities moved against their looters and rapists much more promptly than, say, their Russian equivalents. Individual officers and men protected German civilians. The total number of rapes seems impossible to judge, because so many German women were too frightened and ashamed to report the assaults. There are, however, clues to the true extent. The Koblenz Regional President (*Regierungspräsident*) later counted the instances of 'injury to persons through occupation' (*Besatzungspersonenschaden*) at some three thousand. In the small, picturesque town of Cochem on the Mosel, originally occupied by the Americans but then handed over to the French, the number of babies reported born as a result of rape by French troops was twenty-two.[54]

Unlike the Russians, the French began their time as occupiers with an anti-fraternisation regulation in place, but unlike the Americans and the British they hardly enforced it. Few sentences were passed or fines levied on French troops. In short, reflecting the usual French common sense in sexual matters, very little official attention was paid to liaisons between their soldiers and German women. These occurred, of course. Some even married. Paradoxically, in view of the harsh French attitudes towards the Germans during the early years of their occupation, it seems never to have been an important issue.[55]

Rape did occur in the British and American areas of control, despite strict bans on contact with Germans – although it should be noted that while around two hundred American troops were executed for this crime in Britain and the liberated countries, none were so punished in Germany, despite 284 convictions.[56] All the same, the occupation forces with the most lax fraternisation regulations during the immediate post-war period – the Russians and the French – were clearly responsible for the most rapes of German women. Not that this proves cause and effect. A much more likely reason is to be found in the fact that the Russians and the French had suffered directly at the hands of the German occupiers and therefore felt both greater anger and greater entitlement to inflict such injury and humiliation in the enemy's land.

To see themselves through the eyes of their occupiers, the defeated population in Germany needed only to observe the foreign soldiers' behaviour, and that behaviour did not bode well. If any Germans had really dared to believe that they were to be 'liberated', in a fashion in any way similar to other European nations, disillusionment came quickly and thoroughly.

As for the effect of this on a population of seventy million Germans, quite suddenly relieved of the thrill and the burden of European mastery, it was hard to tell. It soon became clear that the chief task facing the German people was not political or spiritual regeneration, but finding enough food to get through to the next harvest. And then the one after that.

It was equally clear from what the victors said and did after peace was declared, that, unlike in most of the rest of the continent, which was also facing terrible hardship, this was a task that would be down to Germans, and Germans alone. No one planned to help them. No one.

6

Hunger

On the afternoon of 4 October 1942, one of the most well-fed men in Europe gave a speech, recorded in front of an enthusiastic audience and broadcast live on the radio throughout the Greater German Reich and the occupied countries. In this speech he celebrated the fact that during the coming winter, as during the previous one, Germans would eat while millions of their fellow human beings would, in a quite planned and strategic way, starve.

The man was Reich Marshal Hermann Goering, the venue the Sportpalast in Berlin-Schöneberg. The occasion was the 'Reich Harvest Thanksgiving Festival'. Of course, he did not actually say, 'We are planning to starve and kill millions'. He simply told his audience, in his firm but friendly way – Goering was, despite his own wildly excessive, decadent lifestyle, remarkably adept at finding the 'common touch' – that their rations would be increased, and that, as it approached its fourth wartime winter, Germany's problems with food shortages were over.

The reason for this was twofold: first, that year's harvest was better than the previous two; and second, the rest of Europe – especially Poland and Russia – was being systematically robbed to ensure that the German population, far from suffering, lived better than before, as befitted their status as rulers of Europe and as 'the master race'.

What Goering didn't tell his audience was even more significant. Who was paying the price for their continued wellbeing in the middle of such a terrible war? The answer was never revealed during the war, although it was well known among Nazi officials in the occupied countries and also among those responsible for feeding the nation. But it was and is quite clear. So that Germans could eat, Jews and Poles and Russians (and Serbs and Greeks and Dutch people, among others) must and would go hungry or, in millions of cases, die.

Already in the winter of 1941–2, newly occupied Greece had been the first nation to suffer. In peacetime this largely rocky and moun-tainous country had always needed to import food. It was now plunged into crisis by systematic hoarding, soaring inflation, crippling occupation costs and an enforced 'loan' to Germany inflicted upon the collaborationist Greek government – all further exacerbated by ruthless requisitioning of foodstuffs on the part of the Germans and their Italian and Bulgarian co-occupiers.

As a result, Greece suffered the first famine of the Second World War. The 'great hunger' cost the lives of up to 300,000 Greeks, espe-cially in metropolitan Athens, which relied on suddenly non-existent imports from the countryside, and the picturesque but arid Cycladic islands. Viewed in immediate terms, the Germans had not deliberately caused the catastrophe, but they did little to mitigate it, and continued to exploit the country's remaining resources wholly without consid-eration for the starving natives. It was Goering once again who acted as brutally frank spokesman for the Nazi elite: 'We cannot worry unduly about the Greeks,' he said coldly. 'It is a misfortune which will strike many other people beside them.'[1]

In fact, while the German armies appeared everywhere victorious, the year 1942 had been a difficult one when it came to feeding the Reich's population. Two previous consecutive harvests had been poor, and the horrendous cost in money and production of keeping an army of three million fed on the Russian front had led to embarras-sing shortfalls, rations cuts, rapid reduction of the national grain store and widespread public discontent.

An intricately interconnected nexus involving Goering's Four Year Plan Office, Himmler's SS empire and the powerful State Secretary

(later Minister) for Food and Agriculture, Herbert Backe, hummed
with activity as officials spent the first months of that year organising
a solution to this problem. It would be terrifyingly radical.

It was Backe, a cold-blooded technocrat, who had reorganised
German agriculture before 1939 to make it independent of world
markets, as part of the Nazis' master plan for economic autarky, side-
lining the romantic 'blood-and-soil' dreams of his nominal boss,
Minister Walter Darré, in favour of more efficient and 'modern' modes
of food production.

After the outbreak of war, following ruthless racist logic, Backe
and his experts, including leading academics in their fields, developed
plans to cover the supply and feeding of the German army during
the invasion of the Soviet Union. These were frankly genocidal in
tone. It was clear that the people of the Reich could not be fed
comfortably unless the Wehrmacht on the Eastern Front ceased altogether drawing on food supplies from Germany proper, which were
barely adequate for the domestic civilian population. Instead, it must
'live off the land' in occupied Russia. And, if necessary, provide a
surplus that could be sent to Germany to cover shortages there.

The Nazi state's experts were quite clear: if the Wehrmacht was to
be self-sufficient, and German civilians kept well fed, then many
millions of Russians, especially in the cities – which had grown rapidly
during the 1930s as a result of Stalin's programme of rapid industrialisation – would have to starve. On 2 May 1941, at a meeting at which
all the major ministries were represented at State Secretary level, this
murderous policy was agreed. According to a contemporary report,
the conclusions were as follows:

1. The war can only be continued, if the entire Wehrmacht is fed from
   Russia in the third year of the war.
2. If we take what we need out of the country, there can be no doubt
   that many millions of people will die of starvation.
3. The most important issues are the recovery and removal of oil seeds,
   oil cake, and only then the removal of grain.[2]

Backe himself believed that the Soviet Union had a 'surplus population' of between twenty and thirty million that could and must be liquidated in the course of Operation Barbarossa, the campaign against the Soviet Union – this quite apart from any later post-war plans to settle the fertile Ukrainian and White Russian plains with Germans.

Himmler stated openly at a meeting of senior SS officers a few days before 'Barbarossa' was launched in June 1941 that in this fight to the death 'through military actions and the food problems, 20 to 30 million Slavs and Jews will die'.

Goering himself said in November, less than five months after the invasion had begun, that the battle for Russia would bring about 'the greatest mortality since the Thirty Years War'.[3] He repeatedly made gloating remarks to the effect that 'if anyone's going to starve, it will not be Germans, but someone else'.[4] These were echoed by a remark by Goebbels in his diary that before Germany would 'starve . . . a series of other countries will have to take their turn first'.[5]

The fact that, less than three months before Goering's 'harvest festival' speech, the food situation in the Reich itself remained problematic, was further proved by a report that has survived of a meeting at Rovno, the seat of the East Prussian Gauleiter and 'Reich Commissar for the Ukraine', Erich Koch. In his address to his officials, Koch broached precisely that subject. The Reich Commissar, who had just returned from Hitler's headquarters, recounted how he had tried to resist Goering's demands for more imports from Russia. However, the Führer supported Reich Marshal Goering, and, according to the report of the meeting, that was that:

The Gauleiter came direct from the Führer's headquarters . . . The food situation in Germany is serious. Production is already falling as a result. An increase in the bread ration is a political necessity if the war is to be continued with success. The shortfall in grain will have to be made up from the Ukraine. The Führer has made the Gauleiter responsible for ensuring that these quantities are secured. In the light of this situation, the feeding of the [Ukrainian] population is a matter of complete indifference . . .⁶

Koch's remarks to his underlings are not just another expression of the consensus that by then had emerged among all senior Nazi officials. In the early autumn of 1942, farmers in occupied Poland and Russia were placed under enormous pressure from armed foraging groups, in Poland supervised by the notoriously brutal German 'District Captains' (*Kreishauptleute*). Sixty per cent of this already demanding quota was to be supplied by the end of September, and the rest by the end of November. Punishments for withholding of produce, real or imagined, were draconian:

. . . because of the increased pressure, [the District Captains] on their own initiative increased the consignments compulsorily due by 10 to 70%. Moreover, the district farm supervisors had tightened the schedules, so that the farmers had to deliver the 60% by 20 September and the remaining 40% by 1 November. In Garwolin District, the farmers had to deliver as much as 90% of the bread grain by as early as 9 September. The seizures were once again accompanied by terror and violence. In Grójec, several farmers were hanged because they had not fulfilled their quotas. In Lublin District, the terror was particularly severe. Farms were put to the torch and farmers beaten. According to the reports from the [Polish] underground, the shooting and hanging of farmers were everyday events.

The gathering of the harvest in 1942 went satisfactorily for the German authorities . . .⁷

It was not just that Ukrainians, Russians and Jews were to be starved – not to mention the Polish and Jewish inhabitants of the General Government of Poland, who were to suffer a similar fate. Worse, it seems likely that Goering's and Backe's demands for massively increased confiscation of food supplies from the conquered eastern territories led almost immediately to an acceleration of the Holocaust itself.

'Unproductive' individuals in the occupied east, who merely consumed food that might otherwise help support the Wehrmacht in Russia or keep up the standard of living of the population back in Germany, were from now on to be systematically murdered on an industrial scale.[8]

In the second half of 1942, during the campaign known as *Aktion Reinhard* – in honour of the recently assassinated SD Chief and 'Protector' of Bohemia and Moravia, Reinhard Heydrich – the extermination camps at Treblinka and Bełżec, Majdanek and Sobibór reached the peak of their ghastly productivity. At least 1.5 million 'unproductive' Jews died.

The same went – had to a great extent already gone – for the 3.3 million soldiers of the Red Army who had become prisoners after the huge German victories of June–November 1941. By February 1942, 60 per cent of them had perished – starved, shot, even gassed (some of the early experiments with so-called 'gas wagons' were carried out on Soviet prisoners of war).[9]

This treatment was, incidentally, in stark contrast to the fates of Russian prisoners a quarter of a century earlier during the First World War. The Kaiser's government and its military were quite capable of tough, even harsh occupation policy, but they kept to the letter of the Hague Convention when it came to treatment of POWs. Of 1.4 million Russian prisoners then, a mere 5.4 per cent died in German captivity[10] – and this at a time when German civilians were starving in their thousands because of the British naval blockade (roughly 800,000 were reckoned to have died as a result of malnutrition and associated diseases between 1914 and 1918 – more than died from Allied bombing between 1939 and 1945).

By deliberate policy, the German army failed to advance into Leningrad in the autumn of 1941. To do so would have involved decisions about how to either feed or dispose of at least three million Russian civilians. The siege that followed was intended to starve the city's people to death, thus avoiding the unpleasant necessity of liquidating them in some other, more active way. 'For economic reasons, the conquest of large cities is undesirable,' the view went. 'To besiege them is more advantageous.'[11] As Professor Wilhelm Ziegelmayer, nutrition adviser to the Wehrmacht High Command, wrote in September 1941: 'We shall also not allow ourselves in the future to be burdened with demands for the capitulation of Leningrad. It must be annihilated by a scientifically based method.' By January 1942, the people of Leningrad were dying at the rate of nearly 4,000 a day. In the first eleven months of the siege, around 650,000 died of starvation and disease.[12]

So in 1942, the year when millions of Jews from Poland, Russia and elsewhere in Europe were slaughtered, and millions more Slavs died of hunger, a good part of the reason for the urgency of this process lay in the fact that Hermann Goering wanted to announce at the harvest thanksgiving ceremony at the Sportpalast that German civilians would have a bountiful winter.[13] And that they would be suitably grateful to their government.

A report of the SS's *Sicherheitsdienst* following Goering's triumphant ninety-minute peroration at the Sportpalast quoted citizens' conversations to show that his 'comprehensive summary of the ever-improving food situation in the Reich . . . [has] generally consolidated the notion that when it comes to our rationing difficulties we are "over the hump" . . .' This was also, the report added, having the practical effect of improving public morale to the extent that people were 'not worrying so much about the military situation, i.e. the duration of the fighting around Stalingrad'. As for Germany's women, now bearing so much of the burden on the home front, 'the mood among women has become much better, something for which the promise of a permanently improved food and supply situation is principally responsible'.[14]

Above all, the Nazi leadership would not be faced with a rebellious population, as the Kaiser – diligently feeding his own prisoners of war – had been back in November 1918, when starvation and defeat had brought the people on to the streets and cost him his throne. The nightmare of a new uprising by hungry Germans was something that haunted the Nazis throughout the conflict. In the Second World War, unlike the First, the German people never went hungry, in any meaningful sense, until almost the end – although millions, even tens of millions, in the occupied countries did, in order that Germans might eat.

The leadership's calculation paid off. Although, as the news from the front got worse, millions of Germans became increasingly disillusioned with Hitler, only a tiny minority turned to active resistance. Along with the regime's brutally efficient internal surveillance apparatus, and its draconian policing of the black market, its success in organising food supplies on a reasonably fair basis shored up support among the general public in the Reich. Despite the worsening military situation during 1943–4, the constant bombing of the cities, and catastrophic levels of casualties, particularly on the Eastern Front, the only serious uprising against the Nazi government was that of 20 July 1944, an elite affair that had little to do with the masses.

It was not until February 1945 that mothers in bombed-out Berlin started complaining that, for the first time, they 'could not get whole milk on a regular basis'.[15] Whether their ignorance of why they had remained well provisioned for so long was based on lack of information or self-deception, women such as these were not prepared for what the end of the war would bring. 'We were not hungry during the war,' they would insist accusingly. 'Everything worked! It was only afterwards that things got bad.'

These hitherto privileged civilians would soon be faced not just with the end of imports and confiscations from conquered lands that had so long bolstered the German population's standard of living, but with victorious powers who were determined that these citizens would pay for those years of plenty at other nations' expense, and who now had the people of Germany at their mercy.

While the letter of the Morgenthau Plan, as originally conceived in the autumn of 1944, was never wholly adhered to, it would be a long time before its spirit was banished from post-war food policy in Allied-occupied Germany.

As for Roosevelt himself, his health was steadily declining even as he began his fourth presidential term in January 1945. Harold L. Ickes, the veteran Secretary of the Interior, told the President's daughter, Anna Boettiger, that Roosevelt 'did not seem to understand at times what people are saying to him' and that he seemed 'to forget quickly'.[16]

The President was certainly liable to concede to the War/State Department axis one moment, then make fairly outrageous 'Morgenthau' comments the next. On 20 March, over lunch with Morgenthau (and John and Anna Boettiger, who appear to have been contemplating some kind of 'regency' on the ailing President's behalf), Roosevelt seemed confused. Boettiger remarked that the army in Germany was irked by the latest version of JCS 1067, with its clear punitive provisions, which would make it harder to run the country. It wasn't 'workable', and surely Germany couldn't be allowed to stew in its own juice as Morgenthau proposed?

'Let them have soup kitchens!' Roosevelt responded. 'Let their economy sink!' When asked if he wanted the Germans to starve, he retorted: 'Why not?'[17]

A few days later, the President set off for a rest at his holiday cottage in Warm Springs, Georgia. On the early afternoon of 12 April 1945, having awoken with a headache and a stiff neck, he later seemed to be feeling better. The artist who was painting his portrait at the time, Elizabeth Shoumatoff, thought his colour more natural than it had been for some time. He started reading through papers while his secretary and lover, Lucy Rutherfurd, and Roosevelt's old friend, Margaret Suckley, sat nearby. Then, without warning, he bowed forward and said, 'I have a terrific pain in the back of my head.' Within minutes the thirty-second President of the United States was dead. The rush of colour that had been thought to show an improvement in his condition had been a warning sign of the cerebral haemorrhage that killed him.[18]

In February 1945, Hitler had told his private secretary, Martin Bormann: 'An unfortunate historical accident fated it that my seizure of power should coincide with the moment at which the chosen one of world Jewry, Roosevelt, should have taken the White House . . .'¹⁹

Now, in mid-April, the President's death caused a great sensation in the Berlin bunker where Hitler and his cohorts waited, working and praying feverishly for a miracle that would save the Third Reich.

Hitler's fascination with the life and career of the Prussian King, Frederick the Great (reigned 1740–86) – to the end, he kept a portrait of 'Old Fritz' in his study – caused him, encouraged by Goebbels, to leap at the possibility that Roosevelt's death was his 'Tsarina Elizabeth' moment. In January 1762, facing defeat in the Seven Years War at the hands of a coalition made up of Russia, France and Austria, with Russian troops occupying Berlin, Frederick had been plunged in gloom – only to hear, just days later, of the Russian Tsarina's death. The new Tsar, her nephew, Peter III, was an eccentric young man who hero-worshipped all things Prussian, and swiftly – luckily for Prussia, because he was deposed and murdered later that same year – made a favourable peace with Frederick the Great. If something similar happened for Hitler after Roosevelt's death, this would equal that intervention by the goddesses of fate.

The clique in the bunker waited in vain. There was, of course, no miracle, no game-changing crack in the coalition against Hitler. In the meantime, however, the Führer had seen fit to add a few extra twists to the catastrophe he had already inflicted on the country he supposedly loved. First there was the so-called 'Nero Order', or scorched-earth policy, by which Hitler instructed all organs of the Nazi state, political, military and economic, to work together to destroy everything – 'all military, transport, communication and supply facilities, as well as all material assets in territory of the Reich' – so as to deny them to the advancing enemy. Hitler made it clear that the post-war quality of life of the German people, which would obviously collapse if these demolitions were carried out, was of no interest to him:

If the war were lost, the nation would also perish. This fate was inevitable. There was no necessity to take into consideration the basis which the people would need to continue a most primitive existence. On the contrary, it would be better to destroy these things ourselves, because this nation will have proved to be the weaker one and the future belongs solely to the stronger eastern nation. Besides, those who would remain after the battle were only the inferior ones, for the good ones had been killed.[20]

In fact, so Speer claimed, he managed to persuade Hitler to place the continuation of this campaign of senseless destruction in his (Speer's) ministry's hands, thus enabling him to minimise further catastrophic damage in practice, changing orders to destroy into orders to immobilise, and so on.[21]

Amid the sprawling chaos of the German bureaucracy during those last months of the Reich, there were those already planning for the post-war period, for the phase during which the survival of the German economy (and its managing elite) must be secured and German industry's energetic re-entry to the world market prepared.

The activities of these experts were directed (and protected, for such work could involve suspicion of treason) by the powerful figure of Gruppenführer Otto Ohlendorf, head of Department III (SD Inland) of the Reich Main Security Office and Deputy State Secretary at the Economics Ministry.

One of the expert group's leading brains was forty-eight-year-old Dr Ludwig Erhard. Erhard was a complex figure, a Bavarian econo-mist (his Ph.D. dealt with the theory of value), a believer in free markets and global interdependence (not a view welcomed by the Nazis) who had already begun working on 'worst case' economic plans as early as 1942. The study he completed was entitled 'War Financing and Debt Consolidation' and covered such topics as 'refloating' the currency under circumstances of defeat and restoring free-market capitalism after the crypto-socialist autarkic experiment of Nazism.[22] Though a non-Nazi with suspicious contacts to members of the anti-Hitler opposition, his brilliance, and usefulness to the technocrats within the Hitlerite establishment, kept him secure and in employment to the very end – ready, in fact, to face the shining future that awaited him after 1945.*

The great flaw in the post-war plans put together by this expert group under Ohlendorf's protection lay not just in the tainted character of many of their main proponents (Ohlendorf himself would be executed after the war for his part-time activities as a mass murderer in the Ukraine and the Crimea in 1941–2), but in their false assumption that, as in 1918, a defeated Germany would continue to govern itself, albeit under Allied supervision. The same was even more true of plans made by German experts to evercome the problem of feeding the population during the approaching post-war period.

The Reich's food experts knew perfectly well that Germany had never been, and was still not, self-sufficient in food. Even in peacetime, Germany had relied on imports. The country would face grave problems feeding itself from its own, reduced resources – and that was if the situation got no worse.

Well before the full, panic-stricken exodus from the eastern provinces began in January 1945, many millions of other Germans – up to a third of the civilian population – had already uprooted themselves from their normal surroundings, whether in the bombed-out cities or the rural areas threatened by the Allied advances.[23]

This was both good and bad news. Good, because it meant that many more Germans than in the pre-war period were close to the physical sources of food production, and the transport and distribution networks were, therefore, less burdened than might otherwise have been the case. But at the same time bad, because even those not too old or too young for the labour force often found it hard to find productive work in these new environments and as a consequence remained dependent on state welfare of some sort or another.

Luckily for the immediate prospects of the nation, Germany's last wartime grain harvest, although a mediocre one, had mostly been

---

* Erhard became Finance Minister of the Federal Republic of (West) Germany (1949–63) and, less successfully, Chancellor (1963–6). He was known as the 'father' of the post-war economic miracle.

gathered in and stored before the spectacular Allied advances began again in January 1945, and before the Anglo-American air forces' devastating 'transport' campaigns of January–February finally wrecked the rail and canal networks so crucial to the distribution of food and industrial goods alike. It would be another three years before reliable connections were re-established between the crucial Ruhr industrial area and the other urban centres of Germany.[24]

There were, however, serious problems even at this stage. Potatoes, largely coming from the east, could not be transported because of shortages of rolling stock, caused by Allied bombing. And as for the supplies of meat needed to keep the beleaguered Wehrmacht's goulash pots bubbling, these could no longer be requisitioned from foreign sources. Clearly, more of the Reich's domestic livestock had to be slaughtered, thus leaving the national reserve substantially diminished. And this was before the breakdown of normal organised life really accelerated.

There was, finally, another grave, and in the longer term more ominous, problem. In the regime's desperate, heedless attempt to maintain the expansion in the production of explosives and ammunition during the last phase of the war, huge quantities of the nitrogen fertilisers essential to successful large-scale food production within Germany – but also vital to munitions production – had been diverted to the armaments sector. As a result, and despite partially successful attempts by Backe's ministry to protect fertiliser stocks, agricultural yields fell dramatically and would not recover for some years. It was a scorched-earth policy of a kind, perhaps, but, unlike Hitler's noisy *Götterdämmerung* scheme for destroying infrastructure, a silent and covert one that would further hurt average German consumers just when they stood in greatest need.

Minister Backe, the architect of the 'Hunger Plan', had concentrated during the winter of 1944–5 on feeding Berlin, above all other places.[25] And until the dramatic Soviet advances of February–March 1945 robbed them of a large amount of Germany's most productive agricultural land and the final crisis began, the Agriculture and Food

Ministry had viewed the food situation in the Reich as 'sufficient'. Nonetheless, a lot of secret planning had been undertaken to cope with 'worst case' scenarios.

With support from Hans Kehrl, Speer's planning chief, Backe had also secretly been setting up small local plants to process the yeasty sulphite suds that were a by-product of cellulose manufacture. These had previously been sold to breweries, but could be turned into a food rich in protein and vitamins, a substitute for meat.* According to figures from April 1945, just weeks before the end of the war, fifty such plants were in existence, capable of producing 20,000 tons a year – enough to supply the basic protein needs of ten million children. Likewise, Backe managed to get Hitler to sign an order that protected at least part of German agriculture's stock of workhorses from the frantic depredations of the Wehrmacht – which had always used a lot of draught animals but during the final months of the war, when petrol all but ran out, started to requisition farmers' horses as well on a large scale. This threat became severe even as the planting season for the crucial first post-war harvest approached.

So, during these final, bloody months of the Third Reich, the group of intelligent and highly competent technocrats around Speer and Backe – Backe being, so to speak, the 'Speer' of the food sector – knew, for all their loyalty to the Nazi state, that the war was lost. In general, they did their best, without endangering their own positions (not to mention their lives) by confronting the increasingly irrational Führer with this reality, to ensure that the inevitable end of Nazi Germany would not necessarily mean the end of the German people.

The weakness in these managers' plans was that they presupposed, or at least were sustained by the hope, that after the war Germans would still control their own economy and food production. Until the end, both Speer and Backe also harboured delusions that the

---

* It could be spread on bread and, especially if made more palatable with the addition of fruit and spice flavouring, was perfectly edible. Yeast extract in this form was already a popular snack in Britain, branded as 'Bovril' and 'Marmite' (in Australia and New Zealand most well known as 'Vegemite').

victorious enemy would not be able to dispense with their expert services. All these things would not – most emphatically not – prove to be the case.*

To these looming operational and technical problems were added both the prospective hindrance of highly bureaucratic supervision by foreigners unacquainted with local conditions, and the threat of those same foreigners' vengeful, punitive attitudes. This last factor alone would ensure things turned out even worse than feared for the conquered German population.

There seems little question that Backe's and Speer's efforts, in maintaining Germany's food supply and war industries respectively, had kept the Nazi war machine in operation well beyond its expected functional life. The 'miracles' they had so famously performed during this final phase were, however, pointless except in prolonging the war and causing the deaths of hundreds of thousands, probably millions more human beings – who might have stood a chance of survival had the Reich surrendered in, say, autumn 1944.

To the end, production had relentlessly continued wherever humanly (or inhumanly) possible. Labour shortages had been apparent in Germany from the beginning of the war, and had become more and more desperate as millions of German workers, many extremely valuable to the production effort, were sent to the front, their lives and their skills sacrificed to the insatiable needs of the Wehrmacht. They were replaced by foreign labour, either prisoners of war (constant at around 1.5 million) or conscripted civilians from the occupied countries. During the early years of the war, most of the foreigners working in Germany had been POWs, many from France, working on farms. However, by the autumn of 1944, when

---

* Speer would be arrested in Flensburg and brought to trial as a major war criminal at Nuremberg, where his ability to convince the court of his last-minute 'resistance' to Hitler probably saved his life. Backe, knowing he was to be arraigned before the so-called 'Ministries' (or 'Wilhelmstrasse') Trial in November 1947, committed suicide in Allied custody at Nuremberg on 6 April 1947.

the brutally coercive labour programme organised by Gauleiter Fritz Sauckel, the 'General Plenipotentiary for Labour Deployment' (*Generalbevollmächtigter für den Arbeitseinsatz*), reached its height, 7.9 million foreign workers were employed in Germany, more than 20 per cent of the workforce.

It was bitterly ironic that in the systematically racist Nazi state, where homogeneity was close to a religion, foreigners had become a conspicuous feature of daily life to an extent that they had never before been in German history. In the armaments plants, more than a third of the workforce was of foreign origin, and in some sectors even more. Luftwaffe Marshal Erhard Milch, responsible for aircraft production at the height of the war, quipped that the Stuka Ju 87 was '80 percent manufactured by Russians'.[26]

With the arrival of peace, all those foreign industrial workers, concentration camp inmates, servants and POW farm labourers – at least eleven million in all throughout Germany and Austria at the beginning of 1945 – were suddenly free. Some stayed where they were, deciding there was safety in numbers or encouraged to do so by the Allies, who needed their work in the factories and services to keep basic industries going. But the rest ended up either wandering around defeated Germany or streaming home along the crowded, potholed roads and highways that had so recently been the scene of bloody battles and dramatic advances and retreats. These 'displaced persons' (DPs as they were universally known) had to be fed and housed by the newly installed occupation authorities until they could either be sent home or, if for some reason that was not possible or desirable, found permanent shelter and sustenance.

Colin MacInnes described 'Sergeant Mac' coming up against this stream of liberated but still scarred humanity as his unit pushed on into the heart of Germany at the very end of the war:

> . . . I began to meet parties of civilians moving in the opposite direc-
> tion to the Army. Some were in small groups on foot, and others in
> larger bands with belongings heaped on farm carts. It was some time

before I realised they were our Allies – the freed prisoners-of-war and deported workers who were beginning their homeward trek. At first I'd taken them for Germans, and it wasn't so much their dress and the delighted and rather solemn expression I began to notice on their faces that made me realise who they were. They went steadily on as if nothing on earth would stop them.

Then I began to overtake parties of Easterners moving along in the same direction as ourselves, in bodies that were even larger, often riding in a chain of wagons pulled by a tractor which carried a red flag. In some of the villages I passed, they seemed to have taken possession, and I saw whole communities camped in barns by the roadside, cooking themselves meals. I wondered what was happening to the farmers.

These three streams of traffic grew thicker and thicker: our lorries going north-east along the road, the eastern Allies pushing on beside us along the grass verge and the Westerners moving back in the opposite direction. It was as though a day of judgment had come, with the Germans fleeing hopelessly, and the victims rising up and setting out for separate paradises beyond the frontiers.[27]

The distinction between Germans, even displaced Germans, and DPs was clear. According to officials at SHAEF, DPs were defined as those individuals 'obliged to leave their country or place of origin or former residence or who have been deported from there by action of the enemy because of race, religion or activities'. This distinction was especially clear when it came to the matter of feeding. All the Allies acknowledged that the many millions of human beings who had found themselves in Germany against their will as a result of forced emigration deserved to have their further suffering minimised – and their swift return home facilitated.

From the beginning, especially for those DPs who had experienced liberation while still in labour or concentration camps, medical help, however rough and ready, and food, at first from forces rations, was available on an ad hoc basis. For many, transport home was quickly arranged. By May 1945, the United Nations Relief and Rehabilitation Administration (UNRRA), founded with impressive foresight at Roosevelt's behest two years earlier to cater for these eventualities, had already set up five hundred assembly centres for DPs. From these, almost one million DPs had already, officially, been repatriated, even before the end of the war.[28] (This figure did not of course include the vast flood of self-directed returnees encountered by 'Sergeant Mac' on the roads of north-western Germany at this time.)

However, things were by no means perfect, especially for the several hundred thousand Jewish DPs in Germany at the end of the war, who, unlike Poles, most Russians, Yugoslavs and Western European prisoners and forced labourers, did not necessarily have anywhere to go. Their communities in Germany or Poland or Russia had been destroyed, many or even most of their relatives murdered, and for the moment the only places where they felt at home or, on a basic level, safe, were camps – sometimes new ones set up by the victors to accommodate them, sometimes even the same camps where they had been held by the Germans until liberated.

These Jewish DPs were often in very poor physical condition, starving and diseased. In mid-January 1945, after Reichsführer Himmler's order to evacuate the camps in Poland of all but the sickest prisoners, many thousands had been herded on to the roads west. In the final horror that followed, which has gone down in infamy as the 'Death March', many, many died of exhaustion, hunger, or at the brutal hands of the guards who had accompanied them. The Allied soldiers found them – and tens of thousands of other prisoners – packed under the most appalling conditions into the by now obscenely overcrowded camps at Dachau, Buchenwald, Bergen-Belsen and their satellites during the course of April 1945.

The occupiers experienced pity, horror – but also, not infrequently, repulsion.

At Dachau, on the edge of suburban Munich, *Time* magazine's correspondent Sidney Olson found boxcars in sidings, filled with corpses, many still showing whip marks on their bony buttocks and

rumps, and further into the camp, 'half covered by a brown tarpau-
lin . . . a stack about five feet high and about 20 feet wide of naked
dead bodies, all of them emaciated'. That was the dead. Worse were
the unwelcome attentions of the living, who were

> . . . frantically, hysterically happy. They began to kiss us, and there is
> nothing you can do when a lot of hysterical, unshaven, lice-bitten,
> half-drunk, typhus-infected men want to kiss you. Nothing at all.
> You cannot hit them, and besides, they all kiss you at the same time.
> It is no good trying to explain that you are only a correspondent. A
> half-dozen of them were especially happy and it turned out they were
> very proud: they had killed two German soldiers themselves.[29]

At Bergen-Belsen near Celle, 700 kilometres to the north-west, which
the British liberated on 15 April, some 10,000 bodies lay unburied
when they entered the camp. Thirteen thousand more inmates died
in the days and weeks that followed. A Jewish chaplain with the British
Second Army, Leslie Hardman, described the condition of survivors
there. He happened to enter the camp with two young British soldiers,
who were carrying sacks of potatoes meant for the feeding of the
liberated prisoners:

> Almost as though they had emerged from the retreating shadows
> of dark corners, a number of wraithlike creatures came tottering
> towards us. As they drew closer they made frantic efforts to quicken
> their feeble pace. Their skeleton arms and legs made jerky, grotesque
> movements as they forced themselves forward. Their bodies, from
> their heads to their feet, looked like matchsticks. The two young
> Tommies, entering camp for the first time, must of thought they
> had walked into a supernatural world; all the gruesome and fright-
> ening tales they had heard as children – and, not so many years
> since, they had been children – rose up to greet them; the grisly
> spectacle which confronted them was too much. They dropped their
> heavy sacks and fled.[30]

No sooner had the young Tommies retreated than these images of living death, uttering thin, eerie cries, began fighting with the sacks and with each other to get at the precious raw potatoes within.

'All I felt,' said another British officer, in an alarmingly honest appraisal of his own reactions, 'was horror, disgust, and I am ashamed to admit it, hate. Hate against the prisoners for looking as they did, for living as they did, for existing at all. It was quite unreasonable, but there it was, and it gave us one possible explanation of why the SS had done these things. Once having reduced their prisoners to such a state the only emotions the guards could feel were loathing, disgust and hate.'[31]

All the same, away from these absolute extremes of bearable experience, most Allied troops did what they could. The beginnings of a post-war network of refuges for such problematic DPs began to take shape. Towards the end of April 1945, Lieutenant Irving J. Smith, a Jewish-American officer, led his unit into the town of Tutzing, near the Starnberger See and about twenty miles south of Munich. There he found some survivors who had been evacuated from Dachau before the camp was liberated and forced to head south in what was essentially a 'death march'. There were a thousand of them, 'starving, almost raving maniacs, half paralysed with hunger and fear'.

In collaboration with an UNRRA team, the soldiers took over a former Napola* School at Feldafing, drafted many of its German staff, including cooks and medical personnel, and turned it into a refugee camp, with a nearby hotel requisitioned as hospital accommodation. The number of inmates rapidly grew to some 4,000. By the end of May 1945, the camp had experienced its first survivor wedding and those in the hospital – now moved to a former monastery – had been treated to a concert by the Kovno Ghetto orchestra, dressed in their striped concentration-camp pyjamas.[32]

For the Germans among whom these foreigners had lived for the

---

* An abbreviation of *Nationalpolitische Lehranstalt* (National Political Teaching Institution). The Napolas were highly politicised and demanding military academies founded by the Nazi Party with the intention of creating a new Nazi elite. Forty-three of these institutions – including several for girls – were in existence by 1945.

past years, there was no such help. Quite specifically. From the first day of peace until other forms of communication could take over, the language spoken between Germans and Allied occupiers was predominantly that of deprivation, of hunger and restriction and shortages – shortages of shelter and fuel, gainful activity and, above all, food.

After so many millions of others all over Europe had starved, it was now, after 8 May 1945, that defeated Germany's great hunger began.

7

The Price

Deprivation was a short cut, a permanent, unspoken signal that said, on the Allies' part, and eloquently so: you Germans are unimaginably bad and we are good; we will now live well in dwellings and on land taken from you and tell you what to do, while you spend some (unspecified) time suffering and obeying orders and purifying yourselves. We shall impose upon you Germans everything you imposed upon others for so long.

In return, the German population frowned and said: you spoke throughout this war of freedom, but now you impose on us only restriction and deliberate suffering. What do you want with us seventy million? Only to make us suffer more than we already do? Yes, the war was bad. However, we are not just the people of Hitler and Himmler, but also of Beethoven and Goethe. We have lived here in the heart of Europe for hundreds of years, mostly no less peaceably than our neighbours. We shall carry on living – unless you want to kill us all. So, again, what do you want with us?

There was no immediate answer from the Allied side in those days and weeks after Germany's surrender. How could there be, when there was no definite plan? On the big scale that mattered, there was no conversation.

Since the German government was now abolished, and its servants – including Backe, Speer and all the other organisers of Germany's ultimately futile wartime miracles – not just sacked but in the case of the upper echelons arrested, there was no German in authority to talk to. Almost all the Germans who knew which levers to pull to make the machine work had either been Nazis from the start or had ended up that way as the price of staying part of the elite.

Of course, from the first moment Allied troops crossed the border, despite the animosity and the non-fraternisation order and all the rest, thousands and millions of small conversations had taken place – often halting, awkward and even unpleasant, but sometimes, even as the killing continued, informed by hesitant kindness and mutual curiosity. And the number of these tiny conversations began to accumulate. To speak of normality would be wrong – too much had happened and too many innocent people had died unnecessarily to get to this point. There was nothing wholly natural, either, about most of the relationships that arose from these conversations, because they were so unequal. They were fraught with advantage and exploitative intent on the conquerors' side and need and resentment, concealed or open, on the part of the vanquished. But human beings are instinctively, even compulsively, social animals. Even under the very worst of circumstances, in hopelessly beleaguered foxholes and claustrophobic air raid shelters and lice-ridden concentration camp barracks, we still want to make contact. Post-war Germany was no different. But before those millions of small conversations could lead to anything truly positive, the language of deprivation ruled the great affairs of post-war Germany.

Lieutenant General Lucius Dubignon Clay was born in Georgia, son of Alexander Stephens Clay (1857–1910), a member of the US Senate representing that state. The General was an engineer, a logistics man – he had earned his reputation building dams and airfields and, famously, swiftly restoring the wrecked harbour at Cherbourg after it was abandoned by the Germans following D-Day – rather than an old-fashioned battlefield warrior in the mode of George S. Patton.

Clay had risen quickly to become the youngest brigadier general in the US Army because he knew how to handle politicians and he got things done. In the late spring, just after his forty-eighth birthday, he was promoted to lieutenant general and appointed Eisenhower's deputy at SHAEF, a post he continued in as SHAEF merged uneasily into the post-war Allied Control Council, and the Military Government of the American Zone came into being. Clay had gained a reputation as a supporter of 'tough war' measures in America itself, including curfews, restrictions on energy use and bans on horse racing and gambling, and there seemed no reason to believe he would be any easier on the conquered Germans.[1]

Eisenhower had unsuccessfully supported the candidacy of his abrasive Chief of Staff, Walter Bedell 'Beetle' Smith, whom Stimson and his Under-Secretary, McCloy, had thought temperamentally unsuited to such a post-war role. Nevertheless, Clay's appointment had actually been approved by President Roosevelt shortly before his death as the intended Governor of the American Zone, and so it was with the authority of the coming man in Germany that he wrote in June 1945: 'Conditions are going to be extremely difficult in Germany this winter and there will be much cold and hunger.'

Clay's words were nothing more, in a way, than a statement of fact, a logical consequence of the massive human displacement and disruption and the catastrophic damage to the German economy and infrastructure inflicted during the disastrous, drawn-out endgame of the war. But then came the moral message: 'Some cold and hunger will be necessary to make the German people realise the consequences of a war which they caused.'[2]

General Montgomery had been saying much the same thing, at least in public, and issuing declarations to that effect to the population in the British Zone. The Russians, for all their violence in word and deed, tended to be less moralistic.

There had been arguments during the war in Moscow over whether the Germans in general were 'redeemable' at all, but in the longer term a combination of textbook Marxism-Leninism and military pragmatism won the day when it came to occupation policy. Theoretically, of course, the Nazi regime ultimately counted as nothing more than the brutal final phase of capitalism. Those who had foisted it on the German people – Junker landowners, capitalists, militarists and so on – would be found and severely punished in the uninhibited Stalinist fashion familiar from the regime's treatment of 'class enemies' back in the USSR, but the mass of Germans, inasmuch as they had not committed serious crimes, were more or less classifiable as victims.

The Soviets were the only occupiers who, paradoxically – for their mode of conquest, administration and exploitation of Germany's human and industrial resources was anything but soft – allowed some leeway for the German population in the 'guilt question'.[3]

It is difficult to know whether the early phase of post-war Germany's existence would have been perceptibly easier had the Allies done the thing that they were firmly set on not doing: treating conquered Germany on an equal basis with the rest of the continent, which of course was also facing horrendous problems of food supply and economic and structural rehabilitation. Clay and Montgomery were eminently practical men. As his correspondence with Churchill proved, Montgomery was already, by July, growing restless at the restrictions placed upon him by London. All the same, in the push-pull of the post-war crisis, there were times when vengeance trumped pragmatic decency.

This was most apparent in the matter of the German prisoners of war who fell into Western, particularly American, hands. Much of the manoeuvring of German military forces in the very final phase of the war had to do, not with any notion of 'turning the tide' or 'winning', but with reaching the relative safety of the Anglo-American lines and surrendering to the Western Allies. The very luckiest of the Wehrmacht's finest delivered themselves into American hands in time to be put on one of the last transatlantic POW convoys and join the hundreds of thousands of surrendered Wehrmacht personnel in the established prison camp network within the continental USA.

Josef Bischof, for instance, captured near Kaiserslautern in southwest Germany in March 1945, found himself just a few weeks later on the other side of the Atlantic, harvesting sugar beet and beans in Colorado. Later he would wash dishes in a hospital kitchen. By and large, he saw out the war and the immediate post-war era in decent, though not luxurious surroundings. His treatment corresponded to the Geneva Convention, which had until now been more or less adhered to by both the Anglo-Americans and the Germans in the west, although not by the Germans and the Russians on the Eastern Front, resulting in huge losses of POWs on both sides.[4]

At the beginning of April, the transatlantic POW transports were stopped. There was a simple reason, apart from the clearly imminent end of the war: there were now just too many prisoners, too many for this system to cope with anyway. When the German forces of Army Group 'B', besieged in the Ruhr industrial area, surrendered on 18 April, 317,000 men passed into American captivity. This was the largest mass surrender of German troops in the entire war. The total number of prisoners in American hands soared from 313,000 at the end of 1944 to 2.6 million in early April 1945, and over five million at the beginning of May. The 'temporary enclosures' in which prisoners were usually kept before being shipped into captivity in the United States quickly proved utterly inadequate for receiving such numbers.[5]

The problem here was quite clear. Under the terms of the Geneva Convention, the Allies were duty bound to feed enemy POWs at the same rate as their own base troops (and to pay them as well, according to rank). Josef Bischof and his comrades were the last captured Germans to be granted that privilege. But how could this level of treatment be sustained for five million unproductive German POWs, suddenly dropped into a SHAEF-occupied area in the middle of a continent where food shortages were already acute and threatening to take on apocalyptic proportions?

The response to the problem of POW numbers, stated in an order from the JCS in Washington to Eisenhower, was to create a new category, not 'prisoners of war' as stipulated under existing international agreements but 'disarmed enemy forces'. In a coordinated move, the British reclassified their own captives as 'surrendered enemy personnel'. This new category could be fed and maintained at a lower level than stipulated by the Geneva Convention.

Since there was no German government after 8 May 1945, who was there to protest? The German Red Cross, purged of its Nazi leadership, would be allowed to continue some inspection work, but in the post-war context this amounted to a fairly toothless watchdog. Basically, there was little or no recourse for the German soldiers who had fallen (or put themselves, often at considerable effort) into Anglo-American hands in preference to those of the Russians.

Huge numbers of the German prisoners were housed (if that is the word) in the open, with little, or for quite long periods, no food, in a cold, wet spring season. They were often mistreated. That hundreds of thousands, running into millions, of these POWs suffered horribly from hunger, exposure and associated diseases, and that a shamefully large number of them died as a result, cannot be denied. There are wildly differing estimates of the dead, ranging from 8,000 or so up into the hundreds of thousands,* just as there are in the case of those bombed at Dresden – and as in the case of Dresden the post-war political orientation of the estimators seems to be a critical factor.[6]

Until early 1945, it had been usual for Germans captured at the front line to be transferred back to holding camps over the border in France. The massive numbers who surrendered from that time onwards, however, overwhelmed the system. As early as February 1945, the Americans had handed over the administration of these camps to the French authorities. It was a cynical move, since, although the French agreed in writing that they would adhere to international agreements on the care of POWs, everyone was perfectly aware that the French did not have the resources (or perhaps the will) to feed these prisoners at the previous levels – and also that they would reserve the right to use these prisoners as forced labourers. However, with the war rapidly drawing to an end, German retaliation against American troops in their custody – which had earlier always mitigated

---

* This latter figure was publicised by the Canadian writer James Bacque, whose sensational book *Other Losses* is now considered discredited.

against neglecting the letter of the laws of war – was becoming ever more unlikely and would soon be irrelevant.[7]

The numbers of German troops surrendering in the west in the last weeks of the war was unlike anything anyone involved had ever seen. The closest comparison was the millions of Red Army soldiers who had fallen into German hands in the summer and autumn of 1941 and then again during the summer of 1942. This was not an encouraging precedent. There were, however, differences. Firstly, the Americans, though prepared, along with the other Western Allies, to bend the laws of war seriously out of shape when it came to caring for their millions of new captives, had no genocidal impulse. And secondly, unlike in the Soviet Union, where the war continued to rage for years after the great encirclements and mass surrenders of the early months, peace was on the horizon, and that horizon seemed close.

'Unconditional surrender' of Germany had been Allied policy since the Casablanca Conference in 1943. Over the following months, its complex legal implications were the subject of much detailed attention by the EAC's bureaucrats at Lancaster House. By the summer of 1944, the draft instrument of surrender being circulated by the EAC contained a cunning paragraph stipulating that, in case of surrender, the German commander must accept that his men 'shall at the discretion of the Commander in Chief of the Armed Forces of the Allied State concerned be declared to be Prisoners of War'. The obverse of this was, of course, that they might not be so declared,[8] which is where the weaselly formulations of the new surrender conditions, finally introduced in March 1945, come in. Josef Bischof slipped 'under the wire' by surrendering just before this change in the rules. He therefore enjoyed full POW status under the Geneva Convention. Those who followed him into American custody did not.

The reason for this decision on the part of the Combined Chiefs of Staff in Washington (the British did the same, in a coordinated move) was that the numbers of prisoners now pouring in were, they judged, impossible to feed and care for under the relatively generous terms of the Convention. The reclassification was justified in law, not especially convincingly, by saying that because at the end of the war the German government would cease to exist, so would its armed forces. As a result, German soldiers ceased to be part of the German armed forces and therefore did not have to be treated as prisoners of war under the Geneva Convention.

Behind this sophistry lay a simple fact: from now on, any Germans who surrendered to the Allies would have to rely on the decency of their captors rather than any chapter or verse of Hague or Geneva. After Casablanca, Churchill had said with typical eloquence but untypical lack of clarity: 'If we are bound, we are bound by our consciences to civilisation.' The POWs would now find out what the Allied conscience was and was not capable of.

Fritz Mann belonged to what was left of a German unit that gave itself up to the Americans in mid-April at a sheet metal factory at Remscheid near Wuppertal, in the southern part of the Ruhr area. They stumbled over the corpses of those who had not been so lucky, were herded by their captors none too gently from assembly area to assembly area, with the column of prisoners growing dramatically as they progressed, until on the highway leading south towards Hückeswagen the flood of defeated, exhausted troops seemed endless. By the time they reached the outskirts of Wipperfürth, a little more than twenty kilometres from their starting point, they were around ten or twelve thousand strong, and it was early evening. The heat of the day was giving way to a chilly night. And here was a vast camp area, surrounded by an improvised barbed wire fence. This was their first 'cage', and in it they slumped down, without shelter or protection, to spend their initial night of captivity.

Mann, a veteran of the invasion of Russia, still has nightmares about that first, terrible winter, when he saw so many of his comrades die in the snows near Moscow. Now he would have some more to live with. The following morning, despite their protests, they were stripped of their rucksacks and blankets and of anything they could not stuff into their pockets, and put in trucks. Packed sixty per vehicle,

they were driven further south, to Gummersbach. This was the real
thing, the big holding camp, where they joined at least fifty thousand
'disarmed enemy forces' awaiting their fate in a grassy valley snaking
between high, forested crags, with machine-gunners on the heights
to stop prisoners from scaling them, and guards with guns and clubs
to keep those down in the valley in order:

> At mid-day, the sun beats down red-hot upon the valley. But this
> lasts only a short time. Already in the afternoon, the valley finds itself
> in the shadow of the forest. The cool evening is followed by a frosty
> night. – Here and there a few improvised tents have been erected
> with blankets and canvases. They belong to the few lucky ones who
> came from assembly areas where they were allowed to keep all or at
> least a part of their belongings. We others stretch out on the bare
> earth. We lie very close to each other, and the colder the night
> becomes, the more closely we press our bodies together. Thirty, forty
> men lie in a row together. You cannot move or rise. Anyone who
> stands up loses their place, irretrievably. The row immediately closes
> up, slithering and sprawling to fill the gap . . .
>
> . . . From the heights and the outcrops, the camp fires of the guard
> units cast their light down into the valley. The silhouettes of the guards
> stand out against the horizon. Here and there, the tune of an Ameri-
> can song floats over the night air. Down here, however, nothing
> moves. The valley, with its silent guests, lies like a huge mass gravesite
> in the flickering light of the flames.[9]

For four days there was nothing to drink. Then some large metal
tubs, containing around seventy or eighty litres of water, were delivered.
Squads were organised to fetch water for the thousands of men
crowded in the valley. It took hours for anything like a universal
distribution to occur, during which time the thirsty men spent an
agony of waiting. A day later, they got their first distribution of food:
American emergency (known as 'K') rations. Each pack contained
four biscuits, a small can of cheese, a twist of coffee powder, a little

sugar and four cigarettes. It was a beginning, after five days without nourishment of any kind.

There was abuse from some of the guards, and liberal use of wooden clubs to impose what the Americans viewed as 'order' and to move the prisoners around as required. Another account of the same camp has the prisoners being insulted by the guards as they arrived, running a gauntlet of jeers and catcalls in English and pidgin German – *Nazischweine!* and *Hitlerbande!* (Hitler gang) and so on. Otherwise the account is similar. The days without water or food, then the tubs of water and the ration packs finally arriving, just enough to keep the men alive for as long as it takes.[10]

Once some kind of food ration had started being doled out, it was enough to keep most of the men – those who were reasonably young, reasonably fit, not already suffering from wounds or illnesses – from death, though not from malnutrition and its associated ailments. After that, the worst enemy was the weather. At first hot during the day and frosty at night, as April progressed it started to rain, either chilly drizzle or sporadic downpours, and the men still had no shelter worth speaking of. A few lucky ones had managed to hold on to blankets; others managed to purloin cardboard or metal boxes and use them as sheets and blankets. Some dug holes and lay in grave-like trenches, with whatever pathetic, improvised roofs they could find, to keep themselves from the all-pervasive wet.

Gummersbach was one of several larger holding camps used for housing the hundreds of thousands of Wehrmacht personnel captured in the Ruhr Cauldron in mid-April. They were there for a few days. Then most were once more packed into trucks and went on a much longer journey, this time to the left bank of the Rhine. In the area between Wesel, north of Düsseldorf, to somewhere around Bad Kreuznach – more than 300 kilometres – lay the notorious 'Rhine Meadows', where improvised, open-air POW camps – the most infamous of the 'cages' – had been set up among the fields and banks lining the great river.

At the time of the Rhine cages' establishment in early April, the area on the left bank was chosen as a collection point, a processing archipelago for the vast numbers of captives and even large numbers of prospective ones, because most bridges had been destroyed, and so there was little possibility of newly captured German troops escaping (potentially staging mass breakouts), crossing the river and rejoining the Wehrmacht forces at that time still fighting not so far to the east. Altogether, over the next months, it is their stories that show the very worst of what could happen to those who surrendered to the Americans during this chaotic period.

The 'Rhine Meadows' were definitely a black mark against America's otherwise good record of treating enemy POWs. There was chaos and there were terrible shortages and transport difficulties throughout Europe in the immediate aftermath of war. In Austria, Italy and other theatres, German prisoners suffered routine but mostly not life-threatening deprivations during this time. Camps were also established on a temporary basis in southern Germany and Austria by the Americans. Conditions were tough. But the numbers of surrendered troops were not so terrifyingly large and POW survival rates were roughly as expected.

The Rhine camps, however, were something else. The worst of them seem to have numbered six – Bad Kreuznach-Bretzenheim, Remagen-Sinzig, Rheinberg, Heidesheim, Wickrathberg and Büderich – holding hundreds of thousands of German prisoners in the weeks following the mass surrender.[11] Sickness and ill health were undoubtedly rife. At least during the first weeks after the cages were established, the prisoners went unwashed and were perpetually hungry. Rations were similar to those at Gummersbach, or might include milk powder, dried spinach and potatoes (two, often enough all but raw), with bread and a thin soup only becoming available after some weeks had passed.

Many prisoners rapidly deteriorated into skeletal figures, not easily distinguishable from the concentration camp inmates liberated by the Americans and British earlier in the spring (an experience for many Anglo-American troops that may in turn have influenced their attitude towards these same German prisoners). Of the 1,247 officially recorded as dying in the camp at Remagen-Sinzig, many died of dysentery-related illnesses. Some were shot trying to escape. A few others died when 'sleep-holes' dug by prisoners collapsed in heavy rain, burying their occupants alive.[12]

As in all prisons throughout history, there was often admirable solidarity, but theft, intimidation and black-marketeering also quickly became everyday phenomena. The hierarchy that was established was probably the only one possible, but it did give opportunities for exploitation and bullying. The men were split into 'thousands' and the thousands into 'hundreds' and these also into 'tens', each under a leader. It was through this chain of command that water and food distribution was organised. That there was corruption among some of the leaders, and even among the German medical staff, there can be no doubt. Proud soldiers were reduced to begging for cigarette butts thrown away by the guards, who often showed brutal contempt for their charges. Little about the camps reflected nobly on either jailers or inmates, but at least the latter had some excuse for less than immaculate behaviour.[13]

The disaster of the Rhine Meadows camps, which some have blamed entirely on American malice, seems, in fact, to have arisen mainly from two factors. First, inadequate food supplies – bearing in mind that apart from millions of surrendered German soldiers, the Allies in western Germany had the duty to feed huge, largely urban civilian populations that had also fallen into their hands in the previous weeks – exacerbated by transport problems; second, serious overstretching of the personnel available to guard and organise the camps.

The American 159th Regiment, not quite 2,400 men, was given the responsibility of dealing with the 300,000 or so Germans captured in the Ruhr three weeks before the end of the war, when other units were still fighting further east. These same soldiers had to build the vast enclosures at Remagen, where the Americans had first crossed the Rhine so dramatically in March, and Sinzig, five kilometres to

the south – two of the largest and most infamous holding camps –
from scratch.[14] That they consisted of barbed wire stretched between
stakes, a few basic tents for medical personnel and so on, and little
more, was nothing to make anyone proud, but it was explicable.

The entire 300-kilometre sequence of camps large and small,
snaking down the Rhine from Wesel almost to Mainz, was made the
responsibility of one US infantry division, the 106th, with a few more
reserve units thrown in. These were not specialists, nor did they have
experience in this kind of duty. Five hundred and fifty-seven thousand
surrendered German troops were reckoned by reliable post-war
German sources to have been swept into these camps in the weeks
before the end of the war.[15] Because of these serious personnel shortages, and the potential for being overwhelmed (in the military sense
also) by the vast numbers of German troops in the Americans' care,
DPs were also drafted in as guards. Such auxiliary forces, largely Polish
and Jewish, brought with them, in many cases, a real malice – a taste
for making their recent oppressors, now at their mercy, suffer as they,
their families and compatriots had done under the German heel.

On the other hand, as time went on, many prisoners were, in fact,
released. After checks had been made against lists of wanted war
criminals, and forearms checked for SS tattoos, wrongly arrested civilians, elderly and juvenile *Volkssturm* conscripts, and non-German
Wehrmacht soldiers (Poles, Alsace-Lorrainers, Austrians and so on)
found themselves at liberty. Separate camps (with tents) were set up
for women prisoners (Luftwaffe auxiliaries and so on), and likewise,
also with tents, for the under-age boys taken prisoner after being
inducted into Hitler Youth and *Volkssturm* units.[16]

Rations for the prisoners were never generous, but slowly improved.
Despite the chronic grain shortages in Germany and all over the
continent, there arrived, after a few weeks, a real red letter day. As
one former prisoner wrote later:

The teams that bring the rations for the thousand-man units are
hauling strange loads. We have seen nothing like this so far. Among

the usual cans and cartons they carry white paper sacks, with square objects in them. As soon as the carriers turn into the camp, the first curious prisoners start stalking them. – Hey, mates! What you got in those sacks? – But their mates tell them nothing. They just grin – a bit slyly, a bit meaningfully, and they just keep hauling their mysterious cargo on towards the distribution point.

But the haulers' path is soon crowded with more and more curious men; finally, there are so many snuffling around the load that, inevitably, the veil of secrecy can't be maintained. Someone suddenly says just one simple word. Shyly, almost incredulously, with a voice filled with awe, he says it:

Bread!

A second voice joins his: Bread! – a third cries out: Bread! The news spreads through the camp like wildfire: Bread!

Admittedly, there was only a quarter of a loaf per ten men, but it was a powerful moment, a sign of things slowly changing. However, the American position regarding the three million or so German personnel in their custody at the end of the war throughout Europe was clearly put by Major General Robert L. Littlejohn, Chief Quartermaster (European Theatre of Operations): 'Definitely I do not intend to go along with a ration that will cause prisoners to starve to death, or throw them into our hospitals. Neither do I intend to be a party to a ration that will make the Germans fat.'[17]

Large-scale discharges of prisoners began, in fact, just two weeks after the official end of the war. On 23 May 1945, by order of General Eisenhower, women, under-age soldiers and representatives of various professional groups deemed crucial to the post-war survival of Germany were, subject to their not being politically or criminally tainted, proclaimed eligible for release (these groups included farmers, miners, railway workers and officials and telephone engineers).[18]

The releases were then temporarily halted, a result of the French government's demand that some of the Americans' captives be handed over to them as forced labour. A kind of human reparation, their job would be to clear mines and rebuild factories, utilities and infrastructure damaged and destroyed in France as a result of occupation and the consequent fighting during the liberation.

Around 740,000 German POWs would be handed over to the French. The French, in fact, took over the camps in the middle Rhine valley as part of their zone in July, so that many would spend up to two or three years as their effective slaves (though by no means always under harsh conditions).[19] It should be noted that the Americans agreed, on request by the French later that summer, to supply sufficient rations for these German prisoners, even though they were technically no longer their responsibility. When pressed by the French, the Americans even continued with this provision of supplies well into 1946 – hardly the action of a nation with the vindictive intention of starving a defeated enemy.[20]

At least half a million, but perhaps as many as a million, German troops were unfortunate enough to suffer the undoubted privations and horrors of these improvised open-air camps. As for how many died in total? The general figure estimated is usually around 1 per cent, but plausible estimates up to 5 per cent have been made.[21] Particularly if the latter figure is more accurate, this was much higher than it should have been, and a stain on America's reputation.

All the same, to give some idea of how much of an anomaly the Rhine Meadows cages represented, these are the generally accepted mortality rates for soldiers taken prisoner, nation by nation, during the Second World War:

	%
Italian POWs in Soviet hands	84.5
Russian POWs in German hands	57.5
German POWs in Soviet hands	35.8
American POWs in Japanese hands	33.0
German POWs in Eastern European hands	32.9
British POWs in Japanese hands	24.8
British POWs in German hands	3.5

German POWs in French hands	2.58
German POWs in American hands	0.15
German POWs in British hands	0.03[22]

Since the mortality rates for German POWs sent to camps in America (a total of 380,000) amounted to no more than 0.02 per cent[23] (one in five hundred – less than the rate for the equivalent civilian age group within Germany itself), it is not hard to see that fatalities ascribed to the Rhine Meadow cages were, relatively speaking, strongly disproportionate, especially since they existed for a space of just three to four months – but they were much less lethal than falling into Russian, Yugoslav, Polish or even French hands.

The almost equally significant point about the Rhine cages was, in fact, political. What happened there went, for a start, completely against what Allied propaganda had said would happen when encouraging German troops to surrender. The leaflets dropped over German lines in the previous weeks and months were often made up as official-looking 'safe conducts' (*Passierscheine*), which seemed to entitle the surrendering German soldier to some kind of guaranteed special treatment. They varied slightly in details, but the leaflet numbered ZG61 was typical. The Allies printed 67,345,800 of this one, and dropped 65,750,000. Tens of millions of other forms of the *Passierschein* were also dropped between D-Day and April 1945.

The leaflet, impressively printed in either red or green, bore the name and facsimile signature of General Eisenhower and instructions addressed to American troops: 'The German soldier who carries this safe conduct is using it as a sign of his genuine wish to give himself up. He is to be disarmed, to be well looked after, to receive food and medical attention as required and to be removed from the danger zone as soon as possible.' The text on the reverse featured prominently the 'Basic Principles of International Law regarding Prisoners of War':

BASIC PRINCIPLES OF INTERNATIONAL LAW REGARDING PRISONERS OF WAR

(According to the Hague Convention, 1907, and the Geneva Convention, 1929)

1. From the moment of surrender, German soldiers are regarded as P.O.W.s and come under the protection of the Geneva Convention. Accordingly, their military honour is fully respected.
2. P.O.W.s must be taken to assembly points as soon as possible, which are far enough from the danger zone to safeguard their personal security.
3. P.O.W.s receive the same rations, qualitatively and quantitatively, as members of the Allied armies, and, if sick or wounded, are treated in the same hospitals as Allied troops.
4. Decorations and valuables are to be left with the P.O.W.s. Money may be taken only by officers of the assembly points and receipts must be given.
5. Sleeping quarters, accommodation, bunks and other installations in P.O.W. camps must be equal to those of Allied garrison troops.
6. According to the Geneva Convention, P.O.W.s must not become subject of reprisals nor be exposed to public curiosity. After the end of the war they must be sent home as soon as possible.

Soldiers in the meaning of the Hague Convention (IV, 1907) are: All armed persons, who wear uniforms or any insignias which can be recognized from a distance.

RULES FOR SURRENDER

To prevent misunderstanding when surrendering, the following procedure is advisable: Lay down arms, take off helmet and belt, raise your hands and wave a handkerchief or this leaflet.

A bilingual version, with a French translation of the 'safe conduct' instruction, was dropped over areas of the front where Free French forces were serving.[24]

The clash between brute realism, not to mention cynicism, and the letter of the Geneva and Hague conventions, applied to the Allies' handling of the defeated civilian population as well as the military. If anyone in Germany had expected the arrival of the Allies to bring not just an end to violence but a rapid improvement in the supply of food, fuel and other necessities, they were to be terribly disappointed. That disappointment was to last not months but years.

Part of the problem was certainly dislike and vindictiveness on the part of victors against vanquished – that silent but eloquent language of enforced deprivation – of that there can be little doubt. Most of the shortages, economic sclerosis and mass suffering, were, however, probably inevitable. If the Allies had treated the Germans no differently from the other 'liberated' nations of Europe – they could not possibly have treated them *better*, by any rational measure – would the country's and the people's experience in the immediate post-war period have been less gruelling? The question is hard to answer, but worth considering.

And then, of course, there were the political consequences. Just as many German soldiers – but by no means all – felt themselves to be victims of American brutality in the Rhine Meadows cages and similar camps, so, in short order, millions of German civilians inevitably developed a strong sense of victimhood, arising from their suffering during the Allied invasion of Germany and the consequent months and years. Years of punishment, and, as many saw it, unjust persecution.

The massive bombing of German cities and, in the last phase of the war, the destruction of the country's transport system and other infrastructure by bombing and strafing, had helped spread war weariness among the civilian population. It had also created a lasting reservoir of resentment and defiance that carried on into the post-war years. The Allies accused the German nation of atrocities, but what about their own?

In mid-May 1945, the stalwartly anti-Nazi (though socially conservative) Tilli Wolff-Mönckeberg, for instance, complained not just about the pettifogging arrogance of the British after they captured her native Hamburg, but their hypocrisy in:

. . . proclaiming to the whole world that only Germany could have
sunk so low in such abysmal cruelty and bestiality, that they themselves are pure and beyond reproach. And *who* destroyed our
beautiful cities, regardless of human life, of women, children or old
people? *Who* poured down poisonous phosphorous during the terror
raids on unfortunate fugitives, driving them like living torches into
the rivers? *Who* dive-bombed harmless peasants, women and children, in low-level attacks, and machine-gunned the defenceless
population? *Who* was it, I ask you? We are all the same, all equally
guilty . . .[25]

Similar attitudes were widespread, and became even more so when
the Allies' less-than-perfect wartime behaviour was followed by
equally, if not more, flawed attitudes and actions after peace broke
out and they had the whole of Germany to rule.

Fritz Mann, the German POW who had chronicled first the privations of the Gummersbach valley camp and then the Remagen-Sinzig
cage, had helped conquer thousands of square miles of Europe and
Eurasia, and had been part of the occupation force in Holland, France,
Poland, the Balkans and Russia, with all that implied.

Nevertheless, like Tilli Wolff-Mönckeberg, Mann resented the
Allied assumptions of superiority. He saw himself and most of his
fellow Germans as victims, equal in this respect to the formerly
Nazi-occupied populations and the DPs. His dreadful experiences
at the Americans' hands in the Rhine cages merely confirmed him
in this view. Finally released in July 1945, one of the lucky ones not
handed over to the French for forced reconstruction labour, he
hitched a lift in an American jeep that was headed for his home
town. His benefactors were three American soldiers and an older
American woman in uniform, who spoke some German. Having
casually discussed his experiences in the Rhine Meadows – which
he is keen to tell us they did not believe – and the extent of his
'travels' with the Wehrmacht before that, they arrive on the shattered

outskirts of his home city, known in the text only as 'F'.* The woman
gestures at the shattered ruins:

And for all this, she continues, you have to thank one single man.
Terrible! All for nothing!

   Certainly, I think, it was one man who gave the signal for the
beginning of it all; but isn't it a bit convenient for everyone involved
to say: for all this we have to thank one man . . . Do we not all bear
some responsibility for this terrible blow that so profoundly shattered
our western world, and from which it may never properly recover,
all – vanquished and victors alike? – Everything that humanity individually achieves on this earth is always a piecemeal thing, in good
or in evil; it takes all of us together to do the deed . . .[26]

The American woman's apparent attempt to assign the blame to
'one man' – Hitler – is, of course, faintly absurd, but her omni-guilty
Hitler is also the German narrator's welcome straw man. Perhaps, in
fact in all probability, the woman is simply using the Führer, in a
slightly lazy way, as a symbol for Nazism, the ideology to which so
many Germans remained loyal for so long, even as millions died and
their country disintegrated around them. So, Mann is, in the narrow
sense, right, but he is also being deliberately obtuse, exploiting her
dramatic exaggeration in order to slide over the question of Nazism's
responsibility – the party had twelve million members, and many,
many millions more supporters, especially in the early, victorious
years – and move quietly into more amenable territory.

   Within this foggy moral landscape, occasionally warmed by the
milky sunlight of collective blame, victors and vanquished appear
equally tainted. All are guilty and therefore, if one is not careful, none
are. It is clear that the Americans' appalling treatment of himself and
his fellow prisoners between April and July has given Mann permission – at least in his own mind – to do that. In a similar way, the

* From his description and the sketchy geographical details, probably Frankfurt.

apparently indiscriminate bombing and ground attacks carried out by the Allies in pursuit of victory – especially in the final months of the war – cancelled out, for Tilli Wolff-Mönckeberg, notions of the conquerors' moral superiority and Germany's absolute culpability for the recent European catastrophe.

This psychological process was to prove a common resort for many millions of Germans in the post-war years. If some experienced a hunger for democracy, more did so for peace, but the overwhelming majority hungered almost exclusively for – food. The last of these needs would, for some time to come, consume all the mental and physical energy available.

On a purely practical level, the frequent brutality and unfairness of Allied policy – during but especially after the war – seemed to absolve all but the most self-laceratingly fastidious Germans from moral introspection, and effectively freed them up for the struggle ahead – the struggle for physical survival. By a glorious irony, this was the opposite of what the Allies, and particularly the British and Americans, with all their talk of 'teaching Germans a lesson' by deprivation, had intended.

While the Reich had suffered terribly from food shortages in the First World War, and even during the following months – the Allied blockade was maintained after the November 1918 Armistice and not officially lifted until the Treaty of Versailles was signed in June 1919 – the country's governmental apparatus and infrastructure had survived undamaged. Despite severe economic problems and short-term political dislocation, the food situation returned more or less to normal relatively quickly.

In the post-First World War period, in other words, the German people were humiliated and greatly impoverished, but not, once the blockade was lifted, starving. There had been no fighting on German soil (although following the peace there was the nationalist *Freikorps'* futile armed struggle against the ceding of West Prussia and Upper Silesia to Poland) and therefore no destruction of buildings and transportation networks. Moreover, after 1918 the country had remained sovereign, despite the presence of French, American and British forces in the Rhineland and later, from 1923, temporary Franco-Belgian occupiers in the Ruhr.

After the Second World War, the spectre of hunger would have haunted Germany, even had the occupation been a kinder affair. The country's cities were largely wrecked, with between a quarter and a half of urban dwellings seriously damaged or destroyed, its railways operating sporadically or hardly at all, little fuel, and dangerously low food reserves (in the last weeks of the war, as the Allied forces approached, the authorities had opened up many emergency food dumps for the Wehrmacht and the German civilian populations – though not to DPs, prisoners of war or concentration camp inmates).[27] And then there were the internally displaced – up to twenty million – and the other ten million refugees who had fled from the Russian-occupied east, to which, it was rapidly becoming clear, few would want to or be able to return. And the country had no government – or only at the very lowest level, and often, having been cleansed of experienced but politically tainted incumbents, dubiously competent.

So, by their unconditional surrender policy and their decision to abolish the German government, the Allies had ensured that it was upon their own authority – which in practice following the surrender meant their armed forces – that the governance of Germany, including the feeding and care of its people, devolved.

Article 43 of the Hague Rules of Land Warfare (1907) (Section III, 'Military Power over the Territory of the Hostile State') stated: 'The authority of the legitimate power having in fact passed into the hands of the occupant, the latter shall take all the measures in his power to restore, and ensure, as far as possible, public order and safety.'[28] Although feeding the population was not specifically mentioned, it was assumed at the time and later, in the words of an expert testifying to a US Senate Committee, that:

The Hague Conventions . . . are based on the assumptions that when a country has been defeated and occupied, the occupier or occupiers have become responsible for the orderly government of the people in their power. They must safeguard the basic rights of the local population and see to it that their basic needs are met just as they were to the national government of that country. Wilfully to deny them the necessities of life is a violation of international law.[29]

Questions were begged, however, even by this seemingly unequivocal declaration of intent. First, what were 'the necessities of life'? Second, more pragmatically, even if an appropriate level of nutrition were agreed, when – as potential American and British Military Government officers were being told in training schools in England in the final months of the war – most of liberated Europe was existing on 1,600 calories per day or less, how could the Germans be given more, or even the same? (Two thousand calories was the rough life-preserving rule of thumb used earlier in the war for occupied and liberated countries alike by the British and the Americans.)[30]

A senior officer at the training school in London told his students that the German adult would receive '1500 calories as a maximum, although there is no assurance he will get that much; that is all he can have during our occupation'. He continued:

As for supplying the Germans with food, it will only be as a last resort. We are going to treat Germany as a defeated country. We expect to put out food to the German people only where there is no other food available . . . The food problem will cause more trouble from a public safety angle than another one. But we have to be strict with them and we have to watch the food now because later we will have to feed them if supplies become exhausted. We do not want circumstances to force us to import food for Germans.[31]

This was as early as December 1944, when only a tiny proportion of Germany was in Allied hands. Everyone knew then that there would be shortages, possibly on a catastrophic level, because they knew what things were like elsewhere. It was no accident that Franz Oppenhoff, American-appointed Lord Mayor of Aachen, the first German city to fall, spent the March afternoon before he was murdered in his garden, with his wife, breaking soil and sowing seeds for vegetables to keep him and his family alive through the post-war year he would never see.

In the end, feeding the occupied population under the Hague Convention was reinterpreted not to mean providing the best standard of living possible under the circumstances, but, as expressed in the instructions issued to Eisenhower by Washington on 10 May 1945, merely ensuring 'supplies necessary to prevent starvation or widespread disease or such civil unrest as would endanger the occupying forces'.

The Western Allies had baulked at feeding the five to six million Wehrmacht servicemen who fell into their hands in the last weeks of the war on the same level as their own base troops – as the Hague Convention demanded and as had been the case until the last few months of the war – by reclassifying them as Disarmed Enemy Forces or Surrendered Enemy Personnel rather than prisoners of war. So, by a similar token, German civilians were essentially reduced to a new, legally somewhat dubious status, in order to satisfy the twin demands of vengeance and practical necessity.

In 1939, just before the outbreak of war, the average German adult had, as EAC's German Standard of Living Board had calculated, been consuming around 2,900 calories per day. This was 10 per cent above the European average and higher in quality and fat content.[32] The daily ration had remained comfortably above 2,000 calories until the summer of 1944, when the loss of food-producing areas in the occupied east and then of traditionally productive agricultural land in eastern Germany, accompanied by disruption of distribution routes, especially waterways and railways, through Allied bombing, had led to a serious drop in the German standard of living.

Shortly before VE-Day, average rationed consumption was

calculated at around 1,050 calories, and after that it dropped another 200 calories – although American officials of the Public Health and Welfare Branches were aware that unofficial sources of food, from the black market to personal contacts, private stores and private garden production would usually increase the actual consumption substantially, perhaps by up to double.[33] This was fortunate, for otherwise Germans would not simply have been undernourished, but would have starved en masse. In the larger cities, especially, there was a real danger of this even in the early days of the occupation. In Berlin, a week after the end of the war, the food rations were as follows:

Heavy workers and workers in harmful work environments:
Daily ration: 600g bread; 80g processed foodstuffs; 100g meat; 25g sugar.
Monthly ration: 100g real coffee; 100g coffee substitute; 20g leaf tea.
Office workers:
Daily ration: 400g bread; 40g processed foodstuffs; 10g fats; 400g potatoes.
Monthly ration: 25g real coffee; 100g coffee substitute; 20g leaf tea.
Children:
Daily ration: 300g bread; 30g processed foodstuffs; 20g meat; 20g fats; 25g sugar.
Economically inactive family members and other:
Daily ration: 300g bread; 30g processed foodstuffs; 20g meat; 7g fats; 15g sugar.[34]

This was bad enough. It got worse. By the beginning of the following year, the basic calorie allocations per person per day in the various zones were:

US Zone	1,330
Soviet Zone	1,083
British Zone	1,050
French Zone	900

Often supply bottlenecks, transport difficulties and plain bureau-cratic incompetence meant that even these meagre basic rations were not available. Accepted nutritional needs, by present-day standards, run at 3,400 calories per day for heavy work, 2,800 for medium-heavy work (including a housewife with children) and 2,200 for light activity.[35] This meant that the overwhelming majority of people in Germany were not just hungry but starving, slowly. This was true even if some Germans were, in fact, lucky enough to have access to further food through private gardens, hoarded stores, contacts of various kinds, black market purchases and general foraging activity, especially in the countryside (known colloquially as 'hamstering'). The basic ration card, level V, allocated to 'non-productive' adults – housewives, the sick, the elderly, disabled and unemployed – and also those classified as former Nazis, was known in Berlin as 'the death card'.[36]

There was small print on the ration cards, which reminded the consumer that the amounts of each food listed were not a guarantee. Sometimes they were simply not available, or replaced by inferior foodstuffs. Moreover, sausage or bacon or margarine might have been injected with water, so the weight was right but the calorific content less than it was supposed to be.[37]

Given that none of the occupying powers could or would provide guaranteed supplies at a level sufficient for the German population to sustain a satisfactory level of life, it is unsurprising that the black market (and various forms of 'grey market') flourished right from the start.

The Allied soldiers, and later the occupation administrations' imported civilian officials, had food, or at least access to it, and other currencies such as cigarettes, while the German population could offer things in exchange that the occupiers wanted – from radios and cameras, antiques and works of art, to simple pleasures of the flesh.

8

To the Victors the Spoils

Once the initial orgy of looting was over, trading began.

Lieutenant Wladimir Gelfand was among the many who would occasionally stray into the economic shadows, especially the big black markets in Berlin, which existed illegally but surprisingly openly in the Tiergarten in the western part of Berlin near the Reichstag, in the Potsdamer Platz, which straddled the sector border, and around the Alexanderplatz in the east. Of one such visit he wrote in his diary:

I hitch-hiked to Berlin. I got out at the market near the Reichstag [i.e. the Tiergarten] and stayed on the fringes, so as to more easily avoid any patrols. I purchased a few trifles (a fountain pen, batteries) and soon I had spent all my money. Then I decided to sell the watch I had bought from the Rilewskis to a fellow officer, with whom I had travelled from the regimental headquarters, since he was due to go home. I sold him it for the same price I had bought it, and with that I had one and a half thousand Marks in my pocket . . .[1]

On another occasion, this time at the Alexanderplatz, it seemed as if there was no actual black market. Gelfand saw that the entire square was being strictly patrolled by Red Army MPs, who were checking all papers, even of officers senior in rank to them. Frustrated in his aim of purchasing a few desirable items, Gelfand hit upon an idea. There were some shoeshine stands on the square. The lieutenant sauntered over, and one of the expert polishers got to work as Gelfand stood on the spot.

I was immediately surrounded by people, who started offering me goods that they had hidden underneath their coats. I stood there as if I had noticed nothing and just watched while my boots began to gleam like mirrors under the attention of the shoeshine boys.

The crowd was dispersed several times, and several times soldiers with 'MP' armbands came and looked me over – even their commander, an officer. But they simply couldn't find anything wrong.

Meanwhile, I had already succeeded in purchasing a shirt, a leather jacket, three pairs of men's socks and some gloves. And once my boots were through with being polished, the shoeshine boy was told to make himself scarce.[2]

As for the constant hunger that bedevilled the lives of Germans at this time, Gelfand, for all his fastidiousness, seems to have given it scarcely a thought. He had little understanding of the pressures Germans were under, and virtually zero empathy. In fact, he found the neediness of the natives repulsive. Visiting a German girlfriend, Marianne, in the town of Velten, just outside Berlin, he obtained and brought the obligatory food, but was contemptuous of the recipients' reaction to his gift:

Her mother was pleased at the food, as I had anticipated the previous day, but her attitude and her greed robbed me of the last of my patience and poisoned my feelings to such an extent that it halfway extinguished my inclination towards her daughter.

I gave her a small jar of lard and suggested making fried potatoes and then eating them together for supper. She grabbed the jar with both hands, emptied the contents on to a plate and then cleaned out the jar with a spoon and her fingers. There was some kind of liquid already in the pan, so I went over to it, took a knife and cut a slice of the lard I had brought with me. I intended to put it into the pan, but then the old lady winced, let out a cry, threw herself at me, screamed like a thing possessed, and made as if to take it away from me.

'What is wrong?' I asked, perplexed. 'Why?'

She explained it was for her, for tomorrow and other days, and today I must eat her broth.

That didn't suit me. I knew that decent people don't do something like this, and my outrage was limitless, but I pulled myself together, smiled as if nothing was amiss, and nevertheless tossed a piece of lard into the pan. The German woman closed her eyes and moaned.[3]

It is possible that Marianne's mother was, as Gelfand describes her a little later, 'a worthless old woman', but much more likely that she was simply desperate. The lard her guest wasted so carelessly represented rare and precious nourishment for the mother and her family. There was undoubtedly an almost grotesque insensitivity at work here in Gelfand's criticism of her lack of 'hospitality', and also, perhaps, a hint of sadistic retribution on the part of a man who, whatever his virtues compared with his more brutish comrades, was both Russian and Jewish and well aware of how people like him had been treated during the German occupation of his country.

Humiliating as it was, such encounters were, for the Germans, among the few opportunities to raise their standard of living to something near bearable. Either the women found boyfriends among the occupiers, or they simply sold themselves. If they were really lucky, they and any adult males who had either avoided the war or been released from POW camps somehow got jobs as cooks, waiters or cleaners in Allied canteens and billets, or succeeded in gaining employment as secretaries or translators.

Some of the officials of the British occupation administration spoke the language and knew and cared about the country, as George Clare, a German-speaking Austrian Jew serving with the British Army, recalled, but there were also many 'middle-aged middle-class ex-officers, who saw the CCG (Control Commission for Germany) as their last refuge from a Britain so changed they felt strangers in their own country'. He continued:

At that time the Control Commission employed 26,000 British Personnel, of which only a minority, approximately 6,000, actually dealt with Germany. The others made up its swollen bureaucracy, a happy hunting ground for those former majors and half-colonels, some of them of that grand colonial manner so worrying to Kurt Schumacher, the leader of the German Social Democrats. He was only half-joking when he said that the one reason he feared India's coming independence was that her unemployed Pukka-Sahibs might be dispatched to Germany to civilise the natives.[4]

A British officer stationed in the Ruhr explained his own experience:

We did have a weird currency which had no value – occupation currency. It meant nothing to the Germans, but their currency, the Reich mark, meant nothing to anybody. The real thing that made the wheels go round was cigarettes and coffee. The use of this black market was universal at a trivial level. I got my laundry done for ten cigarettes a week – off it went and came back beautifully done for ten cigarettes. I didn't go in much for coffee, but I was a smoker, and you could get cigs cheaply from the officers' mess. To put it simply, you were virtually given free money . . .[5]

Would-be German employees of the occupation were assisted by the fact that soon the Anglo-Americans, in particular, were keen to replace their own personnel with (cheaper) German workers and, where possible, their officials with German officials.[6] It was not the money that drew the Germans – the value of old Reich marks soon fell so low that hundreds or thousands were required to purchase everyday items, even if these were available – but the precious access to leftovers, slops, stores, cigarettes and so on. It seems that most of these jobs went to educated, often upper-class Germans, predominantly women, who before the end of the war would not have dreamed of working as, essentially, servants, but who, at least for now, saw it as a privilege.[7]

As for working-class girls, often bombed out of their homes and unemployed, they were known to more fortunate (and snobbish) compatriots as *Ruinenmäuschen* (literally, little mice of the ruins), and they were desperate to sell rather different skills to the conquerors.

A young American stationed in Berlin with his unit published an article in *The New Republic*. He asked his readers to imagine 'your own 18–19-year-old son removed entirely from your supervision, given an almost unlimited supply of money, granted a power over women equal to that of Van Johnson or Clark Gable, fed a steady diet of lies and stories calculated to inspire suspicion, hate and cynicism, and placed among a people who had lost all moral standards':

> The women of Berlin are hungry, cold, and lonesome. The GIs have cigarettes, which will buy food and coal. The GIs have food – chocolate, doughnuts (taken in large quantities from the Red Cross Clubs) . . . The GIs have warm nightclubs. And the GIs provide a kind of security and meaning in an otherwise meaningless city. The result is an aggressive and wholesale manhunt in the city. They stand in front of the GI nightclubs, parade up and down the streets in front of the Red Cross Clubs . . . 'Ich liebe dich' . . . has become no more meaningful than 'How do you do?' . . .[8]

It was not just in the Russian Zone that the rate of sexually transmitted disease skyrocketed. In one battalion of a Scottish regiment stationed in Germany, around eighteen months after the end of the war, out of 800 men, 108 were under surveillance for possible VD. Becoming infected was not an offence, but failing to report infection was. Miscreants were forced to go on a Sunday morning 'rogues' gallery' march through the town, where German civilians could see who they were – and local women be forewarned about who was 'clean' and who not.[9]

Since tobacco was a far more potent currency than the Reich mark, the job of *Kippensammler* (cigarette-butt collector) became a recognised trade. Waiters in restaurants and clubs frequented by Allied personnel could make a decent supplementary income from such activities. At the Café Wien, they were reckoned to make around $5 per hundred.[10]

The first winter after the war was, fortunately, a mild one, and so the famine conditions feared by many Allied and German officials could be avoided. All the same, in Berlin alone it was reckoned that 12,000 human beings died of hunger or of diseases associated with malnutrition during the first post-war year.[11] Part of the problem was that the Russians refused to allow importation of either fuel or food for the western sectors from their own zone, which surrounded the city, pleading lack of surplus. Coal and food therefore had to be imported into the American, British and French sectors from their respective Western zones.[12]

It may have been true that there were shortages in the Soviet Zone – where, in those months, were there not? – but since eastern Germany had been and remained the most productive agricultural region in the country, the Soviet refusal was yet another straw in the wind, presaging the difficulties that were soon to turn into conflicts, and from there to swell up into the great confrontation that became known as the Cold War.

Things were even worse in the British Zone. The problems there were varied and serious. Britain had been bankrupted by the war it had just won, with huge debts and a crippling shortage of foreign currency. The US had ended Lend-Lease with, so it seemed to the British, shocking abruptness. The advent of peace brought not a relaxation of rationing in the United Kingdom but a tightening of the dietary screws. At the beginning of 1946, the British Ministry of Food announced, on top of reductions in clothing rations, cuts in the allowances for bacon, poultry and eggs – and also told the public that, to save on foreign exchange, dried eggs would cease to be imported from America. Urged on by the largely opposition-friendly press, there ensued something like a housewives' revolt, which eventually resulted in resumed imports of dried eggs.

Later in the year, the British government also introduced rationing of bread, a basic foodstuff that had always been freely available throughout the war years.

The Mass-Observation public opinion sampling organisation carried out a survey in which working-class people in south London were asked whether they would be prepared to give up some food to help people in Europe. 'If it came to it,' said one woman, 'I suppose I'd do it as willingly as the next. But not to help Germany – only the countries that's been overrun. I wouldn't care what happened to the Germans – they've asked for it.' 'I wouldn't go short on half a loaf to benefit Germany,' said another.[13]

So Britain, bankrupt and with a semi-mutinous population that had so far seen little or no benefit from winning the war, was now saddled with a zone in Germany that brought with it quite peculiar problems. It was the most highly populated zone, containing around twenty-two million people, a number being added to daily by the vast influx to the zone of refugees from the east, which would eventually reach around 4.5 million.[14] It also had the highest population density of any post-war political unit except four-power Berlin. Also in the British Zone were several of Germany's largest cities – Hamburg, Cologne, Düsseldorf, Hanover and Aachen – along with the once-mighty (though by 1945 largely destroyed) Ruhr conurbation, whose factories and mines and steel mills had constituted the beating heart of the German military-industrial complex.

Before the war, the Ruhr had been one of the richest, most productive parts of Germany, but for now, in the terrible aftermath of war, its overwhelmingly urban population represented little more than another huge millstone around Britain's neck. It was true that the area of Lower Saxony (including the old province of Hanover), also belonging to the British Zone, was largely rural and quite productive agriculturally, but, along with the other agricultural area, Schleswig-Holstein (north of Hamburg and close to Denmark), it had become a favourite destination for refugees from the lost eastern territories, and could and did plead that it had problems enough of its own without being forced to meet the

American infantrymen march into Germany through the Siegfried Line in early 1945.

German investigators view the bodies of civilians killed at Nemmersdorf by the Russians, after the village is retaken by the Wehrmacht, 20 October 1944 (photograph by one of Goebbels' so-called 'Propaganda Companies').

Distinctly unmilitary looking Volkssturm (Home Guard) recruits at an oath-taking ceremony in Berlin, 12 November 1944, addressed by Josef Goebbels.

USA.-Soldateska drangsaliert deutsche Kinder

Roosevelt stellte Gangster, Kidnapper, Zuchthäusler in die Armee ein —

This cartoon in the Nazi newspaper, the *Völkischer Beobachter*, from January 1945, shows GIs as degenerate hooligans. The captions read (*top*): 'US soldiery molests German children'; and (*bottom*) 'Roosevelt recruited gangsters, kidnappers, jailbirds into the army'.

Richard Jarczyk, a self-confessed spy and Werwolf guerilla, prepares to face execution by an American firing squad, 28 April 1945.

German prisoners are marched down the centre of the Autobahn, away from the front, as the Americans continue their advance towards Giessen, April 1945.

'Surrendered Enemy Personnel'. A huge crowd of German POWs held by the Americans near Salzburg improvise what shelter they can. Conditions elsewhere were even worse, sometimes lethally so.

Citizens of the historic town of Ludwigslust, Mecklenburg, are ordered by soldiers of the American 82nd Airborne Division to view the victims of the Nazi regime at the nearby Wöbbelin concentration camp, 6 May 1945.

Buchenwald Concentration Camp, Germany. Freed survivors and GIs read a welcome message from the camp's political detainees, May 1945.

The Nuremberg Trial. The defendants (*seated in two rows in the right background*) listen to a prosecutor's speech.

Homeless German civilians cook amidst the ruins of Nuremberg, summer 1945.

July 1945. Refugees in transit pass massive posters erected by the Soviet occupiers to celebrate the beginning of the Potsdam Conference. *From left to right*, Truman, Stalin, Churchill.

Fraternisation. British soldiers with German girls, 1945.

Sign warning of the illegality of buying or selling army goods, British Sector of Berlin, 1945. Perhaps one of the most-ignored instructions in modern human history.

Fraternisation. Red Army Lieutenant Vladimir Gelfand and German friend, 1946.

An Allied army wife and her daughter, comfortably ensconced in the dining car of their train, stop in a railway siding in the British Zone, opposite box-cars carrying desperate German refugees from the East. A British soldier looks on, aware of the grim contrast. Early 1946.

German boy checks through the kitchen waste bin from the British Officers ' Club, Hamburg 1946.

The first German women to marry British servicemen arrive in their new homeland. Croydon Airport, near London, June 1947.

A family flees across the wooded border from the Soviet Zone to the West, late 1940s.

Churchill visits Hitler's captured Chancellery in Berlin, accompanied by an entourage including his daughter, Mary (*left*), and Foreign Secretary Sir Anthony Eden (*second left*).

General Lucius Dubignon Clay, Deputy Governor of the American Zone 1945–47, Governor and Commander-in-Chief of US Forces in Europe, 1947–49.

General Marie-Pierre Koenig (*left*), Governor of the French Zone of Germany, 1947. His wartime British mistress remarked half a century later that Koenig 'was never a particularly handsome man, but gosh, did he look like a general'.

Wilhelm Pieck of the German Communist Party and Otto Grotewohl, leader of the Social Democratic Party in the Soviet Zone, shake hands to seal the merger of their parties, April 1946. Communist deputy leader and future dictator of East Germany, Walter Ulbricht (*far right*), looks ahead impassively.

27 January 1946. A long line forms just before polls close as Germans in the American Zone vote in their first free elections since 1932.

A poker-faced Konrad Adenauer consults an aide on the day of his election (with a single vote majority) as Chancellor by the West German parliament, 15 September 1949.

apparently insatiable appetites of miners in Gelsenkirchen and steel-rollers in Essen.

In the autumn of 1945, the British documentary film maker Humphrey Jennings took a film crew to his country's zone and began a project for the government's Crown Film Unit which would end up being released as the influential film *A Defeated People*. He wrote home to his wife of his mixed and, he admitted, confused impressions:

At lunchtime today we were photographing a [German] family cooking their lunch on campfires in dixies on the blitzed main staircase of the Palace of Justice at Cologne – one of the few buildings still standing in the centre of the city – outside apparently deserted – surrounded by miles of rubble and weed-covered craters – but inside voices cries of children and the smell of drifting wood-smoke – of burnt paper – the sound of people smashing up doors and windows to light fires in the corridors – the smoke itself drifting into side rooms still littered with legal documents – finally adding to the blue haze in front of the cathedral.

The cathedral now with all the damage around immensely tall – a vast blue and unsafe spirit ready to crumble upon the tiny black figures in the street below – and then returning to Düsseldorf – much less knocked about – blitzed but not actually destroyed like Cologne and Essen and Aachen – still a beautiful city, returning here to tea we meet sailing through the park-like streets a mass of white Sunday-frocked German school children standing tightly together on an Army truck and singing at the tops of their voices as they are rushed through the streets.

In Essen they still fetch their water from stand-pipes and fire hoses in the streets and the sewers rush roaring and stinking open to the eye and the nose – seep into blitzed houses into cellars where people still live.[15]

Jennings held the German people responsible for their own fate – among his wartime films he had directed *Silent Village*, a powerful dramatised documentary about the German destruction of the Czech village of Lidice after the assassination of Reich Protector Reinhard Heydrich in 1942. He did not, for instance, feel guilty at dining in style in hotel restaurants and British officers' messes while black-clad German waiters (apparently known to the British with cruel humour as 'dwarves') scurried around, desperate to please their new masters. And, rather like Wladimir Gelfand, he commented disapprovingly on the listlessness of the natives without realising how much of a role hunger played in their condition. However, Jennings also knew, as he wrote in another letter home, 'that nothing is clearer straight away than that we cannot – must not – leave them to stew in their own juice . . . well, anyway, it's a hell of a tangle'.[16]

Theoretically, the British Zone – like all the zones – was supposed to be self-sufficient. In practice, however, given the alternative of letting the Germans 'stew in their own juice', London had to feed them, at least in sufficient quantity to stave off famine.

Since Britain itself was forced to import heavily from America to feed itself – one of the reasons for the introduction of bread rationing in 1946 was the effects of the longshoremen's and tugboat men's strikes in the US – it had nothing to spare for Germany from its own domestic resources. Therefore, if Britain was to fulfil its obligations, however modest, to the conquered population for which it had assumed responsibility, it had to use up yet more precious foreign currency to stop them from starving.

The once-strong motive of revenge, not to say any residual attachment to Morgenthau-style de-industrialisation, began rapidly to fade in the light of the terrific burden that a helpless Germany represented for a Britain that was itself economically prostrate. Nor was the planned shutdown or dismantling of 'warlike' industries as straightforward a matter as it had once seemed. In the case of chemical plants necessary to the production of explosives, for instance, it was true that their liquidation would render Germany incapable of waging another war. It was, however, the case that these same plants, using the same ingredients, also produced the fertilisers so vital to the revival of German agriculture and to the feeding of the zone, with its twenty million largely urban inhabitants.

At the beginning of 1946, the inter-allied Control Commission ordered drastic limitations on German production of synthetic ammonia, just such a dual-use chemical. In the last years of the war, on Hitler's orders, supplies of this substance had been diverted exclusively to making explosives, leaving German farmers desperately short of artificial fertilisers even before the post-war crisis. The Control Council's equally short-sighted decision would, it was calculated, cause in the British Zone alone a further shortfall in grain production of three million tons or seven million tons of potatoes.[17]

By spring 1946, the food situation was truly catastrophic. Between March and July 1946 – at the same time as those British housewives were declaring their unwillingness to go without in order to feed the Germans – the zone had a shortfall of about 600,000 tons of grain. Potatoes were simply not available for a while. And this despite the fact that the British were importing an average of 96,000 tons of food monthly to Germany from their own nutritionally beleaguered island.

When in July 1946 the British were the first of the occupiers to appoint a German-staffed 'Central Office for Nutrition and Agriculture' (*Zentralamt für Ernährung und Landwirtschaft*), almost its first task was to take responsibility for practically halving the official ration from its already painfully low level of provision. The daily fat allowance, at seven grams per day, was roughly a quarter of the recommended allowance for maintenance of health.[18] The reports of the busy, overwhelmed British officials trying to cope with this appalling situation show a whole complex of problems that caused these tragic shortfalls.

First came the failure to agree with the Soviets and the French on a central authority that could coordinate the German economy, which meant – among other things – that food surplus areas such as the east of the country (under Russian and Polish control) did not deliver to the urbanised Western zones, especially the British, as they had before 1945. The lack of a central authority and therefore integrated economic and financial policy also meant that the old Reich mark, already seriously depleted before the war ended, rapidly became all but worthless. No one trusted it.

Second, there was the unreliability of imports from abroad. In the exceptionally severe winter of 1946–7, for instance, instead of the usual wheat the British Zone found itself replete with large quantities of North American maize, which local bakers and householders had no idea what to do with. There were few German sources that could make up for this problem.

Third, the British authorities, struggling to feed the industrial cities of the Ruhr, could not even rely on Lower Saxony, a relatively productive agricultural area also under British control, to supply North Rhine-Westphalia (which included the Ruhr) with meat, beet sugar, vegetables and grains. Lower Saxony had food problems of its own, and all the bureaucratic outrage in the world could not make it fulfil its imposed quotas.

As for Bavaria, in the American Zone, then as now a considerable producer of meat and dairy products, although it agreed to supply substantial quotas to the British Zone – substantial enough seriously to benefit the size of the ration available to the population – the produce was simply not delivered. Despite the notionally close collaboration between the British and American zones, culminating in the 'Bizone' agreement that came into effect on 1 January 1947, for month after month the separatist-inclined Bavarians did not keep their promise.

Fourth, even when the food was available, the German Railways (*Reichsbahn*) was often so short of wagons that the provisions sat in ports or storage depots long past the planned date of use.

Finally, there were bizarre background events that could only have happened in occupied Germany, and at a time like this – such as the sudden swoop of a Russian dismantling squad on a factory at Dinslaken, on the northern outskirts of the Ruhr, where tin was produced for making cans. Almost before the British knew it, the entire plant had been stripped and disassembled, then shipped off to the Soviet Union as 'reparations', creating an instant shortage of the cans used in the distribution of nutritionally vital preserved foods throughout the British Zone.[19]

The British fumed impotently at all these blocks and bottlenecks and hindrances, and in early 1947 were forced to announce once more that the ration could not be fulfilled.[20] The result was serious unrest, with food riots and 'food strikes', especially in the all-important but desperately ill-supplied industrial towns of the Ruhr, where there had already been mass meetings to protest at the food and fuel shortages the previous month. In some parts of Germany's greatest industrial conurbation, the daily calorific allowance was down, temporarily, to around 800–850, true starvation level.[21]

The striking workers made it clear that they were taking action not necessarily for themselves – since they were on rations for heavy workers they were relatively well off – but on behalf of their wives and children. In some of the speeches by the workers' leaders, despite their denial of any political aims there were signs not just of a certain naivety but also of a return to wartime attitudes. At the massive Friedrich-Alfred-Hütte steelworks in Rheinhausen on the left bank of the Rhine opposite Duisburg, a trade union official addressed the strikers. His words were recorded in shorthand in English by a German policeman observing the meeting:

Comrades,
The present food situation forces us to this demonstration. We do not believe in transport difficulties. During the war immense quantities of bombs were brought to Germany by Allied aeroplanes. If these aeroplanes would start now to bring food to Germany, the German population would always be thankful to the pilots.

We as your representatives will inform the City Council Meeting of our request. The demonstration shall help back up our request. The Landrat, the government and Mil.Gov are asked to be helpful in getting sufficient food.

Everything shall go on with special discipline. Only cowards do not take part in this demonstration.

This demonstration is not a political one but is only of an economic character.

Within the next few days, demonstrations had spread to Hanover, where an estimated 10,000 protesters turned out, and Braunschweig, where 'though the demonstration was orderly, a gang of hooligans afterwards marched through the town, smashed windows at the Military Government offices, and overturned a lorry and two cars'.[22]

The strikes and demonstrations continued all through that spring, and included workers in Cologne and Hamburg. In Hamburg, half a million, including shipyard workers and dock workers, downed tools and flocked to a mass meeting addressed by a trade union leader, who demanded special rations for Hamburg and the Ruhr. He expressed the widespread distrust for the Germans administering the food supply on the British authorities' behalf by demanding that distribution be controlled by trade union representatives.[23]

It was significant that the British did not use force against the strikers, and nor did they arrest any of the leaders. This contrasted with the situation in the American and especially the French zones, where similar movements were greeted with the use of troops and the infliction of heavy prison sentences.[24] A group of American relief workers, attached to the Quaker Friends' Relief Service (FRS) in Koblenz, made a brief visit to the Ruhr during the winter of 1946–7 and felt both the hostility of the locals to the occupiers and the relative lack of policing compared with the French Zone where they were based:

At the Dortmund railway station we stopped to take pictures of the completely shattered and gutted station building. I wish we hadn't. To get the sun at our backs and get a good view of the building, we stood on the streetcar loading platform in the middle of the street in front of it. There must have been about 100 Germans on it waiting for the next three-car trolley to come. We were all relatively well-dressed, in pseudo-uniform . . . and had fancy cameras hanging from our necks. Our Volkswagen (FRS team's) was the only auto in sight most of the time. Many of the Germans glowered at us sullenly. I could feel their glances like knives in our backs. I felt, probably mistakenly, that the tiniest provocation would result in our massacre at their bare hands . . .

. . . There are very few English soldiers here – perhaps 20 in a town of 200,000. That may have something to do with it. There are 3,000 French, so Dr. Schaffer of the Santé Publique says, in Koblenz, a town of 53,000 . . .[25]

It was broadly true that the left led the fight against hunger in the Western zones. However, perhaps the most grotesque difference between the lives of those Germans who served the Allied presence and the mass of the conquered people occurred not, as might have been expected, in any of the 'capitalistic' Western-controlled parts of the country, but in the Soviet Zone and the Soviet sectors of Berlin. Right from the start, the ready-made German communist elite in the East was openly privileged by their Soviet masters, and in a blatantly elitist fashion.

An eyewitness reported the shock of outsiders who, on being admitted to Communist Party HQ in Berlin during 1945, when the general population was near to starving, found an entirely separate and hierarchical ration system at work. Meals supplied to Party members by the canteen kitchen were graduated entirely according to rank. Thus those of Party Secretary rank, the most senior, received a meal of several courses with wine, while section heads were entitled to a somewhat more modest but still enviably substantial meal. Rank-and-file Party workers got *Eintopf* (a mushy one-pot stew containing potato, pulses and greens, cooked in stock – with meat or sausage if you were lucky).[26] It would have been hard for the average German, learning of such, for them, unimaginable luxury (even the *Eintopf*) not to have felt that the German communists, whatever their pretensions to solidarity, were essentially members of the occupying force.

It was hardly surprising that, despite all the threats and the propaganda, many previously respectable Germans quickly lost all but the most vestigial sense of guilt when it came to trading in or benefiting from the black market. Either they would buy from or barter with dealers who assumed the risk of importing food into the towns, or they would travel out into the countryside and do direct deals with the now all-powerful farmers – naturally, at exorbitant prices. The black market did, of course, favour the relatively wealthy – those who had valuables to sell or barter, or large enough amounts of cash that even in the devalued state of the currency they could buy urgent necessities. Most industrial workers, for instance, had no such advantages.

There was very limited deterrent effect in the fact that joint patrols of the Allied military and the German police visited farms to ensure that no produce was being hoarded for the black market, or that checkpoints were set up on bridges and at railway stations and travellers searched to ensure that they had acquired no black market goods on their travels. In the British Zone, from the spring of 1946, random searches were carried out on the highways by mobile police squads.[27]

In the French Zone, railway stations and approach roads to cities such as Koblenz were also ruthlessly patrolled by the French-controlled police. 'At the station, any food they found on people, they would confiscate . . . the French were horrible [*ekelig*] in that regard,' recalls Marlies Weber (née Theby). As a girl she frequently went on 'hamstering' trips into the countryside around Koblenz with her family as a way of bolstering an unreliable ration that was in any case lower in the French Zone than in any other. They would return with their illegal provisions on foot, often using minor roads to re-enter the city in the hope of avoiding French patrols.[28]

In the British Zone, the story was similar, although it seems that the British and the German police conducted raids on a sporadic but occasionally intense scale. Towards the end of March 1946, for instance, a 'synchronized counter Black Market operation' codenamed 'Second Round' was carried out in Westphalia province, which extended from the agricultural areas to the north and east to the outskirts of the Ruhr industrial area (Münster–Bielefeld–Dortmund–Hagen).

The three-day operation seems to have mainly involved setting up random checkpoints and searching cars and their passengers (approximately 46,000 altogether). One hundred and eighty-eight mobile teams of German police, 'assisted' by British military personnel, arrested 128 civilians, with another 472 charged and 485 summoned to court at a future date for what were presumably relatively minor offences. 'The articles confiscated,' according to a report for the Black Market Standing Committee at Military Government (Mil.Gov) HQ in Münster, 'were mainly items of food, but tobacco and cigarettes were also very much in evidence.'[29]

An appendix to the report painstakingly – in fact excruciatingly – lists every single item confiscated during the course of this obviously time-consuming and expensive operation. Alongside the inevitable '15,325.8 kg potatoes', '52.650 kg leguminous plants' and '747 cigarettes' are strange and surprising items – '10023 combs', '1 tea set', '1 tin of zinc-ointment', '1 play-suit with cap', and so on and on until it seems no simple item carried on the human person was exempt.[30] This Sisyphean task was not helped by the slowness of the German courts, which was put down to staff shortages. At the end of March, before 'Second Round', the progress of current cases against alleged black market dealers stood as follows:

Total cases brought	160	
" convictions	15	
" acquittals	1	
" cases withdrawn	4	
" cases outstanding	140[31]	

There is absolutely no indication that the situation improved as the months wore on. One problem was the doubt in official German legal circles that the sale of cigarettes 'at an excessive price' was, in fact, an offence. The British, overwhelmed here as so often elsewhere in their post-war occupation, were forced to fall back on a set of emergency wartime economic regulations (*Kriegswirtschaftsverordnung*) dating from the Nazi regime (November 1940). When, following the local German State Prosecutor's objections to the use of these regulations against cigarette traders, an opinion was sought from the Control Commission's lawyers at its London headquarters, the eventual advice was predictably ambivalent. To objections that the Nazi-originated regulations applied only in wartime ('objection c'), the report announced in a masterstroke of equivocation:

> It is, of course, true that the object of the Kriegswirtschaftsverordnung was to meet wartime difficulties. However, the ordinance has not yet been repealed and the scarcity of goods which was the reason for the provisions of sections 22 to 28 on 'war prices' still subsists and appears to have been accentuated since 1939. This applies particularly to food and cigarettes. There does not, therefore, seem to be a sufficient reason for assuming that the charge of selling English cigarettes at an excessive price would be dismissed in the German courts on account of objection c. On the other hand, there is no absolute certainty that such a charge would lead to a conviction in the courts.[32]

The only certain way to limit the black market to any extent would have been the reliable provision of adequate rations, and that was never wholly the case in any of the zones. If the Germans did not have enough to eat or keep warm, and were either unable or forbidden by myriad occupation regulations to create the means of paying for these necessities, and German money was more or less without value in any case, then the development of a parallel economy (or, more brutally expressed, black market) was inevitable.

'The cigarette,' said another British report, this time a survey of large-scale black market operations prepared by the CCG's Economic Information Section in Berlin, 'is the begin all and end all of the black market. It has replaced the Reich mark as normal currency. Together with chocolate and alcohol derived from allied stores and canteens, the cigarette is probably one of the biggest single threats to financial stability in the country.'[33]

The writer of the report concluded:

Illegal trading in Germany and from Germany beyond its frontiers in addition to ordinary black market activities have reached unprecedented proportions which threaten to ruin what little remains of her financial and economic structure. Whilst Berlin has developed into the international centre of these illegal transactions, other cities and towns in the Western zones are also of great consequence. In the British Zone, Hamburg is outstanding, whilst in the American Zone Frankfurt and Munich hold the leading places.

All nationalities appear to be involved, including a fair number of Allied personnel now working in Germany in an official capacity.

Practically each individual investigation unearths some new aspect of this black picture and brings forth a further list of personalities who are involved in it . . .[34]

The report is thoroughly bleak in tone. However, as such reports will, it recommended energetic further action. There is no indication that any action which took place then, or later, seriously dented the power of the parallel economy.

And, of course, many Allied personnel were intimately and quite matter-of-factly involved in the black market at all levels. The same soldiers who might one day be manning roadblocks to catch German black market operators would then go back to the NAAFI or the mess of an evening and consume liquor and food obtained at some mutual private profit from those same dubious sources.

According to Lieutenant Maurice Smelt of the Black Watch, stationed in Duisburg, the situation was pretty much universal:

Our mess ran on the black market until the day the SIB* turned up at the Gordons [the Gordon Highlanders, also stationed in Duisburg] and told the Gordons exactly how they had been catering for the past months and they had better change their ways or there would be trouble. As soon as we heard about that we of course cleaned up our

---

* SIB = Special Investigations Branch of the British Military Police.

act so that when they came to us it was all all right. But the moment they had gone, we went back to the old way of operating.

Given that you would pay servants in cigarettes, how can you take a high moral line?

The suffering of the helpless mass provided, of course, an opportunity for a privileged or ruthless few. The fact that, by Smelt's admission, men from his own regiment – many drawn from the least salubrious sections of Glasgow's population – for some time also controlled illegal operations in the Duisburg docks, after a manner not unknown to Al Capone and his disciples, functions as a kind of poisonous icing on that particular cake. Several were finally arrested and, according to Smelt, who acted as a courts martial officer, at least one soldier was executed for what was effectively a gangland murder committed while under His Majesty's command.[35]

If home-grown food supplies in Germany were inadequate, food had to be imported, but who was to pay for this? Not the Germans, because they were unable to produce the coal and manufactured goods that would have supplied the necessary foreign exchange. Why was this? In large part, because Germans simply were not physically strong enough to hew the coal and roll the steel that would build up the country's export trade and pay for food. They were not physically strong enough because rations were inadequate. And German currency was worth only a little more than nothing. Therefore food had to be imported and paid for by the occupying powers . . . and so the story continued.

After Morgenthau, and JCS 1067, and all the talk of making the Germans suffer, just a few months into the occupation the British and the Americans found themselves trapped in the vicious circle that was punitive post-war policy.

The London *Times* expressed the problem clearly in the second autumn after the end of the war:

The evidence of a deterioration in German physique over the last few months as a result of malnutrition is irresistible, and of all the forces inhibiting economic recovery in Germany this is inevitably the most far-reaching. It reduces the efficiency of industrial workers both directly by its effect on health and indirectly by drawing them from their jobs into the search for off-the-ration food. The normal rate of absenteeism exceeds 20 percent; and industrial productivity is at an exceptionally low standard. Food shortages also contribute to the progressive demoralization which can be traced in the economy of the British zone. The lack of a firm foundation, however low, upon which to build and to plan leads inevitably to a frustrating and disruptive effect.[36]

Back in London, powerful voices, including many on the left wing of British politics, were pressing loudly for more aid to Germany and for a freeing-up of restrictions on aid by private individuals and organisations to alleviate shortages among the defeated population.

In the autumn of 1945, Victor Gollancz, a well-known left-wing publisher (and a Jew) and the Labour MP Richard Stokes, who had also protested against area bombing by the RAF during the war and had raised the issue of the destruction of Dresden in Parliament, had founded the 'Save Europe Now' (SEN) campaign. Supporters included the philosopher Bertrand Russell and Bishop Bell of Chichester (like Stokes, a veteran of the wartime Bombing Restriction Committee). Despite the broad nature of its title, SEN in fact campaigned mostly on behalf of the suffering population of Germany and, more specifically, of the British Zone. It proposed, among other things, a scheme for British consumers to voluntarily forego part of their rations for the benefit of unnamed foreign civilians (in practice, as the organisation's activities would show, mostly Germans).[37]

The tireless and in most ways impeccably decent Gollancz, co-founder of the influential Left Book Club and founder of the eponymous publishing house, had led a wartime campaign to save what was left of European Jewry from extermination. Once the war ended, he switched to protesting against the expulsion of Germans from the eastern provinces and the Sudetenland. Neither cause, although wholly justified, succeeded. A skilled publicist for both himself and others, one problem with Gollancz was that the notion of balance seemed alien to him. Once he had decided on his opinion, there was, it seemed, no other to be tolerated. Nevertheless, Gollancz was held in high regard in the leftist circles now in power in London (they included many individuals whose books he had published), and very well connected. 'Emotional but influential', as the British Labour Prime Minister Attlee acknowledged ruefully.

Gollancz's leadership of SEN lent the campaign great energy and passion, but also a proneness to gaffes and insensitivity. When, before Christmas 1946, the British Food Minister, John Strachey – formerly an ally of Gollancz and co-founder of the Left Book Club – announced that hard-pressed British consumers would be granted modest extra rations of poultry, meats, sweets and sugar over the festive season, Gollancz branded the government and his old friend 'shameless'. 'Have our Christian statesmen no idea of what is at present happening in Germany?' he thundered in a letter to the liberal *News Chronicle*. 'Obviously not, or they would not make such idiotic announcements.'[38]

Among other things, SEN also published figures on the prevalence of hunger oedema (swelling due to malnutrition) in British-occupied Hamburg and in the Ruhr, as well as of tuberculosis, both supplied by campaigning German doctors. These turned out, on close inspection, to be seriously exaggerated.[39]

All the same, the efforts of SEN and other pressure groups, including powerful American-based charities, eventually began to pay off. They were clearly right to argue that the occupation authorities alone could not cope with the situation in Germany. In the USA, an alliance of the Cooperative of American Remittances to Europe (identified by the acronym CARE, after which the famous food aid packages would eventually be known), the Quaker American Friends Service Committee, the Catholic Relief Services, as well as Unitarians, Mennonites and others, had been pressing since the summer of 1945 for access to Germany. Under the umbrella title of the American Council of Voluntary Agencies (ACVA), they were permitted early in the new year of 1946 to consult in Berlin with the American occupation authorities.

After Eisenhower's return to Washington to succeed George C. Marshall as Army Chief of Staff, General Lucius D. Clay became de facto Military Governor of the American Zone in Germany. Clay was still technically subordinate to Eisenhower's successor as C-in-C Europe, air force General Joseph T. McNarney, but there was no doubt he was the man in day-to-day charge.

Now fighting a war of attrition of his own against entrenched Washington bureaucracy, determined to overcome persistent transport bottlenecks and raise the quantity of American food imports to Germany, Clay nevertheless resisted the charities' presence. He especially disliked their promotion of certain particularly urgently deserving segments among the German population. The General, a technocrat to the last, also considered that yet more 'bleeding-heart' American charity workers swarming over the zone would not only prove a nuisance but would take food away from the natives – a suspicion that, it has been suggested, may have been related to Clay's Southern roots and inherited dislike of 'carpetbaggers', the bloodsucking northern careerists who had allegedly infested the old Confederate states after they lost the civil war.[40]

Despite the fact that thirty-four US senators had signed a petition demanding Germany and Austria be opened up to the ministrations of private relief organisations,[41] and despite alarming articles by the increasing numbers of American journalists now touring Germany with a brief to expose the conditions there, Clay remained obdurate in not permitting the aid organisations to take over.

Like their counterparts in the British Zone, the American Military Government's employees and their ultimate masters in Washington were aware that the public at home's tolerance of sacrifice on behalf of the Germans was limited. At the beginning of 1946, when questioned by pollsters in three different ways about the food problem,

Americans came up with three noticeably different answers. At first, when reminded that 'the health of many Germans, including children', would suffer under present rations, and asked if therefore Germans should be given more food, 58 per cent answered 'yes', 35 per cent 'no' and 7 per cent had no opinion. When asked if America should send more food even if the British and the Soviets did not increase rations in their zones, the numbers dipped – 47 per cent for feeding, 43 per cent for not feeding and 10 per cent of no opinion. Finally, a dramatic reversal occurred when Americans were reminded that 'People in the liberated countries might get somewhat less food if the Germans got more'. Suddenly only 37 per cent thought the defeated nation should be fed, 52 per cent that it should not – with 11 per cent undecided.[42]

All the same, concessions were made, such as licensing the sending of special aid to starving German children to supplement the extra rations already provided for, a procedure already adopted in the British Zone. It would take until the end of 1946 – as Germany, along with the rest of northern Europe, faced the most severe winter for many years – until all the disagreements were ironed out and the food charities were allowed complete access (as the 'Committee of Relief Agencies Licensed to Operate in Germany' – or CRALOG). The sending of ex-army food parcels (the first of the CARE packages) to individuals and families in Germany had been permitted from June of that year. A few weeks later, the British, despite the problems with their own population's rations, also relented, as, eventually, did the French.

The original CARE package was based on the ration packs that had been stockpiled for use by American troops during the invasion of the Japanese mainland planned for 1946. The A-bombs were dropped on Hiroshima and Nagasaki and the invasion never took place. It was therefore decided to release the packs to individual Americans for sending to friends and relations in Europe (cost, including shipping, $10). When the first packages arrived at Le Havre in May 1946, at this time still exclusively for non-German addressees, they each consisted of:

- 1 lb beef in broth
- 1 lb steak and kidney
- 8 oz liver loaf
- 8 oz corned beef
- 12 oz luncheon loaf (Spam or similar)
- 8 oz bacon
- 2 lb margarine
- 1 lb lard
- 1 lb fruit preserves
- 1 lb honey
- 1 lb raisins
- 1 lb chocolate
- 1 lb sugar
- 8 oz egg powder
- 2 lb whole-milk powder
- 2 lb coffee

By the end of 1946, CRALOG had sent 10,000 tons of food and clothing to Germany. CARE exported to Germany 550,000 packages for distribution, while by December the weight of private food parcels sent directly to recipients had reached seventeen million pounds per month.[43]

The new system produced winners and losers. It alleviated the problem for many, but left others still struggling on the normal ration. This would remain inadequate despite all the imports and charity relief, as well as the Military Governments' increased targeting of vulnerable groups such as children, the elderly and pregnant women. Suddenly, those Germans who had friends or relatives abroad, like those with connections to rural food producers, became a privileged class. It was also true that the Americans used the gift of CARE packages as a way of 'rewarding' their own 'favourite' Germans[44] – not quite as exquisite in its hypocrisy as the privileging by the Soviets of those tame German communists, with their three-course meals (including wine) and requisitioned villas, but all the same a cause of widespread resentment.

When it came to feeding the German people, the Allies' progression from punitive deprivation to reluctant concession, inevitable as it seems with hindsight, had occurred with painful slowness. It was partly a result of common humanity finally outweighing the urge for revenge, an emotion that would always struggle to survive the daily human contact that was the unavoidable result of a long occupation.

It also came from a dawning realisation that unless Germany was allowed to work, and produce, to an extent resembling her pre-war capacity, the country would for ever be a basket case, a mendicant nation dependent on the victors for its physical survival. A nation that might then, as it had after 1918, turn viciously against its tormentors.

Last of all, with the rapidly growing disagreements between the West and Russia (France was another, more complicated case) coming to preoccupy Anglo-American policymakers, there was another plain truth about the problem, which General Clay expressed very early in his rule as America's viceroy in Germany, when the average ration in the Soviet Zone was considerably higher than that in the American Zone:

> There is no choice between becoming a Communist on 15000 calories and a believer in democracy on 1000 calories. It is my sincere belief that our proposed ration allowances in Germany will not only defeat our objectives in middle Europe but will pave the road to a communist Germany.[45]

Or, as Truman's Secretary for the Army put it in a speech a little further down the line, the Allies had a stark set of alternatives when it came to the post-war management of the Germans: 'Starve 'em, shoot 'em, or feed 'em.'[46]

There was never going to be an alternative to the last of the Secretary's options. Allied food policy had been misguided and often vindictive, especially in the early months, and bureaucratic and incompetent at times, too, but Clay and his fellow military governors were no genocidal Goerings, and their advisers were nothing like icy-hearted Herbert Backe. Post-war, the Germans suffered more than was necessary, even given the destruction and chaos caused by Hitler's War. Some died who might and should otherwise have lived. And especially during 1946–7, at a crucial time, when the conquered population experienced the worst deprivations with still no glimmer of hope, many felt a huge resentment against the Allies. There was, ominously, even a stubborn nostalgia for the old Germany.

In surveys carried out on behalf of the American Military Government in the post-war years, when asked the question whether National Socialism was 'a bad idea, or a good idea badly carried out', the population of the American Zone consistently showed a plurality for the view that it had been a 'good idea', and showed an actual majority for that and 'no opinion' combined. The view that Nazism had been simply and unequivocally a 'bad idea' was never held by more than 40 per cent of respondents, and by the end of the third post-war winter that number had declined to around 30 per cent with double that number – 60 per cent – now insisting that Nazism had been a 'good idea' gone wrong.[47]

So much for laying the ghost of Hitler.

Moreover, to the question:

Which of these types of government would you, personally, choose as better:
A) A government which offers the people economic security and the possibility of a good income?
B) A government which guarantees free elections, freedom of speech, a free press and religious freedom?

. . . over a polling period of two years around 60 per cent consistently answered A) and only around 25 per cent, sometimes appreciably less, B).[48]

Despite these discouraging poll results, the facts nevertheless remain that during the occupation there was no Allied 'Hunger Plan' comparable with the Nazis' criminal conspiracy to starve twenty million or more Russians in 1941–2. And there was no equivalent of the Holocaust.

Instead, the Allies' project was indeed to penalise but also at the same time to purify Germany, to make its beaten, hungry population ready for a future in which the country would not be a threat to the world. This was perhaps the most ambitious scheme to change a nation's psyche ever mounted in human history. The process was called denazification.

Whether punishment and re-education could be combined was doubtful. And much of the observable evidence in post-war Germany seemed not to bode well for the country's democratic rehabilitation on this basis.

9

No Pardon

Just short of three hundred years before the Second World War reached its bloody conclusion, Europe had seen the end of a conflict that was arguably even worse, more violent, poisonously divisive and more corrupting of Europe's soul than that started by Adolf Hitler on 1 September 1939.

This seventeenth-century catastrophe involved just about every European country at some stage, including nations such as Turkey, Sweden and Switzerland, which remained neutral in Hitler's War. The fighting also lasted a lot longer, which is why it was known and is still known as the Thirty Years War. The preamble to the comprehensive agreement that finally ended it, the so-called Peace of Westphalia of 1648 (which was actually two treaties, themselves the completion of a sequence of truces and treaties), nonetheless contained a notable paragraph. This declared, according to an English translation dating from the early eighteenth century:

... that there shall be on the one side and the other a perpetual Oblivion, Amnesty, or Pardon of all that has been committed since the beginning of these Troubles ...[1]

The proposal that all participants be forgiven, no matter how appalling their behaviour – *perpetua oblivio et amnestia* in the original Latin text – was not unique, but after a war of such length and ferocity it cannot have been easy to agree. Germany had lost between 15 and 30 per cent of its population through war, famine and disease. Thousands of towns and villages had been devastated. This was recognised as a peace of exhaustion, with no clear outright winner – but perhaps in precisely this lay the possibility for an abandonment of the idea of guilt or the punitive principle.

The end of the Thirty Years War also saw an end to wars of religion between the European states. Another reason to 'leave well alone'. But in May 1945, when the Second World War was declared over, this peace – or perhaps more accurately, absence of war – came about because of the total defeat of Germany and her satellites by the coalition headed by the Soviet Union, the United States, Britain and France, known collectively as 'The United Nations'. Germany could fight no more, and so the war ended. There was no treaty. Unlike the Treaty of Westphalia, which was even incorporated into the body of law of the 'Holy Roman Empire of the German Nation', there was no universal agreement among the war's participants. Not then, and only partially later. Just 'facts on the ground'. And, above all, no 'amnesty and oblivion'.

The notion of a negotiated peace between the Allies and Germany had been rejected more than two years before the end of the war when Roosevelt and Churchill met at Casablanca. Stalin, originally scheduled to attend the conference, had stayed away because of the critical situation on the Stalingrad front, but he too agreed that there could be no conditional end to the war. From January 1943, 'unconditional surrender' was the Allied mantra. It made things easier in at least two respects – solving the moral quandary of who on the German side was fit to be negotiated with, and minimising opportunities for the Germans to divide their enemies by targeted peace offers. In other respects, it made ending the war harder.

Unconditional surrender could be, and was, used by Goebbels as a unifying bugbear. The Allies, he told the German people, were out to 'destroy Germany' (politically though not literally true). Apart from stiffening popular resistance, and thereby lengthening the war, it also weakened the case of those within the ruling caste who planned to overthrow Hitler. After all, if better surrender terms were not to be gained by a revolt against the Nazi regime, what was the point? Was it not better to resist to the bitter end and hope for a miracle? The 20 July plotters suffered from the fact that moral nobility alone was insufficient for most of their fellow countrymen.

But unconditional surrender it was, and the bitter end came in May 1945. The official date was 8 May, but the actual conclusion had come four days earlier. After two meetings on successive days at Field Marshal Montgomery's headquarters on Lüneburg Heath, at 6.30 p.m. on 4 May, four German senior officers had filed into Montgomery's famous caravan in order of seniority to sign the instrument of surrender, followed by the British commander on behalf of the Allied Supreme Commander, General Eisenhower. The document surrendered specifically to Montgomery not just the German forces fighting in north Germany, but also those throughout what was left of the Third Reich and its occupied territories, including Denmark, Norway, the besieged, starving part of Holland – and Flensburg, where Dönitz's tragicomic little Reich government was encamped.[2]

Even before the signing of the surrender, Germans had been tossing away their weapons en masse and giving themselves up to the Americans and the British – anything to avoid the clutches of the Russians. The reasons for the four-day delay until the official announcement of the war's end were fairly simple. First, the Americans based at Reims, hundreds of miles to the south-west, insisted that the Germans surrender to them as well, for formal reasons as well as those of news management. The same went for the Russians. And the Germans themselves were in no hurry either. Few soldiers on either side were being killed as a result of any delay, but every hour without a formal, all-encompassing surrender permitted more Wehrmacht units to place themselves in the hands of the Western Allies. So it was, after a great deal of renegotiating of matters already settled perfectly satisfactorily in the 4 May surrender instrument, that the next big surrender moment came in the small hours of Monday 7 May 1945. At 2.41 a.m., General Jodl, Hitler's former Chief of Staff, finally signed on behalf of Germany; Eisenhower's own Chief of Staff, General Walter Bedell Smith, and General Ivan Susloparov, Soviet representative at SHAEF headquarters, also put their names to the document.

Now the path was clear for the Allies to do with Germany as they wished, and as they had already promised: to eliminate Nazism and to arrest and try its leaders as criminals.

As for Stalin, however, the first criminal charges he announced on 7 May were not against Nazi murderers but against sixteen representatives of the Polish resistance force, the Home Army, which had fought for six long years against German occupation of its country on behalf of the London-based Polish exile government. Arrested some weeks earlier in 'liberated' Warsaw, where the Soviets were busy installing their own puppet regime, these courageous, betrayed patriots – including the Deputy Prime Minister of the Polish government-in-exile – had now been flown to the Lubyanka prison in Moscow. There they were tortured, interrogated and charged with 'diversionary activities against the Soviet State'. Like their fellow captive in Stalinist Russia's most notorious prison, Alexander Solzhenitsyn, they were forced to listen to the victory salvos in Red Square from their NKVD dungeons.[3] The Poles' trial, in June, would include no death sentences – possibly because Stalin was still chary of provoking the West – but put out of action the cream of the anti-communist elite in Poland during the crucial post-war period, which was doubtless its intention.

The reaction in Britain and America was one of mild disapproval mixed with relief that the sentences – from a few months to fifteen years – had been so 'lenient'.[4] Clearly, many in the West had now abandoned any idea that they might be able to influence matters in Poland in any serious fashion, and had moved on to other, more realistic priorities.

From Moscow also came a demand that a second surrender ceremony, this time to the Soviet command in Berlin, must take place on 9 May at its Karlshorst headquarters. And so it did.

Even with Germany now completely at the mercy of the victors, the question of what to do with the main Nazi criminals and the millions of members of the Nazi Party and its affiliated organisations, without whom the regime's occupation of vast areas of Europe and oppression of the continent's people would have been impossible, was not simple.

It was, for instance, a clear-cut matter that crimes committed against Allied nationals, whether military or civilian, should be tried by the appropriate governments. So, for example, members of the German armed forces who had executed Allied prisoners of war out of hand (as had happened notoriously at Malmédy during the Battle of the Bulge), or German police or civilians who had lynched downed bomber aircrew (as had happened fairly frequently, especially towards the end of the war when air raids against an already desperate and highly stressed population had increased in their intensity and apparently indiscriminate nature) would be sought out by Allied intelligence, operating in collaboration with the military police, tried and punished. The same went for war crimes perpetrated on the soil of the occupied countries, from France and the Low Countries to Scandinavia, Greece, Yugoslavia, Poland and the Soviet Union. By May 1945, all of these territories had constituted or reconstituted governments that could take on the official quest for the guilty men.

The problems came in dealing, for instance, with crimes against German citizens by the Nazi regime – especially, but not exclusively, against German Jews. Who was responsible for investigating and punishing these offences? There existed, as of May 1945, no independent German civil power, and when, at some future point, there might be, could it be relied on to prosecute such atrocious behaviour?

Above all, what was to be done with the members of the National Socialist Party? Membership of the Nazi Party at the end of the war totalled more than eight million (around 10 per cent of the overall population), with millions more Germans enrolled in large and small affiliated organisations, such as the German Labour Front (twenty-five million members), the League of German Women, the National Socialist People's Welfare (seventeen million members), and so on. In the twelve years of the Nazi state's existence, the tentacles of Hitlerism had slithered into every town and village, every social nook and cranny of the German people's everyday existence. Who would be responsible for dealing with these people – the individuals who had, essentially, run Germany for the past twelve years, who knew what levers to pull and where the bodies were, literally and metaphorically, buried? How were the truly guilty to be distinguished from the merely conformist and careerist? And perhaps equally problematic, what would be done with them once that distinction had been made?

Lists of Nazi organisations had been drawn up by EAC officials well before the Western Allies set foot on the Normandy beaches in June 1944. The forces that finally crossed into Germany in the autumn carried these lists, marked with notes of which state and party functionaries fitted into the categories leading to automatic arrest as the Allies advanced. These were known leading members of the Nazi Party down to the level of *Ortsgruppenleiter*, senior SA, SS and Gestapo officials. Also, those in clearly delineated leadership positions in separate but affiliated organisations such as the German Labour Front, the National Socialist Welfare, the National Socialist Motor Corps, the Students' and Doctors' Leagues and even the German Red Cross (DRK).

The DRK had been heavily politicised during the Nazi period, used as a political and propaganda tool. Several of its leading officials had been involved in the T-4 Euthanasia and other human experimentation programmes,[5] hence the arrest by the Americans of its president, Duke Carl Eduard [born Charles Edward] of Saxe-Coburg-Gotha, at his castle in northern Bavaria. The British-born grandson of Queen Victoria, the Duke had forfeited a string of British aristocratic titles because, as reigning duke of this tiny state, he chose to stay loyal to Germany in the First World War. He had been a Nazi Party member since 1933 and held high rank in the SA.

The arrests of other survivors of the Nazi elite also came quickly. Goering, having fled his beloved Karinhall – too close to Berlin, too close to the advancing Russians – finally emerged from his castle hideout in Bavaria on 9 May and gave himself up to the local American commander. Bizarrely, and in an impressive example of the Reich Marshal's formidable ability to charm, the officer ended up shaking his captive's hand and giving him lunch. There followed an impromptu press conference at which Goering was permitted to sound off to assembled war correspondents on the subject of post-war prospects ('a black future for Germany and the whole world' was his prediction). It was clear that Goering hoped to create for himself a mediating role in possible future negotiations, but Eisenhower, when he heard of this, put an embargo on the press reports and had the prisoner quickly shipped off to join the other major Nazis in the 'Ashcan'.[6]

Reichsführer-SS Heinrich Himmler had likewise hoped to negotiate, perhaps until the last. He remained at liberty after VE-Day, in Flensburg until it became clear that the game was up for him there, and then for a few more days as a nomadic wanderer, dressed in the uniform of a sergeant major in the Secret Military Police and accompanied by a small group of last-ditch loyalists. They wandered around the Elbe district, until on 22 May 1945 he was arrested in a routine way at a British road checkpoint near Lüneburg and taken to the local intelligence head-quarters for questioning. Realising that, despite his comprehensive set of false papers, he had been recognised by his interrogators, Himmler admitted his identity, then bit down hard on a glass cyanide capsule. Within seconds, the former head of the vast SS empire and engineer of the Holocaust was dead at the age of forty-four.[7]

Albert Speer was arrested along with the other members of the 'Flensburg government' and its hangers-on, when the Anglo-Americans finally closed down that strange enterprise on 23 May. Joachim von Ribbentrop, Hitler's Foreign Minister, was found living in British-occupied Hamburg with his wife and children, and taken from his bed into custody early on the morning of 14 June 1945. The architect of the Nazi–Soviet Pact had apparently spent the last few weeks 'making the rounds of the city, dressed in a double-breasted suit and homburg hat, reviving old acquaintances', presumably from his early days as a champagne salesman.[8]

Other, more obviously criminal types, such as Ernst Kaltenbrunner, head of the SD and the Gestapo, may have taken a more realistic view of their fate once the Allies had triumphed. However, it seems that a surprising proportion of the Nazi elite, including Himmler, Goering and Ribbentrop – plus technocrats such as Backe and Speer – harboured notions that they would prove so indispensable to the Allies in the post-war period that they would not just be spared but somehow be granted an active role, even a new career. They simply did not understand that certain of the Third Reich's crimes, for which they as senior officials were clearly collectively responsible, were so extreme as to preclude forgiveness, in fact to demand their incarceration and punishment. Accustomed to the cold, utilitarian exercise of absolute power, they did not, in other words, understand that what they viewed as realpolitik looked to others like mass murder.

Plans for mass shootings of German officers, and for the summary execution of the main leadership, from Hitler down, had given way in early 1945 – largely at the Americans' behest – to agreement that captured Nazi leaders would be put on trial. The paperwork, mostly put together by officials in Stimson's War Department, allowed for an 'international tribunal' composed of judges from each of the 'Big Four' victor nations.

This was not quite uncharted legal territory. After the First World War there had been calls for the punishment of the leadership of Imperial Germany – 'Hang the Kaiser!' as the slogan had it. Not all commentators on the Allied side agreed with this – not even jingoistic writers such as the journalist Lovat Fraser, who wrote in January 1919 in a patriotic paper, *The War Illustrated*:

Sir Herbert Stephen* points out that, because the Kaiser cannot be 'tried,' it does not in the least follow that it is impossible to punish him. Napoleon had no trial, yet we interned him until his death upon the island of St. Helena. The fact that he was declared an outlaw by the Congress of Vienna, presumably had no legal sanction. I take it that we based our action upon his surrender as a prisoner of war.

* Sir Herbert Stephen (1857–1932), barrister and acknowledged expert on criminal law and practice. Cousin of the writer Virginia Woolf (née Stephen).

Some similar course could probably be adopted with the Kaiser, though as to its legality I can express no opinion. What I am chiefly against is the illegal taking of life; and I cannot recall any case in history where the killing of a monarch under pseudo-legal forms has not in the end done far more harm than good.[9]

Nevertheless, the Versailles Treaty of 1919 provided for an international tribunal to try German officers and officials, including Wilhelm II, mostly for offences deemed to have been committed against Allied troops and the population of the parts of France and Belgium occupied by the Kaiser's armies.

The legal precedent was established – in fact, by international treaty – but things did not go as planned. The government of the Netherlands (neutral in the First World War) stoutly refused to extradite the Kaiser, who had taken refuge within its jurisdiction after being forced by revolution to flee Berlin in November 1918. For its part, the new, democratic German government eventually refused to deliver up the alleged 'war criminals', insisting that they could and should be tried before its own Supreme Court in Leipzig. The Allies agreed. However, the 1921 'Leipzig trials' of a small number of minor military figures led to several acquittals and, even for those found guilty, sentences more appropriate for house-breaking than warmongering. To a man, the defendants were feted by the German public as patriotic martyrs. In general, the Leipzig proceedings combined farce and bathos in a measure that might not bode well for the new work of the new tribunals a quarter of a century later.

In the circumstances of 1945, the strength of these proposed post-war trials was, of course, that the German state no longer existed. Therefore the legal proceedings were completely in the hands of the Allies. No Germans need be involved, except as defendants and defence lawyers. No risk of repeating the Leipzig fiasco. This was, however, also the weakness of the legal process, especially in the eyes of the German population at large. The trials, however punctiliously conducted, were self-evidently 'victors' justice'. The fact that German judges would not be asked to try their nation's most high-ranking criminals – who had committed many crimes against German citizens, too – implied, by this very absence of meaningful participation, that Germans in general shared their leaders' culpability. This fact was not lost on the post-war public.

Nor was it only the aggrieved defeated who found the legal foundation of the trials at best doubtful. Lovat Fraser's qualms in 1919 about the legitimacy of trying a ruler for his life found echoes in 1945. The Chief Justice of the United States, Harlan Fiske Stone, later referred to '[Chief US prosecutor Robert H.] Jackson's high-grade lynching party in Nuremberg'.[10] Stone didn't so much care what Justice Jackson did to the Nazis, but he disliked claims that this was a normal court, proceeding according to common law. So strongly did he feel that, when asked to swear in the American members of the International Military Tribunal, he said he 'did not wish to appear even in that remote way, to give my blessing or that of the Court on the proposed Nurnberg [sic] trials'.[11]

Although Jackson believed strongly in the justice of the trials, he was aware of other weaknesses in the Allies' claim to dispense impartial justice, which might be exploited by the accused. The Allies themselves had 'done or are doing some of the very things we are prosecuting the Germans for. The French are so violating the Geneva Convention in the treatment of prisoners of war that our command is taking back prisoners sent to them. We are prosecuting plunder and our Allies are practising it. We say aggressive war is a crime and one of our allies* asserts sovereignty over the Baltic States based on no title except conquest.'[12]

But how could there be no legal reckoning with the elite of the Third Reich? Clearly, massive and terrible crimes had been committed throughout Europe in the course of the war by German forces at their leaders' behest; crimes that in many cases would be clearly considered as such in all the countries that had signed the Hague Convention forty years earlier, and even centuries before that. Mistreatment of prisoners, violence against and killing of innocent civilians, starvation

* i.e. the Soviet Union.

and brutalisation of occupied populations – all these offences had been perpetrated on a grand scale between 1939 and 1945 by Germans acting on their government's behalf. Surely there must be punishment for those ultimately responsible? Were not justice and revenge in this case the same thing?

The Allies agreed on the final legal basis of the trial of the Nazi leaders at a four-power conference in London on 8 August 1945 – two days after the atomic bomb was dropped on Nagasaki and coinciding exactly with the Soviet Union's final declaration of war against Japan. The opening of the war crimes proceedings was set for 20 November. Less than six months would therefore elapse between the surrender of Germany and the trial, potentially for their lives, of the country's surviving leadership, for multitudes of crimes committed in often obscure circumstances across thousands of square kilometres of Europe and almost six years of war.

By the time the trials began, the first post-war winter was closing in. They were to be held at the Palace of Justice in Nuremberg. With a pre-war population of 420,000 the largest conurbation in northern Bavaria, second city of that ancient kingdom, since the Middle Ages Nuremberg had been a flourishing centre for industry, craft and the arts. Consequently it had become one of the cradles of nineteenth-century German socialism – and in peacetime during Hitler's regime the scene of the massive, overblown annual Nazi rallies known throughout the world as the *Reichsparteitage*.

Each Nuremberg *Parteitag*, held at the vast open space of the Luitpoldhain ('Luitpold Grove') to the south-east of the city, had been named after some supposed major theme of German life during the year concerned. So, in 1933 it was the '*Reichsparteitag* of Victory' (because of Hitler's successful seizure of power), in 1934 – although initially untitled – '*Reichsparteitag* of Will' (associating it directly with Leni Riefenstahl's famous documentary) and so on, through 'Freedom' (from the Treaty of Versailles, not the democratic kind), 'Work', to the '*Reichsparteitag* of Peace'. This had been scheduled to begin on 2 September 1939 and consciously intended to convince the world of

Hitler's pacific intentions despite all indications to the contrary. It was cancelled without explanation towards the end of August.

Hitler invaded Poland on 1 September. No *Parteitage* were staged during the war years.

On a practical level, Nuremberg's large early-twentieth-century court building and its connected complex of holding cells had survived the devastating wartime bombing of the city surprisingly well. On a propaganda level, what better place to bring justice to bear on the Third Reich than in the city where it had celebrated its greatest propaganda triumphs, which had become indelibly associated with Nazi pageantry and oratory, and whose name had even been used to label the notorious set of racist decrees announced by the Führer at the 1935 *Parteitag* and thereafter known as the 'Nuremberg Laws'?

Nuremberg lay in Bavaria, which had been allocated to the American Zone. The Soviets had initially tried to keep the trials themselves in Berlin, but in the end were forced into a somewhat unwieldy compromise: the legal proceedings in the first instance would take part almost 500 kilometres to the south of the Reich capital, at Nuremberg, while the seat of the four-power tribunal authority would remain Berlin.[13]

Three hundred and fifty representatives of the world's press would be granted admission to court room 600 at the Nuremberg Palace of Justice, and four hundred members of the public would also be admitted. Since this was to be a 'fair trial', counsels for the defence of each accused as well as prosecutors would also be present in the spacious chamber, which had been specially renovated and adapted for the purpose. There was no question that the arraignment of twenty-four leaders of the Third Reich (including the missing Martin Bormann, who was tried in his absence, and German Labour Front leader Robert Ley, who committed suicide while awaiting trial) amounted to a 'show trial' in the literal sense. And it was a show on a grand scale. The aim was clearly to impress the world with the crimes of the Nazis – but also with the fairness of Allied justice.

The world might have been impressed, but whether the German public, now realising the full deprivation of post-war life, and with no end in sight, was also impressed, is doubtful. The proceedings, when they began, soon turned out to be long-winded, quite dull to outsiders, and with the evidence overwhelmingly skewed towards the ordering and interpretation of a vast mass of documentation rather than personal testimony. In fact, as one writer has seen it, the entire trial bore more than a passing resemblance to a classic (and classically tedious at times) anti-trust suit, an area of litigation that had become especially common in the United States under Roosevelt's New Deal. This was the kind of case where many of the American lawyers involved had gained most of their experience back home, and it showed. What the trial was not, by and large, was a rousingly emotional moral exploration that might have forced the world (and especially Germany) to examine its conscience.[14]

In one of the odder instances of the importance of translation, or more accurately mistranslation, one of the counts in the indictment – in English 'crimes against humanity' – was consistently rendered into German as '*Verbrechen gegen die Menschlichkeit*', i.e. not 'against humanity' but 'against *humaneness*', thus softening or at least euphemising the accusation (an error that is still found in the German literature to this day).[15] After all, it could be said, was not the Allied bombing of German cities an infraction against 'humaneness'? And was this not also true of the starvation diet which they seemed wilfully to have inflicted upon the conquered German population?

The majority of the inhabitants of the American Zone, according to the Military Government's busy pollsters, followed the trial of the major war criminals in Nuremberg with interest, at least at its beginning and end. A large majority (79 per cent) said they thought the trial fair (procedurally, that is). As for the lesson to be drawn from it, 30 per cent thought it was to avoid following a dictator, and 26 per cent to never again start a war. A mere 3 per cent of respondents mentioned justice and 2 per cent human rights.[16]

The trial went on for almost a year and was extensively covered in the newspapers and newsreels. It was almost like a giant film being projected on to a screen behind the German people, or a radio soundtrack, as the vanquished went about the task of surviving that first post-war winter, spring and summer. Every day, the men who had ruled without pity over the fates of millions sat in their courtroom, crowded in there with their accusers, their defenders and the host of observers in the witness galleries from all over the world, who were hanging on their every word, interpreting their every argument and remark.

As for the Germans on the level below them – the plausible businessmen, the colourless civil servants and the wealthy and powerful backers without whom such criminals could never have taken power – they were also being subjected to a reckoning all over Germany. In many cases justly, but often not, because the victors' justice could be ignorant and capricious.

There were groups of people in Germany, as the Nazi regime collapsed, who could be easily identified as 'guilty' in some way or another, at least so far as the conquerors were concerned. Anyone in an official uniform, anyone who had played an active role in the Nazi Party. Landowners, officers and industrialists, who in the official Allied view had nurtured Hitler and benefited from his dictatorship. Leading artistic, sporting and media figures in Germany who had acted as the attractive face of the regime.

The most horrifyingly immediate retribution against such people occurred in the east. Amidst the general mayhem unleashed by the men of the Red Army, following on the rape, the plunder and the destruction, the treatment of members of the German and more especially 'Prussian' aristocratic elite was merciless. They were triply doomed: as an overwhelmingly nationalist group, whether Nazi or not, seen with some justice as aiding Hitler's rise to power; as the backbone of the German militarism that had allowed Hitler to devastate Europe from the Atlantic to the Volga; and as reactionary class enemies of the communists, Russian or German. Just as the Bolsheviks had massacred the old Tsarist aristocracy during the revolution and civil war more than a quarter of a century earlier, so they and their German protégés now saw little reason to spare the White Russians' German equivalents.

Many landowners understood the danger they were in and took steps, along with their families, to flee to the west. It was hard for them to leave lands where they had been established for many years, perhaps centuries. Marion Gräfin (Countess) Dönhoff, scion of an ancient East Prussian aristocratic family, had already lost a brother to a wartime air crash and a beloved cousin to the gallows at Plötzensee prison, where he had died an agonising death along with other aristocratic leaders of the plot against Hitler's life. Anti-Nazi since her student days, the unmarried thirty-five-year-old Gräfin had spent the wartime years managing the extensive family estates on the flatlands south-west of Königsberg, known as 'Prussian Holland', while the males of the family fought – and in two cases died – for Germany. Ever since Hitler's invasion of Russia, she had expected the tide to turn and her ancestral lands to be lost. Every time she and her sisters and workers bought some new farm machinery, or undertook some improvement on the estate, they had joked: 'The Russians will be pleased.'[17] But old habits die hard, and, despite everything, they worked as if the family would prosper there for another five hundred years.

Even when the end was very close, when the sound of distant artillery could be heard to the east, Gräfin Dönhoff, her sister and her sister's husband, who was home on leave from the front, spanned up the horse sledge and embarked on one last afternoon out hunting across the frozen landscape, tracking wild boar and finally a young fallow buck. That same day, she also heard from contacts among the High Command that a Russian breakthrough was imminent – something she would never have learned from the Nazi-controlled press.

So Gräfin Dönhoff saddled up her horse, Alaric, and with her family and household headed west on a gruelling, fear-driven trek that would take her 1,200 kilometres to Hamburg and a post-war future as a famous journalist. Those who stayed – or fell behind – were not so lucky. In one village in Pomerania, also part of the heartland of the old Junker class, a German witness reported that a Ukrainian boy who had spent three years on one of the local farms as a forced labourer was ordered by the invading Red Army to take them from dwelling to dwelling, from humble cottage to manor house, and report on those who lived there. The witness's father, a small farmer, had treated his foreign labour well and thus escaped with his life. The squire in the manor house had his eyes poked out by the soldiers before a rifle bullet put an end to his misery.[18]

Everywhere, a world unchanged for centuries was forcibly being turned upside down – and not just by the Russian soldiery. Elsewhere in Pomerania, a descendant of another grand Prussian family, Baron Jesko Ludwig Günther Nikolaus Freiherr von Puttkamer, woke up one morning in early March 1945, saw fires spreading across the horizon they had hoped to flee towards and realised there was no escape. He put on his officer's uniform, complete with medals from both wars, and then roused his family – his wife, the Baroness, and his stepdaughter, Libussa, who was pregnant with the child she had conceived with her serving officer husband. 'It is time,' he said. 'Let us go into the park.' Both the women knew what he meant, and what the code of their caste foresaw for such a moment. The Baron's service pistol was loaded and ready. 'It's time,' he explained. 'The Russians will be here in an hour, two at the most.'

Libussa, though, feeling the unborn child inside her, refused to go. 'Mother, wait, please, I can't do it.'

The Baroness tried to calm her daughter. 'It will be quick and painless.'

But Libussa was determined. 'No, no, it isn't that. I'm not afraid. I want to go with you, but I can't. I'm carrying the baby, my baby. It's kicking so hard. It wants to live. I can't kill it.'[19]

Her words changed all their fates. The Baroness decided not to die, but to stay with her daughter. Baron von Puttkamer followed this conversation in a bemused fashion. The decision that the two women had taken was completely alien to his world view. Libussa's brother, born of Prussian Junker stock, who later chronicled her life, wrote of the transfer of power that took place at this moment:

Our notions of right and wrong, our sense of order, our values have for centuries been formed one-sidedly: they are masculine to a fault,

Protestant, Prussian, and soldierly. Self-sacrifice in the name of ideals. Obedience to the state and to superiors. Readiness to serve and fight even unto death. It is from these values that our achievements as well as our destruction have come. Our conditioning pushed us toward an either/or rigidity: friend or enemy, all or nothing, triumph or defeat.

But in defeat, when it suddenly materialises, these masculine principles lose their power and value. Survival in defeat, and ultimately in life itself requires something else.[20]

The Baron looked helplessly at the women. 'And what about me? What am I supposed to do?'

Libussa was firm. 'The first thing you can do is get out of that stupid outfit and throw it in the pond, and the pistols with it! If the Russians find any of those things, we're finished.'

And reluctantly, he did as she told him. The Baron changed into civilian clothes and they waited.

When the Russians arrived, they stole everything, but there was no rape. Then a headquarters unit took over. The aristocrats were in luck. They suffered many further tribulations, but they did not die at the hands of the enemy.

Hundreds of Junkers, sometimes whole families, did commit suicide in these terrible weeks of defeat and violence. Another 1,500 or so have been judged to have died in air raids, in Russian and Polish detention camps, or to have disappeared, presumed murdered, during the trek westward.[21] Most aristocrats who survived the initial flood tide of the Russian advance found their way, in the early days of peace, to the Western zones. They had good reason to do so. They were granted a special place in the demonology of the post-war era, alongside the evil business magnates who had financed Hitler. As early as June 1945, the German Communist Party's first post-war programme called for

... the liquidation of large landholdings, of the large estates of the Junkers, counts and princes and the assignment of their entire ground

and land as well as the living and dead inventory to the provincial or
state authorities for distribution to farmers ruined and expropriated
by war.[22]

These estates would be confiscated without compensation and
redistributed to the less privileged. 'Junker land into farmers' hands'
as the famous communist slogan ran. Towards the end of October
1945, the SMAD (Soviet Military Administration in Germany)
published its decree no. 110 authorising just such a 'land reform'.
There was a small 'escape clause' in the confiscation law that permitted
compensation in the case of proven anti-fascists, but in reality the
break-up of the Junker estates was total and universal. Those landowners who stayed on in the Soviet Zone in hope of being allowed
some kind of role had made a bad decision. The size of landholding
classified as liable for confiscation was fixed at 100 hectares (approximately 250 acres), involving around one-third of the total agricultural
land in the Soviet Zone of Occupation. The landholdings of 'activist
Nazis' could also be confiscated, whatever their extent. Thus when
the 'land reform' began to be implemented, soon after the end of the
war, many thousands, including non-aristocratic, merely prosperous
farmers – essentially, the equivalent of the *Kulaks* Stalin had liquidated
during his collectivisation campaign during the 1930s – from the
decidedly non-Prussian, non-feudal states of Saxony and Thuringia,
were rounded up under the supervision of the Soviet NKVD and in
many cases transported to the island of Rügen in the Baltic. Here
they lived under abysmal conditions, without proper shelter or food.
It was one of the stipulations that the owners of these estates lost not
only their land but *all their other property*. During the winter of
1945–6, one letter written to the communist authorities in Saxony
from Rügen by a Saxon landowner interned there pathetically detailed
the cold, the hunger, the spread of disease. 'Help us, please . . .' it
pleaded. 'We are dying.'[23]

Capitalists could be equally subject to rough justice, especially in the
Soviet Zone. In Berlin during the early days of the Soviet occupation,

a manufacturer of meat-processing machinery, eighty-one-year-old Richard Heike, was identified to a Soviet patrol by 'anti-fascists' and shot on the street in full view. His son, who ran the company, was arrested a little later and disappeared to the Russian Gulag. He was never seen again.[24]

Sometimes Russian officers combined class warfare with other pleasures. The head of the Soviet Information Bureau in Zittau, eastern Saxony, named in the records only as 'Lieutenant R.', invited a group of local German industrialists and their wives to his birthday party. The 'celebration' involved his raping one of the women in front of the other guests. It appears that his 'punishment' amounted to an enforced leave of absence.[25]

Although the initial Soviet line opposed radical social and economic change – Stalin was keen not to frighten either his Allies and co-rulers or the moderate and bourgeois majority of Germans – many industrialists and businessmen were, in fact, immediately subject to arrest and to confiscation of their businesses.

At around the same time as the 'land reform' was being pushed through, the property and businesses of 'fascists and war criminals' were also being declared forfeit. SMAD order no. 124 of 30 October 1945 authorised the requisition of the entire productive property of 'Nazi activists, armaments manufacturers, war criminals, and financiers of the NSDAP (National Socialist German Workers' Party; Nazi Party) in Saxony. The breadth of the definition was, of course, sufficient to include almost any business enterprise the SMAD and its German helpers saw fit, especially as the forced mobilisation of previously harmless, consumer-oriented industry in the interests of the war effort had reached almost every corner of productive manufacturing during the latter stages of the conflict.[26]

A few days later, another order authorised the immediate expropriation of all property of the former Nazi Party and its affiliated organisations. The German communists, meanwhile, began organising a plebiscite that would approve expropriation of the large landowners and farmers as well as this radical move in the direction of industrial collectivisation. In June 1946 this vote – approved by 76 per cent of the electorate – would legitimise the nationalisation of around 1,000 larger business or branches of businesses employing more than 100,000 workers in Saxony alone. These and other concerns, nationalised when the rest of the Soviet Zone followed suit, included holdings belonging to Krupp, IG Farben, and especially the Flick steel and armaments empire, which at its height had 120,000 employees and three-quarters of whose plants were situated in the Soviet-occupied area.[27] Similar developments were afoot elsewhere in the Eastern Zone.[28] A year into the zone's post-war history, major changes were well advanced there, and contrary to the Soviets' protestations they were very radical. Already, despite the Western Allies' insistence on their own commitment to purging their parts of Germany of alleged feudal, militaristic and anti-democratic elements, a clear political and socio-economic divide was emerging between the Soviet Zone and the other three.

Suspected major Nazis and war criminals were subject to arrest by all the victorious powers, under the agreements reached between them before the end of the war. The 'big Nazis' – Goering, Himmler, Speer, Ribbentrop and co. – were obvious targets. And then there were the industrialists in the Western zones. There are no records of any of their wives being publicly raped by the likes of the notorious 'Lieutenant R.', but the spirit of Morgenthau was pretty strong among many men and officers of the American army as it advanced into the Ruhr, the Saar and the middle German industrial areas – especially those who had been the first to enter the concentration camps and see for themselves what horrors the regime and its servants, however respectable seeming, had been capable of.

On Wednesday 11 April 1945, American troops in armoured vehicles and jeeps cautiously advanced into the grounds of the Villa Hügel, on the southern outskirts of Essen in the Ruhr. The palatial, 260-room residence of the Krupp armaments dynasty, grandly positioned above some seventy acres of parklands overlooking the Baldeneysee lake and the Ruhr river, had been completed at the beginning of 1873 after three years of construction. The extended building schedule was largely due to the outbreak of the Franco-Prussian War in July 1870, which, while it may have delayed the family's move into their new quarters, appreciably increased their wealth and power.

Finally, at around 1.45 p.m., troops of the 313th Infantry Regiment approached the Krupp residence, which had suffered no damage despite the extensive bombing of Essen itself. They were reportedly forced to disperse a hundred or so anxious Krupp domestic staff, who were milling around the front entrance. Then the officers in charge, advancing with pistols at the ready, found themselves faced with an imposing figure who by appearance and manner might have been mistaken for the master of the house himself. He was, in fact, merely the personal valet of Alfried Krupp von Bohlen und Halbach.

'Gentlemen,' this German Jeeves said calmly, 'Herr Krupp is waiting for you. May I ask you to step this way?'[29]

Myths abound as to what exactly happened next. Some claim that the American officers were kept waiting for a further twenty minutes, others that threats brought the tall, distinguished, thirty-seven-year-old head of the Krupp concern quickly to the ground floor, where, once his identity had been established, he was taken into custody and driven away in a jeep. A photograph shows the impeccably dressed Krupp, looking slightly bemused in a smart coat and felt hat, his long legs folded awkwardly into an army jeep, sharing the back of the cramped vehicle with a large swing-mounted machine gun and its operator.

The officer who had arrested Alfried Krupp, Lieutenant Colonel Sagmoen, wanted to show him to their CO at 313th Regiment headquarters. 'Colonel,' said Sagmoen, 'I've got Krupp. Do you want to talk to him?'

The CO spat on the floor. 'I don't want to see the son of a bitch,' he snarled. 'Take him to the prison cage.'[30]

Surprisingly, after a few days of interrogation, the iconic industrialist was released and returned to his estate. The divisional command had taken over the main building, but Krupp was allowed to stay under house arrest in the so-called '*kleines Haus*' (little house), a (sixty-room) annexe to the Villa Hügel.

In the weeks that followed, security tightened. It became clear that, with his seventy-five-year-old father, Gustav Krupp von Bohlen and Halbach, too sick to stand trial, the Allies, largely at the behest of Robert Jackson, were discussing whether to prosecute Alfried in his place.[31] Alfried was fortunate only in that, partly because there was little time to prepare his case and partly because the judges were unwilling simply to substitute one Krupp for another at short notice, as if the name 'Krupp' were the sole characteristic required of the accused, he did not stand trial alongside the major Nazi leaders in November 1945. Had he done so, at a time when feelings were still running high, as an exemplar for the willing complicity of German industry in the waging of total war and the mistreatment and starvation of foreign and slave workers – up to 100,000 may have died in the last stages of the war, not forgetting concentration camp inmates – Alfried might have been lucky to escape the gallows.*

Elsewhere, in the case of less celebrated captains of German industry, matters ran less dramatically. In nearby Mülheim, just over ten kilometres to the west of Essen, a week after the peaceful American occupation of the town, leading local industrialists (who were for the most part equally complicit in the criminal aspects of the German war economy) were invited – not ordered – to meet the new city commandant to discuss the stabilisation of the supply situation and the continuation of industrial production. These included Walter Rohland, forty-six years old, General Director of the huge United Steelworks (*Vereinigte Stahlwerke*), dubbed 'Speer's Steel Dictator' or, because of the number of tanks his company produced for the Wehrmacht, 'Panzer-Rohland'.[32] Rohland was eventually arrested and used as a prosecution witness against Krupp. United Steelworks was eventually decartelised, but Rohland was never convicted.

* He was tried at Nuremberg in 1947–8 under less confrontational circumstances and sentenced to twelve years' imprisonment. In the end, he served less than four.

All major industrialists were, in the end, at least subjected to interrogation. There were some who were actively and urgently sought by special Allied investigation teams. Apart from Krupp, there were the directors of IG Farben, the vast dyes and chemicals conglomerate, at one time the fourth largest company in the world after General Motors, US Steel and Standard Oil.

IG Farben had produced poison and nerve gas, explosives and weaponry for the Wehrmacht, as well as the Zyklon B poison gas used in the gas chambers of Auschwitz and Treblinka – even the chemicals used in live human experiments by Dr Mengele and his cohorts. IG had also been notorious for its eager use and cold-hearted abuse of slave labour, most notably at a large plant that made up part of the infamous Auschwitz industrial complex.

Dr Georg von Schnitzler, sixty-one years old in 1945, was a board member of the chemicals giant, closely involved in defence matters and an enthusiastic member of the SA and the Nazi Party. Agents of the American Military Government's Cartel Division finally tracked him down to a country estate near Oberursel, north-west of Frankfurt. A doctor of law rather than a scientist, von Schnitzler had been involved in the ruthless plundering of occupied Europe through mass-kidnapping of slaves, and in organising the forced expropriation of foreign companies. A historian of IG Farben describes the meeting between the predatory lawyer and his nemesis:

He received them wearing his trademark Scottish tweeds and English brogues, sitting with his beautiful wife, Lilly, in a room enhanced by a large Renoir over the fireplace. After offering them a brandy (which they declined), he said he was happy 'all this unpleasantness is over' and that he was looking forward to seeing his old friends at ICI and DuPont again. When he was asked to accompany his visitors back to Frankfurt, he politely declined. As the SHAEF report of the meeting recalled: 'He replied that he was unable to do so as the way was so long and he was so old. The next invitation came from a sergeant with a tommy-gun . . . This time the Herr Direktor did come.'[33]

Hermann Schmitz, sixty-four, was von Schnitzler's superior. Born into a working-class family and with only a basic commercial training under his belt, in the years before the First World War his natural business gifts were such that he had nevertheless forged a meteoric career at Frankfurt-based Metallgesellschaft, the largest producer of non-ferrous metals in the world. Still in his early thirties, he then moved on to a prominent position under Imperial Germany's First World War armaments chief and chair of AEG, Walther Rathenau. Shortly after the end of that war, Schmitz joined BASF, one of the chemicals companies that in 1925 were subsumed into the IG Farben cartel. A devious and hard-nosed negotiator and an expert in company financing, Schmitz was a director of IG Farben for twenty years, a Nazi member of the Reichstag from 1933, and succeeded Carl Bosch as chairman of the company in 1935.

Hermann Schmitz unquestionably bore ultimate responsibility for every criminal act, every ruined life and agonising death the company inflicted. Nevertheless, unlike von Schnitzler, Schmitz was not arrested immediately at his house in Heidelberg. Only after searching the building several times did American investigators find a trunk stuffed with hundreds of company documents, including papers detailing IG's efforts to camouflage its illegal ownership of subsidiaries in the United States.

More sinister secrets were gradually revealed. A British intelligence officer, Major Tilley, managed to extract from Schmitz the location of his personal safe, which was concealed in a cupboard in his office. The documents there included photographs of the branch of IG Farben's Buna Works in the Auschwitz industrial complex, the construction and operation of which had cost at least 35,000 lives.[34]

'Page one,' Tilley wrote, 'had a picture with a narrow street of the old [town of] Auschwitz. The accompanying drawings depicted the Jewish part of the population in a manner that was not flattering . . . The second page began a section entitled "Planning the New Auschwitz Works".'[35]

Schmitz was finally arrested and prosecuted along with other directors and managers of IG Farben – among them, Heinrich Hörlein, a Nobel Prize-winning chemist – on charges including 'enslavement and murder' and 'plunder and robbery'. Only Georg von Schnitzler ever expressed anything approaching remorse for what he and his fellows had done, admitting that 'The IG took on a great responsibility and gave, in the chemical sector, substantial and even decisive aid for Hitler's foreign policy which led to war and the ruination of Germany . . . I must conclude that the IG is largely responsible for the policies of Hitler.' Later, under pressure from other IG defendants, von Schnitzler temporarily withdrew this and similar candid statements, though he later again admitted that they were accurate.[36]

Most major industrialists and managers of German companies in the Western zones were taken into custody at some point after the end of the war and their companies subjected, initially at least, to dismantling, decartelisation or confiscation, as agreed at the Potsdam Conference in August 1945. The list of those arrested by the Americans, the British and the French is long – most of these luminaries, aware of the fate that would await them in Soviet hands, had been cunning enough to ensure they ended the war within the Western Allies' zones. The names of their companies remain in many cases world famous – Krupp, Henkel (detergents and cleaning), Mannesmann (steel piping, later armaments), United Steelworks, the Flick family conglomerate (in whose mills and factories tens of thousands of slave workers are thought to have died of starvation and overwork),[37] the mines and mills belonging to Hermann Röchling, the so-called 'King of the Saar', and so on.

It was relatively easy, in the final analysis, to decide who among the Nazi elite deserved arrest. However, 8.5 million Germans had been members of the Nazi Party, the equivalent of the population of London or New York. Millions more had belonged to associated organisations. What to do with them?

The mesh of the net was accordingly made smaller, to catch all those extra millions. But of those caught, which should be kept and which thrown back into the water to swim on through their tainted lives?

10

The Fish and the Net

It was not too difficult for the Allies to trace the 'big fish' Nazis, militarists and industrial malefactors. Even the second-tier, regional and local bosses were known to intelligence experts. Extensive lists had been drawn up even before the Allies entered Germany at the end of 1944. However, before the millions of minor Nazis – those never mentioned in the Allied monitored press or on lists of prominent functionaries – could be found, investigated and thoroughly categorised as the denazification process demanded, they too would have to be identified. And as the war ended, the Allied investigators still had no foolproof and comprehensive means of tracking down all the eight million or so former wearers of the Party badge.

There were, of course, many non-Nazis (and turncoats) in cities, towns and villages all over the former Reich who would be only too willing to denounce fellow citizens who had been active Nazis, and in many cases this happened very quickly. All the same, this was at best a haphazard way of identifying the guilty, at worst a wearisome and potentially slow method. As for the millions of refugees already pouring westward away from the vengeance of the Russians, Poles and Czechs, they had little to celebrate – except, or so it seemed, for the fact that wherever they were going they were unlikely to be known, which meant that the former Nazis among them hoped to be able to keep their secret and start afresh in some new corner of the Reich. Usually they said that their papers had been destroyed or lost. As

Ulrich Frodien – who had fled Breslau, the Silesian capital, along with his father and hundreds of thousands of others, recalled, one denazification joke in the West after the war went: 'So, were you a member of the Nazi Party, or are you from Breslau?'[1]

When the Americans took Munich at the end of April 1945, the many Nazi Party buildings and office complexes in the city (not for nothing was it known as 'the capital of the movement') were quickly secured and searched by US Army intelligence and security personnel. They did not always find very much of interest, even at the buildings that had housed the main Nazi Party bureaucracy.

At the Nazi Party Treasurer's Munich headquarters, an impressive complex completed in February 1937 to replace three apartment blocks at Arcisstrasse 10–14, extending to the corner of the Königsplatz, row after row of purpose-built steel card-index cabinets had harboured the NSDAP's ever-expanding membership records. They stayed there for more than eight years, until a senior Nazi bureaucrat took a drive out to a suburb at the north-eastern edge of Munich with an urgent request.

On 15 April 1945, an impressive official car arrived at the Josef Wirth paper mill in Munich-Freimann. The man it disgorged into the yard of the factory brought a simple but forceful order. During the next few days, he told the manager, a lot of paper would be transported here, and it must be destroyed immediately. Pulped. Naturally, the manager, Herr Hanns Huber, expressed his consent to this unrefusable command from on high. The bigwig departed, satisfied.

Three days later, trucks began to arrive at the paper mill. Turning up at the rate of twenty a day, one after the other, they contained mysterious bales of paper. The trucks continued to deliver these loads for a total of nine days. In the meantime, Herr Huber, who had originally welcomed the gift of raw materials (which were by this stage of the war in short supply), had checked the bales that had been unloaded into his yard and worked out what was actually in them. These were the cards that had been contained in the steel cabinets in the Arcisstrasse – the membership documents of every member of the Nazi Party since its foundation. Each one with a photograph of the member, with dates of joining and (where applicable) leaving, with personal details about millions of individual careers. There were even cards with red borders, representing a member considered not entirely reliable. And the thing was, Herr Huber was not a Nazi – rather, the opposite. He knew the representatives of the 'Thousand Year Reich' were trying to destroy crucial, incriminating evidence and he determined to prevent them from doing so.

According to his story after the war, Hanns Huber found a way of stalling. He would pile the stuff up in a corner of the yard and then, when the Nazis queried why so much was there when he had been told to destroy it 'immediately', he said the piles were actually pulping paper that had been brought in by other clients, but he had not been able to get to them because he was working on the urgent Nazi Party business. He got away with it. When Munich finally fell on 30 April, with 50 per cent of its buildings now reduced to rubble, Herr Huber still had all the Nazi records. More than fifty tons of them.[2]

Later, Huber claimed to have first contacted the American occupying forces towards the end of May 1945. He was, he said, ignored. He and his staff continued to preserve and where possible put some order to the archival trove they had come into possession of and now could not persuade anyone to take. He persisted, however, and as summer turned to autumn finally convinced Mr Sargent B. Child, a civilian attached to the Third Army's security – a qualified archivist and the army's adviser in such matters – to look at the material. Child did so and was astounded. 'Any goddamned idiot', he later declared to a colleague at the National Archives in Washington, could see that this was of the highest importance.

All the same, Child's superior, Major William D. Brown, did not find it easy to persuade the powers that be in the American Zone of the importance of what they had discovered (or had presented to them by Herr Huber) at the paper mill in Munich-Freimann. Brown had to make a personal visit to American Military Government HQ in Frankfurt, and even then it was some weeks before action was taken. At the end of November 1945, the material was loaded back into a big convoy of trucks and transported from Munich more than three hundred miles to the so-called 'Ministerial Collecting Center' (MCC), a disused former munitions factory complex at Fürstenhagen, on the main Highway 7, south-east of Kassel. Here, since the second week of July, the US Military Government had been storing and attempting to catalogue an ever-increasing mass of German government records, many evacuated from Berlin into the countryside towards the end of the war, which had fallen piecemeal and often under chaotic circumstances into American hands as the army advanced.[3]

The failure of the local American forces to react to Herr Huber's offer was a curious anomaly. Finding useful and/or incriminating documentation belonging to the German military, government and Nazi Party organisations had always been a high priority. In fact, as one of the army archivists proclaimed proudly after the war, he and his team had arrived at noon on 6 June 1944 off Omaha Beach, with the shells and bullets still flying, attached to 49th AAA Brigade and ready to begin work securing enemy files and information.[4] It seems that Huber had simply approached the wrong people, and certainly the oversight was swiftly corrected the moment experts such as Mr Child and Major Brown became involved. They were fortunate – and the guilty, eager-to-disappear Nazis correspondingly unfortunate – that Herr Huber neither destroyed the fifty tons of files nor let them deteriorate while in his care.

The MCC, which now took charge of the Nazi Party files, was subordinate to the Office of the Director of Intelligence in Frankfurt. It had a clear if somewhat general objective, to 'exploit German ministerial personnel and documents for the purpose of Military Government'. This meant that not only were German government documents collected here, but also the German government officials who were familiar with them, who were accommodated at Fürstenhagen along with the American troops. It also quickly became apparent that the main purpose of the archiving of the material was to provide evidence against war criminals and information relevant to the purging of German government, industry and society of Nazis.

The Nazi Party records arrived at Fürstenhagen on 25 November, but they did not stay long. MCC was already scheduled to be transferred to Berlin in the new year, and it was now clear that the NSDAP card index was treasure beyond price – most immediately, in its importance for the war crimes trials already taking place in Nuremberg. As a consequence, at Christmas 1945, the entire mass of Nazi Party documents was loaded on to a fifteen-car military train and shipped by rail through the Soviet Zone to the 'Berlin Document Center' that had already been established, in great part to supply the research and legal staff for the war crimes trials, which were based in Berlin. The MCC's Fürstenhagen complex was closed by the beginning of February and the organisation itself subsumed into the Berlin Document Center.

By the beginning of January 1946, Herr Huber's fifty-ton gift to the Allies – their guarantee that no Nazi could deny Party membership – had arrived in Berlin. So nearly turned to pulp at the Nazis' behest, and then so nearly ignored by the victors, this material would be housed, along with SS personnel records captured after the war, largely unsorted ministerial and military documents, and some other Gestapo and Party records that had fallen into American hands, in a complex of buildings on the Wasserkäfersteig, a leafy dead-end road in Grunewald, in the American sector of Berlin. The material was quickly exploited for the war crimes trials, with many documents – to the disgust of professional archivists – ruthlessly extracted and rearranged for forensic rather than archival convenience. But here the records would stay for almost fifty years, the most valuable resource the Allies had in their mission to cleanse post-war Germany of what they, and anti-fascist Germans, saw as the Hitler plague (and of course a boon to historians).

Denazification could continue with some certainty of success. The Allies, not entirely by their own efforts, had in their possession a golden key, the Nazi Party records filling the vaults of the Berlin Document Center. Now, even the most minor and inconspicuous PG (*Parteigenosse*, or Nazi Party comrade) had no place to hide any more.

* * *

Operation Eclipse was a wide-ranging and sophisticated set of plans developed in 1943–4 by COSSAC (Chief of Staff, Supreme Allied Commander), the joint Anglo-American planning command. It deline-ated structures and modes of operation for when the invasion plan that had been launched on 6 June 1944, 'Overlord', was officially concluded and Germany deemed to have surrendered.

'Eclipse' was, in effect, a blueprint for the immediate post-war role of the victorious Anglo-American forces. As such, though it included plans for securing the occupation against a possible threat from Nazi remnants, and arresting Nazi leaders to that end, the document was otherwise politically more or less neutral. Its principal aims were 'first, to ensure that Nazism was thoroughly destroyed and Germany pacified; and, second, to free combat forces as quickly as possible for military operations against Japan'.[5] After this, it was presumed, military govern-ment would give way to civil administration on a four-power basis. Then would come the political part, the beginning of the cleansing of Germany.

So far as political policy in Germany was concerned, the basic decisions were hammered out, first at Yalta in February 1945, and following that – for the US Zone and rather messily – in Washington during the final battles over JCS 1067, the Chiefs of Staffs' instruc-tions to the American Army of Occupation. This latter detailed political and economic plan was formally imposed on Eisenhower by his masters in Washington in April, just weeks before the final victory.

JCS 1067 remained heavily influenced by Morgenthau. It still presupposed mass dismantling of German industry, sweeping elimi-nation, regardless of possible social and economic cost, of all Nazi influence in politics, business and society, and mass arrests and/or investigations of all Germans thought to have been active Nazis. And it clearly foresaw a period of punitive deprivation for the German people as not merely inevitable but just.

It was true that, at least in the first months of the occupation, the Americans, though not the most violent of the Allies, were the most thorough in their pursuit of the principle that became known as 'de-nazification'. This last was a term that had been minted in 1943 by legal planners at the Pentagon, in its first use apparently referring specifically to reform of the future German legal system. However, it soon became a catch-all phrase, covering plans to dismantle the entire Nazi apparatus, arrest and punish its key officials, and systematically eliminate Nazi supporters from the country's political, economic and cultural life.

JCS 1067's stipulations in this regard, though somewhat modified from the draconian Morgenthau template, were still stern enough:

> All members of the Nazi Party who have been more than nominal participants in its activities, all active supporters of Nazism or militarism and all other persons hostile to Allied purposes will be removed and excluded from public office and from positions of importance in quasi-public and private enterprises . . . Persons are to be treated as more than nominal participants in Party activities and as active supporters of Nazism or militarism when they have 1) held office or been otherwise active at any level from local to national in the party and its subordinate organisations or in organisations that further militaristic doctrines, 2) authorised or participated affirmatively in any Nazi crimes, racial persecutions or discriminations, 3) been avowed believers in Nazism or racial or militaristic creeds, or 4) voluntarily given substantial moral or material support or political assistance of any kind to the Nazi Party or Nazi officials and leaders.[6]

Such dismissals were to be enforced without regard to 'administrative necessity, convenience or expediency'.

For this process to be carried out and the guilty individuals to be identified, every adult German would be issued with a 'Questionnaire' (*Fragebogen*). In filling this out, they were to truthfully answer a host of questions about their past history, political affiliation and activities, on the basis of which their status in the new, cleansed, post-war Germany would be established. The problem was the sheer numbers of Germans involved in the Nazi Party and various other Nazi-controlled organisations (including the Labour Front, the Youth Movements and the likes of the National Socialist Welfare, each of which had more than ten million members). A total of forty-five million has been mentioned.[7] If all were to be penalised by loss of jobs, imprisonment and so on – as some advocates within the US Army suggested – then roughly half the population would be effectively stripped of its civil rights and reduced to virtual economic inactivity at a time when the country needed every productive hand and capable, experienced brain it could muster – if only to gain the foreign exchange to buy food, let alone pay off the vast reparations demanded by the victors.

So, what had been decided was this: were the people who filled in these questionnaires 'real' (i.e. active and/or long-time) Nazis who had joined out of conviction? Or so-called *Muss-Nazis* ('must-Nazis') who had joined in order to keep their jobs? Or simply 'fellow travellers' in some shape or form, who had been nominal members out of convenience? The last two categories naturally overlapped and could be hard to distinguish.

One means of beginning to distinguish between the various graduations of political turpitude was the length of time of membership and the date of joining. After Hitler came to power and then secured his dictatorship in the subsequent March 1933 elections, there had been a wave of applications to join the Party (the so-called *Märzgefallenen*), leading rapidly to orders from the Führer that there be a stop on new members, to maintain the Party's allegedly elite character and avoid its being swamped with politically promiscuous careerists. This generalised blackballing edict was relaxed only in 1937. Thus, almost all who had joined before 30 January 1933 (around 1.5 million) could be reckoned as hard-core Nazis, most of the *Märzgefallenen* as opportunists, and many, if not most, of the post-1937 members as passive *Muss-Nazis*.

These were of course distinctions that any open-eyed Soviet citizen or observer of Stalin's Russia would immediately recognise when comparing the composition of the membership of the Communist Party of the Soviet Union, where to belong was also to open up otherwise closed career paths. This may have been why, although the Red Army could come down brutally, even murderously hard on evident war criminals or recognisable 'class enemies', there was a certain laxity when, perhaps, they read the familiar signs of passive careerism in this or that Nazi.

Thus Götz Bergander's father, the distillery chemist and, since the advent of the Soviets, distillery director, had been a member of the Nazi Party, but a wholly passive one. So passive that the son of Dr Bergander's closest friend, and thereby lifelong friend of Bergander junior, expressed complete disbelief sixty years later that the doctor could have been a Nazi. In his late teens at the time, old enough to understand the essentials of political allegiance, and still remembering downright subversive conversations between their two fathers around the wartime dining table, Steffen Cüppers was staggered by the fact that this serious, independent-minded scientist could have ever joined the NSDAP. But he had.[8]

The Russians were naturally aware of Dr Bergander's background, because he had filled in a questionnaire, but several things counted in his favour. First, he had always treated his foreign workers and servants well, and they had informed the Soviet occupiers of this – just as they also picked out those Germans who had not. Second, Dr Bergander had given a job to a local communist activist after he had been released from a concentration camp, an act of generosity that was technically illegal. Once the Russians arrived, this same man became a power not just in the factory but in the politics of the new post-war Dresden. The man vouched for him. Third, the Soviets decided that they needed Dr Bergander, Nazi or not.

Particularly during the early part of the Soviet occupation, when, for all the mayhem, front-line veterans still dictated a more pragmatic tone and local Red Army commanders had considerable independence in decision-making, it seemed to be all about relationships. This seems also to have been true when it came to matters such as the dismantling of factories.

The distillery in Dresden-Friedrichstadt was marked out for dismantling and shipping to Russia. Dr Bergander protested. The staff, many of them loyal old-style trade unionists and communists, also protested. To no avail. Parts of the factory began to be disassembled and stacked (in all weathers) ready for the first shipment. More protests from the German side. And then suddenly, one morning, Dr Bergander was summoned to Soviet HQ. The NKVD seemed to be involved. When, after some hours, he did not reappear, it seemed the doctor and his family's hitherto considerable store of luck had finally run out.

The rest of the family waited in trepidation in their flat next to the distillery as darkness fell. Still no word. Then, as evening began to turn into ominous night, they heard the sound of vehicles. Doors slamming. Shouting. Boots on the stairs. The door burst open. And in walked – or, rather, lurched – Dr Bergander. The normally taciturn chemist was laughing, talking animatedly to his uniformed Russian companions. They streamed into the room after him, chuckling and back-slapping. They were delighted to be there, delighted that they had been able to decide against the dismantling of the distillery, but right now what they needed was another celebratory drink . . .

The family looked on, open-mouthed. No one had ever seen Dr Bergander the worse for drink before. But quickly young Götz was fetching more schnapps (this was, after all, a distillery) and his mother was raiding their sparsely provisioned post-war larder, seeking snacks for their guests. The distillery was saved. The celebrations went on into the night. The often terrifying but always unpredictable Russians had amazed their new subjects once again.[9]

Most cases were much more bureaucratically complicated, and neither was the by no means straightforward question of Nazi Party membership so easily adjudicated as in the case of Dr Bergander. All the same, when it suited any of the occupiers, they could waive the rules for any German they decided they wanted. The Americans, for instance, removed a great many former German rocket scientists – and eventually their families, too – from their homes and places of work around Nordhausen in the Harz Mountains, the great underground V2 production complex known as the *Mittelwerke*, which was overrun by the US Army in April. Within hours, American investigation teams were swarming over the place like termites – albeit in many cases, termites with degrees from MIT and the like, systematically recruited by the Combined Intelligence Objectives Sub-Committee (CIOS) for just such purposes.

Between April and the beginning of July 1945, when the area had to be handed over to the Russians, these teams and their accompanying T-Force units (whose job was to secure the objectives, clear them of possible booby traps and so on, so that the scientists could move in) worked feverishly to strip it of machines, equipment and what was left of its precious product. Everything – every last nut and plate and bolt and wire – was shipped west into the safety of the US Zone. In one eight-day period, 400 tons of equipment was transported to Antwerp, whence it was shipped to New Orleans.[10] And under a highly secretive programme codenamed 'Overcast' – later changed to 'Paperclip' – 765 selected German engineers and scientists who had worked on Hitler's missile programme were magicked away to America without any denazification process at all, as were the sequestered rockets and their spare parts. Partly this was to complete the debriefing process, partly to keep them from the Russians, but in any case America's post-war missile programme was given a good head start.

These compulsory but often by no means unwilling emigrants were not all apolitical boffins. Some, such as Arthur Rudolph, were also directly responsible for abuse of the complex's slave-labour workforce, whose mortality rate was horrendously high. Initially, Rudolph had been designated a '100 percent dangerous Nazi type' and recommended for internment. He was not alone. Conscientious State Department employees – or fanatical 'Morgenthau boys', depending on your point of view – refused to issue entry paperwork and fought a stubborn battle of attrition with parts of the military to refuse the men residence until they had been properly processed, which would have involved sending them back to Germany. The tug of war went on for many months. Finally, after former Chief of Staff General George C. Marshall was appointed Secretary of State at the beginning of 1947, he broke the log jam by simply declaring that in these cases, national security took priority over the imperatives of denazification.[11]

It was not just in the case of Americans that from a (very) early stage new post-war exigencies undermined noble intentions. The Soviets and the British also scooped up what German rocket and weapons scientists they could find, with scant or no regard to these useful men's previous political allegiances.[12] The Soviet equivalent of 'Paperclip' was Operation Osavakim.[13] The Russians have since been accused of mass abduction. In fact, it seems that many German scientists went willingly, attracted by ration and accommodation privileges, not to mention excellent research facilities, and they were on the whole decently treated by the Soviets.[14]

Neither did this greed for German know-how apply only to rocket scientists. In June 1945, American investigators, driving through the French Zone with Otto Ambros, a senior IG Farben scientist whom they had arrested on suspicion of leading key wartime chemical weapons projects and of involvement with the Auschwitz factory, found themselves stopped, questioned and their arrestee whisked away. Ambros was promptly debriefed by the French at IG Farben's Ludwigshafen factory complex, which happened to be situated inside their allotted territory.[15]

The Americans themselves also effectively abducted not just elite German rocket scientists but a great many other technical and scientific experts from the Thuringia/Saxony area during their brief period of occupation between April and July 1945, in order to find out what they knew and to ensure that what valuable knowledge they had did not fall into Soviet hands.

They promised attractive working conditions, scientific books, equipment and instruments, a salary commensurate with my qualifications, and replacement of the personal items I would have to leave behind. I asked for a few days to think it over, but was told by the CIC agent that I would be taken the next day whether I wanted to go or not.[16]

Extravagant promises were made, but by no means all these experts were offered fat contracts and tickets to California; in fact, many were ruthlessly abandoned in the Western zones, far from their former homes and jobs in the East, once the Americans had finished squeezing them for what they knew. Many such 'rejects' were nevertheless not permitted to return home. These unfortunates were held within the Western zones, often unemployed or at least with no job appropriate for their talents, often for some years, under a kind of semi-arrest. One such, a professor at the University of Jena, complained of life in this professional limbo:

> At 3 p.m. my family, my two assistants, and I left Jena. Only when we were underway did I learn that we were going to Heidenheim, where we were interned. None of the promises made to me . . . have been fulfilled. I lost my position, my income, and about 80 percent of my property. All of my furniture and household utensils and a large portion of my library are gone.[17]

Often the aim of such restrictions was to prevent these men from being recruited by the 'other side' – even though the Americans themselves did not want them. And indeed some, once released, drifted back to the East, drawn by the *payoks* (packages of food and goods) offered by the Soviets, which were of a generosity comparable to those of the rocket scientists recruited under Operation Osavakim.

In varying degrees, the attitude of the Allies changed very quickly from one of fairly good mutual cooperation to open competition. This was most clearly, though by no means exclusively, illustrated in the changes in the relations between the Americans and the Russians. Almost from the outset, the denazification process was directly affected. It could only become more so as passions faded and post-war reality impinged on wartime dreams.

The chore of filling out the *Fragebogen* was, for most Germans, just that. Even for those who had been Party members, the worry was not so much that this fact could come to light as whether, when it did, they would be classified as activists. This revelation could bring serious consequences up to and including imprisonment. Then they could be listed as *Mitläufer* (fellow travellers), which would probably mean a fine, and/or temporary restriction of employment prospects or civil rights.

There were, in fact, five possible levels of classification. The levels were usually referred to by their category numbers, descending from completely innocent to absolutely guilty, as follows:

V. Exonerated, or non-incriminated persons (*Entlastete*)
IV. Followers, or Fellow Travellers (*Mitläufer*)
III. Less incriminated (*Minderbelastete*)
II. Activists, Militants, and Profiteers, or Incriminated Persons (*Belastete*)
I. Major Offenders (*Hauptschuldige*)

Categories I and II included those to be subjected to automatic arrest by any Allied forces that encountered them, on the grounds of either criminal involvement or potential danger to the security of the occupation. The Anglo-Americans also had a huge list, put together from various intelligence sources, held at a central point known as CROWCASS (Central Registry of War Criminals and Security Suspects). This was held on a Hollerith IBM card-index machine based in Paris. The idea was that photographs, fingerprints and personal details of suspects could be sent in from internment and POW camps, compared with those on the list and processed, thus ensuring that no guilty men would escape justice. The system was up and running by the end of June 1945. More or less.

Like such systems before and since, CROWCASS immediately ran into technical problems, not least to do with differing electrical systems and frequent power cuts. The American colonel who ran the data operation in Paris wrote plaintively some months later:

The two buildings (less three floors) occupied by CROWCASS are not adequate for anything like maximum efficient operation. Every reasonable effort has been made to obtain the additional three floors in the building at 53 Rue des Maturins. Neither building is well suited for the IBM equipment. The cyclic rate of the electric current available is not correct for the efficient operation of the machines. Also there are long periods when <u>no</u> current is available at all and this condition is expected to last during the remaining winter months.[18]

It quickly transpired that many prison camps, particularly the British ones, were in any case reluctant to participate in the scheme. In any case, given the vast numbers of prisoners of all kinds falling into Anglo-American hands during the final weeks of the war, the sheer quantity of CROWCASS requests arriving at the Paris offices – some 40,000 per day at one point – quickly proved unmanageable. And that even despite the fact that very few camps were bothering to take the prisoners' fingerprints. Moreover, the existence of CROW-CASS as the supposedly omniscient database of evil had the unforeseen, but with hindsight unsurprising, consequence that if a prisoner was not on this (inevitably by no means exhaustive) list, the overworked and inexperienced personnel back in the detention camps would gratefully assume that their prisoner was 'clean' and no further investigation was therefore required.[19]

A few weeks before Christmas, the Director of CROWCASS in Paris reported that 10,000 forms were being processed daily, and:

To date about 500,000 forms have been processed. Approximately 4,000,000 POW forms are on hand. There is a potential number of approximately 7,000,000.

In other words, even if current rates were maintained, on a seven-days-a-week basis, the checks could potentially take more than two more years. Only a vast increase in resources and machines would give them a chance to get through the backlog within some kind of reasonable timescale. As for the fingerprint section, it should simply be closed, he said. They were paying five fingerprint experts aggregate salaries of approximately $660 per month – this not including the pay of the French civilian clerical staff – and their part of the operation took up four floors of the building. 'So far as can be ascertained, no use has been made of this department, and none is foreseen . . .'[20]

It was not surprising, given this level of chaos and misunderstanding, that, at the other end of the process, the innocent could easily suffer and the guilty equally easily go unpunished. In any case, even by the end of 1945, the Allies were far from united in their detailed approach as to who should be prosecuted, for what, and how. In March 1946, discussions between the 'Big Four' in Berlin led to a document with the title 'Disposal of War Criminals, Militarists and Potentially Dangerous Persons'. It listed and categorised at great length the former enemy citizens who should be prosecuted and what the punishments should be. It also set out the principle by which these trials could be conducted by German courts. This was returning just a little bit of German sovereignty – or fobbing off responsibility, depending on how one saw it.

One who saw it as essential either way was John Francis Warre ('Jack') Rathbone. Rathbone, a thirty-six-year-old solicitor, had spent his nights during the war commanding an anti-aircraft battery in London, and reputedly had been recruited into the legal section of the projected British Military Government by an acquaintance he bumped into while strolling along Pall Mall.[21] He was now, as he described it, in all but name the 'Minister of Justice' of the British Zone. As he later explained his decision: 'They [the Germans] had created the mess, and I thought they should clear it up. It would be jolly good for them.'[22]

And all this time, in the British and American zones some 72,000 Germans had been interned under unpleasant, in fact often harsh, conditions, awaiting a decision. It soon became clear that the British, who had always been in favour of punishing the Germans but strangely reluctant to will the means, had no idea what to do.

In April, Brigadier Douglas Heyman, who rejoiced in the title of Deputy Chief Internal Affairs and Communications Division, Control Commission, Germany, met Rathbone in Lübeck. Rathbone convinced him of the feasibility and desirability of having the Germans try their own people. This was made slightly easier by the decision by the Nuremberg judges that the SA, the mass Brownshirt organisation that had been reduced to political impotence by Hitler's purge in June 1934, should not be considered a criminal organisation along with the SS and the like. Junior Party officials, unless suspected of a particular crime, would also be excluded from this category.

This change reduced the number of automatic internees to 27,000. However, having completed his consultations, Heyman seems to have decided that a further 45,000 Party officials not yet in Allied hands and some 200,000 SS and Gestapo agents should also be arrested and prosecuted. This, he said, could be effected by the local British Army Public Safety Officers, responsible for security and liaison with the German police in specific towns and districts. So far as 'persons at large' (i.e. the general population not interned) were concerned, Heyman added blithely that 'the cases . . . will be individually examined and such persons will be provisionally classified by public safety . . .' These officers were already overworked and understaffed. The notion that they would 'provisionally classify' all people in their areas was beyond possibility.[23]

The minutes of a meeting that Rathbone attended in Lübbecke, twenty kilometres or so north of the British Military Government's headquarters at Bad Oeynhausen, on 4 March 1946, shows the perceived impossibility of this kind of search-and-arrest process even before Heyman's fact-finding committee reported. The report of the meeting, which covered the entire British Zone, also shows the gulf in perception between the Americans and the British, less than a year after the war's end. Under 'Surveillance and Investigation', an intelligence officer present informed the meeting that surveillance of category II and III (i.e. the two levels of definite incrimination) raised 'no particular problem'. However,

Investigation was a far more difficult question, and it would be impossible for the machinery of Kreis* Tribunals to deal with the number of cases envisaged by the Americans, which would approximate to 20,000 per Kreis. It was considered that something in the region of 1,000 to 2,000 per Kreis was the largest number that was practicable.[24]

Heyman's report, drafted six weeks later, supposed not that an average 10 per cent of the population in each averagely 200,000-strong *Kreis* (American supposed figure) or 1–2 per cent (British figure) but *all* civilians would be investigated. His idea was even more of a fantasy than it at first appeared.

Well before this time, the British occupiers were being forced to make compromises. Thus in October 1945 it was agreed by the zone-wide Standing Committee on denazification that '50% of the total number of appointees to the Legal Civil Service in any one *Oberlandesgericht*† District could be nominal Nazis' and noted that 'This concession in fact prevented a complete breakdown in the German Legal Administration'. Given that at its height the *Nationalsozialistischer Rechtswahrerbund* (National Socialist Lawyers' Organisation) had 100,000 members – 90 per cent of the legal profession – this was hardly surprising. And it didn't, in any case, solve the problem. Six months later it was further proposed that, due to continuing shortages and serious backlogs in legal proceedings of all kinds, German law students passing their final examination (*Assessorprüfung*) should be admitted to the Legal Civil Service 'regardless of the 50% restriction . . . provided they could prove that they were not more than nominal members of the Nazi Party'.[25]

The report carried a strong whiff of typical British pragmatism – or hypocrisy.

---

* *Kreis* = District in German. An administrative area between state (*Land*) and community level. In modern Germany there are around 420 of these for a population of 81,000,000, urban and rural, giving an average of slightly less than 200,000 per *Kreis*.
† *Oberlandesgericht* = Higher Regional Court.

At this point, the Americans, even their eminently practical Deputy Governor, General Clay, were still appalled at what they clearly regarded in the latter light. Missionary zeal was still widespread down in southern and south-western Germany, where the American Military Government's writ ran.

Clay himself spent a great deal of late 1945 to early 1946 cancelling exemptions for the likes of railwaymen who had been members of the Nazi Party. He also decided to disenfranchise Nazi Party members when it came to the *Kreis* elections planned for 1946, the American Zone's first, tentative stab at post-war German democracy. In doing this, he ignored both his own advisory committee and the State Department, both of which wanted to exclude from the voting rolls only those Nazis in the 'automatic arrest' category, leaving the vast majority of the so-called 'fellow travellers' or *Muss-Nazis*, while still liable to economic and financial penalties, with full civil rights.[26]

One major problem for the Americans was the pressure both from their own soldiers and from the families they had left behind in the United States to 'bring the boys home'. US forces were supposed to be withdrawn within two years of the end of the war. Wives of absent GIs were organising 'Bring Back Daddy!' clubs that sent baby shoes to congressmen to encourage speeding up the demobilisation process. Where the British faced return to an austerity-racked, pinched home-land where employment prospects might be uncertain – meaning that the relatively well-provisioned life of an official of the British 'Raj' in occupied Germany could appear attractive – their American counterparts had, in general, every incentive, including the generous set of benefits awarded under the GI Bill, to get themselves demobi-lised as quickly as humanly possible. By early 1946, as part of Operation Magic Carpet, a total of around 4.75 million GIs and their officers had been repatriated from the European Theatre of Operations alone by the US War Shipping Administration.

Washington began to panic about the situation in the occupied areas of Europe, including Germany. There were no plans at this point to keep American forces in Europe indefinitely, but the government did try to stem the flow of returnees by extending the tour of duty for '50-pointers'* for at least another three months. There were even attempts to continue imposing the draft on American males, though this later failed in Congress. The slowdown in demobilisation was announced in the US Army newspaper, *Stars and Stripes*, without any reason being given. The result was protests, strikes, even riots, both at home in the USA and in the places where American soldiers were stationed, from the Philippines and Japan to the United Kingdom and Germany.

In Paris, on 7 January 1946, 1,000 '50-pointers', scheduled to be kept on in the forces beyond their assumed demobilisation date, staged a protest meeting, and two days later 4,000 marched on army headquarters in Frankfurt to take their grievance to General McNarney. McNarney was absent attending a Control Council meeting in Berlin. All the same, on 15 January the War Department announced a revised schedule geared to getting all 45-pointers and above home and discharged by April 1946. This meant that by the summer the entirety of the American forces in Europe (USFET) would amount to barely a quarter of a million, and by the end of the year would fall to 200,000 – one-twenty-fifth of its strength when the occupation had begun.

The replacements sent to Europe were mostly unskilled and to a large extent untrained. In November and December 1945, 95 per cent of requisitions had been for men with technical specialities. Of those who arrived, only 13 per cent actually had such qualifications. Beginning in January, replacements shipped out for Europe after eight weeks of training, which was more or less limited to qualification with the M-1 rifle, personal hygiene and sanitation, and 'orientation for occupation duty with emphasis on discipline'.

In the first week of March, after a tour of parts of eastern France and Germany, the army's inspector general reported:

---

* The demobilisation process depended on a system of 'points', which were awarded for length of service, length of overseas duty, number of children, decorations and citations earned by men and their units, etc. Generally, a total of eighty-five guaranteed a man his return to civilian life.

Discipline is generally poor and at this time is below desirable standards. Definite responsibility for maintaining discipline where troops
of various arms and services are stationed has not been satisfactorily
established. Incident to the shortage of personnel, the majority of
replacements are not receiving additional disciplinary basic training
as expected. Many young officers command important installations
and units. Numbers of these have not had sufficient training to carry
out their administrative responsibility. Similarly, there are many
untrained non-commissioned officers.[27]

And with this human material, Clay was supposed to process
millions of *Fragebogen* and ascertain the denazification status of the
respondents, who were filling out the forms in German, which the
overwhelming majority of American troops had little or no knowledge
of? A vast exercise in political and social engineering, affecting more
than five million individual human beings, and carried out entirely
by foreigners?

In fact, the American military managed in 1945–6 to review almost
1,600,000 *Fragebogen*. There were five possible categories of result
from each review: in the most serious cases, mandatory removal; next
in seriousness, discretionary removal with an adverse recommendation; next, discretionary removal with a positive recommendation;
next, non-Nazi; and most desirable of all, anti-Nazi.

This huge and complicated process resulted in the dismissal of
374,000 certified Nazis from their posts.[28] They were to be permitted
only to do 'simple work'. At the end of 1945, with the entire process
still under direct American control, 90,000 of those considered especially dangerous were still held in civilian internment camps awaiting
processing, with another 25,000 picked out as dangerous Nazis or
major militarists from among the POWs and accordingly put into
separate custody, giving some 115,000 individuals detained in the
American Zone as a whole.[29]

This still left, however, some 3.5 million known Nazis waiting to
be classified. In many cases these tainted individuals were unable to

work or reintegrate into society until this was done. They were often respected figures in their communities – business people, farmers, doctors, lawyers, teachers. And they were arguably the backbone of the country, indispensable to its recovery.

Malnutrition was now widespread throughout Germany, energy and sanitation services were still unrepaired in many urban areas affected by wartime bombing and ground fighting, hundreds of thousands of buildings were still in ruins, and the threat, because of these factors, of epidemics and diseases of all kinds was ever present.

Many Americans had started out with missionary intentions. They would punish the Germans, but then they would reform them, turn them into good democrats. Now, like a host of occupiers before and since, these once-optimistic soldier-reformers were starting to think they might just settle for crowd control.

Realising that, for all his determination to cleanse the American Zone of Nazis, he would soon have neither the quantity nor the quality of manpower to achieve this through American personnel alone, at the end of November 1945 General Clay had done what many decision-makers do when a tough decision presents itself – he had appointed a commission.

The 'Denazification Policy Board' began considering the possibilities through that first post-war winter, and especially consulting with the appointed German officials of the three *Länder*, or states, that made up the American Zone: Bavaria, Hesse and Württemburg-Baden.

Wilhelm Hoegner, the appointed Bavarian Premier, was a fifty-eight-year-old former Social Democrat Reichstag deputy, a lawyer who had spent the war in Switzerland. His denazification expert was a communist by the name of Heinrich Schmitt, who had spent ten years in jail during the Nazi time. Hoegner thought that the fervently anti-Nazi Schmitt might act as a counterbalance in Bavaria, with its reputation as a stronghold of the nationalist right. It was a bold move. Schmitt was reliably anti-Nazi but too left wing for many Bavarians, and also some Americans. Nevertheless, along with their colleagues from Hesse and Württemberg-Baden, these appointed post-Nazi officials put together a law that effected some compromises between German interests and concerns and the still-dominant punitive intentions of the 'Removal from Office and from Positions of Responsibility of Nazis and of Persons Hostile to Allied Purposes' directive that the four-power Control Council had promulgated in January 1946.

As a result of these consultations, in March 1946, the 'Law for Liberation from National Socialism and Militarism' followed, drafted by officials of the Office of Military Governor US Zone (OMGUS) but processed through the nascent German political organs, who thus took co-responsibility.

The 'Liberation Law', as it was known (*Befreiungsgesetz*), was the first to provide a framework for the Germans themselves to cleanse their own body politic. It took upon itself the right to speak in the name of the German people in proclaiming its aim:

(1) To liberate our people from National Socialism and Militarism, and to secure a lasting base for German democratic national life in peace with the world, all those who have actively supported the National Socialist tyranny, or are guilty of having violated the principles of justice and humanity, or of having selfishly exploited the conditions thus created, shall be excluded from influence in public, economic and cultural life and shall be bound to make reparations.

(2) Everyone who is responsible shall be called to account. At the same time he shall be afforded opportunity to vindicate himself.

Clay was aware that this handover to the Germans was necessary for hard-headedly practical reasons. He also knew that, when it came, it would attract attention at home, and not necessarily of a positive nature. This was clear from the transcript of a frank phone call with General John H. Hilldring, who had been head of civil affairs under him but had just been appointed Assistant Secretary of State for Occupied Areas:

CLAY: You will find that we will get a tremendous amount of abuse from those of us that will say that we are turning back responsibilities to the Germans too quickly. Actually, if you gave me 10,000 people over here, I couldn't do that job. With 10,000 people I couldn't do the job of denazification. It's got to be done by the Germans.

HILLDRING: Yes.

CLAY: This is a good law and I am going to approve it over here, and specifically not send it back to you because I'm going to take the responsibility for it myself.

HILLDRING: Yes, OK.

CLAY: But I just want to warn you on it because it will hit the press on the 5th of March and I want you to know about it.

HILLDRING: Yes.

There was another hidden problem here. A large number of the US Army's best denazifiers in Germany, and its most suitable administrators – given their knowledge and language skills – were German Jews. Many of them had left Germany after the Nazis came to power, and then returned with the conquering forces.

To many Germans such émigré Jews were near-mythical beings, inspiring fascination yet at the same time somehow especially resented and feared. During the war, fantasy tales had abounded in the Reich of these émigrés acting as guides to the Anglo-American bomber fleets, often directing the deadly aircraft to the towns and cities where they had grown up and been persecuted because of their race.[30]

Now that these exiles were returning in foreign uniforms to their native Germany or Austria, they were assumed by many of their one-time compatriots to be highly vengeful, and, moreover, likely to favour the Jewish survivors, whether German-Jewish or DPs, over native Germans. This strange mixture of communal guilt and residual anti-Semitism seems to have been widespread among a German population still conditioned by Nazi ideology but nonetheless striving to adapt to a new, post-Hitler world where they were the villains and not the heroes.

Nor was this suspicious attitude confined to Germans. The more or less oblique criticisms from Secretaries Stimson and Hull, centring on Morgenthau's Jewish identity, that had greeted his plan for post-war Germany, were reflected in the American and British armies on the ground in occupied Germany. Here, both the genteel and the less subtle kinds of anti-Semitism were not uncommon. Professional soldiers were and remain most commonly conservative in their social and political inclinations. The keenest denazifiers, the 'Morgenthau boys' or 'Chaos boys' as disapproving comrades called them – including Saul Padover in the early days in Aachen – were Roosevelt's New Dealers in uniform, and many of them, again like Padover, Jewish New Dealers at that.

In fact, American denazification policy itself had been influenced by the 'Frankfurt School' of exiled German leftists, a group who were mostly but not exclusively Jewish. One major architect of the policy was the Marxist political scientist Franz Neumann, along with his colleague Herbert Marcuse, both adherents of the Frankfurt School, who were recruited to the Office of Strategic Services (predecessor to the CIA) to consider the internal situation in Germany during the war years and come up with ideas.

Neumann, author of an influential Marxist analysis of the National Socialist state, *Behemoth*, and Marcuse (who twenty years later would become a guru of the 1960s 'New Left') saw Nazism not as a 'top down' power structure foisted on the passive populace by an elite of relatively few charismatic individuals, with Hitler at its apex, but as a more diffuse, virus-like phenomenon that had spread widely throughout various sectors of society, including the military, industry, bureaucracy and so on. This made it, in a way, more difficult to deal with and post-war Germany harder to change. Just getting rid of the Nazi leaders who had, according to the opposite theory, dictated to and corrupted the German people, would not suffice to eliminate the ideology. Root and branch work, delving into every corner of the country, every aspect of German life, was the answer. Denazification, New Left style. The aim: to purify Germany through revolutionary inquisition. Or, as one German commentator put it, 'the Nuremberg of the common man'.[31]

There was, of course, a great deal of common-sense opposition within the American military to these extreme forms of denazification, which would have involved the imprisonment, perhaps indefinitely, of hundreds of thousands of Germans, but sometimes this reluctance was clearly tinged with anti-Semitism. This could take on grotesque forms.

The brilliant but unbalanced American General George S. Patton, as military governor of Bavaria in 1945, rapidly began talking of another war against the 'Mongol savages' of Russia and soft-pedalled denazification to the best of his ability. 'What we are doing,' Patton wrote to his wife, 'is to utterly destroy the only semi-modern state in Europe so that Russia can swallow the whole.'[32] He especially expressed his loathing for the DPs, who were still present in the occupied zones in their hundreds of thousands and were undoubtedly causing political and public-order problems.

After the former Dean of the University of Pennsylvania and United States Commissioner of Immigration, Earl G. Harrison, toured the DP camps, often former concentration camps, in the summer of 1945, he reported back unfavourably to the President at the end of August, saying that 'as matters now stand, we appear to be treating the Jews as the Nazis treated them except that we do not exterminate them'. The defeated Germans, Harrison added, might even suppose from this that 'we are following or at least condoning Nazi policy'.[33] He also recommended that Jewish DPs be allowed to emigrate to Palestine, although since that country was under British mandate, and the British were keeping Palestine firmly closed to Jews, his suggestion had no immediate force.

Patton wrote in his diary, just after the publication of Harrison's report:

Harrison and his ilk believe that the displaced person is a human being, which he is not, and this applies particularly to the Jews, who are lower than animals.[34]

When, after further ill-advised remarks about the defeated Nazis being just like members of an American party who had lost an election, Patton found himself faced with Eisenhower's disapproval, he remarked in a letter to his wife in October 1945 that 'The noise against me is only the means by which the Jews and Communists are attempting . . . to implement a further dismemberment of Germany'.[35]

Shortly after this incident, Patton was dismissed from his post as governor. He had not much longer to live. The General died from injuries sustained in a traffic accident while on a hunting trip in Bavaria a few days before Christmas 1945. He was not, however, alone in taking a negative view of DPs in general and Jews in particular. They were, to many occupation officials, an irritation and a threat, who suffered by comparison with the apparently meek and law-abiding Germans. As a representative of a Jewish children's charity wrote:

If one can understand, though deplore that fact, that the American soldiers prefer the company of German men and women, clean, healthy, well dressed, to that of the D.P., dirty, destitute, in frayed garments, and torn shoes, we must, however infer that the attitude of the responsible officers, benevolent and sometimes even – horribile dictu – obsequious towards the Germans, but impatient, severe, incomprehensible, intolerant and often hostile towards the religious and political victims of these last – is due to the anti-democratic and pro-fascist mentality of many responsible commanders and their subordinates.[36]

This problem remained largely undiscussed, at least in public, but it did not go away. Former President Hoover's adviser on press and relations with the Military Government in Germany, Frank E. Mason, returned early in 1947 to Washington and spoke with, among others, General Eisenhower, who was now Chief of Staff. Shortly after, Eisenhower wrote to Clay about his conversations with Mason, who had told him:

. . . that many of our civilians are German-speaking people of a rather undesirable type. Among other things they say that many of these people have been citizens of the United States for only two or three years and are using their present positions either to communise Germany or to indulge in vengeance. One very conservative man recommended that we should allow no one to be in our Military Government unless he has been a citizen . . . for at least ten years.[37]

The coded message seems to have been read and understood. On 7 April Clay gave secret instructions to reduce the number of German-born refugees in the employ of the American Military Government. His deputy, General Frank L. Keating, sent out a 'highly confidential' memorandum to the effect that Clay had 'decided we shall not employ anyone or renew the contract of anyone who has been naturalized since 1933'. Even where special technical expertise was required, 'we should try to find a way out'. In carrying out this instruction, Keating continued, officers must 'refrain from general discussion of the subject or issuance of any orders. It is not necessary for us to indicate why we do not intend to rehire anyone [but] see that diplomacy is used in handling each case.' The document in the file was later marked 'recalled' but a sudden wave of dismissals among AMG officials of a certain background ensued.

In the British Zone, too, and in the British sector of Berlin, there were worries in certain circles about 'over-zealousness' on the part of Jewish officers and men of the Military Government. George Clare, a Jew who had left Vienna at the time of the *Anschluss*, was now, eight years later, a British Army officer involved in denazifying the cultural sphere in Berlin and Hamburg, with special attention to press and radio. One day in 1946, Clare was called into his superior's office. Major Sely discussed Clare's new role – the young man had just been in London on a course and getting his British naturalisation papers – and then unlocked his desk and handed him a letter he had been keeping safe for this moment. Clare read it carefully and recalled later:

Addressed to Colonel Edwards, Deputy Chief of PR/ISC,* it was
from Public Safety, the CCG's police division. Couched in somewhat
more diplomatic language than my summary of it, its author, a Public
Safety Commander, accused our section of denazifying with – in his
words – 'excessive zeal'. Was PR/ISC Group aware of this, he enquired,
or – and there was the sting – the fact that the officer in charge, a
Major Sely, his Hamburg representative, a Mr Felix, as well as his
man in Hanover, one Staff-Sergeant Ormond, were all of German-
Jewish extraction, which might well incline them to act in a spirit of
revenge? Did PR/ISC consider it advisable that such a delicate task
should be entrusted to people of such background?[38]

Clare asked Sely if he should therefore pack his bags and take the
next train back to London.

The major laughed. No, Colonel Edwards, a fiery Welshman, had
already sorted out the 'bloody ignorant jumped-up bobbies', telling
them that he chose his own staff and they had his full confidence. 'And
since,' Sely added, quoting their boss, 'they had his full confidence he
had to refute the Commander's aspersions on their integrity with the
same determination with which Public Safety had refuted reports that
it allowed former Gestapo officers to seep back into the German police.'

Apparently, no more was heard from Public Safety on this issue.

---

* PR/ISC = Public Relations/Information Services Control.

11

Persil Washes White

The determined denazifiers were lucky in one sense. Unlike Patton, the otherwise conservative General Clay held on to his conviction that a political purge of the occupied areas was a necessity.

Clay believed in business, he wanted to modify JCS 1067 as much as he decently could so that Germany and its industries could pay their keep, and he was decidedly in favour of a capitalist post-war Germany. All the same, he also felt strongly about cleansing the political Augean stables in the zone as thoroughly – but also as quickly – as possible so that the country could genuinely move on to a democratic as well as a more prosperous future.

That much of the policy carried out by the AMG and its officials in the summer and autumn after the victory was very tough is hard to deny. There were officers, like Patton, who sympathised with the Germans (though perhaps not in quite such extreme terms), disliked the DPs (sometimes with good day-to-day reasons) and thought that denazification was paving the way for communism. There were equally many, if not more, who believed passionately in the most thorough-going of purges.

Certainly, the effects of investigation by the AMG's denazification teams could be devastating so far as incriminated individual Germans and their families were concerned. From the substantial town of Kempten in Allgäu, south-western Bavaria, AMG officials reported:

1. On 31 Oct 45, Dr Bernhard Wagner, former city treasurer, and his wife and child attempted triple suicide. Morphine had been taken by all three but the dose was lethal to the child only. Since the morphine failed to kill, Frau Wagner opened the veins on Dr Wagner's wrist. He died the next day in hospital. Frau Wagner is recovering and will be tried for attempting suicide and murder.

2. The suicide was evidently caused by the removal of Dr Wagner from his position and his imminent re-arrest by CIC. He had returned only a few days before from several weeks in an internment camp having been taken into custody by CIC as a mandatory arrest. The day before the suicide, he had been summoned by CIC for another interview and as a result he evidently assumed that he would be interned once more.[1]

By the end of the winter, more than 42 per cent of public officials had been summarily dismissed by the occupation forces. It was all very well cleansing the Augean stables, but who was going to run them once they were cleansed?

With political parties for Germans now licensed at local level, and communal elections set for January 1946, so far as general attitudes in Bavaria regarding denazification were concerned, American intelligence led with several examples chosen to typify different views in the *Land*:

a. Among small and humble Nazis the reaction is mainly one of anxiety and fear. A railway switchman, for example fears that he may lose his job and his home, and reports, in a manner inimitably Bavarian: 'Ich will meine Ruhe haben' [I want my peace]. He now sympathises, he says, with the Social Democrats, and hopes to see Germany rebuilt.

b. A middle-aged working woman, wife of a PG [*Parteigenosse*, or Nazi Party member], and a refugee from the Sudetenland, plaintively asks: 'How did we earn this? We always tried to do the right thing and didn't know the party was so bad'.

c. More spirited Nazis are beset by similar fears, but do not deny their principles. 'The Americans are seeking to destroy Germany,' says a female high-school teacher bitterly, 'and this is one of their techniques of doing it'. A former Nazi official says: 'Yes, we are guilty of being Nazis and must suffer for it'. A former Professor of the alleged science of Rassenkunde [literally: racial lore] warns that the purge will produce an intelligent proletariat which will be communistically inclined and which will prove a menace.[2]

The resentment and fear of the power of the AMG was not necessarily combined with a desire by Germans at this point to rule themselves. In fact, another report, from Friedberg, a suburb of the city of Augsburg, stated:

There is frequent comment concerning the handing over of the civil administration from the Military Government to the civilians [that] is being made soon. One comment is that the American authorities are not interested enough in the affairs of their occupation zone and want to release themselves of the burden of responsibility as soon as possible. It is noticed that the semi-step of self-government is being taken only by the American forces.[3]

It seemed that, in the eyes of the defeated, the occupiers could not win. The catch was, of course, that without structured German involvement, governing the zone except on the most basic level would be impossible. Similarly, if the Americans persisted in pursuing denazification alone, the process would take several years, perhaps even longer, and would, moreover, always be seen as an alien imposition.

As we have seen, millions of American troops had already been repatriated and demobilised. Final American withdrawal from Europe was still planned for 1947. German self-denazification was therefore convenient, even essential, for the American occupiers, but it was also consciously part of democratisation. The Soviets had been the first to set up (appointed) German-run *Land* governments in their zone in July 1945. The Americans were acutely aware of invidious comparisons, should they – the world's democratic paragons – delay the transition to German self-rule in their own zone.

The Soviets were also the first to allow the formation of post-war political parties. The Communist Party (KPD) was officially refounded in Russian-controlled Berlin a little more than a month after the end of the war, followed rapidly by the Social Democratic Party (SPD), then a Christian Conservative Party (the Christian Democratic Union = CDU) and a Liberal Party (Liberal Democratic Party of Germany = LDPD). However, the uniquely close relationship between the Russians and their ready-made German communist allies – many of whom had returned after years of exile in the USSR – assured the KPD of a crucial, though not yet openly dominant role. The rapid consolidation of the parties in the Soviet Zone into the 'Unity Front of Anti-Fascist Democratic Parties' was early evidence of this covert control. On 9 July, the Russians instituted five provinces, or *Länder*, and appointed German officials to head them. In October, the German authorities were supposedly given 'full powers'.

The US authorities followed piecemeal with their own appointed *Land* governments – in Bavaria, Greater Hessen and Württemberg-Baden – composed of supposedly 'clean' German politicians (mostly from the pre-Hitler period) and officials. These bodies also made up a *Länderrat* (Council of *Länder*), constituted under American supervision at a conference in Stuttgart on 17 October. The council's task was to liaise with and take instructions from the occupiers on a zone-wide level, though General Clay emphasised in his speech to the founding conference that the Germans should assume responsibility for their own government as soon as possible, and that the establishment of a free press and broadcasting system were also a high priority.[4]

Political parties were permitted, though at first only on a district basis and subject to a licensing procedure to ensure their democratic credentials. Within three months of that, the military administration had begun the process of holding free elections on the American model, the first of the occupiers to do so. Parties on a *Land* level were allowed from January. Organisation on zone level had to wait.

That the Americans took the lead in the race to give post-war Germans the chance to vote freely was hardly surprising, given the almost religious importance the US placed on democracy, but the speed with which the AMG did so was impressive.

In January 1946, elections took place on a village level, in April on the *Kreis* level and in May for city councils. Finally, in June there followed elections to constitutional conventions for each of the *Länder*. It was a consciously decentralised model. Like the individual American states, the *Länder* were to have the right to promulgate their own laws and define their own governmental systems. Referenda on these *Land* constitutions, combined with legislative elections, would take place at the end of the year.

The plans for German self-denazification ran parallel with these political developments. Democratisation and denazification were intimately connected imperatives. One legitimised the other – certainly as far as the outside world was concerned, and hopefully, the occupiers thought, so far as the average German in the American Zone was concerned, too.

The permanence and legitimacy of these developing institutions had now to be clearly established. When the Germanised version of the 'Law for the Liberation from National Socialism and Militarism' – drafted by the AMG's lawyers under consultation with German colleagues – was approved by the *Land* premiers on 5 March 1946, the signature ceremony was symbolically located in the metropolis that had been the birthplace of Nazism and Hitler's favourite city: Munich. Each of the three state governments now acquired a Minister for Denazification. Under him extended a network of 545 denazification tribunals (*Spruchkammern*), organised at *Kreis* level, and with a total German staff for the entire system of around 22,000. Each of these thousands of officials was implausibly supposed to have been thoroughly vetted by the US Army Special Branch.

The highly unpopular *Fragebogen* (literally: question sheet) was now renamed a *Meldebogen* (report sheet). The tribunals could classify their subjects as major offenders, offenders, lesser offenders, fellow travellers – or as exonerated of all involvement. Oversight would still be exercised by Military Government officers at a regional level, but the local Germans were indeed allowed a lot of freedom – more than in any other zone.

There were also some concessions on principle. It was now assumed that only around a quarter of Germans in the zone counted as contaminated.[5] The possibility was also conceded, for the first time in the post-war period, that denazification should be about rehabilitation, not just punishment. While any German who had 'contributed to the development or support of National Socialism or militarism' would be 'called to account', he would also be given the opportunity to vindicate himself on the basis of a 'just consideration of his individual responsibility and his actual conduct, taken as a whole'.[6] This was either a masterstroke of sensitive humanitarianism or a licence to acquit. Only time, and the tendencies of individual tribunals, would tell which.

Things were made easier for the tribunals, as the year went on, by the exemption of Party members born after 1919 (unless they had committed serious crimes), who were considered to have been subjected to brainwashing, and to disabled veterans. A reasonable and humane exemption, preserving many genuinely devastated lives from further misery, this nevertheless represented a useful loophole for the truly guilty.

So the new-model denazification took off, a little slowly at first. There were all kinds of problems. These included shortages of office space, of office furniture and equipment and, significantly, of professional qualified and educated staff. Many otherwise suitable candidates were tainted by Party membership and could not join the tribunal system until they had themselves been cleared. Since each tribunal had, according to the law, to be headed by a qualified judge, the Americans immediately ran into exactly the same problem as the British – the difficulty, given sky-high rates of Nazi Party membership among lawyers, of finding 'untainted' law officers.

The tribunal process was not technically a legal proceeding, though it involved a prosecutor, an accused, a defender and a jury (the tribunal, or *Spruchkammer*, itself) and could take place in public with all the adversarial trappings of a 'trial'. The difference was that tribunals technically decided 'responsibility', not guilt – a concession to the Germans who objected to *ex post facto* laws being applied.[7] However, by no means all cases got so far. The flood of business would simply have overwhelmed the system, which even as things stood was stretched up to and beyond its limits. It was generally only when the prosecutor decided to charge a former Nazi in one of the serious categories that a hearing was necessary. This could be held in public, if based on oral evidence, or in private if based on written evidence. The tribunals decided in secret by a majority vote. In fact, in the first five months after they were set up, of 583,985 cases that came before the tribunals, 530,907 were dealt with without the necessity of a trial. So less than 10 per cent went to public hearings.[8]

Perhaps it was inevitable that Germanised denazification would run into so many problems right from the start, and grow worse as the process rolled out. In the early months of the occupation, the opponents of Nazism had been able to expect that, if they could gain the support of local American military officials – particularly public safety officers – they could bring about some changes in their communities and make sure that at least some of the guilty were punished for what they had inflicted on their fellow citizens and the wider world between 1933 and 1945.

In Bavaria, there was a period even after the 'Germanisation' of the process where the appointment of a communist, Heinrich Schmitt, as minister promised to turn denazification into a genuinely radical process. But Schmitt, though efficient and incorruptible, operated in an openly political way, which disturbed many both among the populace and within the Military Government. He was also openly radical in his goals, an unabashed social engineer. Schmitt believed strongly that it would only improve society if former Nazi big shots were forced to slide down to unskilled labourer level – the result of being found guilty of activism and banned from government service and the professions. This would act as a warning to others, a case of elementary social justice, and give an opportunity for decent, untainted Germans with hitherto limited life chances to climb the post-war social ladder.

Schmitt did not last long in his post. American intelligence investigated his department and found he was stuffing it with fellow communists. With elections now taking place, Bavaria's post-war conservative party, the Christian Social Union (CSU) – founded from a collection of old Catholic Centre Party members, veterans of the pre-war Bavarian People's Party and former Nazis – was gathering a dominant political momentum, and also flexing its muscle. In May, Schmitt's ministry was purged. In June, Schmitt himself was forced out, despite the personal respect in which he was held by Major Walter Louis Dorn, the American history professor who had spent the war years with the CIA's predecessor, OSS, and was adviser on denazification first to Eisenhower and then to Clay. Schmitt, Dorn admitted, was simply too controversial and was seen as a barrier to wider public acceptance of the programme.[9]

The new minister, Anton Pfeiffer, was a pre-war Catholic politician of the familiar anti-Nazi but strongly nationalistic and socially conservative type. A member of the CSU, 'untainted' Pfeiffer may have been, but like the CSU itself he disliked the denazification law they had been forced to accept, seeing it as little more than victors' justice, and did his best to render it all but ineffective. He insisted to his American overseers that only 30,000 Nazis in Bavaria belonged to categories I and II, and snubbed tribunals run by leftists.

While Pfeiffer was minister (until December 1946), the tribunals reclassified at least 60 per cent of senior Nazis, often only fining them, and reinstated more than 75 per cent of the officials formerly dismissed by the Americans. It got so bad, from the Americans' point of view, that in October Premier Hoegner had to be warned to report improper behaviour by the tribunals to the US authorities.

The fact was, Germanised denazification rapidly descended into a farce, and not just in Bavaria, as Clay himself was forced to admit.

Nazis, often comfortably situated and able to hire clever lawyers to represent them at the hearings, ran rings around the untrained and often relatively uneducated members of the tribunals. A torrent of denazification certificates – popularly known as *Persilscheine* ('Persil certificates' – after the well-known detergent produced by Henkel & Co., which naturally washed white) – descended on the guilty in Bavaria and elsewhere in the American Zone. The tribunals, hated as they were in many circles, in fact proved so forgiving that they were known satirically as 'follower factories', producing from once-rabid Nazis hundreds of thousands of mere political passengers of convenience or compulsion who were deemed worthy of the mildest punishments.

There was evidence, as American intelligence realised from censoring letters sent abroad from the zone, as well as listening in on phone calls, that the tribunals were in many cases not only incompetent and politically lax, but corrupt. CIC Region IV Munich reported in August 1946: 'Censored letters make clear the existence of a black market in securing statements of innocence for former Nazis; dozens of intercepted communications seem to indicate that Nazis trade endorsements of their guiltlessness and mutually certify to their anti-Nazi attitude and anti-Nazi activities in the past.'[10] The report continued damningly, in a snapshot of the bleak situation in the tribunals and a Bavarian government machine that was rapidly becoming a tool of the conservative-nationalist CSU:

Letters from smaller communities seem to indicate that the CSU very commonly gives aid and comfort to former [Nazi] party members. In several letters the CSU is called the CNSU, i.e. the Christian National Socialist Union. Many communications complain that former Nazis still occupy leading positions in Bavaria. Letters from returned Prisoners of War, who have participated in re-education courses as, e.g. Ft Mead in the United States, express disappointment with the Bavarian political situation and a feeling of hopelessness that PW's returning from America, indoctrinated in American democracy, are not utilised or employed by Military Government.[11]

Within months of the end of the war, denazification, initially quite popular among the disillusioned and angry German masses, had lost a lot of public support. In the early days, almost everyone rejoiced at the humiliation of former Nazi big shots, known as 'golden pheasants' for their ornate uniforms and lavish lifestyles. Now, leftists thought the purge didn't go far enough, Nazis hated it for understandable reasons and non-Nazi conservatives came to see it as just another otherwise pointless ruse by the control-mad occupiers to 'keep Germany down'.

Half-starved, largely unemployed, seemingly with few prospects and looked down upon by the foreign bringers of 'freedom', ordinary Germans soon began to see themselves as victims and to reject the notion of indiscriminate 'collective guilt' that they saw as lying at the heart of denazification.

It was this problem – the awareness that if one has 'collective guilt' then there is for the individual often no guilt – that led the Austrian-born liberal journalist Hans Habe, who had returned from exile as a GI in 1945 and almost immediately became the editor of the American-licensed German-language newspaper in Munich, to observe that 'in fact, if the Germans were collectively guilty, we should have concealed it from them'. Habe was sceptical about the effectiveness of denazification in the form it took. The defensive reaction that it gave rise to would not produce genuine reflection and readiness for re-education on the part of the German people.[12] The writer and political scientist Eugen Kogon, a devout Catholic who had spent six years in Buchenwald for his opposition to the Nazis, observed that the Allied mission to cleanse and re-educate the Germans was starting to have the opposite effect:

Because of the awful clamour around it and because of its own blindness, they [the German people] wanted to hear nothing of self-examination. The voice of their conscience did not awaken.

American polling in their zone saw approval of denazification slip from 54 per cent in early 1946 to 32 per cent in 1947. It would reach its lowest level in 1949 at 17 per cent.[13]

Denazification was especially unloved in conservative, inward-looking rural communities, in essence for quite primitive, unpolitical reasons. There respected and trusted local figures were often among the accused, and community solidarity often – in fact usually – trumped the demands of a political justice that few locals, whether Nazi supporters or not, recognised. The doctor, the teacher, the policeman or the agricultural merchant may have been Nazis, but they were the people villagers relied on. To have them removed from such crucial positions in the community by a bunch of opportunists and/or unpatriotic German troublemakers – as rural folk often viewed the denazification tribunals – caused deep resentment.

In many parts of the American Zone, those who served the denazification tribunal were treated as social lepers. It was therefore hardly surprising – especially given the shortage of lawyers and officials untainted by Nazi pasts – that there were serious shortages of qualified personnel; in fact, of any personnel at all. An American Special Branch report from October 1946 on the *Spruchkammer* at Steinach, a small town about an hour's drive west of Nuremberg, summed up one particular tragicomic case:

> The Spruchkammer of this Landkreis is one of the most incompetent Spruchkammern in the entire Land. The chairman and Public Prosecutors are ordinary farmers who are practically illiterate. There is one young law student, who, until now, has carried by himself the entire responsibility for operations. Since neither the Public Prosecutor nor the Chairman are capable of drawing up anything approaching adequate charges or a decision, this man has alternated between writing charge sheets for the Public Prosecutor and decisions for the Chairman. Thus he has found himself in the peculiar position of first drafting up charges and then drafting a decision opposing his own charges. This legalistic 'Jekyll and Hyde' situation has been much of a strain and now, after four months of it, he is close to a nervous breakdown. In addition to his other duties, he has been in charge of all administrative matters.[14]

By this time, cases of violent outrages against tribunal property and even tribunal members themselves had become fairly common-place. Threats were also an everyday occurrence. In Schwetzingen, near Heidelberg, the head of the local denazification board received a letter in which he was warned about the 'serious crime' he had committed by taking on this role:

Should an opportunity arise, you will have to bear the consequences of your actions. Think of your family.

In another small town, tribunal members were warned that 'a gallows will be erected in the market place . . . and all of you will hang there with heads down . . .' At Mainburg, not so far from Steinbach, the deputy chairman of the tribunal resigned 'because he was afraid of the consequences'. Tribunal offices were burgled and vandalised. There were even cases of a chairman's car being blown up (a crime traced to some fanatical former Hitler Youth members) and of a prosecutor being stoned while visiting a village on tribunal business.[15]

In the case of Vilsbiburg, a small community in the Alpine foothills, 100 kilometres or so north-east of Munich, there were indications that the local Nazis were taking on both the tribunal and the American occupation official in charge, and winning. A letter from a Lieutenant Colonel Bradford, Chief of the Governmental Structures Branch at Office of Military Governor, Munich, to Albert C. Schweizer, Director of Civil Affairs, on 10 October 1946 described the arrival of a delegation of anti-Nazis, including the local *Landrat* (District Supervisor), a former police chief, and the prosecutor from the denazification tribunal. They were in despair that the local American Public Safety Officer, a Lieutenant Brooks, obviously an ally of the anti-Nazis, seemed to have been withdrawn at the behest of the reactionaries in the town. Bradford wrote:

They stated that the transfer of Lt. Brooks, former Public Safety Officer with that detachment, had been openly flouted [sic – probably an error for 'flaunted'] by the Nazi elements in that community as a victory for them. The democratic elements, who have been trying to carry on their duties in that highly Nazified community are accordingly completely discouraged. It had been said to the Landrat 'that if an American officer can be disposed of so rapidly it won't be long before you will go also'. The public prosecutor of the Spruchkammer stated that unless something is done to strengthen the prestige of the anti-Nazi forces he would be forced to resign inasmuch as it would be impossible for him to carry on his task because of such open opposition.[16]

Bradford called for immediate action.

The undersigned officer is convinced that the transfer of Lt. Brooks by Military Government, no matter for what reasons, has resulted in a situation in this community entirely contrary to our policy. Some action must be taken to effectively continue the investigation and prosecution of the Nazi elements there that Lt. Brooks had begun in order to restore the confidence of the people in the strength and purpose of Military Government and in the democratic principles we are trying to inculcate in every community. This division has requested Col. Hastings to send Lt. Brooks back to Vilsbiburg to prosecute the charges against Herr Feistle, Bürgermeister of Vilsbiburg, in the forthcoming trial before a Military Government Intermediate Court. Col. Hastings has agreed. However, it is to be doubted that this in itself is all that is required to better the situation. Of the many Nazis in that area, some are firmly entrenched and much more effort will be required by a tough and thorough investigator before any true progress can be achieved in clearing up the highly disturbing condition that exists there.

The next day, Bradford was able to inform Schweizer that Brooks had been intercepted just before he was due to return to the US. A coalition of the lieutenant colonel and three intelligence officers was able to prevail on Colonel Hastings to retain Brooks for another month, and for the Vilsbiburg mayor's case to be brought forward. 'Thus the Feistle case seems well taken care of,' Bradford reported with limited satisfaction, 'but the more long range problem of the other entrenched Nazis in Vilsbiburg still exists.'[17] It might be supposed that this case was a successful exception. There is an air of hopelessness about many such reports.

Worse, even if Nazis were properly arraigned, there were problems with proportionality in their punishments. The system of fines, for instance, took no account of the almost absolute worthlessness of the post-war Reich mark. Fifty Reich marks, which before the war might have constituted, for around two-thirds of German workers, the loss of almost two weeks' wages,[18] was now small change. Earlier in the summer of 1946, an editor at Hans Habe's *Neue Zeitung*, Robert Lembke, complained to a government press conference:

> It is apparent from very many letters to our editorial department that people do not understand tribunal verdicts that inflict a fine of 50 Reich marks. They say, for 50 Reich marks we could have indulged ourselves too [i.e. we could have been Nazis]. If people are really guilty of so small an offence, maybe it would be better if we let them work off the penalty – rather than penalising them with this sum of 50 Reich marks, which feels like an absolute mockery, what these days almost anyone would spend on a pack of cigarettes.[19]

A spot check by the Army Special Branch in Heidelberg showed that 80 per cent of those cases where Nazis had been sentenced as 'fellow travellers', probably leading to fines similar to the ones complained about by Robert Lembke, should have led to their being classified in more serious categories.

In a survey of the progress of denazification, the AMG's *Weekly Information Bulletin*, trying to take a positive tone despite acknowledged problems, tackled the case of a fifty-year-old teacher at an industrial school who appeared before a Bavarian denazification tribunal. The man had been:

. . . a party member since 1 May 1933, propaganda leader from 1938 to 1945, member of the NS Lehrerbund (teachers' organisation) 1935–1940 and its trustee 1937–40, NSV and NSKOV since 1934, and Reichskolonialbund 1935–38. He was engaged in the fortification programme in Italy from 1 September 1944 to 30 November 1944. He was an honorary cultural adviser in the state guild of painters from 1934 to 1937. Also he was a teacher at the Academy of Painting. He was made a civil servant by the city administration of Munich in 1935. He was active in the Ortsgruppe.[20]

A middling fish, then, but definitely an active Nazi rather than a token one.

The prosecutor had asked for the accused to be classified as an Offender – the second most serious category, liable for permanent exclusion from state employment and the professions – but the tribunal demurred, reducing their verdict to that of Lesser Offender. He was fined 5,000 Reich marks (or fifty days' labour) and ordered to pay costs amounting to 7,000 Reich marks, but – most importantly – was simply sentenced to three years' probation and exclusion from responsible posts, after which – presuming he behaved himself – he could resume his career. The tribunal's reason for mitigation was that he 'according to the evidence of reliable witnesses . . . proved to be of unselfish assistance to everyone without making propaganda for the party. He extended his help to a woman who had four children and, after having been denounced to the Gestapo, was arrested for a considerable period of time by a special court.' He might, it concluded, 'be expected, because of his character, after he has proved himself in a period of probation, to fulfil his duties as a citizen of a peaceful, democratic state'.[21]

Soon, the denazification tribunals were overcome by a tidal wave of 'mitigating circumstances' – alleged favours done to dissidents and anti-Nazis, kindnesses shown to the poor and persecuted. Even dyed-in-the-wool Nazis could usually come up with someone to speak for them.

Occasional dissolution of especially notorious tribunals, and attempts at intervention by Special Branch, seemed to have little effect. A directive in September 1946, insisting that German officials involved in denazification show 'political and moral qualities capable of assisting in developing genuine democratic institutions in German' made little difference.[22] The next month, a selection of popular jokes reported from the Munich area showed the contempt in which the tribunals were widely held. One went:

> Question: What is the difference between a *Spruchkammer* and a fish-net?
> Answer: A fish-net catches the big ones and lets the little ones get away!

A CIC agent in Berchtesgaden collected some more witticisms. People there were saying that 'The erection of a monument to the *Spruchkammer* is being contemplated by grateful Nazis' and 'The salute "Heil Hitler!" being temporarily out of fashion, thankful Nazis suggest in its stead "Heil Hoegner!".'[23]

That an American appointee such as Hoegner, the 'clean' post-war Bavarian Prime Minister, could be mocked in this way was symptomatic of a serious problem. A few weeks later, in a speech to German politicians in the *Länderrat*, the all-zone political forum, Clay lashed out at these failures, declaring himself 'sorely disappointed'. The General had personally investigated 575 cases of 'major offenders' put before the tribunals, he said, and found out that almost two-thirds had been reclassified as 'fellow travellers' and another forty-nine acquitted altogether. He declared a sixty-day deadline, beyond which, if the tribunals did not shape up, direct American control of the process would be reinstituted.

During this time, there were intense discussions within the Military Government in Frankfurt about the degree of control that might be reintroduced, but in the end little came of it. Despite Clay's threat, no one suggested taking the denazification process out of German hands. It was simply too difficult to contemplate. The most meaningful concrete decision was to forbid the tribunals from continuing to re-instate Nazis who had been dismissed by the Americans before German organs took charge in March 1946.[24]

There was a distinct lack of natural justice in this last stipulation. It meant that those Nazis suffered most who, for some reason or another, had been the first in line for denazification. Any Nazis who, while just as deeply incriminated, had managed to evade the tentacles of the American denazification system until the spring of 1946, stood a good chance of suffering much less draconian punishment from their fellow countrymen after March of that year – and especially after June, when Schmitt, the communist zealot, was ejected from the minister's office.

Almost a million Germans resident in the American Zone were subject to the attentions of tribunals during the course of the denazification process, although not all had to appear in person. Of these, a mere 25,000 were classified as 'major offenders' or 'offenders', which involved mandatory exclusion from public life and from offices of responsibility. Almost 600,000 were put in the category of 'lesser offenders' or 'followers' and suffered mostly temporary suspensions from responsible employment, supplemented by fines, which were payable in near-worthless Reich marks. According to one set of AMG figures, one-third of ex-Nazis in the American Zone were dismissed from their employment between 1945 and 1947 – although almost all had been re-employed by the end of the latter year.[25] The fact was, had this not been the case, the public and private infrastructure of the zone would have been faced with crippling difficulties, and possible total collapse.

During the initial period, when denazification was being pursued with real determination by the US Army, another method of delaying (and thereby possibly avoiding) serious punishment had been to take refuge in the British Zone. Here things were very much less strict, even during the early stages of the occupation.

It was not that the British did nothing. They were very determined, for instance, to find those Germans who had committed war crimes against British POWs or captured Allied aircrew.

Mobile investigation teams swept through the British Zone in the late spring and summer of 1945. In one particular case, meticulously recorded in British files and including word-for-word transcripts of statements and of the trial itself, a German reserve policeman, Hans Renoth, was tried and convicted by a British military tribunal for the murder of an RAF pilot. The airman had crash-landed his aircraft, a single-seater fighter-bomber, in the north-west German countryside, not far from the Dutch border, on 16 September 1944.

Although Renoth, a reserve constable, admitted shooting the airman, the case was not straightforward. Several other officials had been involved. They had come from the small town of Elten, near Emmerich, after Renoth had taken a phone call from a farmer, who telephoned the police station to report the crashed plane. They drove to the crash scene in a car belonging to two signals captains who were based in the town. A senior constable and two customs officials who were also Nazi political leaders came in the signals captains' car, too, making six officials at the crash site. At first, Renoth reported in his statement to the British investigators in July 1945:

We saw the fallen aircraft but the pilot was not to be seen. During the search for the latter we had to take cover as other aircraft were flying over. After these aircraft had flown past, we continued our search for the pilot. The pilot was located about 50 metres from the aircraft in a ditch in the direction of the AA [anti-aircraft] site. I told him to come with me, which he immediately did. I searched him first but I found no weapons. I went with the pilot in the direction of the aircraft towards the captains. On the way the pilot was taken away from me by two soldiers, the two political leaders, and [Senior Constable] Pelgrim, with the remark 'You want to be friendly with the dog who has murdered our women and children.' I assume the soldiers came from the railway (or the main road). A beating ensued. The following were present: the two soldiers, the two political leaders and Pelgrim. The pilot was beaten nearly to death. I took no part in the beating, but withdrew and went to the captains. We conversed briefly; I can no longer remember the subject of the conversation. I saw that the rifle model 98 was broken in two pieces. (Pelgrim was in possession of the rifle.) It is my opinion that the pilot had been beaten so severely that the rifle broke. Captain Koerkes ordered me to give the pilot the coup de grace and I carried out this order. In accordance with my oath, I had to carry out the order. I made no protests but received a letter from Captain Koerkes. I passed this on to the Kreisführer of the Gendarmerie Harmann by name in Wesel at the office of the Landrat. I fired a shot into the pilot's chest from a range of 5–7 metres. The pilot died immediately without uttering a sound.[26]

Four of the men present at the incident stood trial in January 1946. The two signals captains were not mentioned in the account of the proceedings. After a two-day hearing, only the hapless Auxiliary Constable Renoth was found guilty of murder and sentenced to death. Pelgrim, who had apparently carried out the fatal beating with his service rifle, was given fifteen years in prison, and the two political leaders, as accessories and possible participants, got ten years each.

Renoth was hanged in 7 March 1946, despite his protests that the pilot was already dead when he fired the shot (which had been confirmed by medical tests carried out on the court's behalf) and the prosecution's acknowledgement that he had been obeying a superior order. The brigadier who forwarded the verdicts to the C-in-C Rhine Army for confirmation noted only: 'I think there was justification for the death sentence on Renoth, but I should have felt happier about it had Pelgrim also been sentenced to death.'[27]

By this time, the usual executioner for the British Zone was the well-known British hangman, Albert Pierrepoint. Already involved in a busy career in England, he travelled to British-occupied Germany and Austria to carry out around two hundred hangings of war criminals between December 1945 and the end of 1947. These included several instances of individuals held responsible for killing downed RAF aircrew like the pilot who crash-landed near Elten. He also hanged the British traitor John Amery, and William Joyce, known as

'Lord Haw-Haw', an American-born British fascist who had broadcast propaganda for the Nazis from Berlin. In between these commissions, which made him something of a contemporary celebrity, Pierrepoint ran a public house in Lancashire called Help the Poor Struggler.[28]

The Elten trial counted as harsh justice – one example of many – but the forensic process itself, judging from the records of this and similar trials, was on the whole sound. In terms of jurisdiction, it was also straightforward enough. The RAF pilot was a lawful combatant who had been killed after surrendering to the enemy, and so, whoever was held responsible, a war crime had been committed.

But what about other, less clear-cut cases? Through the winter of 1944–5 there had been a debate about whether crimes committed by Germans, not against British or other Allied nationals (including French, Belgian, Dutch, etc., citizens), but by Germans against those who were technically German citizens (Jews, for instance), could be tried by Allied courts, and if so by what right. Could they be called 'war crimes'? Apparently not.

In the first major trial of those involved in the mass murder of concentration-camp inmates – the so-called 'Belsen trial' – which began on 17 September 1945, at Lüneburg in the British Zone, the accused were not charged with crimes against peace or against humanity but with being involved in the murder of specific Allied nationals. In other words, they were held responsible in much the same way as the unlucky country policeman Hans Renoth. The accused were thought to have been responsible for thousands of deaths, but, in order to get around this legal problem, they actually stood trial for the murder of a small sample number of Allied nationals, whose deaths could be classified as war crimes. The short list of twenty victims, including three British nationals and others of Polish, Hungarian, Belgian, French, Dutch and Soviet nationality,[29] who actually appeared on the charge sheet, stood in for unknown thousands of innocent dead of all nationalities, including Germans and Austrians.

As the introduction to the United Nations War Crimes Commission report on the Belsen trial put it: 'Jurisdiction was asserted under the military law, which entitles the Court to punish war crimes, limited under the Royal Warrant to crimes against Allied nationals.'[30] This also meant that the trial was carried out under British law, under its habitual adversarial conditions, which included the right for witnesses to be subjected to hostile cross-examination. The British lawyers appearing for the defence of Josef Kramer, formerly of Auschwitz-Birkenau and commandant of Bergen-Belsen in its last terrible months, and his fellow defendants, therefore took every opportunity to argue often obscure points of legal principle, to place their 'clients' in the best possible light, and to discredit the testimony of the prosecution witnesses – even if these were hollow-cheeked, still-traumatised camp survivors who had waited months in DP camps to tell their harrowing stories.

The adversarial nature of the trial led to horrors such as the assertion by Josef Kramer's lawyer, Major T. C. M. Winwood, that his client's behaviour might be explicable by the fact that he dealt with 'the dregs of the ghettos of Eastern Europe'. The lawyer defending Ilse Grese, a sadist who had been in the habit of whipping prisoners to death at both Belsen and Auschwitz, maintained that she was not the 'beast' but the 'scapegoat' of Belsen, and that, since the camp was a prison, corporal punishment was 'reasonable conduct in the circumstances'.[31]

The trial summing-up by the British Army's Judge Advocate-General, C. L. Stirling, a civilian, erred to an extraordinary degree in the direction of 'fair play', reminding the five-man military tribunal who would judge the cases that much evidence was 'vague'. The court, he added, 'would have to be satisfied that a person on the staff of Auschwitz or Belsen concentration camp was guilty of deliberately committing a war crime; just being a member of the staff itself was not enough to justify conviction'.[32]

Stirling's remarks caused international uproar, especially in France and Russia. A reminder from the bench regarding standards of proof in a trial at the Old Bailey of, say, a suburban murder suspect of hitherto blameless character, was one thing. To speak in this way under such circumstances was simply incomprehensible to millions awaiting justice for the crimes of the concentration camps.

When the trial finally reached its conclusion two months later, thirty of the accused were convicted and fourteen acquitted. Eleven prisoners – including Grese and two other women warders – were sentenced to death, one to life imprisonment and the rest to prison terms ranging from one to fifteen years. The hangings took place at Hameln prison, with Pierrepoint once again officiating.

By contrast, the Americans began their first concentration-camp trial on 15 November and concluded it on 13 December. Of the forty accused staff of the infamous Dachau camp, all were found guilty. Thirty-six were sentenced to death, and twenty-eight death sentences were carried out.

Even the British Prime Minister, Clement Attlee, was moved to send a note to his Secretary of State for War, the Judge Advocate-General's ultimate superior, expressing concern at the lack of 'drive and energy' being shown and citing the example of the Belsen trial. Sir Hartley Shawcross, the British Attorney General (and British Chief Prosecutor at the Nuremberg Trial of Major War Criminals), called for an 'accelerated war crimes programme', but he knew they would never find all those responsible for the numberless and often nameless cruelties committed during the Nazi occupation of Europe.

There are tens of thousands of Germans responsible for millions of murders. We must set ourselves an absolute minimum of prosecuting at least ten percent of those criminals in the British zone. That is about two thousand people. I am setting as an irreducible minimum that we try five hundred cases by 30 April 1946.[33]

Attlee was not pleased with this, pointing out that such a deadline meant that this 'would surely have the effect of leaving a large number of criminals unpunished and at large'. The Prime Minister's instinct was correct. Even this relatively modest target was never met. Just a year after the end of the war, the British Army in Germany stopped investigating any non-British cases. There would be no repeat of the Belsen trial. From then on, it would be up to the foreign nations whose people had been murdered to pursue the cases.

So far as general denazification in the British Zone was concerned, influential figures, especially in the London Foreign Office, had always opposed a wide-ranging purge.

John Troutbeck, head of the German section at the Foreign Office, had warned in 1943 that this would 'lead us into incurring greater responsibility for administration than is wise or necessary'.[34] He was backed by senior figures in the Treasury, too, including Edward (later Sir Edward) Playfair, who also fought the Morgenthau Plan and prophesied national bankruptcy if Britain dismantled the German government machinery and tried to run its zone alone.[35] A *Time* magazine journalist gave a coyly bowdlerised version of a British official's words: 'We tell the bahstads what to do, you know, so their political beliefs make no difference really.'[36] Traditions of realism clashed, in the British case, even more strongly with traditions of natural justice than in other zones, and as the drama of denazification played out after 1945, this battle turned into something of a tragicomic fiasco.

The situation was complicated by the fact that a left-wing Labour government had been elected in July 1945. Its ranks were packed with passionately anti-Nazi and in many cases idealistic souls, who looked forward to radical and positive change both at home and in defeated Germany.

Public opinion, war-embittered and appalled by the spectacle of the concentration camps as the Allied advance uncovered the full extent of Nazi atrocities, was also a factor in inhibiting the FO's natural tendency to surreptitiously favour what might work and make life easier over what might be right but difficult. Churchill's temporary (though, it seems, for a while genuinely enthusiastic) espousal of Morgenthau's 'Carthaginian Peace' and the full force of the 'Morgenthau boys'' intervention in the planning process as the war ended caused problems for the Foreign Office mandarins. However, the punitive view did not quite manage to dominate planning as it did in Washington during 1945–6.

The British policy, admitted or not, was to dismiss all senior officials in occupied Germany, but to reinstate them if subsequent checks established that they were nevertheless 'acceptable' (a fine Foreign Office adjective). Various forms of words were also found to permit some discretion for British officials on the spot in Germany, while at the same time appearing severe, such as: 'Germans who are permitted to remain in, or are appointed to, official posts (e.g. in the police or the administration) should understand that they hold office only during good behaviour.' The Americans accepted this but at Potsdam, Molotov, the Soviet Foreign Minister, justifiably pounced on it as a possible loophole for the retention by the Western Allies of 'useful' Nazis.[37]

Unlike the Americans, who initially showed a strong moral/ideological aversion to keeping Nazis in offices or in comfortable jobs in industry and commerce, the British tended to see former Nazis as above all a potential security problem. The Americans also had a large pool of German speakers to draw on, be they 'Aryan' German-Americans or German-Jewish refugees who had made their home in the US after 1933. With the exception of émigrés like George Clare and his colleagues, who tended to be inserted into obvious areas where German-language skills were required, most British officers remained resolutely monolingual, and the civilian officials who were increasingly brought in to oversee German industry, as expropriations of companies progressed during 1946, were little better.

One advantage the British undoubtedly possessed was General Sir Gerald Templer. Aged forty-six and with a successful war record behind him as a divisional commander, Templer was appointed Director of Military Government – largely responsible for the day-to-day running of the British Zone – by Montgomery in March 1945, initially with a staff of only fifty officers.[38] Something of a martinet, and certainly a man of great energy and determination, Templer specialised in challenging complacency. In the words of a colleague, the historian Noel Annan, then a senior intelligence officer: 'Military Government officers who had previously spent happy hours commandeering the best houses and stocking up the messes with wine and schnapps, found themselves working late hours reconstituting the German administration and putting Templer's plans into operation.'

Not that all of this solved Germany's post-war problems in any short order. Here is Annan's verdict on one particular burst of energy on General Templer's part:

> Horses were gathered at three centres and sent by train to the main agricultural areas; 800 railway bridges and 7000 miles of track were repaired by the end of the year [1945]. But the food crisis did not disappear, the black market raged, and people left work to deal in it or went to farms to barter their possessions.[39]

On the other hand, without such leadership, things might have been even worse. Templer would go on to become the organising genius of a successful British campaign against the communist uprising in Malaya, a model for counter-insurgency efforts from Vietnam to Afghanistan.

Annan, based in Berlin and speaking fluent German, wrote a number of very influential reports. He was in a good position to observe the vices and virtues of the British handling of their slice of the defeated Reich, and to compare the British view of the country's problems with the rather different perspectives held by the Germans themselves.

Annan was also on close terms with the Political Adviser to the Military Governor, Sir William Strang, who had risen from a humble state-school background to the heights of the Foreign Office's elite. 'He looked,' recalled Annan, 'like a confidential clerk, but if he considered his opponent on the other side of the table obstructive he became a terrier and tore his arguments to shreds.'

Annan accompanied Strang on a tour of Germany in October 1945.

It was assumed, he reported, that the occupation of Germany would last for twenty years, during which time the Germans would have to learn to rule themselves again slowly and from first principles. Accordingly, a former colonial civil servant, Harold Ingrams, was drafted in and set up appointed councils of supposedly reliable Germans, drawn from business men, trade unionists, religious leaders, lawyers and so on, all over the zone. Little initiative was expected of them. They were there, Annan recalled, essentially to carry out British orders.

Ingrams was apt to treat Germans as if they were a specially intelligent tribe of Bedouins. Discussion in the shady tent was permitted until the Resident Officer struck the ground with his stick and gave his decision. This attitude exasperated the Germans.

Kurt Schumacher, the Hanover-based anti-Nazi who quickly became the leading figure in the post-war Social Democratic Party, was outraged. '*Wir sind kein Negervolk*' ('We are not blacks') the fiery former concentration-camp inmate told Annan.

The overriding object of Military Government was to make things work, to keep their zone stable.

. . . The British were technocrats. They preferred the status quo. From the start they regarded the SPD (Social Democratic Party) with suspicion, because the left endangered the status quo. 'It therefore had to be discouraged and it was.' Works councils were forbidden, Nazis might be turned out of their flats by the British, but not by zealous Germans. Some city administrators tried to compel known Nazis to clear rubble: Military Government forbade it. When a committee of concentration camp victims was formed to supervise releases from the camps it was at once banned . . . There was therefore no sense of a new beginning. When Military Government called on the ordinary German citizen to help them distinguish between repulsive, fervent Nazis and merely nominal members of the party, the ordinary German citizen replied '*Ohne mich*' – count me out.[40]

The appearance of denazification in the British Zone was, in fact, superficially similar to that in the American Zone: the interminable *Fragebogen*, the five categories of Nazis, and of course the arrests of those thought to have been serious supporters of the Hitler regime. However, the British, uninfluenced by the beady-eyed social engineers of the Frankfurt School, did not compel all Germans over eighteen years old to fill out the *Fragebogen*, as in the American Zone. It applied only to those employed by or seeking employment in public offices and enterprises.[41]

This rule led to some bizarre anomalies. George Clare, involved with denazification for the media and entertainment branches in post-war Berlin, reported the scene that greeted him when he entered his office one day and found it full of people who in the unenlightened 1940s were still called midgets:

Tiny men and women standing on the chairs around the big table were bending over it filling in their Fragebogens; another group in the middle of the room agitatedly discussed in squeaky voices whether such questions as 'Did you serve in the general or Waffen SS?' or 'What was the last rank you held in the Wehrmacht?' needed to be answered by them at all; two little chaps, obviously fed up with this nonsense, practised handstands in a corner and as there were not enough chairs for so many – some were reading their questionnaires lying comfortably on their tummies on the carpet.[42]

It turned out that these artistes were part of a troupe known as the 'Lilliputians' from a well-known circus. Clearly someone had decided that since they performed for the public they counted as security-sensitive media operatives and therefore needed to be checked for political reliability.

Like the Americans, though rather more reluctantly, the British introduced German involvement, setting up 'denazification panels' in January 1946. There was even a German appeal body, although the British could and did overrule its decisions if they felt it necessary.

By June 1946, 66,000 Germans had been arrested and placed in civil internment camps or, in the most serious cases, prisons. In a month, 24,000 were cleared, leaving 42,000 still detained. Five hundred were put on trial. Over the entire two years and a bit after VE-Day, two million *Fragebogen* were evaluated and some 350,000 Germans excluded from office.[43]

British policy was less rigorous than the American, but it was also slow and it was inconsistent, which in some ways was worse from the point of the view of the German population. The inconsistency was remarkable.

In 1945–6, in the British-occupied province of Oldenburg, 41 per cent of those involved in food production and distribution, 31 per cent of railway employees and 30 per cent of postal employees were dismissed because of their Nazi records. The pattern was followed elsewhere in the same zone. So, for instance, a highly efficient local potato merchant in the North Rhineland by the name of Paul Kistermann – his role in food distribution admitted even by the British authorities as vital to his large, semi-rural community in a time of hunger and shortages – had his licence withdrawn because of past Nazi involvement. The result was that – again as the British themselves admitted – 'immediate ill effects were felt'.[44]

Meanwhile, in bizarre contrast, only 9 per cent of teachers and 8 per cent of police officials in Oldenburg were sacked.[45] Given the high proportion of Nazis known to have been active in both these latter professions, the contrast is absurd and in its way quite sinister.

As for the slowness of the British denazification, it was not only the job prospects of ex-Nazis that were blighted. The civil internment camps where many were held while awaiting processing were truly grim places, often crowded and unsanitary, with ration allocations for inmates dropping to 900 calories per day – more serious for detainees than for the rest of the civil population, who were also kept on dangerously short rations but could at least forage and trade and grow their own food.

Although the British-run internment camps were not comparable with those where wretched millions had been incarcerated, tortured and murdered during the years of the Nazi regime, they were scandalous by the standards which the Western Allies had themselves set (the Soviets, as we shall see, were a very different matter). A House of Commons committee condemned the state of the camps and pointed out that it was damaging the prestige of the British occupiers as well as doing nothing to 'attract Germans to the British way of life'. A senior Military Government official conceded that these lengthy detentions without trial were 'not compatible with the professed restoration of the rule of law and the professed abolition of Gestapo methods'.[46]

It must be admitted that there were, in fact, cases where precisely those 'Gestapo methods' were being used by British military men and officials operating in the name of justice and security. No. 74 Combined Services Detailed Interrogation Centre (CSDIC) was opened in June 1945 at Bad Nenndorf, a once-elegant spa town near Hanover. The unit was housed in a hotel centred around a *Schlammbad* (mud bath) complex, with the rooms formerly reserved for guests undergoing expensive health cures now fitted with special steel doors and functioning as cells. The aim was initially to detain and interrogate suspected former Nazis or SS members who might become involved in post-war resistance activities against the occupiers.

Not only did No. 74 Combined Services Detailed Interrogation Centre rapidly become a torture centre used against ex-Nazis, but in surprisingly short order, considering that the Soviets had been British allies so recently, also against suspected communists agents and infiltrators. Inmates were tormented with cold, with whippings and beatings, with sleep deprivation, with threats against their wives and children (justified by the perpetrators on the grounds that such threats were never carried out), with starvation, and even with the use of 'thumb-screws' and 'shin-screws'. Some weighed less than 100 pounds when investigators finally gained access to the detention centre. Three died as a result of their privations.

The strange thing was that many of the victims were not even

German. One, allegedly a Frenchman, turned out to be a Russian intelligence agent. Others were Germans who had crossed from the Soviet Zone and, appalled by what they had witnessed, offered to spy for the West. They were tortured to see if their defection was genuine. One detainee, who had previously spent two years in Gestapo captivity, declared afterwards: 'I never in all those two years had undergone such treatments.'

It might have been a clue that all the German inhabitants – including many homeless refugees – were expelled from Bad Nenndorf when the Centre was opened. However, it was the death of an internee and the serious illness of others in January 1947 in a local hospital that caused the alarm to be raised and the London government to send over a police inspector to carry out an investigation. The result, to the intense embarrassment of the British, was news coverage, the closure of the camp and a court martial.

The commander of the Bad Nenndorf camp was forty-five-year-old Colonel Robin Stephens, known as 'Tin Eye', a former luminary of the Peshawar Division of the Indian Army turned MI5 officer. Stephens was put on trial along with several of his interrogators. It turned out that Bad Nenndorf had become a dumping ground for soldiers subject to suspended sentences for assault or desertion, a group liable to be less inhibited in the use of violence than your usual Tommy. Several of the interrogators were also German-Jewish émigrés, and others Polish and Dutch in origin, and therefore hardly likely to go easy on their captives.[47]

The shameful story of Bad Nenndorf became known in a bowdlerised form at the time of the court martial (only in the twenty-first century did the Freedom of Information Act allow journalists to make it fully public), but for Germans in the British Zone it was one among many instances that tended to give rise to a certain cynicism.

There were good things about British rule – a certain principled fairness on a daily basis, a keenness to promote education and democratic institutions, a healthy pragmatism – but it also drew on the country's imperial traditions in other, less attractive ways. Much behaviour reminded critical observers, including post-war Germans, of British arrogance and of the empire's brutal treatment of recalcitrant natives in India and Africa and South-east Asia. These flaws would become manifest once more in the post-war empire, most obviously in Malaya, Aden and Kenya. Scandals such as Bad Nenndorf did little, in German eyes, to reinforce the right of the British to 're-educate' them.

Of the officers prosecuted for the Bad Nenndorf excesses, only the camp doctor, Captain Smith, was penalised. Although found not guilty of manslaughter at the court martial, he was convicted at a secret internal hearing of neglect and dismissed from the army at the age of forty-nine. One of the interrogators, Lieutenant Langham, a German-born émigré, denied mistreatment and was acquitted. 'Tin Eye' Stephens himself, who was tried in camera, was also acquitted of two charges and two others were dropped, enabling him to re-apply to join MI5.

Three months after the closure of No. 74 CSDIC, a new, purpose-built interrogation centre was opened near the British garrison town of Gütersloh. The inmates would not be Nazis but suspected Soviet spies. Most of the interrogators employed had previously worked at Bad Nenndorf.[48]

In other areas of denazification activity, again British policy swung between extremes. While initially the British had taken a relatively laissez-faire attitude with the ownership and management of major German companies, especially in the Ruhr – on the pragmatic basis that production needed to be maintained – by the autumn of 1945, partly under the influence of the American JSC 1067, the line was becoming harder.

In September, most of the Krupp senior management was rounded up and dumped unceremoniously in an internment camp to await investigation and/or trial. Meanwhile, a British comptroller took over and the few Krupp bosses who had never joined the NSDAP or the SS struggled to continue managing the company. On 1 December, seventy-six senior executives from other major Ruhr conglomerates, including Thyssen, Hoesch and the United Steelworks (Rohland himself had been picked up in the French Zone and handed over to the Americans), were arrested. Once in custody, they experienced the rigours of Bad Nenndorf, although they were not among those subjected to torture. Hundreds more executives were forced out from Krupp and other major heavy industrial concerns in these months, though not all were subject to arrest.[49]

At heart, the British policy in denazifying German industry was two-pronged: first, to investigate and, where a case existed, to dismiss management; second, to strengthen the role of the trade unions, by additionally – after the initial bureaucratic objections mentioned earlier had been overcome – agreeing to grass-roots demands in Rhine-Ruhr heavy industry for works councils (*Betriebsräte*) that had some genuine power in decision-making within companies.[50] These new labour organisations also played a role in humanising the process of denazification on a day-to-day level in factories and plants, giving non-Nazi workers a chance both to accuse particularly tainted managers or to intercede on behalf of managers or foremen who were considered decent despite their political records.

The role of the workers was especially significant in the Ruhr mines, upon which so much depended in post-war Germany. From the mines came coal to give the stricken Reich electricity, heat, domestic and industrial gas supplies, and finally transport, in the form of steam-powered railway engines. Without coal, normal life in Germany – as elsewhere in the advanced industrial world in the 1940s – was simply not possible.

In 1945 the Poles took over the other great source of high-quality coal in pre-war Germany, the Silesian fields. This was why the Ruhr, after 1945 in British hands, was so crucially important not just to the British Zone but to the whole of Germany. It was also why both the French, very stubbornly, and the Russians, though in a less consistently obstructive fashion, continued during the immediate post-war years to push for internationalisation of the Ruhr industrial area under four-power control. They withheld cooperation in other vital areas of inter-Allied collaboration in the hope of forcing such a settlement, thus preventing the political integration that might have made four-power occupation work, for the Germans as well as the victors.

The denazification of the management of the Ruhr mines was intensive, and many managers and supervisors were dismissed in the period up to early 1946. This led to undoubted problems, in an industry where knowledge and experience affected not only productivity but safety. In January 1946, forty-six miners were killed at Peine, over the border in Lower Saxony, when a cage (elevator) carrying them to the surface suddenly plunged back into the depths of the mine. The disaster was blamed on inadequate safety measures.

The next month, at Unna, twenty kilometres east of Dortmund, an even worse catastrophe saw almost five hundred miners trapped underground by a coal-dust explosion. Many of the mine's inspectors had been sacked due to their Nazi affiliation. Temporary replacements had been recruited from among staff already in retirement, some of whom, it seemed, were no longer up to the exacting job. The same went for the rescue crews, who were also lacking key skills. The most senior inspector still surviving had just recently come out of a detention centre and was said to have had some kind of breakdown. When it came to the final phase of trying to fight the fires, the mine's expert in this area, one Dr Stodt, also an ex-Nazi, had to be fetched directly from jail to the pit to lead the last-ditch struggle. He refused to cap the shaft and was rewarded with a handful more miners rescued to join the fifty-seven who had somehow been pulled out alive. In the end, the Unna disaster claimed 418 lives, the worst pit accident in German history.

It was not absolutely certain that denazification had caused all, or even any, of these deaths, but the possibility existed. In March 1946 the British halted active denazification in the mining industry. A joint British–German commission was set up, including experts and miners' representatives and a broad spread of political opinion, to consider where to go next. It was decided that revisions and appeals would be permitted – with nominations for this process accepted from the North German Coal Control, the overall supervisory body run by British technocrats, but also from the trade unions and works councils.

During the course of that spring and summer, the commission considered 337 cases, ruling for reinstatement or retention in all but sixteen of them, although twenty-five men who remained employed suffered punitive demotion. Many hard-case Nazis did not apply for reinstatement, perhaps because they knew that a commission composed in part of their former work colleagues would be harder to fool than some blow-in Military Government official or small-town *Spruchkammer*.[51]

The mining industry, though it ended up keeping many of its Nazis, at least underwent a reasonably thorough process. Things elsewhere could be farcical. At the Volkswagen factory in Wolfsburg, near Brunswick, Hitler had planned to produce his KdF, or 'people's car' (*Volkswagen*). A few specimen civilian models had been made before the war began, after which the plant manufactured nothing but vehicles for the Wehrmacht all through the war years. The plant was heavily bombed. However, as early as the autumn of 1945, light vehicles were being produced for British personnel under Military Government supervision. As part of the pepped-up denazification drive that went on throughout the spring and summer of 1946, there was a purge of the workforce: 179 key executives and other employees were sacked. By the beginning of the next year, 138 had been reinstated. Without them, the place simply didn't function.[52]

By not insisting on the universal filling out of *Fragebogen*, the British never had to deal with the numbers the Americans did. On the other hand, by 1946 they had 26,000 military officials administering their zone, as against the Americans' mere 12,000. There were accusations at home in Britain that a bloated occupation bureaucracy was living well in requisitioned villas and profiting from the defeated enemy's misfortune. There was also a suspicion that clever Nazis could hide more easily in the British Zone, because so long as they didn't apply for a senior or sensitive job they would not have to submit to denazification. 'Numbers of ardent Nazis,' as Annan observed from his own experience, 'learnt that their best chance was to lie low, to be employed as a clerk, and wait for the heat to die down.'[53]

However, the size of the British military bureaucracy did mean that, for good or ill, it could retain more control of the denazification programme than could the Americans, for whom rapid transfer of power to the Germans was not just a democratic duty but a practical necessity. Whether this led to a more thorough denazification in the British Zone is doubtful, and although the British did keep more control of their German denazification panels than the Americans, there is no evidence that this led to less corruption or less inappropriate leniency. After all, few British officials spoke German. They were highly dependent on 'their' German officials and employees, who spoke English and were probably better educated and altogether more charming and entertaining than the embittered victims of the regime and the rough-and-ready socialist trade unionists who wanted a genuine purge in the zone. It must have been easy, especially as time went on and there were so many other critical practical problems pressing for solutions, to become tired of the anti-Nazis' constant demands, protests and apparent obstruction.

The results of British denazification were less spectacular in sheer numerical terms than those in the American Zone. Around 200,000 Nazis were either dismissed from their jobs or refused employment. The problem was that somehow most of those were 'small fish'. In the extremely populous province of North Rhine-Westphalia, with around twelve million inhabitants, a total of only ninety accused were, after all was said and done, categorised within the two most serious categories as 'major offenders' or 'offenders'. By early 1947, the British had decided to withdraw as completely as possible from the process.

The government minister responsible for the zone, Chancellor of the Duchy of Lancaster John Burns Hynd, a former railway clerk and trade union official of no particular distinction, was replaced in April by a very different kind of politician, the aristocratic and high-minded Francis (Lord) Pakenham. Pakenham, a convert from conservatism

to labourism and from Anglicanism to Catholicism, assured Germans
of his goodwill and told his fellow peers in the British House of Lords
that denazification was a 'horrid tiresome business':

> But I find in Germany to-day, on all levels – in the political Parties, in
> the Land governments, in the trade unions, in the universities and
> elsewhere among humbler people – many people coming forward, or
> going about their business, who are deeply conscious of their sad herit-
> age, and who are deeply resolved to set things right, to wipe clean the
> slate and enable Germany to make a worthy contribution to Europe. [54]

In October 1947, the British formally handed over denazification
to the now-elected *Land* governments of their zone, though they kept
the power to categorise and try former Wehrmacht criminals, and
also to administer the Civil Internment Camps, which still held
19,000 detainees. No new denazification processes would be initiated
after January 1948.

12

Divide and Rule

The two 'outsider' nations among the victors were consistently the French and the Russians – and of these two the French, during the first two years of the occupation, remained the more obstructive on matters of principle. Although the British and the Americans disagreed on many issues, they rarely actively blocked each other's post-war plans. This was, of course, partly because the British depended on American help in terms of food aid and also financial back-up when it came to the ruinous costs of running theirs, the most populous and urbanised of the zones.

One reason why, for the first years of the occupation at least, the French remained 'outsiders' was because, despite having been offered their own zone in Germany, they had not been invited to join the 'Big Three' at Potsdam. Within days of the conference, France formally signalled its agreement with most of the Potsdam decisions, but, because it had not been part of the decision-making process, it felt entitled to cherry-pick which and to what extent.

The aim of General de Gaulle, who led a broad-based post-war coalition in France between 1944 and 1946, was in any case different from that of any of the other three powers involved in the administration of Germany. His priority was that Germany never again be capable of attacking France. To this end, he wanted to keep Germany as weak and divided as possible for as long as possible – ideally, permanently. Alone among the victors, the General did not pay even lip service to the notion of a single post-war German entity run from Berlin by the four Allied powers. He wanted to annex the Saar to France; to encourage the division of Germany into independent mini-states, taking the country back to the eighteenth century; to ruthlessly extract industrial and financial reparations from Germany and to internationalise the Ruhr.

The other three powers may have harboured their own conflicting ambitions, may have conspired against each other in this and that way, and had their own reasons why they desired to retain as much freedom of action as they could in their own zones, but none of them took a principled stand against a single Germany under four-power control, as France did during the first post-war years.

Therefore, in the summer of 1945 de Gaulle made it clear – visiting Truman in August, shortly after the Potsdam Conference – that France would oppose the establishment of central agencies in Berlin and any treatment of Germany as an 'economic unit'.[1]

One of the 'opt outs' from Potsdam upon which the French insisted related to the situation of the Germans expelled from Eastern Europe and from Germany's forfeited eastern provinces as a result of the post-war settlement. Since France was not a party to the agreement of the 'Big Three' that victims of 'the orderly and humane' expulsions would be accommodated in the occupied zones, it essentially refused to take any. In fact, during the winter of 1945–6, thousands of refugees from the East already living in the French Zone were put on trains and dumped in neighbouring zones, mainly the British. Many had been in the area some time and had put down roots, even found employment.[2]

Apart from a lack of desire to be swamped, as wide swathes of the other three zones already were, by a tide of refugees from the East – who of course would all need feeding and housing – the French were also concerned that their part of Germany be kept relatively homogenous. They had plans to encourage separatism here, to bring the people of the southern Rhineland into the French cultural and political orbit. When forced by protests from the British and the Americans to take some of the refugees in late 1945 and into 1946, the French managed to ensure that Catholic refugees were given preference, thus avoiding the danger of hordes of Prussian Protestants changing the character of the French-governed provinces. In this they had the support of many local German officials and politicians. In December 1945 the German government president for the Koblenz district declared in a report to his French masters:

From a denominational point of view, the catholic character of the Rhineland would be strongly diluted by the resettlement of the mostly protestant eastern Germans, which in view of your relationship with overwhelmingly catholic France would be highly undesirable. This congruence in religious matters is extremely important from a cultural point of view. The dangers of such a solution being imposed arise from the alien mentality of the eastern population. This has long been militaristic and nationalistic, and latterly much more inclined towards national socialism than the western population. In among the flood of refugees, countless National Socialists of all shades would be resettled here, and secretly act as carriers of Hitlerian ideas.[3]

The French Zone was by no means the only part of Germany where the way eastern refugees were viewed verged on racist. Many Silesians and East Prussians were sneered at, especially in the inward-looking rural areas of western and north-western Germany, as 'Polacks' or 'Russkies'.[4] However, it was only in the French Zone that the occupying authorities colluded in such prejudice.

As for the notion that eastern Germans were somehow more Nazi than the westerners, there was in that a grain of truth. Not so much in the case of relatively heavily Nazified Koblenz, which differed in some regards from the surrounding area, but certainly in most of the rest of the French Zone, where Nazism, partly for religious reasons, had been less strong than in other regions such as Bavaria, Saxony, Silesia and East Prussia. This, plus a tradition of anti-Prussian particularism in the westward-looking Rhineland, did give the French rule certain advantages.

For the French, like the British, denazification was regarded as chiefly a security concern. They had a long border with Germany and a history of mutual invasion going back many hundreds of years. In the French case, therefore, the question of security was geographically immediate in a way that it was not for the Russians, with their newly acquired cordon sanitaire of satellite states in Eastern Europe, nor, across the other side of the Channel, the British. And certainly not for the Americans, who, whatever happened in the future, would continue to enjoy the safety of 5,000 kilometres of Atlantic Ocean between them and a resurgent Germany.

The rule of the *grande nation* in defeated Germany had started violently and in some cases chaotically. Rape and pillage had accompanied the French armies' advance through west and south-west Germany in the spring of 1945. And there was the small matter of the French occupation of the capital of Württemberg, Stuttgart, on 21 April – and their refusal to evacuate it, despite the fact that it lay in the zone allocated to the United States and that the French General Lattre de Tassigny had been ordered by his superior, the American General Devers, to do so. De Gaulle seems to have seen the city as some kind of useful bargaining counter. Only on 8 July did the French finally leave, after Eisenhower had threatened to cut off all their supplies.

The French record as a hoarder of German prisoners of war, whose services it claimed for reconstruction work back in France, was also extremely dubious. At least 30,000, possibly more, German POWs may have died in French captivity, of starvation and malnutrition, of disease and neglect and mistreatment. Around 5,000 are thought to have been killed during work on clearing minefields alone. The International Red Cross certainly considered the French, after the Russians, the most reprehensible of the major powers in their treatment of German prisoners of war. The French claim that most of the POWs concerned had died of wounds acquired before their capture did not inspire special confidence in their official figures.[5]

All the same, once they settled into their curious, hourglass-shaped zone bordering Alsace and Lorraine, by far the smallest with fewer than six million inhabitants, the French found the task of running it, from their capital in the elegant spa town of Baden Baden, not quite so onerous as did their fellow Allies. The zone's towns had remained for the most part relatively undamaged, with Koblenz as the great exception. The region was favoured with rich agricultural resources, including the famous vineyards of the Middle Rhine and the Moselle valleys, and – because of the French refusal to accept any of the millions of Germans displaced after VE-Day – unlike the other zones, its population had actually fallen since 1939.

The French denazification programme was characterised by a curious mixture of cynicism and idealism. There was cynicism in the sense that, unlike the British and the Americans, many French officials and military men were so convinced of the bad character of the German nation as a whole that it seemed hardly worth their while to distinguish between Nazis and anti-Nazis. Tellingly, the French did not call their process 'denazification' but simply *épuration*, or 'purification'. On the other hand, there was idealism in the sense that the French could not resist trying to export the country's proud republican rationalism to their zone in Germany – especially since this might draw the traditionally more liberal folk of the Rhineland and Swabia and Baden towards the longer-term French goal of their permanent detachment from the rest of Germany.

There was also the Saar area with its steel-making and coal-mining wealth, which Paris hoped to absorb into France on a much shorter timescale – so much so that rations for the population there were kept artificially high (higher than in metropolitan France, in fact). This favouring of the Saarlanders was calculated to encourage pro-French feeling as well as to increase vital coal production. Understandably, it caused huge resentment among the rest of the population of the French Zone.[6] It also didn't work. Most Saarlanders voted for a return to Germany once they got the chance.

So far as rations, dismantling of industry and day-to-day routine went, especially in the early stages of the occupation, the Germans inside the French Zone also had a tough time. Onerous reparations in the form of transfers of German industrial machinery and entire factories into French hands continued beyond the time when the British and the Americans gave up on their reparations demands in kind. Within a little over two years of the end of the war, the French had dismantled thirty entire factories, with another ten former armaments and fifty-eight other factories earmarked for the same fate. Ships and German property in France to the value of some five billion francs* were also confiscated.[7]

General Tassigny and his successors were determined to exhibit French strength and firmness at all times. The Germans were to recognise who was master. In June 1945 an instruction was issued through posters in public places:

> The German civilian population is to salute Generals and official cars bearing a general's insignia (men by removing their hats). Failure to obey this order will be penalised by collective fine or personal punishment.[8]

German civilians were to give way to French soldiers, right down to the rank of private, under all circumstances and at all times.

Perhaps to counterbalance the macho posturing, there was also a cultural offensive. French teachers and advisers were parachuted into places of education, the study of French became compulsory in schools, replacing English, and most schools had at least one French *assistant(e)* to ensure that young post-war Germans did not fail to appreciate the beauties of their new masters' language. Local appreciation of this cultural force-feeding was mixed, likewise the students'

---

* Exact value equivalents are difficult to estimate. The French franc had been steadily sliding in value since 1936 and would continue to do so until the 'new Franc' was introduced in 1960 and its worth stabilised. The exchange rate was around 120 to the American dollar in 1945 and by 1949 had slid to some 350 to the dollar. Choosing a mean value of around 250 to the dollar, this sum might represent $200 million, i.e. some $2–3 billion at current prices.

regard for what seemed like pampered representatives of the occupying power stationed in their classrooms.

Helmut Schnatz, then twelve years old and in his second year at the *Gymnasium* (selective secondary school) in Koblenz, recalls his freezing classroom during the fierce winter of 1946, when wood and coal were reserved mostly for the occupiers, with all the students huddled at their desks in sweaters and coats. He still treasures the vision of an elegant young French *assistante*, new to her job, as she turned up wearing little more than a light dress and a cardigan – the clothing which, presumably, had more than sufficed in the generous warmth of her requisitioned apartment. She was forced, out of pride, to sit through the class without complaint, even though her teeth were chattering and her lips turning blue with cold. The boys laughed. To see the privileged representative of the victors suffer was something of a tonic.[9]

All the same – and Dr Schnatz is clear about this as well – as time went on, relations between the French and the Germans improved. They got used to each other. A popular feeling among Germans in the French Zone was that, as the battle-hardened veterans of the Maquis who had made up a considerable part of the French army that conquered south-west Germany were replaced by post-war conscripts and other, more well-disposed types, so the attitude of the occupiers softened.

The fact that many French commanders – and officials – had also served the country's collaborationist Vichy regime (in some cases quite happily) and got used to familiar relations with Germans during the occupation years, also played a part. A common assertion by contemporary German witnesses is that, after the war, many Frenchmen who had been POWs between 1940 and 1945 rejoined the army. These men, who were in many cases sent to labour on German farms in wartime, had often ended up on extremely good terms with their employers and their families. They were, so the popular perception went, therefore far less hostile towards Germans than their predecessors, more likely to treat them as human beings like any others.[10]

None of this indicated a lack of toughness, where necessary. After all, it was the French who in their first months in Germany, against all the rules of war and occupation, took hundreds of hostages from among captured Nazis, as a guarantee for their comrades' behaviour. This was, of course, publicly denied, even in the face of the fact that four such hostages were shot in the market square of Reutlingen, near Stuttgart, in retaliation for the murder of a French soldier.[11]

Even Egon Plönissen's father, the innocuous Koblenz dentist, was forced to flee out of the back door of his home one day a few months into the occupation when French gendarmes turned up with a warrant for his arrest. The family is still not sure whether he had been confused with his cousin, the Nazi *Ortsgruppenleiter*, or whether the French planned to take him hostage until the guilty party made himself available. In any case, Herr Plönissen did not stay around to find out. He fled over the border into the British Zone – by now known as a relatively safe haven to miscreants from the French Zone as well as the American – and stayed with relatives there, in Krefeld, for a couple of weeks until the fuss died down. By the time he returned home, the matter had been sorted out. The *Ortsgruppenleiter* Plönissen was in custody, and his cousin the dentist Plönissen's professional and family life resumed its orderly and relatively comfortable rhythm.[12]

This lack of regard for regulatory inconveniences could also apply when it came to respect – or lack of it – for the integrity of other Allies' jurisdictions. American records report French gendarmes appearing at a house in the suburbs of Munich and hauling a German teenager off in a staff car. He was later found to be in prison in the French Zone. It turned out that the boy's brother-in-law had escaped from a French POW camp. The family were told frankly that if the fugitive did not return himself to French custody, the boy would be shipped off to do labour in France in his place.

To the outrage of the American authorities, no permission had been sought by the French, no notification made of their journey into the American Zone. Even aside from the kidnapping of the boy, the very unnotified presence of the French officials in the American

Zone was illegal. When challenged by the boy's relatives, who enjoyed the full support of the American authorities, the French liaison officer in Munich replied smoothly that he would, of course, do his best to right this grave wrong, but it would, equally naturally, help a great deal if the escapee would give himself up as the gendarmes had originally requested . . .[13]

In the first months of the occupation, moreover, there was some 'wild purging' of the administrative and economic machine reminiscent of the recent vengeance against French collaborators after the liberation. It was, however, at the heart of the French denazification system that the character of the suspects, not simply their paper membership of the Nazi Party, be taken into account. In fact, unlike in the other zones, simple membership of the Nazi Party as such was of no material interest to the French authorities. As the French representative to the Berlin four-power *Kommandatura* put it: 'We can't ignore our directives . . . but we can interpret them with a little more attention to the individual and his circumstances.'[14]

It was also true that the French were willing to make good their mistakes. Thus, after enthusiastically sacking three-quarters of all teachers in their zone in the weeks after victory, faced with a crisis when reopening the schools again in September the French authorities simply rehired them en masse – albeit initially without job tenure. The same applied to technical experts with shady political records. These were hired on a month-to-month basis, with their supervisors held responsible for their conduct.[15] French flexibility on matters of principle, like British pragmatism, distinguished their denazification activity from the American and, in a different way, Russian programmes.

It was also in the French Zone that the Germans were earliest involved in the process. A semi-devolved system ('*auto-épuration*') was introduced as early as autumn 1945. There were ebbs and flows of strictness – often when the politicians in Paris saw fit to shake things up, or one of the other occupiers criticised the French Zone as 'an El Dorado of tolerance' or similar – and the procedural bureaucracy, imported wholesale from France, could be stifling.

Particularly in the *Land* of Württemberg-Hohenzollern, with its capital in the picturesque university city of Tübingen and presided over between 1945 and 1947 by the local SPD leader, Carlo Schmid (who had been born in France and lived there until he was five), the denazification scheme was considered a model one, a 'golden mean between an excessive degree of severity and an inadequate standard of leniency'. It was flexible, but could be harsh when the situation seemed to call for strict measures.

In the end, after a shaky start, and appearances often to the contrary, French *épuration* may well have been as thorough (a relative judgement) as the best of the American system.[16] The manageable size of the French Zone undoubtedly helped, as did the fact that only one in seven Germans had to fill out a *Fragebogen*. In the two years up to the spring of 1947, the French had processed a little more than half a million of them, but they processed them successfully and thoroughly.

In contrast to the French treatment of German POWs and internees, the actual result of their denazification campaign was relatively mild. Three years after the end of the war, some 133,000 inhabitants of the French Zone were classified as above 'fellow traveller' status, but eventually only 18,000 ended up classified in a way that brought automatic penalties. Even then, demotions and fines were a more popular punishment than imprisonment, leading to general agreement that, despite the French reputation for revenge and occasional individual brutalities, the denazification in their zone may well be classed as the least harsh.[17] So, for instance, only thirteen Germans throughout the entire French Zone were found guilty of being 'major offenders' – against 1,654 in the American Zone.[18]

There was one final note about the French denazification campaign. The relatively personal and subjective nature of the process could lead to absurdities, anomalies and injustices (as could its opposite elsewhere in occupied Germany), but as Perry Biddiscombe wrote, 'its humanism and recognition of the individual set the tone for a policy that would eventually take shape as Franco-German reconciliation'.[19]

So, for France and Germany – the ancient intimate enemies – a time that had begun with violence, revenge and oppression led, in a remarkably few years, to a friendship that would survive into the twenty-first century.

And the other outsiders, the Soviets? The system in the Soviet Zone, being a creature of Stalinism, all too often went beyond harshness and into sheer brutality. All the Allies, democratic or otherwise, had their civilian internment camps, their 'holding pens' for the denazification process. The Soviet ones turned, in many cases, into nothing less than concentration camps. In fact, they included the former Nazi concentration camps of Sachsenhausen and Buchenwald, as well as the notorious Gestapo prison at Bautzen, which were emptied of their wartime inmates only to be filled in short order with real or perceived enemies of the Soviet occupation.

Between 1945 and 1950, according to official figures, 122,671 Germans passed through 'special camps' set up by the Soviet MVD (as the NKVD secret police were known after February 1946) in their Zone of Occupation. Of these, 42,889 were claimed to have died 'of sickness'. Two years after the end of the war, a further 10 per cent of the prisoners in the Soviet Zone Gulag, mostly those judged fit enough to work, were creamed off and sent to labour camps in the Soviet Union itself.[20] Only a small fraction were actually tried by Soviet tribunals.[21]

The numbers of dead and disappeared may, in fact, be gross underestimates. Estimates by American intelligence and the West German Social Democratic Party's own usually reliable network of informants inside East Germany come to about double that. Mass graves unearthed since 1989, representing by no means all the dead of the camps but already pointing to tens of thousands of victims – including 16,000 sets of remains found in the vicinity of Bautzen prison alone – also indicate that the death toll may have been much greater. Only the opening of secret Soviet archives will bring some certainty into these estimates.[22]

They died, those who were not executed, of disease (especially tuberculosis, which was endemic, but also dysentery), of starvation and cumulative malnutrition. Conditions were bad in the West – they were bad for most Germans, imprisoned or not – but here they were lethal. The denazification laws were used ruthlessly not just against former Nazis but against anyone whom the post-war rulers of eastern Germany wished to crush or discredit.

The camp inmates were supposed to be Nazis or suspected security threats of various kinds, but it quickly became clear that the Soviets and their German protégés were using the Nazi smear as a way of dealing with anyone who appeared to threaten the rapid 'Sovietisation' of the zone. There were, of course, the 'class enemies' such as aristocrats, bourgeois or prosperous landowners – the remnants, who had failed to flee westward, of the groups expropriated in the winter of 1945–6. However, after the allegedly voluntary merger of the Social Democratic and Communist parties in the Soviet Zone, at Stalin's behest, in April 1946, dissident Social Democrats and other activists who refused to join the communist-sponsored 'block' parties also found themselves targeted by the MVD as 'hostile elements' liable for arrest under the denazification directives.

Torture was common. 'As a rule, interrogations took place in the night from eight pm to around five am,' recalled a former inmate of Bautzen prison. With one man, who had lost a leg in the war and wore an artificial limb, the camp's interrogators '. . . worked on his leg as they questioned him, in such a way that after a while there was just a bloody stump'.[23]

The MVD remained in overall charge until 1948. However, soon alleged enemies of the post-war state also began to be pursued by a nascent secret police force run by East German communists. This began in Saxony as 'K-5' and would eventually morph into the notorious Stasi.

Also especially at risk from the Soviet Zone authorities were dissident elements among German youth. All the occupiers were concerned about how to handle the 'brainwashed' young, who had grown up under Hitler. Young people, many of them only recently enthusiastically involved in the Hitler Youth or the League of German Girls, seem to have represented a particularly thorny problem for the Soviets and their German allies. In the Western zones, the main source of friction with this section of the population seems to have been envy and sexual jealousy, arising from the attraction of young German women to the nylon, chocolate and cigarette-toting British and American occupiers. In the east, it was more socially and ideologically based. The MVD was aware of this, and typically chose to list it all under the drastic rubric of '*Werwolf* activity', thereby justifying draconian measures.

In fact, although there was a tendency among the youth to sing the old Hitler Youth songs (sometimes with satirical lyrics aimed at the new rulers), to loiter around, as young people will, in a vaguely disreputable fashion, and to engage in low-grade black market activity, their main crimes consisted of posting anti-communist and anti-Soviet graffiti. Clandestinely circulating critical leaflets and pamphlets was also fairly common.

Dissatisfied and bored young people would also sometimes heckle Soviet films when they were shown in cinemas. In one case, in Dresden, a group of 'young rogues' (*Lausejungen*) hissed at a documentary film lauding Soviet food deliveries to Germany. The local German communist leader organised a check to ensure that these were not 'paid agents'. In Leipzig, a circular complained that Soviet films were 'being sabotaged by the public, which in itself is a victory for the enemy'.

Again, youths arrested were charged with membership of *Werwolf* groups.[24] In Chemnitz, a group of young 'reactionaries' were arrested for asking awkward questions at a meeting of the new communist youth movement, the FDJ ('Free German Youth'). They were delivered straight to the not-so-tender ministrations of the MVD.

Others who did the same thing were luckier. Ulrich Frodien, for instance, who had escaped from Breslau to Berlin, to Göttingen and then to the small town in the Soviet Zone where his doctor father now practised, also attended FDJ meetings. He was a little cleverer than the young people who ended up in the local Gulag. Ulrich and some friends became active in the youth movement, and appeared to be loyal, but remained critical when it came to some important political questions. The new regime, still not willing to drop its democratic façade and hoping gradually to draw even 'tainted' youth into its orbit, tolerated them, even though they were regularly overruled at meetings and conferences and increasingly heavily criticised. Attempts were made to nudge young Ulrich in the 'right' direction. When he attended a regional conference, he was even granted a brief interview with the Russians' cultural dictator in conquered Germany, Colonel Tiul'panov.

The paranoid brutality of the new regime when it encountered opposition only grew as the 'gradualist' and relatively tolerant policy of the early post-war months was abandoned.

A key moment was the Soviet-encouraged merging of the Communist and Social Democratic Parties in April 1946 at a thousand-strong congress in Berlin to form the so-called 'Socialist Unity Party of Germany' (*Sozialistische Einheitspartei Deutschlands* = SED). With 1.3 million members, the two left parties were more or less equally represented in the new movement (in fact, the SPD made up a slight majority), and initially Party posts were appropriately divided up between social democrats and communists. All the same, it fairly rapidly became clear that the communists had the upper hand, and it would become even clearer in the years that followed. Many social democrats in the Soviet Zone and also in Berlin did not support the merger, but only in West Berlin were they able to organise themselves properly without being harassed by the Soviets and their German allies.

The elections in the Soviet Zone in October 1946 – the last more or less free choice for its citizens until after the fall of the Berlin Wall – gave the SED a strong vote, but not the majority the Soviets had anticipated. In Greater Berlin, where the Soviet writ did not run as completely as elsewhere, and the SPD continued to put up its own candidates, the SED failed spectacularly, gaining fewer than 20 per cent of the vote, with the SPD managing 48 per cent.

Aware that it could not win a free vote – elections in Hungary and Austria had also ended in the defeat of communist 'united front' movements – the Soviet-installed regime began to tighten the political screws. Ulrich Frodien and his friends, realising the dangers they were running, gradually dropped out of political activity. Most of them went to the West in the end, including Ulrich in February 1948, escaping at great risk from a sanatorium near the border with the British Zone, where he was undergoing treatment for bronchial problems arising from a war wound to his lung.[25]

That denazification was a tool for economic transformation and an instrument of political control for the Soviets and their German communist allies could not now be denied. It was also a means of changing German society, making a clean sweep through the two areas of public life where until now the right had been especially firmly entrenched: the legal and educational systems.

Since the nineteenth century, Germany's courts, and its schools and universities, had been strongholds of the nationalist, authoritarian right. As in the West, a strong majority of teachers and legal officials were known to have been Nazis. The French made a brief, early attempt at a comprehensive purge, but then changed their minds when they saw that there would be no teachers in the zone's schools when they reopened. The Russians and the German communists were less timid, perhaps because for them there was more at stake. To the totalitarian mind, it was clear that the education and legal systems were essential for their future control in the zone – the first, key to their control of young people's minds; the second, key to their control of the whole people's liberties.

There was some justification for a radical transformation in both areas. In the Weimar Republic, the courts had often been a centre of hard-line resistance to democracy, as had the schools. In both cases, professionals in these areas had flocked to the Nazi Party. In fact, in the area of the Soviet Zone, 70 per cent of teachers had been Party members, as opposed to 55 per cent on a nationwide basis. In Mecklenburg-Pomerania and Thuringia, membership had touched

85 per cent. But how to purge these areas in the required radical fashion without bringing teaching in the zone to a halt? Teachers and judges were, after all, highly trained and qualified people, as were doctors. Except that in the case of doctors – also a strongly Nazified group – the results for their patients of dismissing so many qualified people would be, quite literally, fatal. So the medical profession remained more or less untouched.

In late summer 1945, the Soviet Zone authorities hastily trained thousands of 'reliable' candidates – usually socialist or communist activists – in three-week courses covering the basic teaching skills. They called them *Neulehrer* (new teachers). Joachim Trenkner remembers most of his former teachers just disappearing. They were replaced by *Neulehrer*, whom he described more than sixty years later as 'bizarre'. And they were not all politically reliable, either:

> I remember one thing. Russian language classes started . . . and it was hard to get Russian teachers in the Thuringian provinces. And so we got most of them from Lithuania. Refugees, most of them came from the Baltic states. I remember our very first refugee teacher was an old man, white hair, thick glasses, and he started the first lesson with words I shall never forget: 'Children, I have to teach you the language of our common enemy!' I don't know how long *he* lasted there . . . [laughter][26]

By the same token, established judges or prosecutors – around 80 per cent of whom had been Nazis in each case – were replaced with *Volksrichter* (people's judges), again proletarian candidates selected by the SED, who began their work with as little as six months' legal training. Unlike in the Western zones, in the East the rule was that *any* judge or state prosecutor who had been a Nazi must be dismissed, and this stipulation was overwhelmingly kept to.[27]

All these changes could be presented as a necessary radical social transformation, which arguably they were. However, they also, through the appointment of committed loyalists wholly dependent on the administration's favour – an Eastern-trained 'new teacher' or 'socialist' judge would not find employment in the West – gave the new powers in the land direct control over vital levers of the post-war social machine.

In the universities, the remaining teaching staff were also ruthlessly purged. Many had already headed west. By the beginning of 1946, three-quarters of professors in the Soviet Zone's six major universities had either been purged or had fled.[28] The politicisation of higher education was soon impossible to ignore. The quality of teaching declined drastically. Affirmative action quotas were introduced, systematically favouring working-class over 'bourgeois' applicants.

Universities and colleges were used as social portals through which only those socially or politically acceptable to the new communist rulers would be allowed to pass. Unlike in the Western zones, where the post-1919 generation was presumed to be the product of Nazi brainwashing and therefore less than fully responsible for its own political crimes and errors, in the East a close watch was kept on the past politics of applicants for university places.

Lothar Löwe, considering applying for the prestigious Humboldt University in East Berlin, was warned by a friend, who had himself narrowly escaped arrest, that the authorities there were not just refusing any would-be students who had risen to the rank of Pennant Leader (*Fähnleinführer*) or above in the Hitler Youth – as Löwe had – but were also liable to take them into custody. Since the foundation of the Free University of West Berlin still lay in the future, Löwe accordingly abandoned plans for university study and went straight into journalism with one of the newspapers recently licensed by the Americans in West Berlin. It was the beginning of a distinguished career.[29]

Although historians concede that the Soviet purge was probably the most thorough, as in all the zones the 'normal' procedure for denazification varied from lax to harsh. When the Soviets wanted people – the case of the rocket scientists and other specialists is typical – then they got them, Nazis or not. In that, they were no different from the other powers. More than half a million Nazis out of a population of eighteen million were banned from all but menial employments between 1945 and 1948 – at least temporarily.[30]

The thing about the communists, however, was that, like the Church, they allowed for the possibility of redemption. After all, given the attitude of the communists towards Nazism as the final, desperate phase of capitalism, there was always a kind of moral opening for those who admitted their mistake – who repented. So (usually minor or so-called 'fellow traveller') Nazis who, after a year or two, were willing to turn to the true church of the SED, stood a chance of being rehabilitated. Especially if the new regime decided it could use their services. Goering had once quipped, 'I decide who is a Jew'; Ulbricht and co. might equally have joked, had their sense of humour been more obliquely developed, 'I decide who is a Nazi'. Think of the rocket scientists and, on a more localised, personal level, the efficient – but once Nazi – chemist Dr Bergander in his Dresden distillery.

As early as the winter of 1945–6, when the leaders of the German Communist Party visited their masters in Moscow, Stalin had suggested, on the above lines, that there should be a political bolthole for ex-Nazis to go to in the Soviet Zone; a special party organisation that would permit repentant ex-Nazis to contribute to the new world that was opening up in post-war Germany.

Stalin's suggestion was too cynical even for Ulbricht and his comrades. They were, of course, busily attacking the Western Allies for alleged laxity towards former Nazis in their zones, and did not want to undermine their own propaganda.[31] However, a little over two years later, as relations between East and West deteriorated further, and the SED's control had reached a level where it could manipulate public opinion much as it wished, the unthinkable happened. The NDPD (National Democratic Party of Germany) was added to the 'block' of parties (all ultimately controlled by the SED, of course) that made up the pseudo-democratic political landscape in the Soviet Zone. In the NDPD, ex-Nazis whose past crimes were demonstrably not too terrible, and who were prepared to swear allegiance to the communist regime, were permitted to participate in the new society. And the transfer from allegiance to totalitarianism of the right to totalitarianism of the left often proved, perhaps understandably, not so hard as the pre-1945 world might have imagined.

During the previous two years, even before their existence was officially recognised, and even while they still lived in fear of the denazification courts, this group had been quietly courted. 'Minor' Nazis had been encouraged, for instance, to vote the right way in the Saxon plebiscite of June 1946 about 'land reform' by timely concessions from the Soviet Zone authorities regarding the security of their own property. The implication was: if you, the small Nazis, vote for the big Nazis to be expropriated, then you will receive fair treatment. There is every indication from the plebiscite results that this strategy worked.[32]

The Soviets, like the other occupying powers, were torn between the dream of denazification and the necessity, in the developing struggle for power in post-war Europe, for which control of Germany would be crucial, of stabilising 'their' Germany and drawing 'their' Germans together.

In the final analysis, like the Western powers they criticised so savagely – and sometimes rightly – the communists were prepared to cut deals and compromise. By the late 1940s, Germany was no longer just a defeated nation to be disposed of as the victors willed, but the cockpit of the Cold War.

13

Hope

In May 1946, General Clay cabled Chief of Staff Eisenhower a memorandum, in which he attempted to sum up the situation of Germany one year after Victory in Europe. It was a far from optimistic communication. Clay wrote:

After one year of occupation, zones represent airtight territories with almost no free exchange of commodities, persons and ideas. Germany now consists of four small economic units which can deal with each other only through treaties in spite of the fact that no one unit can be regarded as self-supporting, although British and Russian zones could become self-supporting. Economic unity can be obtained only through free trade in Germany and a common policy for foreign trade designed to serve Germany as a whole. A common financial policy is equally essential. Runaway inflation accompanied by economic paralysis may develop at any moment. Drastic fiscal forms to reduce currency and monetary claims and to deal with debt structure are essential at earliest possible date. These cannot be obtained by independent action of the several zones. Common policies and nationwide implementation are equally essential for transportation, communications, food and agriculture, industry and foreign trade, if economic recovery is to be made possible.[1]

In practice, he said, the only possibility of economic integration was with the British Zone. 'In theory' the Russians should find it acceptable 'though in detail many difficulties will arise with the Russian representatives'. The proposals would be unacceptable to the French, who were still insisting that the Rhineland and the Ruhr be detached from Germany, a suggestion Clay dismissed without reservation. It posed the prospect not just of a German crisis but of 'a world disaster'. Clay's cable makes it clear that, in reality, the French were seen as more of a problem than the Russians. The Russians might be obstructive on detail, but not at this point on basic principle. The French, however, refused point-blank to accept either a unified administration in Germany or a unified economy. It could be argued with hindsight that the Soviets let the French do a lot of their 'dirty work' for them, but that was not apparent to contemporaries.

Clay continued:

However, if agreement cannot be obtained along these broad lines [i.e. general integration of all four zones], we face a deteriorating German economy which will create political unrest favourable to the development of communism in Germany and a deterrent to its democratisation. The next winter will be critical under any circumstances and a failure to obtain economic unity before the next winter sets in will make it almost unbearable.

The General from South Carolina was clearly in favour of a merger with the British Zone before the next winter was upon Germany, however many problems it caused with the Russians and the French. He and his masters in Washington had not yet fully given up on the hope that Germany could be run as a whole, but there were so many complications and disagreements that optimism in this regard was becoming harder to sustain.

In Washington things were also moving in a new direction, away from four-power to unilateral action, or at best joint action with the British. At Paris in April, when the four powers' foreign ministers (plus China) met yet again to try to agree on a unified approach to fulfilling the detailed provisions of the Potsdam Agreement, the result remained one of stalemate. The US Secretary of State, James F. Byrnes, held out against new reparations demands from the USSR, telling Stalin's Foreign Minister, Molotov, that the US and Britain were having to pay half a billion dollars a year to feed 'their' Germans because the Russians were refusing to supply them with food. Molotov also rejected Byrnes' suggestion that Germany be demilitarised and remain that way for twenty-five years. With America still due to withdraw its troops from Europe within the next couple of years, the most likely conclusion to draw from that was that the Soviets were simply waiting for them to leave before they made their real move on Germany.

Whether this suspicion of aggressive Soviet intentions was justified is uncertain. Stalin's exhausted but triumphant country continued to tighten its grip on Eastern Europe as well as on its own zone in Germany, and to look for advantage in an opportunistic fashion, either directly or through political proxies. The question was not if Stalin would have liked to have seen a united, communist Germany, but if he was prepared to use force rather than persuasion and subterfuge to get it.

By the beginning of 1946, there were plenty of indications that Stalin was not going to cooperate with the Anglo-Americans, however, and not just with regard to Germany. Russia was refusing, for instance, to carry out its part of the post-war agreement when it came to Iran. The country had been occupied by British, American and Russian troops during the war years, with an agreement that all would withdraw as soon as peace came. The British and American forces duly complied within the time agreed, but the Soviets did not, and, moreover, showed signs of trying to expand their area of occupation. Two ethnically based 'soviet republics' were set up by Soviet agents on Iranian territory during early 1946. These were liquidated by the Iranian army, with American encouragement, and their leaders either executed or put to flight, but the crisis atmosphere lingered on for months before Stalin quietly withdrew. The Iran crisis was a key factor in the deteriorating relationship between the Anglo-American axis and its former Soviet allies. While it was still simmering, President Truman reinforced his case by sending the US battleship *Missouri* to the Mediterranean. The *Missouri* came to form the core of the Sixth Fleet, which is still there.[2]

At around the same time, the Soviet Union abruptly withdrew from the discussions at Bretton Woods about future international financial stability, which led to the foundation of the International Monetary Fund and the World Bank.[3]

On 9 February 1946 Stalin made a speech in Moscow in which he began to retreat from the grand alliance with the capitalists that had won the war, and by the same token from any economic arrangements that would leave capitalism intact. It was a traditional Marxist-Leninist rant in which he repeated Lenin's claim that capitalism always brought war, and that, even though the Nazis had been beaten, peace would come only when communism triumphed throughout the world. He reminded his audience of the pre-war industrialisation of the Soviet Union – achieved, of course, at appalling social and human cost – and how this had enabled Russia to win the war with Germany (Stalin made no mention of the Anglo-American aid that had also made a great, perhaps decisive difference to the Soviet war effort). And he called for preparations for the new struggle that, given the contradictions of capitalism, would surely be necessary in the future.[4]

It was at this time, February 1946, that America's deputy chief of mission in Moscow, George Kennan, sent a cable to the US Department of the Treasury, which had requested some insight into the Soviet thinking that had caused the Russians to pull out of Bretton Woods. The cable, a remarkable 8,000 words long, went far beyond financial matters and into the politico-military problems exemplified in situations such as the Iran crisis and the increasing tension in Germany. It ended up exploring what Kennan saw as the entire, complex psychopathology of Soviet/Russian behaviour, and making suggestions as to how America should handle the deteriorating relationship with its erstwhile wartime ally and 'contain' the Russian power that now extended over half Europe and into Asia, too. Kennan's influential cable became known as 'The Long Telegram'. It would play a crucial role in post-war American policy.

Even months before the German surrender, Kennan had favoured not trying to run post-war Europe in concert with the Russians but dividing the continent into spheres of influence, so that '. . . within whatever sphere of action was left to us we could at least . . . [try] to restore life, in the wake of the war, on a dignified and stable foundation'.[5] Just over a year later, he wrote of 'containing' the Soviet Union, whose view of world affairs was 'neurotic'. He proposed a more forward stance than the simple drawing of lines and demarcation of spheres. To do this, the counter-forces – cultural, economic, political – had to be consciously strengthened and promoted. In the penultimate paragraph of his telegram he wrote:

> It is not enough to urge people to develop political processes similar to our own. Many foreign peoples, in Europe at least, are tired and frightened by experiences of the past, and are less interested in abstract freedom than in security. They are seeking guidance rather than responsibilities. We should be better able than the Russians to give them this. And unless we do, the Russians certainly will.[6]

Of the 'foreign peoples' Kennan referred to, few fitted his bill in terms of their anxieties and hopes more closely than the Germans. They needed encouragement and hope, and for its part America needed to realise that, in dealing with the fifty million people who were now crowded into the Western zones of Germany, it had to offer them more than just moralistic finger-wagging, war crimes trials, heatless winters and the 'soup kitchens' Roosevelt had thought sufficient back in late 1944. Germany – because of its position, its people, its industrial capacity – was the key to Europe.

A little more than two weeks later, on 5 March, in Fulton, Missouri, Winston Churchill delivered a speech in which he called for Britain and the USA to unite against possible Soviet aggression. He referred to an 'iron curtain' stretching from Stettin on the Baltic to Trieste in the

Adriatic, behind which the resubjugation of the recently liberated peoples of Eastern and Central Europe was being accomplished with consummate ruthlessness by Stalin's henchmen. Churchill's electoral defeat the previous July had relegated him to the post of Leader of the Opposition in Britain, but as a statesman his words held vast authority and served as another indication of the shift in Western attitudes. The speech was actually received downright sceptically by many Americans, who were not looking for more foreign entanglements at this point, but his words hung in the air, and they were closely listened to in Europe.[7]

There was a problem implicit in this new forward stance being proposed by Kennan. The thoughtful diplomat did not dwell on military factors, but they were a significant part of the equation. Officially, America was still committed to withdrawing all its troops from Europe, and soon. At the end of the war there had been ninety-seven American divisions on active duty in all theatres. That number had already been reduced by some eighty divisions, and demobilisation was continuing. The British Army's strength would fall from five and a half million to a little over a million in the same period. The French continued to expand their post-war army, but they would soon be distracted by adventures in the Middle East and Indo-China. In any case, feeling in much of France was pro-Soviet. The coalition government in Paris, which included communist ministers until May 1947, frequently cooperated with Moscow to present an obstructionist united front in German affairs.

The Soviets, actually, had also gone a long way towards demobilising their own huge army, which by the end of 1947 would be reduced from a wartime strength of more than eleven million to one of just under three million – in absolute terms, of course, still greatly outnumbering the military manpower of the other three victor nations. As Churchill said in his speech in Fulton, Missouri, the Russians might not want war, but they did want 'the fruits of war and indefinite expansion of their power and doctrines'. Whether or not Stalin was preparing to use this still-formidable force, and from what we know now this seems unlikely, it remained a highly visible and threatening phenomenon.[8]

In October 1945, only 7 per cent of the American electorate thought that foreign policy concerns should take precedence over domestic problems.[9] The discussions that were going on within the inner circles of the State and Defence Departments during early 1946 would probably have horrified the average American voter, but that did not make them any less necessary. So long as the Americans continued to plan their withdrawal from Europe, their policy towards the Soviets was shaped by the necessity of establishing some kind of modus vivendi with Stalin that would offer a measure of security for Western Europe against possible Russian aggression. This necessity placed Moscow in an altogether advantageous position, and weakened the American stance.

Clay knew this. He also knew that somehow the French and the Russians had to be stood up to. On 19 July he put together a long letter to his Civil Affairs Director, General Echols, which he intended using as the basis for a speech that would be distributed throughout the occupation administration as well as to the German public.[10] Clay, it is clear from some of his letters at this time, was feeling frustrated and even depressed by his inability to make the progress in Germany that he felt lay within his and America's grasp.[11] He was even considering early retirement.

The need for this statement arose from a speech by Soviet Foreign Minister Molotov in Paris the week before, one day before the Allied foreign ministers' conference there broke up in some confusion on 12 July. Molotov said that the creation of a united independent Germany had become urgent, complete with a (highly centralised) democratic central government and a full programme of economic reconstruction. To this end, for the first time, the Soviet Foreign Minister surprised everyone by stating clearly that the Ruhr should not be separated from Germany, thus leaving the French isolated in their demand for detachment and internationalisation of the Reich's richest and most productive industrial area.

Molotov also, however, refused Secretary of State Byrnes' suggestion that, as a first step, zonal boundaries be dismantled and intra-German free trade finally introduced. And, in the metaphorical

small print, the Russian demanded that reparations from Germany
be increased to ten billion dollars and also be supplied in part not
just, as hitherto, from dismantling and confiscation but from current
German production. Molotov's declaration was, in truth, a mixed
message of a typically Soviet sort – a seemingly generous offer that
was liable to vanish in a fog of Russian bureaucratic obstruction,
procedural attrition and semantic nit-picking once it came to actually
putting the thing into practice.

The problem for the Americans was that, for all its ambiguities,
Molotov's statement seemed to play well with the German press, West
as well as East. It seemed more decisive, and therefore potentially
more attractive to the German population, than anything the divided
Western Allies had to offer. 'While occupied Germany is busily
discussing the Molotov statement,' Clay wrote in the preamble to his
letter, 'our own military government people have no real up-to-date
summarized version of our policy or objectives which they could use
in discussions with our German people.'

In the draft of his summary, Clay made it clear, while paying lip
service to Potsdam and JCS 1067, that Germany was not to be squeezed
if that meant its people starved. And he included an interesting aside:
'The United States recognizes the need for the occupation of Germany
until Allied objectives have been accomplished. It believes that with the
return of responsibility to the Germans, the size of the occupation forces
can be reduced soon thereafter . . .' The implication was of a longer-term
American military presence of some size in Germany. A united, democratic and self-governing Germany was reckoned, even under more
favourable conditions than those currently pertaining, to be years away.

On Clay's instructions, the letter was copied to the Defence and
State Departments. At the latter, the Assistant Secretary, Howard C.
Peterson, commented, 'My only criticism of Clay's proposed statement is that it tends a bit in tone towards wooing the Germans.'[12]
When it was discussed at the highest level, however, it was decided
that the proposed material was too political, that this kind of thing
was international policy – in other words, the Secretary of State's job.

Clay got no reply for some time. On 7 August he wrote to the Civil Affairs Division at the War Department in Washington to protest about this, but again no instructions seemed forthcoming, even though, Clay said, this was merely a 'statement of policy we are operating now'.[13] On 12 August, the War Department ordered Clay not to publish his 29 July statement and said it would send a delegation to Berlin to discuss things. Clay complained bitterly, but there was little he could do.

Except that the General's opinions had not gone unheeded. 'Wooing the Germans' was, in fact, coming gradually into fashion, even in faraway Washington.

On 6 September 1946, what had once been Hitler's personal train made a stately arrival at the still bomb-shattered main station in the south-west German metropolis of Stuttgart. Aboard was James F. Byrnes, US Secretary of State. He had slept in the Führer's bed during his overnight trip from Paris. There he had spent the past few days at peace conference proceedings that had already lasted since 29 July and would continue until 15 October, leading eventually to comprehensive treaties with former German wartime allies such as Italy, Hungary, Bulgaria, Romania and Finland.

Byrnes' last public appointment in Paris had been a discussion with the Hungarian Prime Minister, Ferenc Nagy,* about the internal situation there and the progress being made towards post-war rehabilitation. Now, after his nearly 700-kilometre train journey, Byrnes stepped into an official car outside Stuttgart station. Preceded by an escort of 'screeching US army jeeps', as *Time* magazine's man had it, he rode 600 metres or so to the city's Staatstheater, the only major opera house in Germany still functioning after five years of

---

* Ferenc Nagy (1903–79) was the leader of the Smallholders' Party, which won a majority in the free elections held in November 1945. He was in office from March 1946 until May 1947, when he succumbed to a mix of threats and bribes (the Russians had kidnapped his son), resigned, and finally went into exile in the United States. New elections ensured a communist majority in parliament.

Allied bombing. Here an audience was waiting for him, consisting not just of American officers and diplomats but of invited German officials and civilians, plus a wide range of the international press, including Russian journalists. Significantly, the speech was also to be broadcast on German radio, with a simultaneous translation.[14]

Byrnes was supposedly in Stuttgart merely to discuss occupation matters with senior US officers and AMG officials, but this was clearly something more deliberately public and much more important. He was accompanied, for good measure, by two US senators, the Democratic Chairman of the Foreign Relations Committee, Tom Connally of Texas, and his Republican counterpart, Michigan's Arthur Vandenberg.

Byrnes looked tired, as well he might, but the sixty-seven-year-old South Carolinian read his speech slowly and clearly, helping even non-native speakers to understand. What he said transformed the American view of their mission in occupied Germany and, more to the point, revolutionised the view of the Germans themselves.

'It is not,' Byrnes said, 'in the interest of the German people or in the interest of world peace that Germany should become a pawn or a partner in a military struggle for power between the East and the West.' This was an interesting statement. It admitted a conflict with the Soviets, but it was not the key statement. More interestingly for most Germans, he proclaimed that the German people should not be 'denied . . . the possibility of improving their lot through hard work'. He admitted that, without Germany becoming a unified economic unit with a common financial policy, it was impossible for this to be properly achieved. And a democratic government in Germany was the aim, too. Then he came to another of his crucial points:

Security forces will probably have to remain in Germany for a long period. I want no misunderstanding. We will not shirk our duty. We are not withdrawing. We are staying here. As long as there is an occupation army in Germany, the American armed forces will be part of that occupation army.[15]

America was staying in Europe. Maybe not for ever, but there was no more talk of a two-year withdrawal.

The Secretary's speech gave concessions to the Russians, accepting territorial changes in East Prussia in their favour, but cast some doubt as to whether the Poles would be able to hold on to all the areas of eastern Germany they were currently occupying. This must await the final peace treaty negotiations. He also conceded the Saar area to France – though emphatically not the Rhine and Ruhr.

Ever since, analysts have argued about the exact origins and meaning of the Byrnes speech. There is little doubt that it was based on Clay's original letter to Echols. In some places, it reproduces the letter's phrasing almost word for word. It still talks about a unified administration and pushes for all the things that had been pushed for ever since Potsdam. Some have argued that it was directed, despite a few little jabs in the direction of the uncooperative eastern neighbours, mainly at the French rather than the Russians.[16]

Byrnes' promise that the Americans would not withdraw before things in Germany had been settled was an enormous boost to most Germans in the Western zones (Communist Party members perhaps excepted), as was the change in tone of the references to the German standard of living and the Germans' right to work hard and see the fruits of their labour. Even the Secretary of State's equivocation about giving all the rest of East Prussia, Pomerania and Silesia to the Poles might be seen as a comfort to the defeated nation. Now there was, at least, some hope.

This appears to have been the main aim of the speech. To encourage the German population to feel that they were no longer just being punished, but could actually have ambitions to live as other peoples lived, and perhaps in the not too distant future. As such, although applause at the Staatstheater was described by *Time* as 'mild', Byrnes instantly became a very popular man in Germany. After the speech, he was greeted with 'enormous enthusiasm' and mobbed by locals. 'Here,' Clay later recollected, 'was an American Secretary of State out there signing autographs for the Germans, little over one year after the end of the war.'[17]

It was remarkable. A little more than a year after the end of the war – and not quite two since Sergeant Holzinger and his platoon had been the first American soldiers to splash across the river Our into Germany – an Allied leader had spoken convincingly to the defeated and apparently eternally disgraced German nation about hope.

The fact was, of course, that the country's worst post-war winter still lay ahead of it. By the spring of 1947 there would be food riots and more bitter criticism of the Allies. But lines were being drawn and plans modified. Within ten days of Secretary Byrnes' speech, Clay was in correspondence with the War Department in Washington discussing a revision of the draconian JCS 1067 and suggesting that the Stuttgart speech 'be taken as a basis for a positive policy statement'.[18]

On 4 October 1946, premiers of the German *Länder* from the British and American Zones met in Bremen to discuss coordinating their political systems in a '*Länder* Council' along the model followed in the American Zone. On 2 December, Secretary Byrnes and his British counterpart, Ernest Bevin, would sign an agreement leading to the economic unity of their zones, to take effect from 1 January 1947.

On 16 October 1946, eleven of the defendants arraigned the previous year at the Trial of Major War Criminals in Nuremberg were hanged. Goering cheated the noose by committing suicide in his cell. Three of them were acquitted, the rest sentenced to terms from ten years to life. It was the last of the war crimes trials to be conducted under four-power auspices.

The discussions in Paris ground on, finally leading to peace treaties with the former Nazi satellites, but the discussions over Germany rumbled on and on. Kennan was now back from Moscow and becoming an increasingly important figure in Washington. There the Republicans had wiped out the Democratic majority in Congress in the November 1946 elections. Of the pair who had backed Byrnes at Stuttgart, Senator Vandenberg of Michigan, once a staunch isolationist but now an equally fervent anti-communist internationalist, had replaced Connally at the head of the Senate Foreign Relations Committee.

In January, Truman replaced Byrnes as Secretary of State with the formidably hard-headed General George Catlett Marshall, who announced to Molotov in March 1947 at the latest foreign ministers' conference that America was 'opposed to policies which will continue Germany as a congested slum or an economic poorhouse in the centre of Europe'. The continuing move towards a more humane and realistic assessment of Germany gained further momentum from Hoover's second trip to Germany in the winter of 1946–7, when the ex-President issued dire warnings about conditions there. Elsewhere, announcements of huge aid packages for Greece and Turkey, which were seen as threatened by communist aggression, showed that a new, tough Western line was now in place.

JCS 1779 finally replaced JCS 1067 in July 1947, formalising a policy that was already in operation at ground level. The new orders for Clay, who had recently succeeded McNarney as Governor of the American Zone and C-in-C Europe, now stated quite clearly that 'an orderly, prosperous Europe requires the economic contributions of a stable and productive Germany'. The Clay/Byrnes line had triumphed. Morgenthau was officially a dead letter.

But how to ensure that Germany became 'stable and productive' and democratic, too? The answer was given when Secretary Marshall delivered an address to the graduating class at Harvard on 5 June 1947. He used the occasion to outline the administration's proposals for European recovery from the world war.

George Marshall had a plan, one which would become the most famous in modern history. The better future for Europe that this plan envisaged included a place for a new, post-war Germany. And, as it turned out, this latest reincarnation of Germany would be prosperous and peaceful beyond most contemporaries' wildest dreams.

Epilogue:
The Sleep Cure

On 15 September 1949, Konrad Adenauer was elected Chancellor of a new state that called itself the 'Federal Republic of Germany'. Adenauer, at seventy-three long past the age when most politicians would take on such a job, had been approved by the 402-seat parliament with a margin of just one vote – his own. When the result, 202 votes for him – with 142 against, 44 abstentions, one invalid ballot and thirteen deputies not present – was announced by the parliament's speaker, Adenauer turned, seemingly unperturbed, to his neighbour on the parliamentary benches and commented in his strong Rhenish accent: 'Things have always turned out all right.'

By that autumn, four and a half years after the war ended, the various victors had truly gathered all 'their' Germans in. The state over which Adenauer so narrowly came to preside was formed from the three Western zones – American, British and French – with a population close to fifty million. It was federal, it was a republic, but it was not Germany. As if to emphasise the fact, it took as its (allegedly temporary) seat of government the university town of Bonn on the Rhine, rather than the much larger Frankfurt, which in the Middle Ages had been seat of the Holy Roman Empire, and might well have made a permanent capital.

The Russians' protégés to the east founded their own state less than a month later, on 7 October, but they called it something subtly different: the German Democratic Republic. Again, two out of three words were correct. It was German, it was a republic, but it was not democratic.

Officially, the Western state had come into being in May 1949, when the three zones' German representatives had passed a Basic Law that enabled elections for a parliament to take place throughout the areas concerned. The *Länder* that made up the Soviet Zone were invited to follow by a careful wording that said: 'The entire German people remains invited to complete the unity and freedom of Germany in a process of free self-determination.' They wouldn't be allowed to do that for more than forty years, until free self-determination actually became possible.

Born in January 1876 in Bad Honnef near Bonn, Konrad Adenauer had followed a career as a legal civil servant in the service of the Prussian kingdom, of which his native Rhineland had become a part after the Napoleonic Wars. However, he was by religion a pious Catholic and by cultural inclination Westward looking. He had become High Burgomaster of Cologne in 1917, when the last Kaiser was still on the throne of Germany, and remained in office until 1933, elected repeatedly on the ticket of the Centre Party.

Adenauer's politics may have been Catholic and conservative, but he became an energetic, progressive leader for the city. Among other achievements, it was Adenauer who persuaded the Ford Motor Company to establish a major car plant in Cologne, rather than expanding their small facility in Berlin. And the dignitary privileged to open the first four-lane, intersection-free highway in Germany – the country's first *Autobahn* – on 6 August 1932 was also Adenauer. The highway, the first exclusively for the use of motor vehicles (its official name was *Kraftwagenstrasse*, or automobile highway), ran almost dead straight for twenty kilometres from Cologne to Bonn. 'This is how the road of the future will look,' proclaimed the Cologne High Burgomaster, who had been closely involved in the conception of the new route.[1] Six months later, Hitler took power – and the credit as 'inventor' of the *Autobahn*.

Deposed by the Hitler regime, Adenauer spent the next twelve years sporadically hiding from its violence or in its custody (for instance, after the June 1934 'Night of the Long Knives' purge and the 20 July 1944 plot against Hitler's life). At the same time, however, he was confident enough to write long, rather flattering self-exculpatory letters to the Nazi authorities, by means of which he managed to retrieve his mayoral pension entitlement and gain compensation for his rather grand house in Cologne, which had been seized by the regime.

When the Americans occupied Cologne in March 1945, Adenauer was reappointed High Burgomaster of the city, only to fall foul of the British, into whose zone it was absorbed after the war ended. They sacked him that autumn, ostensibly for failing to master the food supply situation, and for some time banned him both from the city and from political activity.

A curious letter in British archives, dating from July 1945 and contained within a file dealing with Adenauer's dismissal, throws a little light on the tense relationship between the High Burgomaster and the new rulers on the Rhine. It is from a General Ferguson, who had been British Military Governor of Cologne from December 1918 to July 1919, and contains some fascinating misinformation. Despite saying he 'came to know him well', Ferguson states that Adenauer was 'a Prussian, not a Rhinelander by birth' (untrue), that he had 'served in the war and been severely wounded' (untrue), and that he had 'a metal lower jaw wonderfully camouflaged' (also untrue).* The octogenarian retired general, who had spotted an interview with Adenauer in the *Scottish Daily Express*, warned his colleagues in Germany:

Adenauer was, and probably still is a man of great influence and undeniable ability. It may be true that he hates the Nazis, in fact if as I believe, he is of the Junker class, it probably is the case, but I am

---

* Adenauer had actually suffered serious facial injuries in 1917 when his mayoral limousine collided with a streetcar in Cologne. His bones and nose were 'pushed in' as a result, a slight but permanent disfigurement that gave him an oriental look.

quite certain that unless he has changed very much in the last 25 years
his hatred of Britain is far deeper than any other feeling. He is clever,
cunning, a born intriguer and dangerous. I suggest that too much
reliance should not be placed on him, and that in their dealings with
him, our authorities should be on their guard.[2]

That Adenauer didn't like the British very much seems likely, and
not entirely surprising. That he disliked both the Russians and the
Prussians much more is probable. Noel Annan had a meeting with
him when Adenauer, rehabilitated by the occupation authorities early
in 1946, was Chairman of the post-war Christian Democratic Party
in the British Zone. In an exchange of small talk, Annan, who was
planning to return to his teaching post at Cambridge University in
the near future, asked the venerable ex-Burgomaster what was the
worst mistake the British had made in their relations with Germany.
Adenauer answered that the mistake had been made 130 years before:

It was at the Congress of Vienna, when you so foolishly put Prussia
on the Rhine as a safeguard against France and another Napoleon.[3]

At the same meeting, Annan also gently queried Adenauer's activities after the First World War (being an intelligence officer, had he
seen General Ferguson's somewhat excitable letter?). The future Chancellor denied being anti-British, though he admitted he found it
difficult to regard Britain as a properly European state.

Prussia, at the time of this discussion, had just ceased to exist, on
the insistence of the Allies (on 25 February 1947). It would have been
missed by many, though not so many the further south and west the
news travelled. In Bavaria, where the term 'Saupreuss' (pig of a Prussian) has been a generally accepted insult for centuries, in Saxony, the
Catholic Rhineland, and many parts of south-west Germany, the Iron
Kingdom had been admired and respected, but never popular.

The only true Prussian to figure prominently at the time Adenauer
became Chancellor was Kurt Schumacher. The Social Democrat leader

and Adenauer's greatest opponent had been born in West Prussia, a region lost by Germany to Poland in 1918. This fact made Schumacher no less a democrat, but perhaps more of a nationalist, and more liable, despite his fervent anti-communism, to look East as well as West in his search for his country's advantage. Had the SPD not gained only 29.2 per cent of the votes against the CDU/CSU's 31 per cent in the August 1949 elections, and had Schumacher consequently become Chancellor, the new West German state might have looked quite different. Under Adenauer, it turned its gaze west to France, and then even further westward. To America.

The French had finally been forced to give up their dreams of a permanently harmless Germany of small states and of an international-alised, exploitable Ruhr, when they realised that they could not carry anyone with them – not even the Russians, and certainly not most Germans in their own zone. In any case, like the British, by early 1947 the French were in deep financial trouble and suffering from a serious case of imperial overstretch. They needed more American money, on the tempting scale that was already being talked about and which would eventually begin to become available after Secretary Marshall's great speech in June 1947.

The price Paris paid for American support was abandonment of its grand post-war plan for breaking up Germany into a multiplicity of states and thereby ensuring that it would never again be an economic or military threat. The British–American 'Bizonia', which had existed since January 1947, had now to become a British–American–French 'Trizonia'. Although the expression 'Trizonia' was current from mid-1948 on, the French took their time making it all the way to the altar for this exercise in politico-economic troilism. France partici-pated in the currency reform in June 1948 and helped the Anglo-Americans break the Soviets' blockade of Berlin, and was engaged in increasingly close de facto economic and political collabo-ration with London and Washington in Germany throughout 1948 and into 1949. Nevertheless, the final, conclusive legal steps for the three-way merger were put into place only in the spring of 1949. The way was now clear for the three Western zones to become a West German – possibly, ultimately, an all-German – state. This was the very thing Paris had spent the first years of the occupation trying to avoid, and represented, in the circumstances of the time, a major sacrifice for the French political establishment.

Meanwhile, the German population managed to glean some fun from the uncertain national situation, which had its absurd side. One of the great pop music hits of 1948 was the popular Cologne singer-songwriter Karl Berbuer's humorous ditty, *'Wir sind die Eingeborenen von Trizonesien'* ('We Are the Natives of Trizonesia'). With its play on the name of Indonesia, the new South-east Asian nation that had just emerged from the wreckage of the Dutch East Indies, it became, for many, a sort of substitute national anthem for the not-yet-born new German state.

French convergence with the Anglo-American unified zone accelerated shortly after Stalin, frustrated by the clear progression of the Western zones towards self-reliance, and by the introduction of a new, hard currency in all three Western zones, gathered up his chips and put them all on the bet of getting the Western Allies out of the former German capital. In June 1948 he blockaded Berlin.

The eleven-month-long Berlin blockade, during which the Anglo-American air forces succeeded in carrying out an 'air lift' of supplies to the beleaguered Western-ruled sectors – but during which the black market skills of the Berliners also came into the equation – provided the basis for a significant act of defiance against Soviet aggrandisement. Apart from the more furtive business of Iran, this was the first instance since 1945 where Stalin had failed to get what he wanted.

The blockade also made heroes of the Berliners. Instead of being cast in the minds of their former enemies as the dark denizens of Hitler's capital, his helpmeets in atrocity, Berliners became heroes of the free world. Noble, stoical, cheerful under pressure. Rather like the British in 1940. Cockneys with a German accent. Survivors. For the first time, ordinary post-war Germans – not just anti-Nazi martyrs – garnered an unreservedly positive press in Western Europe and

America. Stalin stopped being the wartime 'Uncle Joe' and became the villain of the piece.

The currency reform of June 1948 took a little while to translate itself into jobs and security for ordinary people. But now that the money in circulation was suddenly worth something, items from coffee to candles, typewriters to textiles, appeared miraculously for sale. The cigarette economy did not quite die overnight, but the speed with which it became relatively insignificant was amazing. This showed the value of a sound currency, but also the size of the hidden 'real' market economy that, after years of concealment, could burst into plain sight once it was allowed to do so.

Germans in the Western zones rolled up their sleeves. They had already cleared the rubble from their streets and patched up their buildings, even when money was worth nothing and they were permanently hungry. Now they had the chance actually to get their country and their lives back. They even had a government of their own again: limited in its powers, subjected to an ultimate veto by military governors who had now turned into 'High Commissioners', but a government all the same.

So what did the population of former Trizonia, now the Federal Republic of Germany, feel when it came to confronting the past, almost five years after Zero Hour?

The answer was, in most cases, nothing at all. The country had decided to take the sleep cure.

On 20 September 1949, five days after his election as Chancellor of the new, democratic German state and hours after his first Cabinet had been sworn in, Konrad Adenauer gave his first official address to the Federal Parliament (*Bundestag*). It was a policy statement on behalf of a coalition that included the Christian Democratic Union (CDU), the right-wing Christian Social Union (CSU) – the party that had given the American denazifiers so much trouble – the liberal, market-oriented Free Democrats (FDP) and the national-conservative German Party (DP).

Adenauer talked a lot about the law-making that lay ahead of the parliament, cleaning up the legal mess of Nazism, about the practical problems the country faced, and about the tasks of rebuilding bombed and shelled cities and reviving German industry and farming. What the new Chancellor did not do was indulge in breast-beating about German guilt. True, he talked about the mistreatment of the Jews, within the context of general mistreatment by the Nazis, and abhorred the fact that there were still anti-Semites in post-war Germany. But he did not believe in purges. In fact, he told the deputies:

> Much unhappiness and much damage has been caused by denazification. Those truly guilty of the crimes committed during the national socialist time and in the war should be punished with all rigour. But for the rest, we should no longer have two classes of human beings in Germany: the politically flawless and the politically flawed. This distinction must disappear as quickly as possible.

He went on to plead even more clearly that the denazification process be all but nullified:

> The government of the Federal Republic, in the belief that many have atoned for a guilt that was subjectively not heavy, is determined where it appears acceptable to put the past behind us.[4]

To loud cries of approval from his own side of the chamber, Adenauer suggested that he would consider the possibility of petitioning the three Allied High Commissioners about an amnesty for those sentenced by their military courts in the immediate post-war period.

If this seems like complacency on Adenauer's part, it is worth remembering that he was himself a social and economic conservative. Moreover, in his somewhat unsteady coalition, he was reliant on parties such as the CSU, which had not distinguished itself in the denazification process in Bavaria, the DP and the FDP. Finally, as Adenauer well knew, the five million or more expellees from the eastern provinces, who were still adjusting to life in alien environments hundreds of miles from their established roots, were already turning into a powerful political force. They were for the most part, and perhaps understandably, among those voters least inclined to support a Chancellor who apologised all the time for Germany's past.

Even the FDP, in favour of free markets and socially liberal, nevertheless contained a strong intermix of old-fashioned nationalism. As for the DP (German Party), it was a strange combination of a regional ultra-conservative pressure group and a collection point for Nazi remnants (it had originally been re-founded in 1946 as a direct successor to the so-called 'German-Hanoverian Party', which between 1866 and 1933 had campaigned for the restoration of the Hanoverian monarchy that had been dispossessed by Bismarck).*⁵ Given the tight parliamentary situation, even the extreme national-conservative DKP/DRP (*Deutsche Konservative Partei/Deutsche Reichspartei*), with only five seats, had to be taken into account.

Under these circumstances, the Chancellor's position, and the position of this new democratic experiment in Germany, still felt precarious. Adenauer needed a broad consensus and this kind of talk ensured he got it.

Perhaps it was just that, in the end, many of the (mostly) men who had suffered at the hands of the denazifiers were, like Adenauer, middle-class university graduates, usually in law, who continued to see themselves, whatever political choices they had made on the way, as disinterested servants of the people. Unless there was direct evidence of terrible offences against humanity, the Chancellor just could not bring himself to see them as criminals, and, given his own conservative values, he wanted these men to return to the country's service as soon as possible, just as he had.

Kurt Schumacher, in his reply to Adenauer's big speech, attacked the Chancellor's apparent complacency about the Nazi regime's crimes

---

* When the DP finally collapsed in the 1960s, some of its prominent members joined the CDU, while others helped found the neo-Nazi NPD, which has survived into the second decade of the twenty-first century.

and doubted whether its victims, especially the Jews, would ever be properly compensated. The barbaric Hitler regime, he said, 'had dishonoured the German people by its extinction of six million Jews'. Oddly, though, Noel Annan records:

> I remember being surprised that in a ten-page memorandum which Kurt Schumacher wrote in May 1946 setting out what his party wanted the British to do there was, except for one request to move a particular police chief, no reference to denazification.[6]

The American military official Walter Dorn observed the same of Schumacher's lack of real interest in denazification.[7] Annan admired Schumacher greatly for his moral stature, whereas he respected Adenauer for his practical political abilities. But there is something subtle here about why denazification did not work, even for those Germans who hated the Nazis. And there is also something about the way that occupiers, especially English-speaking occupiers during the twentieth and twenty-first centuries, do not understand what unites the people of the countries they occupy, no matter how violently, often lethally, those people disagree among themselves. The history of 'de-Ba'athification' in Iraq tells its own, echoing story, too.

So it was that in May 1951 the CDU and SPD combined to pass the *Entnazifizierungsschlussgesetz* (law to end denazification), which allowed all but categories I and II of Nazi miscreants, i.e. major war criminals and incriminated individuals – in the event, a tiny proportion of those punished by denazification panels – to return to their jobs in the country's civil service.

Even before this, many convicted Nazis had been restored to their old jobs by German-run administrations. According to an American report, in Hesse in 1949, 85 per cent of civil servants originally removed by the denazifiers were back at their jobs. In May 1949, at the time the West German state and constitution were coming into being, between 30 and 60 per cent of officials of the Bavarian *Land* government were ex-Nazis.[8] After the passing at federal level of the

Entnazifizierungsschlussgesetz, the way was also free for ex-Nazis in the central government civil service. In August 1950, a quarter of all departmental heads in the Bonn ministries were ex-Nazis. Three years later, the proportion had reached 60 per cent. In the Foreign Ministry in 1952 the proportion was two-thirds.[9] It must be mentioned that, despite the torrent of accusatory East German propaganda on this issue, by the middle of the 1950s in many regions of that communist state up to 15 per cent of SED members were former Nazis.[10]

The outbreak of war in Korea in June 1950 was another turning point in the history of post-war Germany. Germany, like Korea (and Vietnam), was divided between communist and capitalist regimes and therefore also at risk. In Washington, opinion switched away from post-war moral niceties and towards getting as many 'useful' Germans on the Western team as possible. Freedom needed German industry and German manpower.

Alfried Krupp and other leading industrialists were released from their prisons during 1951, on the initiative of the American High Commissioner to Germany, John McCloy. Soon most had had at least some property returned to them. Krupp suffered losses from the breaking up of his giant company, but with a fortune of more than a billion dollars (estimated in 1960, the equivalent in today's money of between seven and eight billion) he remained the richest man in Germany, and probably in Europe, until his death in 1967.[11]

IG Farben was also broken up.* However, almost all of the IG executives put on trial in 1947–8 enjoyed profitable and respected post-release careers. Again, High Commissioner John McCloy played a part in their early release, though he claimed that he had decided this on purely legal grounds. Fritz Ter Meer, who had been closely involved in planning IG's Auschwitz satellite camp, was released in February 1951 from Landsberg prison in Bavaria. Landsberg was the same not especially rigorous institution in which Hitler had served

---

* Decartelisation restored BASF, Bayer, Agfa and Hoechst as separate companies. Hoechst has recently merged with the French pharmaceuticals giant Rhône-Poulenc SA to become Aventis.

time after his attempted Munich coup in 1923. Ter Meer may have been a war criminal, but he was no fool. He said very little to the reporters gathered outside the prison gates, but did find time to observe: 'Now that the Americans have Korea on their hands, they are a lot more friendly.'[12]

The Korean War unleashed a huge rearmament programme on the part of the US and its allies. Armies that had been allowed to run down were reinforced, budgets massively increased. Washington's armed forces budget near enough quintupled from $17.5 billion in 1950 to $70 billion at the end of 1951. Defence expenditure as a share of the American gross national product went up from 4.9 per cent in 1949 to 17.8 per cent in 1952–3.[13] The British also raised their defence budget. The Labour government, narrowly re-elected in 1950, was divided over the new taxes and charges raised to cover the increased military spending, and was soon out of office.

The Federal Republic, aka West Germany, was rapidly developing into one of the bulwarks of the European resistance to Stalin. There was talk in government circles as early as 1950 of a new West German army (in East Germany there already existed a paramilitary police force – the so-called 'People's Police in Barracks').[14] It no longer mattered nearly so much that an official or a businessman had been a Nazi. All hands were needed to rebuild Germany. The danger from the East was all too clear.

It certainly did not matter at all if that same official or businessman had been in the Wehrmacht. The cult of a 'pure' Wehrmacht that had been led astray by Hitler, but whose soldiers had nevertheless done their duty, flourished from the late 1940s onwards, even though it did not wholly accord with the facts about the Second World War. It was, however, undoubtedly true that, just as not all Allied forces that fought in that just war did so in a just fashion, so, in the case of the Wehrmacht, by no means all of those who fought in the Führer's criminal war were war criminals.

However, by the early 1950s in West Germany there were many who sought to deny that there had been war crimes at all. The Free

Democrats, who had set out to target former Wehrmacht soldiers and POW returnees as potential supporters, fell in with a group of former Nazis, including a circle based around Werner Naumann, former State Secretary at Goebbels' Propaganda Ministry, who had been agitating in favour of a general amnesty for 'so-called war criminals'. Another pillar of Adenauer's power, the GB/BHE,* which entered the parliament (and the government) in 1953, represented many expellees. It also flirted with the far right (several of its leaders were former Nazis). Along with the much larger, supposedly apolitical refugee organisation, the BdV (*Bund der Vertiebenen*, Federation of Expellees), the GB/BHE represented a powerful pressure group in Germany right through to the 1970s, blocking any roads that might have led to a post-war settlement of the 'German Question' through recognition of the post-war territorial losses to Poland and Russia. The GB/BHE even opposed diplomatic relations with Poland and Czechoslovakia until the 'stolen' territories were returned.[15]

A campaign for total amnesty rumbled on, but by now such a thing would have undermined Adenauer's fence-mending foreign policy, and releases and pardons were at best piecemeal. A push before the 1953 elections in West Germany achieved much, but not enough for the Chancellor's nationalist opponents, and in the elections Adenauer's party gained an extra 10 per cent of the vote, greatly strengthening his position. Many real war criminals remained in prison until the late 1950s, but eventually all were released from Allied jails. The last four – SD killing-squad leaders who had been condemned to death at Nuremberg but then had their sentences commuted – left prison in 1958.[16]

One of this final quartet of the pardoned, Dr Martin Sandberger, had personally commanded the killing squad that rendered Estonia 'Jew-free' in the winter of 1941–2, and been SD commander and head of the security police there. As it happened, he had studied law, back in the early 1930s, at Tübingen University with the social democratic

* *Gesamtdeutscher Block/Block der Heimatvertriebenen und Entrechteten* (All-German Bloc of Expellees and Dispossessed).

politician Carlo Schmid. Schmid remembered him well and with a degree of affection. Some years before Sandberger's release, Schmid was among those who submitted statements in support of his repeated pleas for clemency. The impeccably democratically minded Schmid's portrait of the mass murderer Sandberger as a middle-class, educated German led astray could have stood for many thousands of others:

> He was a hard-working, intelligent and gifted lawyer, who on the one hand had succumbed to the intellectual nihilism of the time, and on the other clung firmly to the formal world of middle class behaviour conditioned by his family tradition. Had it not been for the irruption of national socialist rule, Sandberger would have been a decent, conscientious, hardworking official like so many others . . .[17]

Sandberger, Schmid pleaded, should be 'given the chance to prove himself in life anew'. And in the end, he was – 'like so many others'.

The 1950s in West Germany were a time for what might be kindly called 'reintegration' but could also have been called, as it was by some left-wing commentators, 'restoration'[18] – not so much of Nazism, but of the old authoritarian, conservative Germany out of which Nazism had grown. Just as the Bourbons, when they were restored in France after Napoleon's overthrow in 1814–15, ended up pardoning and employing some of Napoleon's most talented soldiers and officials, so Adenauer's Germany was prepared to let Nazis in on the power structure of the Bonn Republic – so long as they behaved themselves and acted as if they were prepared to become democrats. Which most of them, given the chance for a 'second career' after such uncertain times, did.

The benign differences that became apparent in the formally democratic West Germany of the 1950s – contrasting with the equivalent period after the First World War, the 1920s – were threefold.

First, after a shaky start amidst an economy still recovering from the post-war breakdown, with shortages still widespread and industry

only slowly picking up capacity, within a couple of years of its foundation the Federal Republic was booming. Its democratic predecessor,
the Weimar Republic, had never quite achieved sustained economic
growth – not even in the mid-1920s, when it came as close to economic
and, as a result, political stability as it ever would. West Germany's
long boom continued from 1950 to 1965, as Germans, chastened by
war and determined never to go hungry again, worked as never before,
and correspondingly benefited more than any other country (with
the possible exception of Japan) from the enormous resurgence of the
world economy following the Second World War. The period of uninterrupted German growth and prosperity lasted, in fact, a little longer
than the entire Weimar Republic and a lot longer than the 'Thousand-
Year' Third Reich. Even the relatively mild recession of the mid-1960s,
though it caused dismay at the time, was a mere pause in a road to
national riches that continues, with some indigestion as a result of
the absorption of East Germany after 1989, to this day.

Second, the birth of the second German democracy happened in
the shadow of the Cold War. The collapse of the wartime capitalist/
communist alliance and the subsequent nuclear stand-off with Russia
made West Germany a valued partner for the US and its allies. Fear
of communism also stampeded all but the far left and the very far
right of the German political spectrum into supporting the form of
government that the Americans supported: democracy. That was, in
effect, the deal. Even those West Germans who still harboured doubts
about the ultimate efficacy of democracy – the polls taken around
the time of the Federal Republic's foundation indicate there were at
that point quite a few – nonetheless realised that rebuilding it in their
country was the price of membership of the American-led anti-
communist club that guaranteed the safety of their increasingly
prosperous society. The wave of rape and violence that had followed
the Soviet invasion of eastern Germany – horrific first-hand accounts
of which were brought west by masses of refugees – had served to
propel millions of Germans in the Western zones towards their new
American, British and French masters, no matter how unimpressed

by them they might have otherwise been. The rapid imposition east of the Elbe River of a communist puppet state, complete with the full apparatus of police repression and economic semi-serfdom, further reminded the Westerners that, whatever the imperfections of their own post-war state, it was better than the only other alternative currently on offer.

Two million more eastern Germans followed the wartime refugees to the West from the then Soviet Zone between 1949 and 1961, often at considerable personal risk – two million more reminders, if needed, of how unattractive the alternative really was to Western-style democracy.

And third, there was a growing, genuine conviction in the West that this time democracy might work and be found good. Especially among the young, the very 'brainwashed' Hitler Youth products that the Allies had originally feared would prove irreconcilable in a post-Nazi world, there grew a willingness to try the new post-war democratic political diet that had originally been forced upon Germany but which after a while started to taste a little better than it had amidst the bitter reek of defeat.

For Ulrich Frodien, for instance, who, after finding his Silesian refugee family in Soviet-occupied Thuringia, spent almost three years there, increasingly chafing against the new thought-dictatorship that was the developing East German communist state. He desperately wanted to write and express opinions he was not, in this part of Germany, allowed to express. Ulrich's father, after practising medicine in the East under conditions of professional and personal hardship, managed to escape across the border into the West. Ulrich followed some while later, making a dramatic winter escape, on crutches, across the snowy border between the Soviet and British zones from a sanatorium where he had been undergoing treatment for lung problems. By the time young Ulrich, now twenty-one, collapsed on a road he believed to be in the West – he knew for sure that he was safe only when a military vehicle stopped to pick him up, and he saw to his immense relief that it bore British Army number plates – he was half dead with fever and exhaustion, but he survived to begin a new life in the West.[19]

Less than two years later, Ulrich began work at the liberal *Süddeutsche Zeitung* in Munich, where he would later found and manage the paper's picture agency. Likewise, Lothar Löwe, three years younger and also once a fanatical Hitler Youth leader, who had avoided study at Humboldt University out of fear of arrest, also went into journalism, although from a more unsteady start. His first ever encounter with an American GI, on a Berlin tram, had not been encouraging. Seeing this smartly uniformed, conspicuous figure smoking a cigarette next to him among the drab crowd of commuters, young Lothar decided to try out his school-learnt English. 'How do you do, sir?' he said brightly. As Löwe now recalls with retrospective amusement:

> He said nothing. He looked at me like I was a piece of sh*t . . . And then he threw his cigarette on the floor and stepped on it . . . This was the moment I knew we had lost the war . . .[20]

However, spending the first couple of years after the war in the eastern part of Berlin was enough to persuade Löwe that the Soviet-imposed version of 'freedom' held little appeal. After moving with his mother to the US sector, he met an altogether friendlier kind of American. He was drawn into the youth clubs set up by the US military authorities precisely with the purpose of encouraging teenagers like him, who had grown up under Hitler, to learn about America and to involve themselves in a new, democratic post-war Germany. It helped, in those times of shortage, that the youth clubs offered hot drinks (real coffee and hot chocolate) and snacks.[21]

Once the connection with the occupiers was made, Löwe became involved with an American-sponsored youth newspaper, and after that he was hooked. By his early twenties, he was employed as a reporter by the popular Berlin daily newspaper *Der Abend* (The Evening – even though it appeared at midday), which had been founded in 1946 under licence from the American authorities by Hans

Sonnenfeld, a former executive of the Ullstein publishing house, and Maximilian Müller-Jabusch, a veteran editor from the pre-war liberal newspaper of record, the *Vossische Zeitung*. Müller-Jabusch had extra reason not to love the Nazis, who had mistreated his Jewish wife. Löwe learned his trade, he recalls, from the Americans ('learning by doing') and from Müller-Jabusch and the other 'old gentlemen' from the Weimar press, who were now able to return to their desks.[22]

Reporting from a democratic but firmly anti-communist stand-point on Berlin and regional matters, including the 1953 workers' uprising in East Germany, young Löwe quickly made a local reputa-tion. In his thirties he became a national figure as the correspondent of ARD (German state television) in America, from where he reported on the American reaction to the building of the Berlin Wall in August 1961 and two years later on the assassination of President Kennedy. He was then ARD's man in East Germany, whence he was expelled because of his brutally frank accounts of conditions there and espe-cially the East German government's secret 'shoot-to-kill' policy at the border.

It was perhaps in the rise of a lively, and in many cases highly politicised, press in West Germany that the new three-quarter-country's idiosyncratic route to democracy was most vividly expressed. Of the hundreds of newspapers and magazines licensed by the Western Allies in the years immediately following the war, several would form the basis of internationally important newspaper concerns.

In a country hungry for information and eager to express itself freely after twelve years of dictatorship, dynamic proprietors could quickly carve out profitable and influential niches for themselves. Most arose in the British Zone, where press regulations were from the outset more liberal than elsewhere. And it was in the north-western part of the British Zone, in the autumn of 1948, that a group of concerned German journalists from Hamburg and its surrounding area got together, along with local academics, churchmen and psychol-ogists, for a conference at which the theme was 'the journalist as entrepreneur', but which most importantly dealt, in an amateur sociological kind of way, with what they, as newspapermen, could do to help prevent a recurrence of the Nazi rise to power. The general conclusion was that the press in the Weimar Republic, written mainly by earnest liberal intellectuals (including many of the participants in the conference), had failed to attract a mass readership and thus to influence the general public in a positive way. In other words, for all its good intentions, it had been boring. This must change.[23]

Whether this was correct or not, certainly the evolving press in the Western zones was not all boring. Sometimes both the Allied occupiers and the nascent West German government would come to wish it had been. Whatever the serious gentlemen who had proposed the 'journalist as entrepreneur' in 1948 had actually expected, what they got was – in the left corner – Rudolf Augstein, and – in the right – Axel Springer.

Rudolf Augstein was just twenty-three, a former artillery observation officer who ended the war as a deserter from the Wehrmacht, when he founded *Der Spiegel* (The Mirror), a weekly news magazine, in British-occupied Hanover in January 1947. He had spent the previous year writing for British-controlled newspapers, and he consciously based *Der Spiegel* on the British news magazine *News Review* and its even more famous American equivalent, *Time* magazine. Critical, satirical, left-liberal, *Spiegel* acquired a devoted readership as the 1940s turned into the 1950s and it moved its headquarters to Hamburg, which was once more thriving as Germany's second city after Berlin.

Axel Cäsar Springer, born in Altona near Hamburg in 1912, son of a successful printer and newspaper publisher active in liberal politics before Hitler came to power, was thirty-four when, courtesy of the British authorities, he launched *Hör Zu* (Listen), a popular radio (and later TV) listings magazine, in Hamburg in 1946. This was followed by the women's magazine *Constanze*, and then, two years later, by the daily *Hamburger Abendblatt*. Finally, he put in place the cornerstone of the Springer concern, the mass-circulation, heavily illustrated *Bild-Zeitung* (Picture Newspaper). This garish broadsheet, consciously modelled on highly successful, sensationalist British newspapers such as the *Daily Mirror* and the *Daily Sketch*, soon gained the biggest sales (2.5 million by 1956, 5 million by the 1980s, fifty years later still 3.5 million) of any European newspaper outside the United Kingdom, and second in the world only to the Japanese daily *Yomiuri Shimbun*.

In 1953 Axel Springer acquired the British-owned paper *Die Welt*. This had been the official mouthpiece of the occupation authorities in the early post-war days, based on the London *Times*, and was reckoned, unlike most of Springer's titles at this point, to be a serious publication. He turned it into the 'respectable' (but loss-making) flagship of his empire. By 1968, the Springer Publishing House was responsible for nineteen major publications, making up 88 per cent of all Sunday newspapers in West Germany, 81 per cent of all newspapers sold at street outlets such as tobacconists (many Germans subscribed to and received their newspapers by mail), 70 per cent of all newspapers sold in Berlin and Hamburg, and 56 per cent of all radio and television listings magazines.[24]

Augstein's *Spiegel* and its sister papers were left-liberal and oppositional, critical of Adenauer's West Germany, while Springer's papers, like the man himself, were vehemently anti-communist and conservative – in the case of *Bild-Zeitung*, when it chose to turn its attention away from scandal, shock and celebrity stories to deal with political matters, aggressively and raucously so. His papers opposed recognising the Russian and Polish acquisition of Germany's eastern provinces, and for decades would print the name of the East German state only as 'DDR' (in inverted commas), thus constantly emphasising the illegitimacy of Walter Ulbricht's 'German Democratic Republic'. Augstein, by contrast, was in favour of recognising the communist regime, and formalising the loss of the eastern territories, and even of conciliatory negotiations with the Eastern Bloc over the status of West Berlin.[25] Not so Springer. He moved his headquarters to West Berlin, where he built an eleven-storey office block yards from the Berlin Wall, from where he could see and be seen by East Berlin's citizens and their guards. It was a typically quirky and clever move, a permanent reminder of what he and his papers stood for – and what

Augstein and his liberal friends, as Springer saw them, did not.

All the same, despite its relentless muckraking and shrill right-wing bias, even the Springer Press could not be accused of encouraging a Nazi revival. Springer himself was, superficially at least, not the tough, ruthless press baron one might expect to own a paper such as *Bild*. Spare-framed, dandyish, with an interest in religion and esoteric philosophy, Axel Springer was also possessed of a powerful charm, which he used with great success on those he liked or needed – from the British newspaper controllers who gave him his licences in the early days to politicians, journalists and also women (he was married five times).

According to George Clare (who later worked for him), Springer picked up his first newspaper licence from the British in Hamburg, against stiff competition from other would-be proprietors, because he was the first applicant not to complain loudly and often unconvincingly about being persecuted by the Nazis. The officer asked Springer, in German, with ill-suppressed sarcasm if he too had been persecuted by anyone (the German verb *verfolgen* can also mean 'pursued' or 'chased'), to which young Springer replied cheekily, 'Only by women'. He got the licence.[26]

After he became Germany's most important and richest newspaper proprietor, Springer spent Christmas every year in Jerusalem and was the recipient of several awards from the Israeli government and Jewish charities.

Under the Weimar Republic, swathes of the popular press had been owned by extreme, anti-democratic nationalist figures, most especially Alfred Hugenberg, former director of Krupp Steel, leader of the German National People's Party, and ally of Hitler. Springer was different. His was consciously a post-war, post-Hitler version of what it meant to be German and of the right. In the 1960s Springer himself drafted four articles of faith that summed up his media group's commitments, which changed little in the next twenty years and still appear on its website today in a form amended to suit changing historical circumstances:

1. Advocacy of German reunification.
2. Reconciliation between Germans and Jews.
3. Rejection of all forms of political totalitarianism.
4. Defence of the social market economy.[27]

Adhering to basic freedoms, but conservative, often socially intolerant, and nationalist within certain limits – this echoed the tone of
the parliamentary-democratic restoration state ruled over by Konrad
Adenauer between 1949 and 1963, when the 'old fox' finally (reluctantly) resigned as Chancellor at the age of eighty-eight.

Adenauer's state may not have been what the more idealistic Allied
planners dreamed of when they first brought their democratic ideas
into occupied Germany, but it functioned, it prospered and it
provided a protective environment for the first stage of West
Germany's healing process.

Adenauer himself devoted a great deal of attention to foreign policy.
This was not unimportant. The new republic, isolated and still
distrusted by its neighbours, and only incompletely sovereign, needed
to find a way forward into a new Europe and a new world. Luckily,
in the French Foreign Minister Robert Schuman he found a partner
not just willing but eager to create a peaceful, united Europe that
included Germany.

Schuman was a perfect fit for Adenauer, a man with multiple
cultural allegiances. A patriotic Frenchman who had risked his life in
the wartime Resistance, Schuman was nevertheless no stranger to
Germany and its people. He had been born in 1886 in Luxembourg,
a German citizen (his French father came from Lorraine, which was
part of Germany between 1871 and 1918), and grew up in the Grand
Duchy, where he learned French and German as well as the local
language. He completed his education at various German universities,
but chose to become a French citizen when Alsace-Lorraine was
returned to France in 1919, and was elected to the Paris Chamber of
Deputies that same year. A member of Paul Reynaud's wartime

Cabinet in 1940, he later had an adventurous war with the French Resistance, which included imprisonment by the Gestapo.

In 1948, Schuman was serving as Foreign Minister in the post-Gaullist, post-communist government that negotiated the formation of Trizonia and acceded to the establishing of a West German state. Even before the foundation of the Federal Republic, Schuman declared France's readiness to create a democratic European organisation of which a democratic, rehabilitated Germany could be a part. This represented a radical change from the 'Divide and Rule' principle that had dominated France's obstructive attitude in Germany in the years immediately after 1945.

In May 1950, Schuman announced an offer to the Germans and other European countries to manage the sinews of Europe's recovery, their iron and steel industries, in a collaborative and democratic fashion: a common market. It gave France a stake in the Ruhr, the guarantee of co-responsibility she had always hankered after, while leaving the industrial megalopolis in German hands. Adenauer was pleased to accept. He wanted what Schuman wanted, which was a Germany tied inside a peaceful European family and therefore unlikely to go rogue again.

Six countries – France, Germany, Belgium, the Netherlands, Luxembourg and Italy – signed the Treaty of Paris in April 1951. From this came the European Community, which became the European Union, and, later, allowed for West Germany's accession to the American–West European alliance system, NATO.

In the early 1950s, Adenauer, despite his initially lukewarm attitude towards compensation for Nazi crimes against the Jews – he habitually spoke of Jewish suffering, but hardly ever about German perpetrators – carried out negotiations with the Israeli government, mostly behind closed doors. In September 1952 he agreed to a deal that would, over years to come, compensate Jewish Holocaust survivors to the extent of some 100 billion Deutschmarks. The Chancellor's difficulty came when he tried to get the settlement through the Bundestag in Bonn the following March. The deal was unpopular among many in the country at large.

A year earlier, only 5 per cent of Germans had admitted feeling guilty about the fate of the Jews. Although 29 per cent felt that some restitution was owed by Germany to the Jewish people, 40 per cent felt that any compensation should be paid for 'by those responsible', and 21 per cent felt that 'the Jews themselves were partly responsible for what happened to them during the Third Reich'. Many of Adenauer's own party and of the CSU voted against it, the Free Democrats abstained and Adenauer had to rely on the social democratic opposition to get the bill through.[28]

It was a difficult and momentarily embarrassing beginning for a decades-long West German policy that was both morally right and diplomatically cunning – committed support of Israel in foreign policy and a determined philo-Semitism at home. Again this was reflected in the German press, including the Springer concern's massively influential but otherwise strongly conservative newspapers.

Adenauer's true personal feelings on this issue remain not entirely clear, except that his personal method of operating, according to Annan, was *do ut des*, Latin for 'I give so that you give'. And as far as West Germany's self-image and international reputation were concerned, the compensation bill was the gift that kept on giving.

Meanwhile, amid the nervous silence and the hard work and the quiet 'restoration' of those who had been punished after 1945, Germany began to prosper once more. Professor Erhard, who had been part of the clandestine wartime cabal preparing for the post-war crisis, was made economic director of the Bizone and pushed through price deregulation in 1948 against the advice of the Allied experts. He was right, as the rapid improvement showed. In September 1949, Erhard became Minister of Economics in Adenauer's government, a post he would hold for fourteen years with huge success.

After January 1950, food was no longer rationed (in Britain, rationing did not finally end until mid-1954). A construction boom was under way. With the pump primed by the Marshall Plan and Europe eager to get back to work, the German 'social market economy' took off. The generation of young managers who had learned their skills in the Nazi armaments boom of the 1930s and early 1940s now turned to peaceful, export-led manufacturing in a post-war world crying out for machine tools and high-quality manufactured goods.

As one writer has recently noted, 'The social market economy of Ludwig Erhard had its roots in the policies of Albert Speer'.[29] And it did no harm that the bombing and the chaos of 1939–45 had swept away much old plant and factory space as well as rusting infrastructure. In contrast, Britain continued with antiquated industrial practices, factories and equipment. Its long decline as a manufacturing nation accelerated, at the same time as Germany's revival went into overdrive.

Germany in the 1950s, like America and Britain and other Western countries during this decade, experienced a conservative interlude, where relations between the sexes appeared to retreat to something like their pre-war shape. Women had worked in factories and offices during wartime, and experienced financial as well as sexual freedom. Now, in most cases, they returned to home and children. German men had suffered the humiliation of defeat, the frustration and deprivation of long periods in Allied prison camps – the last, weary German POWs were not repatriated from the Soviet Union until 1955 – and many also experienced the shock of returning home to see that 'their' women seemed to prefer occupation soldiers.

Adenauer's Christian-conservative government, eager to turn the clock back to social 'normality', got the vote of the majority. The complaining rebels, pointing to society's amnesia about the Nazi past, got little attention. The magazines were full of domestic bliss, sanitised war stories, consumer desire and portraits of Germans as victims led astray by the Nazi leadership. One of the runaway bestsellers in the Germany of the early 1950s was Ernst von Salomon's brilliant *Der Fragebogen* (1951), an autobiographical novel and *apologia pro vita sua*, satirising the Allied denazification questionnaire and thereby the victors' right to rule and judge Germany. Von Salomon, although a former far-right-wing activist convicted in his youth for involvement in the murder of Weimar Finance Minister Walther Rathenau, was a curious political beast. Although sympathising with many of Hitler's aims, he had never joined the Nazi Party – for whose leaders he expressed an open, fastidious contempt – and had lived openly throughout the war with his Jewish female companion. *Time* magazine's reviewer expressed the revulsion of many when he described the book's American translation as redolent of 'self-pity mixed with arrogant self-righteousness'. Distaste for *Der Fragebogen* was widespread in liberal circles in Germany and throughout the former Allied countries, but others in Germany and elsewhere applauded this conservative intellectual's hard-headed, even cynical analysis of why Hitler had come to power and its exposure of alleged Allied hypocrisies.[30] This was literature for the new post-Hitler German right.

The government itself spent some time dealing with the past – but this mostly in the form of lengthy and thorough reports, based on the collation of hundreds of eyewitness reports, enumerating the sufferings and injustices suffered by Germans expelled from the eastern territories and from the Sudetenland during the brutal twilight of the Third Reich. It was mostly true, of course, but only one part of the past.

As for Adenauer, his slogan during his successful re-election campaign in 1957 was: 'No experiments!' The double-edged meaning again expressed the spirit of the time. Nothing radical to the left – or right. The new West German state, under the Adenauer–Erhard duopoly that lasted until 1963, made a bargain with its citizens: we provide prosperity and social stability, and you accept democracy. And why shouldn't you? Things are good.

The price for this longed-for normality was conformity. Not the kind of draconian conformity demanded by the Nazis, but more like the Eisenhower-era, socially encouraged conformity in America – except with added Jesuits, given the clerical influence in the Adenauer government. And Axel Springer.

Into the 1960s, members of the West German government still at times behaved, if not like Nazis, then in a way reminiscent of the authoritarian acolytes of the old 'deep state', who had undermined Germany's last attempt at democracy during the Weimar Republic. The social and cultural focus of West Germany for the first fifteen years or so of its existence was deeply, at times oppressively, conservative. This manifested itself most notoriously in the 1962 '*Spiegel* Affair', in the final months of Adenauer's chancellorship. In October of that year, Rudolf Augstein, now a middle-aged, wealthy rebel but on this occasion no less a hero for all that, was arrested along with several of his *Spiegel* colleagues on possible treason charges. Their 'crime' was to have published a damning critique of the *Bundeswehr*'s ability to defend the country against a Russian attack, based on leaked documents originating from a recent NATO exercise.

Augstein spent 103 days in custody, released only after press and popular outrage – and revelations of ministerial high-handedness – caused the near-collapse of Adenauer's governing coalition. The price for the government was the resignation of Bavarian CSU politician Franz-Josef Strauss, the dynamic, ultra-conservative forty-seven-year-old Defence Minister, who, despite his initial denials, was proved to have been the driving force behind the prosecution and to have wildly exceeded his powers in the process. Strauss remained an important figure, but he never fulfilled his ambition of becoming Chancellor. The price for Augstein? Naturally, the uncomfortable days in a prison cell in Hamburg, but also the consolation of hearing large crowds gathering outside the jail every day to demand his release (and the prosecution of Minister Strauss). So embarrassed was the government that it felt forced to move Augstein to Koblenz to get him away from the sympathetic crowds.[31] The press campaign on his behalf, and the widespread demonstrations and protests, were something new in postwar Germany. And there was a further consolation for Augstein the magazine proprietor – *Spiegel*'s circulation, already half a million, doubled. In 1965, the Federal Constitutional Court absolved Augstein and his colleagues of any guilt.

There was a phenomenon in West Germany during the 1950s, after the abolition of the ration system at the very beginning of the decade, called the *Fresswelle*, the 'eat wave'. After the near-starvation of the immediate post-war period, West Germans went crazy for food. Suddenly they could eat their fill, and then maybe some. And they did. This eat wave went on through the 1950s and into the 1960s.

The playwright Berthold Brecht has a saying in his *Threepenny Opera*: '*Erst kommt das Fressen, dann kommt die Moral*' – 'First comes filling your belly*, then morality'. In other words, those with a full stomach find it easier to be good. By the 1960s, Germans had full stomachs. And some of them wanted very badly to be good. The mobilisation of public outrage over the '*Spiegel* Affair' – sometimes described as 'the beginning of [post-war] German democracy' – was one indication, perhaps the greatest, that things were changing.

The patient began to awake from the sleep cure and look around. The patient began to remember . . .

There was already the first of several generational changes going on in Germany. The survivors of Hitler's generation – those born in the 1880s and 1890s – were now old and fading from public life. Those of the following generation, the energetic achievers of the Nazi regime such as Speer, born around 1900–1905, too young for the First World War but acutely aware of its humiliating aftermath, were moving into late or very late middle age. The next generation, those who had been born around 1920, who had spent their adolescence in Nazi Germany and served in the war as young men, were on the threshold of their 'best years'. And then there was the generation that was around thirty, out in the world but not yet quite ready to make its mark, the so-called 'Flak Auxiliary' generation, born in the late 1920s, who as schoolboys had been drafted in to man the anti-aircraft guns against the Anglo-American bombers. Finally, there was a really new generation: the generation born in the early to mid-1940s. The student generation of the 1960s.

---

* In German there is a distinction between '*fressen*' meaning eating (by animals) and '*essen*' meaning eating (by human beings). Brecht's use of the first coarsens the expression deliberately, as it does in the word '*Fresswelle*'.

It is often said that Germany's re-examination of itself began in the mid-1960s. In fact, it seems, rather, to have begun in 1958, amid the late period of Adenauer-era conformity, when the 'Central Bureau of the *Land* Justice Authorities for the Investigation of National Socialist Crimes' was set up at Ludwigsburg, just north of Stuttgart.

The Central Bureau had been founded in response to the trial at Ulm in Bavaria, that same year, of former members of a killing squad in Russia. The state's interest in them had been aroused, it seems, only because one of them had attempted to rejoin the civil service and reaccess his pension rights. Investigations uncovered a whole network of former killing squad members living law-abiding, productive lives in plain sight in West Germany. These men stood trial. The Ulm case, the first case of mass murder to go to trial since the foundation of the West German state, aroused real public interest in Nazi crimes, for the first time since the immediate post-war period.

The task of the Ludwigsburg office was to deal systematically with crimes committed outside of normal German jurisdiction, for instance in concentration camps and other crime scenes not directly associated with warlike activity. Its role was to coordinate such investigations: it had, technically, no power to prosecute. Nonetheless, its work identified many more West German citizens, apparently living peacefully in various parts of the country, who had been involved in the working of Auschwitz extermination camp. These men had somehow escaped the original trial of Commandant Höss and his henchmen in 1947. Following a laborious process of legal and jurisdictional wrangling, they were taken into custody and a trial prepared.

Meanwhile, Israeli agents had kidnapped Adolf Eichmann in Argentina, to where he had fled in 1950 after years living under an assumed name in northern Germany. Eichmann, a senior SS officer who had been in charge of the transportation of Jews to the extermination camps, was tried in Jerusalem and executed, on 31 May 1962, after an internationally reported trial. A year later, the Auschwitz Trial (usually called the 'Second Auschwitz Trial') of twenty-two defendants

began in Frankfurt. It lasted for 183 trial days, and the verdicts – six
life sentences, various sentences from three years and three months
to fourteen years, and three acquittals – were pronounced on 19
August 1965. The daily appearance at the stand of a total of 360
eyewitnesses with chilling stories to tell, and the presence of television
cameras and newspaper journalists, brought home with shuddering
immediacy to the German public, after twenty years of silence and
forgetting, the full horror of what had been done in the name of the
German people by these apparently ordinary men during those shameful years.

The children of the war, the ones who had survived the malnutrition and disease that had led to such terrible infant mortality in the
immediate post-war years, were now young workers and students.
They began to ask questions of their parents and grandparents. They
were not satisfied with many of the answers.

It was and is often said of the Germans, with more than a hint of
sarcasm, that they 'denazified themselves' on 8 May 1945. During the
advance into Germany that year, an American major told the photo-
journalist Margaret Bourke-White: 'The Germans act as though the
Nazis were a strange race of Eskimos who came down from the North
Pole and somehow invaded Germany.' Many observers at the end of
the war would, like White, have remarked, tongue in cheek: 'I have
yet to find a German who will admit to being a Nazi.'[32]

There is, of course, a non-cynical truth in this, to the extent that
most Germans did, by the time the immediate post-war period began,
wish to distance themselves from the Third Reich. Many – probably
most – despised Hitler and the other leaders who had led the country
astray and their people into such misery. At that moment, perhaps
that was enough of a prophylactic against a recurrence of the Third
Reich. Then, closing their ears to the arguments of the well-meaning
Allied denazifiers, most submerged themselves in work, in reconstruction, recreating 'normality'. These were physical as well as psychological
imperatives.

The Auschwitz Trial, however, and the great questioning that began in the 1960s, led to something else: a proper self-denazifying (or as the French put it: '*auto-épuration*'). Now large numbers of Germans really did start to look at and study the behaviour of their nation between 1933 and 1945, and try to draw conclusions. They had food in their bellies, roofs over their heads, jobs (or student bursaries), and they were not to be fobbed off with bland explanations.

This led to excesses. The rebellious alternative culture in Germany in the 1960s and 1970s could be especially oppressive and obsessive. It dropped out of the Mom-and-Pop, glad-to-have-enough-to-eat conservatism of the Adenauer era and into a future where Mom and Pop's ideas were not just boring but evil (hadn't Mom and Pop been Nazis?).

There was truth in the rebels' accusations. Critical Germans were still in a minority, albeit a growing one. The '*Spiegel* Affair' might have brought many thousands out on to the streets to demand more freedom, but according to a poll in 1966, 54 per cent of West Germans agreed with the statement that 'In politics there is too much talk and not enough action. We need a strong man at the top, who will make short shrift of trivialities', and 44 per cent were convinced that German youth lacked 'discipline and good order'.* A total of 59 per cent agreed with the idea that 'It is finally time to get a firm grip on all trouble-makers, and not using kid gloves, as we have until now'.[33] Even at this point of transition, the echoes of those same longings that had made Hitler's regime so popular had by no means died away.

To balance this continued presence among many Germans of old-fashioned nationalist-authoritarian values, it was true that by the 1960s the right-wing fringe parties that formed part of Adenauer's coalition back in the early 1950s – the 'German Party', the GB/BHE and so on – had either dwindled or been subsumed into the larger parties. The expellee groups, while still influential, were no longer quite such a crucial element in the political equation, as the expellees

---

* The German phrase *Zucht und Ordnung*, though going back hundreds of years, was common in the Nazi period and implied 'good breeding' as well as discipline.

and their children integrated into West German life and began to vote accordingly. German politics was now a three-way contest, with the two big 'people's parties', the centre-right CDU and the centre-left SPD, potentially dependent on the parliamentary support of the socially liberal but pro-enterprise FDP for any government they might form. Neo-Nazi groups experienced local revivals, but never made it into the federal parliament, let alone the government.

From 1966 to 1969, Germany had one of the most paradoxical governments of any Western state. Or perhaps it simply expressed the feel of the country. Adenauer had gone in 1963, and Ludwig Erhard's government was not a success. In the grip of West Germany's first recession since 1945, with more than half a million unemployed – considered shocking at the time – it had fallen as a result of disagreements with its FDP partners about the tax increases needed to balance the budget (the tax-cutting FDP was against them). Under these circumstances, only one other possible partner existed: the SPD. Hence the idea of a so-called 'Grand Coalition', which took office on 1 December 1966.

On the one hand, the administration was headed by a CDU Chancellor, Kurt Georg Kiesinger, who was a former Nazi Party member. The silver-haired Swabian lawyer had been a liaison man between Goebbels' Propaganda Ministry and the German Foreign Office. Obviously a *Muss-Nazi*, but a Party member nevertheless. On the other, as his Foreign Minister in their so-called 'Grand Coalition', there stood Willy Brandt, the Social Democrat leader. Brandt had been forced to flee Germany for Scandinavia when Hitler came to power, and had even taken Norwegian citizenship. He had returned to Germany after the war as a major in the Norwegian army before deciding, at the low point of his birth-country's fortunes, to revert to German nationality and help the reconstruction effort. Many conservative Germans still viewed him as a traitor.

It was a pivotal moment. The joining, as it seemed, of anti-Nazi Social Democrat with ex-Nazi conservative caused purest disillusionment among many sensitive citizens. It led to the formation of an 'extra-parliamentary opposition', composed of many thousands of West Germans, who had decided that, with the Social Democrats' 'selling out' to the right, a slip of paper dropped in a ballot box just didn't make anything happen.

Before long, a group of 'urban guerrillas' who called themselves the 'Red Army Faction' (also known as the Baader-Meinhof Gang) were going around stealing cars and kidnapping and shooting anyone they disapproved of, particularly ex-Nazis. Nazi methods for violent denazification. Such was the group's revulsion at the hypocritical conservatism, as they saw it, of the German political and economic establishment, that they also rebelled against the privileged position of Jews in this despicable new Germany's world view, allying themselves with Palestinian groups and even setting off a bomb at a Jewish Cultural Centre in Berlin.

Germany subtly changed again in 1969. Willy Brandt finally became Chancellor, in coalition with the Free Democrats – the first Social Democrat to take office as head of a German government since Hermann Müller in 1928.

Brandt made treaties with West Germany's eastern neighbours that recognised the post-war borders. He visited Warsaw and dropped on to one knee in front of the memorial honoring the victims of the Warsaw Ghetto Uprising. It was clear that Brandt's apology extended not just to the Jews who died but to the entire Polish people. The conservative right and the refugee organisations didn't like it, but they were no longer the power in the land that they had been in the 1950s when Adenauer put his uneasy coalition together and started post-war German democracy on its way. Brandt's West Germany also finally recognised the reality of the East German state, though it never formally gave up its claim to represent all Germans.

This was a different Germany, one starting to feel secure in its wealth and its institutions. A Germany that was now prepared to talk about the past, and to recognise what had gone wrong, without necessarily feeling that this undermined its right to exist. In the mid-1970s,

Holocaust, a well-meant American mini-series chronicling the fate of the Weisses, a middle-class Jewish family in Berlin, pierced the German television-viewing public to its heart. Where there had once been so little, now a flood of books and articles and television documentaries covered every aspect of Nazi malfeasance, and did not spare the German nation for its complicity. They continue to this day. Paradoxically, the further the nation moved from its ugly past, the more diligently Germans confronted it. 'First comes filling your belly . . .'

The generational change continued. From Chancellor Willy Brandt (born 1914), the resistance fighter, to Chancellor Helmut Schmidt (born 1918), who served with the Wehrmacht but converted to social democracy as a returned soldier in the British Zone. Then, abruptly, came Helmut Kohl (born 1930), a child throughout the Nazi period and therefore the first West German Chancellor to be blessed with no possible responsibility for what happened before 1945. Perhaps appropriately, Kohl was also the first post-war West German Chancellor to become truly leader of all Germany.

It was in November 1989, as Helmut Kohl attended a state dinner in Warsaw, that the Berlin Wall opened, the citizens of the failed state of East Germany poured through to the West, and a new era began for Germany and the world.

After the building of the Berlin Wall in August 1961, the haemorrhaging of its population to the West all but ceased. If the reaction to the '*Spiegel* Affair' in West Germany was hailed as the rebirth of West German democracy, the Wall was seen as East Germany's 'second birth'. They were, of course, two revealingly different phenomena – the flowering of critical consciousness in West Germany after 1962, a creative, positive thing; and the imprisonment of the East German population after 1961, a terrible suppression of possibility that permitted only the unimpeded continuation of a politico-economic tyranny.

Nevertheless, the East German state seemed, in the 1970s, at its strongest. Aware of the regime's unpopularity, the state planners had permitted some growth of consumer goods production after the Wall went up. A modest prosperity followed. Ten years later, most East German households had a refrigerator, a TV, a washing machine and even a car – though the waiting time for this might be seven years. It was even claimed, at one point in the mid-1970s, that the German Democratic Republic had overtaken Great Britain in its living standards. East German athletes were successful in the world's arenas far beyond the country's size and resources – a prominence that the regime naturally attributed to communism's production of exceptional human material, but which later, it became apparent, was actually down to elaborate and subtle doping programmes in which the government itself was totally complicit.

Above all, the East German state considered itself morally superior to its Western equivalent. Theirs was a totally cleansed, post-Nazi state, they claimed, whereas the Federal Republic was still tainted by the role Nazis played in its affairs. In the East, for instance, East Prussians, Silesians, Sudetenlanders and other expellees had from the start never been allowed to call themselves that, or even 'refugees'. Their official title was 'resettlers'. They were not permitted to form special organisations or write or speak about their suffering, or complain about their fate. If they did so, they were prosecuted. Organisations in the West such as the BdV, which continued to protest at the injustice of the post-war status quo, were attacked from East Germany as 'revanchists' or worse. East Germany might be a dictatorship, but it was the 'better Germany'.

East Germany was, however, also the less rich Germany. In fact, it was the broke Germany. It turned out that the impressive economic figures put out by its officials were more or less fraudulent. By the 1970s the country was massively in debt, getting by with foreign loans, some from the West, and by such stratagems as selling political prisoners to West Germany for as much as a hundred thousand marks apiece.

Then the Soviet Union met its fate. Eastern Europe was no longer a fortress. East Germans could leave via Poland, Hungary and Czechoslovakia. And the German Democratic Republic itself came, in the fatal autumn of 1989, as it grandiosely celebrated its fortieth anniversary, to the end of the line.

By the autumn of 1990, Germany was reunited under a Christian Democrat Chancellor, Helmut Kohl. Many years earlier, Axel Springer had maintained, 'I shall reunite Germany, whether you believe it or not.'[34] Springer himself died in 1985, just four years before his seemingly impossible dream came true, but for all his sins it must be said that he kept the faith. Forty-five years after Year Zero, Germany – not all Germany because the lost eastern provinces would never be regained – was one country again.

After Kohl came Schröder. The wartime generation was beginning to disappear. Even the Flak Auxiliaries, the loyal but increasingly sceptical teenagers of those last wartime months, were ageing into their sixties and beyond. Chancellor Gerhard Schröder (born 1944) was not quite a post-war baby. His father died a few months after his birth, killed in action with the Wehrmacht in October 1944. He grew up in straitened circumstances in a single-parent family, but the opportunities provided by the post-war 'social market' system enabled him to make it to the top. Schröder lived two-thirds of his life under the American defensive umbrella that guaranteed West German security and prosperity. All the same, he proved as friendly to Russia as to America.

Germany's first post-Nazi Chancellor, in the fullest sense, was and is Angela Merkel. Born in Hamburg, brought up in East Germany as the daughter of a Lutheran pastor, she is a qualified scientist, conservative and patriotic without being nationalistic. Her East German heritage is important. She was not brought up to feel any particular guilt about the German past – this had been largely dealt with by forty years of the communist government's official 'sin-eating' ceremonies. Neither, though she recognised the importance of Germany's role in the European Union, did Merkel have that visceral, bred-in-the-bone commitment to ever-increasing European integration that was so important to politicians brought up in the West, where the process was seen both as a defence against communism and a prophylactic against the return of Nazism.

No longer feeling compelled to write cheques to every nation or individual that Germany ever wronged, a loyal European but also a loyal German, Frau Merkel is, like most Germans since 1945, also reluctant – for reasons all too apparent from the terrible story of the Third Reich's defeat – to go to war. The international interventions in Kosovo in 1999 and Afghanistan in 2001, in which the German *Bundeswehr* has taken part, have been passionately opposed, and not just on the far left.

Germany in the twenty-first century is, like everywhere else, imperfect. The absorption of the East after 1989 has, in a sense, proved no easier in the short term than dealing with the legacy of Hitler. By this time, most West Germans had accepted not just the formal externals of democracy, but had taken it to their hearts and become active democratic, often highly critical, citizens. The friendly takeover of East Germany (some saw it otherwise) involved hurt feelings, and the rejoining of seventeen million compatriots after almost half a century of separation was always going to be a tricky process.

East Germans were often quickly disillusioned with the democratic experience after 1990. They had, in fact, spent almost sixty years as subjects of a dictatorship, starting in 1933 with the Hitler adventure and then moving more or less seamlessly into Ulbricht's austere and intolerant, though slightly less violent, version. Whether they liked it or not, many had become accustomed to a top-down command economy where mechanisms such as the market could be ignored or circumvented, and daily life, while it might sometimes be tedious and restrictive, had the feeling of security and the illusion of permanence. They had not had the Westerners' forty years of deciding to accept, even love, capitalist democracy with all its faults and flaws as well as its virtues. And in the 1990s, they experienced nothing like the economic miracle the Westerners had benefited from in the 1950s – in a very different global market – and which had so aided acceptance of the post-war status quo in the Bonn Republic.

Progress has been remarkable in some areas of the former German Democratic Republic, much less so in others, but there are signs that the East, though it has undergone painful changes and still faces serious challenges, is slowly integrating. Just as some had naively believed the Germans could be converted into instant democrats by discussion and education immediately after 1945, so there were those who had anticipated, in accordance with Chancellor Kohl's never forgotten and often rued election promise, 'blooming landscapes' as the East's future immediately after 1990. In fact, both evolutionary processes needed at least twenty years, and, in the East's case, then some.

Like the rest of the advanced world, modern Germany is concerned about being able to absorb immigrants. It worries about its identity. It struggles to deal with economic problems arising from the crisis that has hit the advanced world towards the end of the century's first decade. But Germany also observes that its citizens have not gone rushing towards extreme-right solutions during the current serious economic crisis. Despite a few local successes for neo-Nazis in the troubled parts of the East, this is no replay of the 1930s in that regard. In fact, the far right in Germany seems to be meeting with appreciably less support than elsewhere in Europe, including in countries that were once part of the anti-Nazi coalition in the Second World War.

From unpromising beginnings in 1945, when for the most part it simply succumbed to the inevitable and obeyed, Germany's political and official class – the same pillars of society who once hated the Weimar Republic and set out to destroy it – along with most of the country's voters, have come to believe that democracy works. Or at least, that it is less of a bad solution than dictatorship.

In 1945, the official policy had been that Germany 'will always be treated as a defeated, not a liberated, country', and Eisenhower's declaration to the German poeple had reflected this. Exactly half a century later, Germany begged to disagree. According to a poll in 1995, a little more than half the population saw VE-Day, 8 May 1945, as a 'day of liberation', while a further 28 per cent saw it as a 'day of liberation but also of defeat'. Only 13 per cent regarded the end of the Second World War as purely a 'day of defeat'.

Has Germany exorcised Hitler? Perhaps that is up to its people to decide. If it is any indication, Germans certainly feel inclined to continue their cleansing rituals on a regular, precautionary basis. But even if the old demon who died in 1945 has not yet disappeared completely, modern Germans seem to have banished his restless, malevolent ghost to somewhere very, very far away.

NOTES

INTRODUCTION

1 See Michael Balfour, 'Another Look at Unconditional Surrender', in *International Affairs*, vol. 46, no. 4 (October 1970), p. 720n. The Russian dictator had been invited but, pleading preoccupation with defeating the Wehrmacht at Stalingrad, declined. The first conference of the 'Big Three' did not take place until late November of that year in Tehran.

2 Cited in Balfour, 'Another Look at Unconditional Surrender', p. 728.

3 See Michael Beschloss, *The Conquerors: Roosevelt, Truman and the Destruction of Hitler's Germany 1944–1945*, p. 13. Beschloss points out (ibid., p. 11) that Roosevelt, as a young Assistant Secretary of the Navy, had also taken a hard line at the end of the First World War, insisting that the Germans must be 'cut down and purged, and arguing unsuccessfully for an Allied advance into Germany'. 'The one lesson the German will learn is the lesson of defeat', he had proclaimed.

4 *Hansard*, HC Deb 22 February 1944, vol. 397, cc663–795 (Adjournment Debate): Prime Minister's Address on The International Situation.

5 Roughly translatable in the English phrase '. . . then I'm a Dutchman'.

I INTO THE REICH

1 Klaus-Dietmar Henke, *Die amerikanische Besetzung Deutschlands* (Quellen und Darstellungen zur Zeitgeschichte, Herausgegeben vom Institut für Zeitgeschichte, Band 27), p. 122.

2 Charles B. MacDonald, *The Siegfried Line Campaign*, Washington, 1961, p. 3. And for the following.

3 Quoted in Volker Koop, *Besetzt: Amerikanische Besatzungspolitik in Deutschland*, pp. 25f.

4 Henke, *Die Amerikanische Besetzung Deutschlands*, pp. 169f.

5 Eyewitness description of the border crossing in A. Eaton Roberts, *Five Stars to Victory: A True Story of Men and Tanks*, ch. III, 'Rhineland' (no page number), an account of Task Force Lovelady's exploits, privately published 1949 and now available online at http://www.3ad.com/history/wwll/feature.pages/five.stars. htm. Captain Roberts, a qualified doctor, served as the Task Force's Chief Medical Officer throughout its campaigns.

6 Henke, *Die Amerikanische Besetzung Deutschlands*, p. 170.

7 Roetgen town website http://de./lokales/geschichte03.php.

8 See Kudryashov, Sergei, 'Stalin and the Allies: Who Deceived Whom?', *History Today*, vol. 45, no. 5, May 1995. Sir Archibald Clark Kerr, British Ambassador in Moscow, described him to Churchill as 'a rude, inexperienced and bad-mannered fellow'.

9 For the early part of the battle for East Prussia see Evan Mawdsley, *Thunder in the East: The Nazi-Soviet War 1941-45*, pp. 374f.

10 See Bernhard Fisch's contribution, 'Nemmersdorf 1944, nach wie vor unge-klärt', in Gerd Überschär, ed., *Orte des Grauens: Verbrechen im Zweiten Weltkrieg*, pp. 161f.

11 For a discussion of this question and others see Fisch, 'Nemmersdorf 1944', pp. 155 ff. Fisch even seriously considers – though ultimately does not embrace – the possibility that the entire event was a German provocation, carried out by undercover units. See also Guido Knopp, *Die grosse Flucht: Das Schicksal der Vertriebenen*, pp. 37ff.

12 Quoted in *Der Spiegel*, 2.2002 1.6.2002, 'Der Treck nach Westen', p. 10.

13 Report of Major Hinrichs, 26.10.1944 – facsimile copy in the possession of the author.

14 Cf. Isabel Denny's *The Fall of Hitler's Fortress City: The Battle for Königsberg, 1945*, 2007, p. 177. Ms Denny claims that 'all the women were captured and raped and some were left crucified on the doors of houses and barns . . . When the German Army retook the village two days later they claimed to have found nearly all the 635 inhabitants dead.' Since it is well established that almost all Nemmersdorf's inhabitants had left before the Soviet incursion, it is hard to know where she obtained this information or why she chose not to question it. It also seems well established that, while women were indeed tortured and murdered in this way, the atrocities occurred elsewhere. Nemmersdorf, like other symbolically important scenes of violence, was fated to have a whole amalgam of extra horrors loaded upon it.

15 Henke, *Die Amerikanische Besetzung Deutschlands*, p. 155.

16 Horst Boog, Gerhard Krebs and Detlef Vogel, eds, *Das Deutsche Reich und der Zweite Weltkrieg*, Bd 7: *Das Deutsche Reich in der Defensive*, p. 615.

17 Cf. Max Hastings, *Armageddon: The Battle for Germany 1944–45*, p. 107.

18 Henke, *Die Amerikanische Besetzung Deutschlands*, p. 142.

19 Perry Biddiscombe, *Werwolf! The History of the National Socialist Guerrilla Movement 1944–1946*, p. 23.

20 Boog, Krebs and Vogel, eds, *Das Deutsche Reich in der Defensive*, p. 615.

21 Perry Biddiscombe, *The Denazification of Germany: A History 1945–1950*, pp. 44f.

22 *New York Times*/AP, 31 October 1944: 'Aachen Mayor Sworn In; Anti-Nazi's Office in Cellar'.

23 Biddiscombe, *The Denazification of Germany*, pp. 45ff. unless otherwise stated.

24 Henke, *Die Amerikanische Besetzung Deutschlands*, p. 158.

25 Ralf Georg Reuth, ed., Josef Goebbels, *Tagebücher*, Bd 5, 1943–45, p. 2108.

26 See Boog, Krebs and Vogel, eds, *Das Deutsche Reich in der Defensive*, p. 622.

27 Paul Fussell, *The Boys' Crusade – American GIs in Europe: Chaos and Fear in the Second World War*, p. 126.

28 Henke, *Die Amerikanische Besetzung Deutschlands*, pp. 158f.

29 See Frederick Taylor, *Dresden: Tuesday 13 February 1945*, p. 155.

30 G-5 report of September 1944, cited in Henke, *Die Amerikanische Besetzung Deutschlands*, p. 151.

2 HOO-HOO-HOO

1 See Biddiscombe, *Werwolf!*, pp. 12ff. and for the following unless otherwise stated.

2 Quoted in Rolf-Dieter Müller, ed., *Das Deutsche Reich und der Zweite Weltkrieg – Der Zusammenbruch des Deutschen Reiches 1945, Band 10, Zweiter Halbband: Die Folgen des Zweiten Weltkrieges*, p. 14.

3 Biddiscombe, *Werwolf!*, p. 18.

4 *The Times*, 20 October 1944: 'Nazi Force for Last Stand' (From Our Military Correspondent).

5 Quoted in Robert Gellately, *Backing Hitler*, pp. 253f.

6 Ibid., p. 231.

7 Quoted in Henke, *Die Amerikanische Besetzung Deutschlands*, p. 265.

8 Perry Biddiscombe, *The Last Nazis: Werewolf Guerrilla Resistance in Europe 1944–1947*, p. 126. And for Himmler's threat.

9 Ibid., pp. 127f. And, especially if the putative sex lives of the squad are of interest, Charles Whiting, *SS Werewolf: The Story of the Nazi Resistance Movement* – written in racy thriller style with suspiciously comprehensive dialogue, but based in part on interviews with surviving participants during the 1960s – pp. 103ff.

10 Biddiscombe, *The Last Nazis*, p. 129.

11 *New York Times*, 11 February 1945: 'Hitler Youth Learns of American Justice'.

12 See Richard Matthias Müller, ed., *Der Krieg, der nicht Sterben Wollte: Monschau 1945*, especially ch. 7, 'Ardennenschlacht' by Joseph C. Doherty, pp. 243ff.

13 *New York Times*, 16 February 1945: 'German Girl Vows Vengeance on U.S.'. See also Henke, *Die Amerikanische Besetzung Deutschlands*, pp. 167ff. Maria Bierganz's later reflections date from 1983, when she wrote a memoir of her experiences, and are also found in Henke.

14 For this and the following account of the mission see Biddiscombe, *The Last Nazis*, pp. 129ff., and Whiting, *SS Werewolf*, pp. 7ff.

15 According to Whiting, *SS Werewolf*, as above.

16 *New York Times*, 29 March 1945: 'Non-Nazi Mayor of Aachen Killed By 3 German Chutists in Uniform'; *The Times*, 29 March 1945: 'Aachen Burgomaster Murdered: Shot by Three Germans'.

17 See *New York Times*, 4 April 1945 (the wire had been sent four days earlier but was marked 'Delayed', presumably due to censorship): 'Nazis Tell Rhine They Will Return'.

18 Goebbels, *Tagebücher*, Bd 5, p. 2164.

19 Ibid., p. 2170.

20 See Whiting, *SS Werewolf*, pp. 157–62, and Biddiscombe, *The Last Nazis*, pp. 131f.

21 Ibid., p. 167n.

22 Biddiscombe, *Werwolf!*, pp. 153f.

3 THE GREAT TREK

1 Andreas Kossert, *Kalte Heimat: Die Geschichte der deutschen Vertriebenen nach 1945*, pp. 39f.

2 Ruprecht von Butler, quoted in Joachim Käppner, *Die Familie der Generäle: Eine deutsche Geschichte*, pp. 226f. And for the further remark.

3 Quoted in Antony Beevor, *Berlin: The Downfall 1945*, p. 34.

4 Quoted in Norman M. Naimark, *The Russians in Germany: A History of the Soviet Zone of Occupation, 1945–1949*, p. 78.

5 Mawdsley, *Thunder in the East*, p. 216.

6 Ibid., pp. 216f.

7 Naimark, *The Russians in Germany*, p. 72 and for the following.

8 Ibid., p. 74.

9 Alexander Solzhenitsyn, *Prussian Nights*, translated by Robert Conquest, p. 7.

10 See his obituary in the *New York Times*, 20 June 1997: 'Lev Kopelev, Soviet Writer in Prison 10 Years, Dies at 85'. Kopelev died in Cologne, Germany, where he had lived since being exiled from the Soviet Union for dissident

activities – which included writing about his experiences in occupied Germany – in the early 1970s.

11 For the story of Wanda Schultz (later Hoffman) see Ingeborg Jacobs, *Freiwild: Das Schicksal deutscher Frauen 1945*, pp. 83ff.

12 Kossert, *Kalte Heimat*, p. 40.

13 Naimark, *The Russians in Germany*, pp. 90f.

14 'Wenn du's nicht aushältst, dann geh in die Alle'. See Jacobs, *Freiwild*, p. 53.

15 Ibid., pp. 57ff.

16 Full text available at http://avalon.law.yale.edu/20th_century/dec939.asp along with other documents relating to the Nazi-Soviet Pact and its consequences.

17 Alfred M. de Zayas, *Nemesis at Potsdam: The Anglo-Americans and the Expulsion of the Germans* (revised edition 1979), pp. 40f.

18 Ibid., p. 50.

19 To be exact, 9,955,000, according to the detailed tables in Kossert, *Kalte Heimat*, pp. 22f.

20 Quoted in Norman Davies and Roger Moorhouse, *Microcosm: Portrait of a Central European City*, p. 380.

21 See most recently Giles Milton, *Paradise Lost: Smyrna 1922. The Destruction of Islam's City of Tolerance*, and for a concise account of the catastrophe, Norman M. Naimark, *Fires of Hatred: Ethnic Cleansing in Twentieth-Century Europe*, pp. 44ff.

22 Giles Milton, *Paradise Lost*, p. 315.

23 Quoted in ibid., p. 326.

24 Ibid., p. 311.

25 See Denny, *The Fall of Hitler's Fortress City*, pp. 202f. Gustloff was German by nationality but resident in Switzerland. The ship itself had been converted for military use as a barracks ship and was painted naval grey.

26 For a potted biography of Hanke, see Davies and Moorhouse, *Microcosm*, pp. 373f.

27 Quoted in Knopp, *Die grosse Flucht*. This estimate is based on a saying that 'ten died for each metre of runway', and the runway was 1,300 metres, so is more likely to be a figure of speech than a figure of fact, but there can be no doubt that thousands of German civilians died in this and other unspeakable horrors inflicted on them by their own leaders.

28 For a biography of Hanke see Karl Höffkes, *Hitlers Politische Generale: Die Gauleiter des Dritten Reiches*, pp. 120ff.

29 Knopp, *Die grosse Flucht*.

30 Ulrich Frodien, *Bleib übrig: Eine Kriegsjugend in Deutschland*, p. 124, for their
    encounter with the barricade and for the drama at the railway station, pp. 143ff.

31 Davies and Moorhouse, *Microcosm*, p. 408.

32 See Müller, ed., *Das Deutsche Reich und der Zweite Weltkrieg . . . Band 10, Zweiter
    Halbband*, pp. 336f.

33 Figures in Hans-Werner Mihan, *Die Nacht von Potsdam: Der Luftangriffbri-
    tischer Bomber vom 14. April 1945, Dokumentation und Erlebnisberichte*, p. 119.

34 De Zayas, *Nemesis at Potsdam*, p. 87.

35 Müller, ed., *Das Deutsche Reich, Band 10, Zweiter Halbband*, pp. 347.

36 See Davies and Moorhouse, *Microcosm*, p. 416; for Breslau specifically and in
    detail, de Zayas, *Nemesis at Potsdam*, p. 88.

37 See Helmut Schnatz, *Der Luftangriff auf Swinemünde: Dokumentation einer
    Tragödie*, p. 138, for the author's final analysis of numbers killed, and in general the
    chapter Teil VI: 'Rezeption und Bewertung des Angriffs', pp. 87–138, for its masterly
    exercise in demythologisation. The attack by 661 American bombers was propor-
    tionately one of the heaviest of the war in terms of tonnage dropped. It was carried
    out at the specific request of the Soviet High Command, whose own aircraft were
    busy with the ground support role to which they were in any case more suited.

38 Davies and Moorhouse, *Microcosm*, p. 408 and p. 413.

39 Ibid., p. 420.

40 Ibid., p. 424.

41 Testimony of Zdena Nemcova, cited in *Europe's Forgotten War Crime*, first
    broadcast on BBC Radio 4, 9 February 2004, details available at the BBC
    website: http://news.bbc.co.uk/1/hi/world/europe/3466233.stm.

42 Knopp, *Die grosse Flucht*, p. 369.

43 Dr Anton Sum quoted in ibid., p. 368.

44 Müller, ed., *Das Deutsche Reich, Band 10, Zweiter, Halbband*, p. 622.

45 See the account in ibid., p. 625.

46 Ibid.

47 Ibid.

48 See Ota Filip, 'Die Stillen Toten unterm Klee bei Pohrlitz: Auf den Spuren des
    Brünner Todesmarsches', in *Frankfurter Allgemeine Zeitung*, 30 May 1990; and
    Knopp, *Die grosse Flucht*, pp. 392f.

49 Knopp, *Die Grosse Flucht*, p. 393.

50 Ibid., p. 395.

51 Letter, 'Future of Minorities in Czechoslovakia' to *The Times*, 14 June 1945,
    from Wenzel Jaksch, Eugen de Witte and Franz Katz, members of the last
    freely elected Czechoslovak Parliament. Jaksch, a Social Democrat, later settled
    in West Germany, where he became prominent in the Sudeten German Expel-
    lees' Organisation and was a Social Democrat member of the Bundestag in

Bonn. In the last free elections in Czechoslovakia in 1935, Konrad Henlein's proto-Nazi Sudeten German Party (SdP) received 60 per cent of the German vote. By 1938, the Sudeten-German Social Democratic Party, once the largest of the German parties, had shrunk into near-insignificance. All other Sudeten-German parties then merged with the SdP, whose leader then became Gauleiter of the Sudetenland after the Munich Agreement awarded the area to Germany. That in 1945 the Czechs regarded all Sudeten Germans as Nazis was unjust, but under the circumstances not entirely surprising.

52 Quoted in *The Times*, 7 August 1945, 'Germans in East Europe: Many Expulsions'.

53 *New York Times*, 13 November 1946, Anne O'Hare McCormick, 'Problem of Places for Refugees'.

54 Müller, ed., *Das Deutsche Reich, Band 10, Zweiter Halbband*, p. 622.

55 Ibid., p. 624. These comments are likely to represent a matter-of-fact professional observation rather than an expression of human sympathy. During his long career, Serov was involved in the state-instituted Ukrainian famine of the early 1930s, in the massacre of Polish officers at Katyn, the deportation of thousands from the Baltic states, the wartime displacement of Crimean Tatars and many other Stalinist atrocities, climaxing in the bloody suppression of the Hungarian Revolution in 1956.

4 ZERO HOUR

1 Frodien, *Bleib übrig*, p. 175.

2 Ibid., p. 179.

3 Ibid., pp. 232ff.

4 Ibid., p. 181.

5 Interview with Joachim Trenkner, Berlin, 24 March 2008.

6 Interview with Egon Plönissen, Koblenz, 12 June 2009.

7 See Martin Middlebrook and Chris Everitt, *The Bomber Command War Diaries: An Operational Reference Book 1939–1945*, p. 615.

8 Helmut Nassen, *Tagebuch des Helmut Nassen vom 6.3.45 bis 30.4.45*, Dr H. Schnatz, ed. (typescript, reproduced with permission of Dr Schnatz and Herr Nassen).

9 Ibid.

10 Ibid.

11 For details of these and later events in Penzberg see Biddiscombe, *The Last Nazis*, pp. 168ff. except where otherwise indicated.

12 Biographical details for Giesler in Höffkes, *Hitlers politische Generale*, pp. 87ff.

13 Ibid., p. 89. Hitler would commit suicide the next day. Accounts of Giesler's suicide vary, but he may have attempted to kill himself at least twice, and after the second (a botched pistol shot to the temple) to have lingered for some days before expiring on the last day of the war in a military hospital near Berchtesgaden.

14 Earl F. Ziemke, *The U.S. Army in the Occupation of Germany*, pp. 257f.

15 See Henke, *Die Amerikanische Besetzung Deutschlands*, p. 968.

16 Müller, ed., *Das Deutsche Reich, Band 10, Zweiter Halbband*, p. 320.

17 Ziemke, *The U.S. Army in the Occupation of Germany*, pp. 262f.

18 Ulbricht's explanation quoted by a member of the group, Wolfgang Leonhard, in an interview published sixty years later, in *Der Spiegel*, no. 16, 2005 (8 April 2005): 'Zurück in die Zukunft'. Leonhard, brought up in the Soviet Union as the child of German communist émigrés, became disillusioned and eventually fled to the West.

19 For a thorough outlining of the political chess game surrounding the withdrawal plans, see Henke, *Die Amerikanische Besetzung Deutschlands*, pp. 716ff.

20 Müller, ed., *Das Deutsche Reich, Band 10, Zweiter Halbband*, p. 324.

21 See Henke, *Die Amerikanische Besetzung Deutschlands*, p. 719.

22 Ziemke, *The U.S. Army in the Occupation of Germany*, pp. 265–7. And for the following details of the Wendenschloss meeting.

23 Henke, *Die Amerikanische Besetzung Deutschlands*, p. 724.

24 Ziemke, *The U.S. Army in the Occupation of Germany*, p. 267.

25 For this and the following see interview with Joachim Trenkner.

26 Interview with Egon Plönissen.

27 Ibid.

5 THROUGH CONQUERORS' EYES

1 These figures cited in Jeffry K. Olick, *In the House of the Hangman: The Agonies of German Defeat, 1943–1945*, pp. 42f.

2 Quoted in Maureen Waller, *London 1945: Life in the Debris of War*, p. 112.

3 Quoted in ibid., p. 113. And for the following.

4 Olick, *In the House of the Hangman*, p. 71.

5 Ibid., p. 106.

6 Günter Bischof and Stephen E. Ambrose, eds, *Eisenhower and the German POWs: Facts against Falsehood*, p. 30.

7 Cited in ibid., p. 25n.

8 George Clare, *Berlin Days, 1946–1947*, p. 210.

9 Frodien, *Bleib übrig*, p. 204.

10 See Ziemke's remarks in *The U.S. Army in the Occupation of Germany*, pp. 88f.

11 Ibid., p. 90.

12 Text of JCS 1067 (Directive to Commander-in-Chief of United States Forces of Occupation Regarding the Military Government of Germany) in *Department of State: Foreign Relations of the United States, 1945*, vol. 3, European Advisory Commission; Austria; Germany, pp. 484ff.

13 Signed memorandum from Henry Morgenthau to President Roosevelt n.d. but before 4 September 1944 in: President's Secretary File (PSF) Safe Files: German Diplomatic Files 1944 (January–September), Franklin D. Roosevelt Library and Museum Website; version date 2009.

14 Memorandum from Henry J. Stimson to President Roosevelt, 5 September 1944 in: President's Secretary File (PSF) Safe Files: German Diplomatic Files 1944 (Jan.–Sept.), Franklin D. Roosevelt Library and Museum Website; version date 2009. And for the following.

15 See Cordell Hull's Memorandum for the President (Presented by the Secretary in person to the President on 1 October 1944) dated 29 September 1944 in: President's Secretary File (PSF) Safe Files: German Diplomatic Files 1944 (Jan.–Sept.), Franklin D. Roosevelt Library and Museum Website; version date 2009.

16 Olick, *In the House of the Hangman*, p. 31.

17 Michael Beschloss, *The Conquerors*, p. 173.

18 Lord Moran, *Winston Churchill: The Struggle for Survival 1940–1965*, p. 200.

19 Ibid., p. 131.

20 Olick, *In the House of the Hangman*, pp. 31f.

21 Cited ibid., p. 32.

22 *Time* magazine, 2 July 1945: 'Leave Your Helmet On'.

23 *Pocket Guide to Germany*: copy in the author's possession. Also available in facsimile in English and as a German/English parallel text with commentary by Hg. Sven Felix Kellerhof.

24 Henke, *Die Amerikanische Besetzung Deutschlands*, p. 194.

25 See John Willoughby, 'The Sexual Behaviour of American GIs during the Early Years of the Occupation of Germany', in *Journal of Military History*, vol. 62 (January 1998), p. 170.

26 'German Girls: US Army Boycott Fails to Stop GIs from Fraternizing with Them', in *Life*, 23 July 1945, no. 35.

27 *Time* magazine, 30 July 1945: 'Ban Lifted'. And for the following.

28 Facts in the article at DW-World.de http://www6.dw-world.de/en/2099.php: 'Sleeping with the Enemy'.

29 Point (15) in Montgomery's 'Notes on the Present Situation no.2' 6 July 1945, a letter to his Corps Commanders and Control Council Heads of Divisions. In Montgomery's papers in the Imperial Museum and also quoted extensively in Christopher Knowle of London University's highly informative blog on

aspects of the British occupation of Germany, http://howitreallywas.typepad.com/, entry for 14 March 2009: Field-Marshal Montgomery and the fraternisation ban.

30 Alex Danchev and Daniel Todman, eds, Field Marshal Lord Alanbrooke, *War Diaries 1939–1945*, p. 682, 10 April 1945.

31 Volker Koop, *Besetzt: Britische Besatzungspolitik in Deutschland*, pp. 157f.

32 Account by Lieutenant Christopher Leefe, quoted in Douglas Botting, *In the Ruins of the Reich*, p. 257.

33 Colin MacInnes, *To the Victors the Spoils*, p. 189.

34 Ibid., pp. 183f.

35 Botting, *In the Ruins of the Reich*, pp. 47f. And for the following.

36 MacInnes, *To the Victors the Spoils*, p. 55.

37 Letter of 17 May 1945, in Mathilde Wolff-Mönckeberg, *On the Other Side: Letters to My Children from Germany 1940–46*, p. 140.

38 Jacobs, *Freiwild*, p. 154.

39 Cited in Paul Steege, *Black Market, Cold War: Everyday Life in Berlin 1946–1949*, pp. 23f.

40 Account by Pastor Dr Karl-Ludwig Hoch, then aged fifteen, resident at Löschwitz, taped interview with FT on 30 October 2001 (in author's possession).

41 Interview with Götz Bergander, Berlin, 25 March 2008.

42 Interview with Lothar Löwe, Berlin, 25 March 2008.

43 Jacobs, *Freiwild*, p. 170.

44 See Frederick Taylor, *The Berlin Wall, 13 August 1961–9 November 1989*, p. 34.

45 *Time* magazine, 9 July 1945, 'Foreign News: What Is to Be Done?'

46 Anonymous, *A Woman in Berlin*, translated from the German by Phillip Boehm, p. 140.

47 Wladimir Gelfand, *Deutschland-Tagebuch 1945–1946: Aufzeichnungen eines Rotarmisten (Ausgewählt und kommentiert von Elke Schersjanoi)* (translated from Russian to German by Anja Lutter and Hartmut Schröder), p. 79f.

48 Gelfand, pp. 61f. And for the following.

49 Ibid., pp. 200ff.

50 Naimark, *The Russians in Germany*, p. 92.

51 See Richard Evans, *The Third Reich at War*, p. 709.

52 Quoted in Volker Koop, *Besetzt: Französische Besatzungspolitik in Deutschland*, pp. 40f. And for the Sindelfingen outrages.

53 Ibid., p. 46.

54 Ibid., p. 47.

55 See Perry Biddiscombe, 'Dangerous Liaisons: Occupation Zones of Germany and Austria, 1945–1948', in *Journal of Social History*, vol. 34, no. 3 (Spring 2001), p. 618, n.56.

56 See J. Robert Lilly, *Taken by Force: Rape and American GIs in Europe during World War II*, p. 161. For the numbers of convictions, ibid., p. 117.

6 HUNGER

1 Quoted in Mark Mazower, *Hitler's Empire: Nazi Rule in Occupied Europe*, p. 280. See also by the same author, *Inside Hitler's Greece: The Experience of Occupation, 1941–44*. The wartime experience still rankles in Greece – see the remarks by Greek Deputy Prime Minister Theodoros Pangalos in February 2010 in response to what he saw as a lack of generosity in modern Germany's attitude towards Greece's economic difficulties. 'They [the Nazis],' Pangalos claimed, 'took away the Greek gold that was in the Bank of Greece, they took away the Greek money and they never gave it back.'

2 Secretariat's report of the meeting quoted in Adam Tooze, *The Wages of Destruction: The Making and Breaking of the Nazi Economy*, p. 479. And for the following quotes from Backe and Himmler.

3 Götz Aly, *Hitlers Volksstaat: Raub, Rassenkrieg und nationaler Sozialismus*, p. 198.

4 Ibid., p. 197.

5 Goebbels diary entry 24.5.1942, quoted in Christian Gerlach, *Krieg, Ernährung, Völkermord*, p. 213.

6 Ibid., p. 241.

7 Markus Roth, *Herrenmenschen: Die deutschen Kreishauptleute im besetzten Polen – Karrierewege, Herrschaftspraxis und Nachkriegsgeschichte*, pp. 166f.

8 See Gerlach, *Krieg, Ernährung, Völkermord*, especially pp. 191f., p. 197, pp. 219–21, pp. 237–40.

9 Figures in Aly, *Hitlers Volksstaat*, p. 201.

10 Ibid.

11 Cited in ibid., p. 198. And for the Ziegelmayer quote.

12 Tooze, *The Wages of Destruction*, p. 485.

13 See Gerlach, *Krieg, Ernährung, Völkermord*, pp. 241ff.

14 Aly, *Hitlers Volksstaat*, p. 202.

15 Ibid., p. 206. And for the following observation.

16 Beschloss, *The Conquerors*, p. 194.

17 Ibid., p. 196.

18 Ibid., p. 214.

19 Cited in Tooze, *The Wages of Destruction*, pp. 657f.

20 From Speer's testimony at Nuremberg, 20 June 1946 (translation p. 497), available at http://avalon.law.yale.edu/imt/06-20-46.asp.

21 See Tooze, *The Wages of Destruction*, p. 654. And for a detailed account of Speer's complex motivations and his relations with other members of the Führer's entourage, 'Die Machtprobe mit Hitler im März 1945', in Müller, ed., *Das Deutsche Reich, Band 10, Zweiter Halbband*, pp. 85–106.

22 See Müller, ed., *Das Deutsche Reich, Band 10, Zweiter Halbband*, pp. 57–9.

23 Ibid., pp. 60ff. For this and the following unless otherwise stated.

24 Tooze, *The Wages of Destruction*, p. 651.

25 Ibid., p. 654.

26 For this and the other 'foreign worker' figures see ibid., pp. 517f.

27 MacInnes, *To the Victors the Spoils*, pp. 180f.

28 Atina Grossmann, *Jews, Germans and Allies: Close Encounters in Occupied Germany*, p. 133.

29 *Time* magazine, 7 May 1945, 'Foreign News: Dachau'.

30 William I. Hitchcock, *Liberation: The Bitter Road to Freedom, Europe 1944–1945*, pp. 302f.

31 Ibid.

32 Grossmann, *Jews, Germans and Allies*, p. 136.

7 THE PRICE

1 See *Time* magazine, 9 April 1945, 'Stern Man for the Nazis'.

2 J. E. Smith, ed., *The Papers of General Lucius D. Clay*, vol. I, p. 24.

3 Naimark, *The Russians in Germany*, pp. 252f.

4 See Bischof and Ambrose, eds, *Eisenhower and the German POWs*, pp. 8f.

5 Ibid., p. 9.

6 See James Bacque, *Other Losses: An Investigation into the Mass Deaths of German Prisoners at the Hands of the French and the Americans After World War II*. Bacque claims that almost a million were deliberately starved to death and the mass murder covered up.

7 See Rüdiger Overmanns, 'Das Schicksal der deutschen Kriegsgefangenen des Zweiten Weltkrieges', in Müller, ed., *Das Deutsche Reich, Band 10, Zweiter Halbband*, p. 427.

8 Bischof and Ambrose, eds, *Eisenhower and the German POWs*, p. 60.

9 Fritz Mann, *Frühling am Rhein Anno 1945*, p. 8. And for the accompanying events described.

10 See the account by the East Prussian Kurt Baltinowitz, unpublished typescript 39 pp. in possession of author courtesy of Herr Wolfgang Gückelhorn, pp. 13f.

11 The Maschke Commission, appointed by the West German government. Their

multi-volume work appeared in several volumes between 1962 and the mid-1970s. See Rolf Steininger, 'Some Reflections on the Maschke Commission', in Bischof and Ambrose, eds, *Eisenhower and the German POWs*, pp. 170ff.

12 Wolfgang Gückelhorn, *Das Ende am Rhein: Kriegsende zwischen Remagen und Andernach*, pp. 145ff.

13 See Rüdiger Overmans, 'German Historiography, the War Losses, and the Prisoners of War', in Bischof and Ambrose, eds, *Eisenhower and the German POWs*, pp. 138ff.

14 Günter Bischof, 'Bacque and Historical Evidence', in Bischof and Ambrose, eds, *Eisenhower and the German POWs*, p. 217.

15 Overmans, 'Das Schicksal der deutschen Kriegsgefangenen des Zweiten Weltkrieges', in Müller, ed., *Das Deutsche, Band 10, Zweiter Halbband*, p. 419.

16 See Gückelhorn, *Das Ende am Rhein*, p. 146.

17 Overmans, 'Das Schicksal der deutschen Kriegsgefangenen des Zweiten Weltkrieges', in Müller, ed., *Das Deutsche Reich, Band 10, Zweiter Halbband*, p. 420.

18 Gückelhorn, *Das Ende am Ehein*, p. 146.

19 Figures in Overmans, 'German Historiography, the War Losses, and the Prisoners of War', in Bischof and Ambrose, eds, *Eisenhower and the German POWs*, p. 150.

20 Ibid., p. 152.

21 Overmans, 'Das Schicksal der deutschen Kriegsgefangenen des Zweiten Weltkrieges', in Müller, ed, *Das Deutsche Reich, Band 10, Zweiter Halbband*, p. 421, estimates between 5,000 and 10,000 out of roughly a million. Bischof, in 'Bacque and Historical Evidence', as above, allows up to 56,000, making the total around 5 per cent.

22 Figures according to Niall Ferguson in 'Prisoner Taking and Prisoner Killing in the Age of Total War: Towards a Political Economy of Military Defeat', *War in History*, vol. 11 (2004), part 2, p. 186 (Table 4: Prisoners of War: percentage and chances of dying in captivity).

23 Overmans, 'Das Schicksal der deutschen Kriegsgefangenen des Zweiten Weltkrieges', in Müller, ed., *Das Deutsche Reich, Band 10, Zweiter Halbband*, pp. 442f.

24 For an illustrated collection of these *Passierscheine* (with texts and explanations) see the website 'The Allied *Passierschein* of World War 2' by SGM Herbert M. Friedman at http://www.psywarrior.com/GermanSCP.html. Many sources thought this the single most effective propaganda leaflet of the war.

25 Wolff-Mönckeberg, *On the Other Side*, p. 140.

26 Mann, *Frühling am Rhein Anno 1945*, p. 27.

27 See Müller, ed., *Das Deutsche Reich, Band 10, Zweiter Halbband*, p. 62.

28 Full text of the Hague Convention on Land Warfare available at http://avalon.

law.yale.edu/20th_century/hague04.asp#iart1. And see Richard Dominic Wiggers, 'The United States and the Refusal to Feed German Civilians after World War II', in Steven Béla Várdy and T. Hunt Tooly, eds, *Ethnic Cleansing in Twentieth-Century Europe*, p. 274.

29 Quoted in Wiggers, as above, p. 275.

30 Ibid., p. 276.

31 Ibid., p. 277.

32 Ibid., p. 279.

33 See Trent, 'Food Shortages in Germany and Europe', 1945–1948, in Bischof and Ambrose, eds, *Eisenhower and the German POWs*, p. 99 and n.9.

34 See Jörg Echternkamp, 'Im Schlagschatten des Krieges. Von den Folgen militärischer Gewalt und nationalsozialistischer Herrschaft in der frühen Nachkriegszeit', in Müller, ed., *Das Deutsche Reich, Band 10, Zweiter Halbband*, p. 661.

35 For average ration figures in 1946 and current estimates of calorific requirements see ibid., pp. 662f.

36 Steege, *Black Market, Cold War*, p. 42.

37 Ibid., p. 43.

8 TO THE VICTORS THE SPOILS

1 Gelfand, *Tagebuch eines Rotarmisten*, pp. 211f.

2 Ibid., p. 176.

3 Ibid., p. 191.

4 Clare, *Berlin Days*, p. 146.

5 Interview Penzance, England, 4 October 2008, with Maurice Smelt (lieutenant in the Black Watch 1945–8, stationed at Duisburg).

6 See Clay for McCloy, 16 September 1945, in Smith, ed., *The Papers of General Lucius D. Clay*, vol. I, p. 78.

7 See Willoughby, 'The Sexual Behaviour of American GIs during the Early Years of the Occupation of Germany', p. 171.

8 Walter J. Slatoff, 'GI Morals in Germany', in *The New Republic*, 13.5.1946, vol. 114, issue 19, p. 686 and p. 687. Slatoff was later a professor at Cornell University and Chair of its English Department.

9 Interview with Maurice Smelt.

10 David Clay Large, *Berlin: A Modern History*, p. 390.

11 Taylor, *The Berlin Wall*, p. 46.

12 See Steege, *Black Market, Cold War*, p. 38.

13 David Kynaston, *Austerity Britain 1945–1951*, pp. 106f.

14 Figures from tables of 1950 census in Germany (West) in Kossert, *Kalte Heimat*, p. 59.

15 Kevin Jackson, ed., *The Humphrey Jennings Reader*, p. 101.

16 Ibid., p. 102.

17 Kopp, *Besetzt: Britische Besatzungspolitik in Deutschland*, p. 173.

18 Ibid., p. 174.

19 Ibid., p. 178.

20 For a snapshot of this crisis period see the memorandum from North Rhine-Westphalia Food and Agriculture Minister Heinrich Lübke, 20 March 1947 in NA Kew FO 1013/1038 Food and Agriculture, Food Situation – 99th and 100th Periods.

21 NA Kew FO 1013/1038, as above, telegram from REO Düsseldorf-Hamburg, 31.3.1947. Düsseldorf-Mettmann and Wuppertal were the lowest at 834 and 827 respectively. Other cities in the Ruhr area varied between 1,028 and 1,336.

22 *The Times*, 2 April 1947, p. 3, 'Germany's Food Supply'.

23 Kopp, *Besetzt: Britische Besatzungspolitik in Deutschland*, p. 188.

24 Ibid., p. 189.

25 Joel Carl Welty, *The Hunger Year: In the French Zone of Divided Germany 1946–1947*, pp. 155f.

26 Steege, *Black Market, Cold War*, p. 85.

27 Kopp, *Besetzt: Britische Besatzungspolitik in Deutschland*, p. 178.

28 Interview with Frau Marlies Weber (née Theby), 12 June 2009.

29 NA Kew FO 1013/1499 Black Market Standing Committee 1945–1946 Report of 23 April 1946.

30 See Appendix 'B' to the report of 23 April 1946, NA Kew, as above.

31 NA Kew FO 1013/1499 Black Market Standing Committee 1945–1946, p. 43, Major Birtwhistle to Commander, 17 April 1946.

32 NA Kew FO 1013/1499 Black Market Standing Committee 1945–1946, p. 39, British Special Legal Research Unit (London) to Mil.Gov Münster, 1 March 1946.

33 NA Kew FO 936, Operation 'Sparkler' and Large Scale Black Market Activities, 17 July 1946, p. 7.

34 Ibid., p. 8.

35 Interview with Maurice Smelt.

36 *The Times*, 13 November 1946: 'Hand-to-Mouth in British Zone'.

37 See the copy of the appeal made by SEN at its founding meeting in October 1945, in John Farquharson, '"Emotional but Influential": Victor Gollancz, Richard Stokes and the British Zone of Germany, 1945–9', in *Journal of Contemporary History*, vol. 22, no. 3 (July 1987), pp. 514f.

38 Quoted in George Clare, *Berlin Days*, p. 191.

39 Farquharson, '"Emotional but Influential"', as above, pp. 506–8.

40 Bischof and Ambrose, eds, *Eisenhower and the German POWs*, p. 108.

41 Wiggers, 'The United States and the Refusal to Feed German Civilians after World War II', p. 282.

42 NARA College Park RG407/270/69/23/01 Box 1118 US Opinion Concerning Police Toward Germany Report no. 6, 31 January 1946, p. 3.

43 Ibid., p. 283.

44 Steege, *Black Market, Cold War*, p. 46.

45 Clay, Personal to Maj. Gen. Echols and Assistant Secretary Petersen, 27 March 1946, SECRET in Smith, ed., *The Papers of General Lucius D. Clay*, vol. II, p. 184.

46 Secretary Kenneth Royall as quoted in Wiggers, 'The United States and the Refusal to Feed German Civilians after World War II', p. 286.

47 NARA College Park RG407/270/69/23/01 Box 1118 HICOG Public Opinion Surveys – Summary of German public opinion trends 1945–1949, p. 6.

48 NARA College Park, as above, p. 8.

9 NO PARDON

1 Text available online in Latin, German, English and other languages at http://www.pax-westphalica.de/ipmipo/index.html.

2 See Gregor Dallas, *Poisoned Peace 1945 – The War That Never Ended*, pp. 495f.

3 Ibid., pp. 508f.

4 See Norman Davies, *Europe at War 1939–1945: No Simple Victory*, p. 195.

5 Thus the Head of Operations of the German Red Cross from 1937 to early 1945 was Professor Dr E. R. Grawitz, who was also Chief Physician of the SS and perpetrator of notorious 'scientific' atrocities at Buchenwald. His successor, Karl Gebhardt, was a senior SS doctor and personal physician to Himmler, and was in charge of lethal human experiments at Ravensbrück and Auschwitz. For Grawitz, see Benno Muller-Hill (translated by George R. Fraser), *Murderous Science: Elimination by Scientific Selection of Jews, Gypsies and Others, Germany 1933–1945*, p. 82, and Evans, *The Third Reich at War*, p. 607. For Gebhardt see Evans, p. 604f. and p. 612.

6 Evans, *The Third Reich at War*, p. 728.

7 Ibid.

8 John Weitz, *Joachim von Ribbentrop: Hitler's Diplomat*, p. 295.

9 Quoted from Lovat Fraser, 'Shall We Hang the Kaiser?', in *The War Illustrated*, 11 January 1919, available online at http://www.greatwardifferent.com. Fraser (1871–1926) was a former editor of the *Times of India* and a prolific journalist who at this time was also a regular foreign correspondent for the London *Times*. See his obituary in *The Times*, 21 April 1926.

10 Ann Tusa and John Tusa, *The Nuremberg Trial*, p. 69.

11 Jeffrey D. Hockett, 'Justice Robert H. Jackson, the Supreme Court, and the Nuremberg Trial', in *The Supreme Court Review*, vol. 1990 (1990), p. 258.

12 Quoted in Robert E. Conot, *Justice at Nuremberg*, New York, 1993 (paperback edition), p. 68.

13 See Charter of the International Military Tribunal – Annex to the Agreement for the prosecution and punishment of the major war criminals of the European Axis, Article 22: 'The permanent seat of the Tribunal shall be in Berlin. The first meetings of the members of the Tribunal and of the Chief Prosecutors shall be held at Berlin in a place to be designated by the Control Council for Germany. The first trial shall be held at Nuremberg, and any subsequent trials shall be held at such places as the Tribunal may decide.'

14 Daniel Bloxham, quoted in Olick, *In the House of the Hangman*, p. 109.

15 Ibid., p. 109, n.37.

16 Cited in ibid., pp. 112f.

17 See Marion Gräfin Dönhoff, *Namen, die keine mehr nennt: Ostpreußen, Menschen und Geschichte*, pp. 26ff. And for the following.

18 Jacobs, *Freiwild*, p. 86.

19 For an account in English of this incident see Christina von Krockow, *The Hour of the Women* (translated by Krishna Winston), pp. 45f.

20 Ibid., preface (unnumbered).

21 See Naimark, *The Russians in Germany*, pp. 142f.

22 See Arnd Bauerkämper, 'Zwangsmodernisierung und Krisenzyklen, Die Bodenreform und Kollektivierung in Brandenburg 1945–1960/61' in *Geschichte und Gesellschaft*, 25. Jahrg., H. 4, Ostdeutschland unter dem Kommunismus 1945–1990 (October–December 1999), p. 560.

23 Ibid., p. 153.

24 See Taylor, *The Berlin Wall*, p. 195.

25 Naimark, *The Russians in Germany*, p. 93.

26 See Winfrid Halder, '"Prüfstein . . . für die politische Lauterkeit der Führenden?" Der Volksentscheid zur "Enteignung der Kriegs- und Naziverbrecher" in Sachsen im Juni 1946', in *Geschichte und Gesellschaft*, 25. Jahrg., H. 4, Ostdeutschland unter dem Kommunismus 1945–1990 (October–December. 1999), pp. 592f.

27 Halder, '"Prüfstein . . . für die politische Lauterkeit der Führenden?"', as above.

28 Figures in ibid., p. 589.

29 For Krupp's arrest, see Henke, *Die Amerikanische Besetzung Deutschlands*, pp. 483f. The valet's words were: '*Meine Herren, Herr Krupp erwartet Sie. Darf ich Sie bitten, näherzutreten?*'

30 William Manchester, *The Arms of Krupp: The Rise and Fall of the Industrial Dynasty that Armed Germany at War*, pp. 605f.

31 Tusa, *The Nuremberg Trials*, pp. 138f.

32 Henke, *Die Amerikanische Besetzung Deutschlands*, p. 481.

33 Diarmuid Jeffreys, *Hell's Cartel: IG Farben and the Making of Hitler's War Machine*, p. 301.

34 Ibid., p. 290.

35 Quoted in ibid., p. 301.

36 Ibid., pp. 315f.

37 See Thomas Ramge, 'Totaler Krieg, Totaler Profit', at http://www.thomasramge.de/texte1/kriegprofit.htlm.

IO THE FISH AND THE NET

1 Frodien, *Bleib übrig*, p. 239.

2 For this and the following see Astrid M. Eckert, *Kampf um die Akten: die Westalliierten und die Rückgabe von deutschem Archivgut nach dem Zweiten Weltkrieg*, Transatlantische Historische Studien 20, pp. 59f., and Sven-Felix Kellerhof, 'Brisante Papiere aus dem Müllhaufen', in *Die Welt*, 2.11.2005.

3 See Lester K. Born, 'The Ministerial Collecting Center near Kassel, Germany', in *The American Archivist*, vol. 13, no. 3 (July 1950), pp. 237–58. Born, a trained archivist as well as a captain (later major) in the army, had played a major role in the foundation and operation of the MCC.

4 Born, p. 244.

5 Kenneth O. McCreedy, 'Planning the Peace: Operation Eclipse and the Occupation of Germany', in *Journal of Military History*, vol. 65, no. 3 (July 2001), p. 739.

6 JCS 1067 text, as cited above.

7 Biddiscombe, *The Denazification of Germany*, p. 47. And for the extreme advocates.

8 Interview with Steffen Cüppers, Dresden, February 2003. Faced with this passionate denial, the author returned to check with Götz Bergander. Herr Bergander confirmed that, although it was never discussed in the family, his father had indeed been a Party member of the passive sort.

9 Interview with Götz Bergander.

10 Tom Bower, *The Pledge Betrayed: America and Britain and the Denazification of Post-War Germany*, p. 98.

11 Biddiscombe, *The Denazification of Germany*, p. 77. Rudolph went on to design the Saturn V rocket that took the first American astronauts to the moon.

12 See Dolores Augustine, 'Wunderwaffen of a Different Kind: Nazi Scientists in East German Industrial Research', in *German Studies Review*, vol. 29, no. 3 (October 2006), pp. 579–88. The author went to school (from 1959) with several

sons of German scientists who had worked on the V2 but by then were
employed at the rocket research station at Westcott, near Aylesbury. Despite
invariably being known to their fellow pupils as 'Fritz', they were otherwise
popular and well integrated.

13 See Bower, *The Pledge Betrayed*, p. 97.

14 See Naimark, *The Russians in Germany*, pp. 214ff.

15 Jeffreys, *Hell's Cartel*, p. 298 and p. 298n.

16 John Gimbel, 'US Policy and German Scientists: The Early Cold War', in
Political Science Quarterly, vol. 101, no. 3 (1986), p. 441.

17 Ibid. pp. 441f.

18 NA Kew FO 1032/787 Colonel G. E. O. Elms to Commanding General,
European Theatre of Operations and Commanding General, British Army of
the Rhine, 6 December 1945.

19 Bower, *The Pledge Betrayed*, pp. 101–3.

20 NA Kew FO 1032/787 CROWCASS Colonel G. E. O. Elms, as above.

21 Bower, *The Pledge Betrayed*, p. 171.

22 Ibid., p. 278.

23 For remarks about Heyman's report see ibid., pp. 278f. For the draft text of
the report see NA Kew FO 371/55436 Denazification Measures: Meetings of
Denazification Committee Appendix 'A' to HQ/06101/9/Sep P of 16 May 1946:
Report of Heyman Working Party, Disposal of Criminals, Nazis, Militarists
and Potentially Dangerous Germans.

24 NA Kew FO 371/55436 Denazification Measures: Meetings of Denazification
Committee 1946. Monday, 4 March 1946.

25 NA Kew FO 371/55436 Denazification Measures: Meetings of Denazification
Committee Appendix 'A' to SCD/P(46)30 dated 23 May 1946, Denazification of
Legal Profession.

26 Biddiscombe, *The Denazification of Germany*, p. 60.

27 For this account of the demobilisation process and the condition of the army
in early 1946 see Ziemke, *The U.S. Army in the Occupation of Germany*,
pp. 223–4.

28 Biddiscombe, *The Denazification of Germany*, p. 61.

29 Clay personal to Hilldring, 8 December 1945, in Smith, ed., *The Papers of
General Lucius D. Clay*, vol. I, p. 130.

30 See Schnatz, *Tiefflieger über Dresden: Legende oder Wirklichkeit?*, pp. 145f., 'Ursachen
der Legendenbildung'.

31 The role of Neumann and the quote 'Nuremberg of the Common Man' (Jörg
Friedrich's phrase) appears in Olick, *In the House of the Hangman*, p. 119. For
the involvement of Marcuse as well as Neumann see Biddiscombe, *The Denazification of Germany*, pp. 23–5. See also Barry M. Katz, 'The Criticism of Arms:

The Frankfurt School Goes to War', in *Journal of Modern History*, vol. 59, no. 3 (September 1987), pp. 439–78.

32 Mark Blumenson, *Patton: The Man Behind the Legend 1885–1945*, p. 281.

33 Grossmann, *Jews, Germans and Allies*, p. 138.

34 Blumenson, *Patton: The Man Behind the Legend*, p. 281.

35 Ibid., p. 282.

36 Report of *Oeuvre de Secours aux Enfants* (OSE), cited in Grossmann, *Jews, Germans and Allies*, p. 140.

37 See Joseph W. Bendersky, *The Jewish Threat: Anti-Semitic Politics of the US Army*, p. 391. And for the following information about Keating's memorandum.

38 Clare, *Berlin Days*, p. 152. And for the major's further remarks.

II PERSIL WASHES WHITE

1   NARA College Park RG 260 390/47/19/1 Box 168 Records of the Office of Military Government, Bavaria, Weekly Intelligence Reports 1945–47 Intelligence Annex to Weekly Report for Period 8–15 Nov 45, p.5.

2   NARA College Park, as above, pp. 7f.

3   NARA College Park, as above, p. 12.

4   Account of conference in Koop, *Besetzt: Amerikanische Besatzungspolitik in Deutschland*, p. 111.

5   Biddiscombe, *The Denazification of Germany*, p. 64.

6   *Military Government Information Bulletin Number 64/21 October 1946*, p.27.

7   See Biddiscombe, *The Denazification of Germany*, p.72.

8   Ibid., p. 73.

9   Ibid., p. 69.

10 NARA College Park RG 260 390/47/19/1 Box 168 Records of the Office of Military Government, Bavaria, Weekly Intelligence Reports 1945–47 Periodic Report for Week Ending 28 August 1946, p. 18.

11 Quoted from report, as above.

12 Quoted in Olick, *In the House of the Hangman*, p. 183.

13 Biddiscombe, *The Denazification of Germany*, pp. 191f. And for the poll figures.

14 Ibid., p. 193.

15 Ibid., p. 199.

16 NARA College Park RG 260 390/47/15-16/6-3 Box 7 Public Safety 23 October–13 December 1946, Memorandum John P. Bradford to Mr Schweizer, 10 October 1946 Subject: Situation in Landkreis Vilsbiburg. And for the following quotation.

17 NARA College Park, as above, Memorandum John P. Bradford to Mr Schweizer, 11 October 1946.

18 Tooze, *The Wages of Destruction*, pp. 141f: 'In 1936 . . . 62% of all German taxpayers reported annual incomes of less than 1,500 Reich marks, corresponding to weekly earnings of just over 30 Reich marks.'

19 NARA College Park RG 260 390/47/15-16/6-3 Box 8 Denazification. Press conference of Bavarian government 22 June 1946.

20 *Military Government Information Bulletin Number 64/21 October 1946*, p. 8 (cont. p. 27).

21 Ibid., p. 27.

22 Biddiscombe, *The Denazification of Germany*, p. 73.

23 NARA College Park RG 260 390/47/19/1 Box 168 Records of the Office of Military Government, Bavaria, Weekly Intelligence Reports 1945–47 Periodic Report for Week Ending 16 October 1946, p. 18.

24 Biddiscombe, *The Denazification of Germany*, p. 74.

25 Figures in ibid., p. 81.

26 NA Kew WO Elten (War Crimes) Trial Petitions. Translation of signed statement by Hans Renoth 12 July 1945.

27 NA Kew WO 235/55, as above. Submission to C-in-C (2 pp.) and note initialled (illegible) by a brigadier of the Department of the Judge Advocate-General, 29 January 1946.

28 See entry by Brian Bailey in *Oxford Dictionary of National Biography* online edition 2010.

29 Law-Reports of Trials of War Criminals, The United Nations War Crimes Commission, Volume II, London, HMSO, 1947 (Case No. 10 . . . Trial of Josef Kramer and 44 Others) Part I p.4 B: THE CHARGE.

30 Ibid., Foreword, p. x.

31 Both quotations from lawyers' remarks at the Bergen-Belsen trial from Bower, *The Pledge Betrayed*, p. 182.

32 Law-Reports of Trials of War Criminals, The United Nations War Crimes Commission, Volume II, London, HMSO, 1947 Part XI, pp. 119f.

33 Bower, *The Pledge Betrayed*, p. 187.

34 Biddiscombe, *The Denazification of Germany*, p. 87.

35 See obituary of Sir Edward Playfair by Noel Annan in the *Independent*, 23 March 1999.

36 *Time* magazine, 12 November 1945, 'The Nations: Temperature Down' (satirical rendering of British accent the magazine's, not this author's).

37 Biddiscombe, *The Denazification of Germany*, pp. 89f.

38 See entry by Michael Carver in *Oxford Dictionary of National Biography* online edition 2010.

39 Noel Annan, *Changing Enemies: The Defeat and Regeneration of Germany*, p. 150.

40 Ibid., p. 163.

41 Koop, *Besetzt: Britische Besatzungspolitik in Deutschland*, pp. 76f.

42 Clare, *Berlin Days*, pp. 148f.

43 Figures in Annan, *Changing Enemies*, p. 206.

44 See the case of Paul Kistermann in the Aachen district 1946/47 in NA Kew FO 1013/303 Public Safety, Denazification (Farmers and Farm and Agricultural Workers), especially the report by Lt Col. C. H. Gilbert, Commander of North Rhine-Westphalia Regional Food Teams, to Regional Economic Officer, 22 March 1947, which details the lengthy history of this case.

45 Koop, *Besetzt: Britische Besatzungspolitik in Deutschland*, p. 77.

46 Biddiscombe, *The Denazification of Germany*, p. 109.

47 Report by Ian Cobain in the *Guardian*, 17 December 2005: 'The interrogation camp that turned prisoners into living skeletons'.

48 Ibid.

49 Biddiscombe, *The Denazification of Germany*, pp. 100f.

50 This volte-face seems to have been a conservative rather than a radical move by the British officials, who had become increasingly concerned about serious political and economic unrest in the Ruhr. The co-decision-making (*Mitbestimmung*) was in part designed to head off demands for wholesale nationalisation of the iron and steel industry. See Diethelm Prowe, 'Economic Democracy in Post-World War II Germany: Corporatist Crisis Response, 1945–1948', in *Journal of Modern History*, vol. 57, no. 3 (September 1985), pp. 451–82.

51 Biddiscombe, *The Denazification of Germany*, pp. 103–5.

52 Annan, *Changing Enemies*, p. 205.

53 Ibid.

54 For both quotes see *Hansard* online, HL Deb 12 November 1947 vol. 152 cc587-646. Lord Pakenham (1905–2001) later succeeded to the earldom of Longford. He served in Labour governments 1945–51 and 1964–8, but became especially well known to the general public in Britain for his quixotic campaigns, first against pornography and then for the release from prison of the serial child murderer Myra Hindley.

12 DIVIDE AND RULE

1 See John Young, 'The Foreign Office, the French and the Post-War Division of Germany 1945-46', in *Review of International Studies*, vol. 12, no. 3 (July 1986), p. 224.

2 Koop, *Besetzt: Französische Besatzungspolitik in Deutschland*, p. 181.

3   Quotation from ibid., p. 183.

4   See Kossert, *Kalte Heimat*, pp. 71–86, 'Deutscher Rassismus gegen deutsche Vertriebene'.

5   See Overmans, 'Das Schicksal der deutschen Kriegsgefangenen des Zweiten Weltkrieges', in Müller, ed., *Das Deutsche Reich, Band 10, Zweiter Halbband*, p. 464, for the IRC figures and opinions, and an analysis of the official death figures, which are contradictory. Koop, in *Besetzt: Französische Besatzungspolitik in Deutschland*, takes an uncharacteristically naive view of James Bacque's work in this regard, describing it as belonging to an 'independent study' (whatever that means in this context) and giving credence to the Canadian writer's sensational figure of between 167,000 and 300,000 – i.e. roughly one-fifth to one-third of all German prisoners of the French.

6   Koop, *Besetzt: Französische Besatzungspolitik in Deutschland*, p. 81.

7   Ibid., pp. 120f.

8   See *Der Spiegel*, 19/1970 4.5.1970, 'Ist das nicht ein wüster Traum? Spiegel-Report über das Ende des Zweiten Weltkriegs 1945'.

9   Interview with Dr Helmut Schnatz (born 1934), Koblenz, 11 June 2009.

10 Interview with Helmut Nassen (born 1928), Koblenz, 11 June 2009.

11 Biddiscombe, *The Denazification of Germany*, p. 160.

12 See interview with Egon Plönissen.

13 See NARA College Park RG 260 390/47/15-16/6-3 Military Government of Bavaria Record of the Intelligence Director/Records of the office of Director Intelligence Records 1946 Box 7 Memorandum Major Peter J. Vacca to Brigadier General Walter J. Muller, Director, 19 April 1946. And depositions by Frau Franziska Rösner and Frau Elisabeth Schmidtbaur.

14 Biddiscombe, *The Denazification of Germany*, p. 158.

15 Ibid., p. 164.

16 Ibid., p. 182.

17 Ibid., p. 181.

18 Lutz Niethammer, 'Schule der Anpassung: Die Entnazifizierung in den vier Besatzungszonen', in *Spiegel Special*, 4/1995, p. 93.

19 Biddiscombe, *The Denazification of Germany*, p. 182.

20 See Niethammer, 'Schule der Anpassung'.

21 Naimark, *The Russians in Germany*, p. 376. And for the following.

22 See *Der Spiegel*, 40/1992, 'Straflager: Vorhöfe zur Hölle', pp. 77–9.

23 Ibid., p. 81.

24 Naimark, *The Russians in Germany*, p. 383.

25 Ulrich Frodien, *Um Kopf und Kragen: Eine Nachkriegsjugend*, pp. 173ff.

26 Interview with Joachim Trenkner.

27 See Hermann Wentker, ed., *Volksrichter in der SBZ / DDR 1945 bis 1952: Eine*

Dokumentation, Schriftenreihe der Vierteljahrshefte für Zeitgeschichte, Bd 74, 1997, p. 10.

28 Biddiscombe, *The Denazification of Germany*, p. 137.

29 Interview with Lothar Löwe.

30 Ibid., p. 152.

31 Ibid., p. 143.

32 See Halder, '"Prüfstein . . . für die politische Lauterkeit der Führenden?"'.

13 HOPE

1   CC5797 Secret 'Conditions in Germany', 26 May 1946 From Clay to Chief of Staff, in Smith, ed., *The Papers of General Lucius D. Clay*, vol. I, pp. 212–17. And for the following.

2   John Lewis Gaddis, *The Cold War: A New History*, pp. 28f.

3   See Tony Judt, *Postwar: A History of Europe Since 1945*, p. 108.

4   For Stalin's speech see Gaddis, *The Cold War: A New History*, p. 94.

5   Kennan from Moscow, 26 January 1945, quoted in ibid., p. 106.

6   Text of Kennan's 'Long Telegram', 22 February 1946, available online at http://www.gwu.edu/~nsarchiv/coldwar/documents/episode-1/kennan.htm. (Some definite articles added by this author in lieu of cable's abbreviations.)

7   For the American response see Judt, *Postwar*, p. 110.

8   Figures in ibid., pp. 120f.

9   Ibid., p. 109.

10 Clay to Echols, 19 July 1946 (letter), in Smith, ed., *The Papers of General Lucius D. Clay*, vol. I, pp. 236–43.

11 See Clay to Byrnes (handwritten letter), 19 August 1946, in ibid., p. 255. Clay and his wife had visited the Byrnes on 10–12 July in Paris, where the Secretary was slogging through yet another meeting of foreign ministers (which meant that Clay would have been directly familiar with Molotov's manoeuvres). In the letter he thanked Byrnes for managing to 'raise my spirits' and for lending an ear to his local problems in Germany when the Secretary had the whole world picture to consider.

12 Ibid., p. 237, n.2.

13 From Clay personal to Schulgen, ibid., p. 247.

14 See *Time* magazine, 16 September 1946, 'Foreign Relations: Journey to Stuttgart'.

15 James F. Byrnes, speech in Stuttgart, 6 September 1946. Available online at http://usa.usembassy.de/etexts/ga4-460906.htm.

16 See John Gimbel, 'Byrnes' Stuttgarter Rede und die amerikanische Nachkriegspolitik in Deutschland', in *Vierteljahrshefte für Zeitgeschichte*, 20. Jahrgang, H. 1 (January 1972), pp. 39–62.

17 Lucius D. Clay, quoted in Beschloss, *The Conquerors*, p. 227.

18 From Clay for War Department, 16 September 1946, CC3769, in Smith, ed., *The Papers of General Lucius D. Clay*, vol. I, p. 263.

EPILOGUE

1 See article by Lars-Broder Keil in *Die Welt*, 6 August 2007: '*Vor 75 Jahren wurde in Deutschland die erste Autobahn eingeweiht. Von Adenauer. Und Hitler hatte nichts damit zu tun*' (75 Years Ago in Germany the First Autobahn was Inaugurated. By Adenauer. And Hitler Had Nothing to Do With It).

2 NA Kew FO 1013/701, 'German Officials: Dr Adenauer', Memorandum from (Sir) Charles Ferguson, General (retired), 10 July 1945. The writer of the letter (1865–1951) had gone on to be Governor-General of New Zealand.

3 Annan, *Changing Enemies*, p. 172.

4 Full text available at the website of Stiftung Haus der Geschichte der Bundesrepublik, http://www.hdg.de/lemo/html/dokumente/JahreDesAufbausInOstUndWest_erklaerungAdenauerRegierungserklaerung1949/index.html (in German).

5 Kossert, *Kalte Heimat*, p. 171.

6 Annan, *Changing Enemies*, p. 210.

7 Biddiscombe, *The Denazification of Germany*, p. 210.

8 Ibid., p. 211.

9 Ibid., p. 212.

10 Herausg. Norbert Frei, *Hitlers Eliten nach 1945*, p. 278.

11 Manchester, *The Arms of Krupp*, p. 780.

12 For the post-war careers of the IG executives see Jeffreys, *Hell's Cartel*, pp. 346ff.

13 Judt, *Postwar*, pp. 152f.

14 See Frei, *Hitlers Eliten nach 1945*, p. 284, for Adenauer's first memoranda of August 1950 regarding a possible 'contribution to defence' (*Wehrbeitrag*).

15 Kossert, *Kalte Heimat*, p. 171.

16 See in general ibid., pp. 266–305, 'Die Abwicklung des Kriegsverbrecherproblems'.

17 Quote from Schmid, ibid., pp. 299f.

18 See ibid., p. 277.

19 Frodien, *Um Kopf und Kragen*, pp. 180ff.

20 Interview with Lothar Löwe, Berlin, 25.03.2008 (these words in English).

21 Ibid.

22 Ibid.

23 For an account of this conference see Hans Dieter Müller, 'Ich werde Deutschland wiedervereinigen, ob Sie es glauben oder nicht: Geschichte und Analyse des Springer-Konzerns', part 1 in *Der Spiegel*, 3/1968 (15 January 1968).

24 Figures in *Der Spiegel*, Nr 17/1968, pp. 44f.

25 See Rudolf Augstein, 'Ist der Staat noch zu retten?' in *Der Spiegel*, 39/1967 (18 September 1967), a transcript of his lecture to the 'Freie Gesellschaft' of Hamburg at the Auditorium Maximum of the University of Hamburg, 7 September 1967.

26 For Springer in 1967 see Ben Witter, 'Mit Axel Springer am Wannsee', in *Die Zeit*, 49/1967, and for his charm in the early days, see Clare, *Berlin Days*, pp. 159–60. Clare ended up working for Springer after he left the army, and stayed with Springer-International as the company's UK representative until his retirement.

27 See http://www.axelspringer.de/artikel/Unternehmensgrundsaetze_40574.html (German) and http://www.axelspringer.de/en/artikel/Corporate-principles-for-a-liberal-world-view_40575.html (English). There are now five, with the reunification ambition replaced by one of German integration in Europe, and since 11 September 2001 a clause specifically emphasising support for the trans-atlantic alliance with America.

28 Judt, *Postwar*, pp. 271f.

29 Ibid., p. 355.

30 See *Time* 10 January 1955, 'It just happened'. The full English title was 'The Answers of Ernst von Salomon to the 131 Questions in the Allied Military Government "Fragebogen"', translated by Constantine Fitzgibbon with a Preface by Goronwy Rees.

31 See 'Es war ein Kampf: Rudolf Augstein über die Spiegel-Affäre und ihre Folgen', in *Der Spiegel*, 43/2002 (21 October 2002).

32 Margaret Bourke-White, *Dear Fatherland, Rest Quietly: A Report on the Collapse of Hitler's 'Thousand Years'*, p. 5.

33 Cited in part 4 of the *Spiegel* series by Peter Brügge on the 'new nationalism' in Germany, 'Rechts ab zum Vaterland', in *Der Spiegel*, 21/1967 (15 May 1967).

34 See the series in *Der Spiegel* about Axel Springer's rise, entitled 'Ich werde Deutschland wiedervereinigen, ob Sie es glauben oder nicht', in *Der Spiegel*, 3–8/1968.

BIBLIOGRAPHY

Diaries, memoirs and autobiographies

Alanbrooke, Field Marshal Lord, *War Diaries 1939–1945*, Danchev, Alex, and Todman, Daniel, eds. London, 2002.

Anonymous, *A Woman in Berlin* (translated from the German by Phillip Boehm). London, 2004.

Bourke-White, Margaret, *Dear Fatherland, Rest Quietly: A Report on the Collapse of Hitler's 'Thousand Years'*. New York, 1946.

Clare, George, *Berlin Days, 1946–1947*. London, 1989.

Dönhoff, Marion Gräfin, *Namen, die keine mehr nennt: Ostpreußen, Menschen und Geschichte*. Kreuzlingen/München, 2005.

Frodien, Ulrich, *Bleib übrig: Eine Kriegsjugend in Deutschland*. München, 2002.

— *Um Kopf und Kragen: Eine Nachkriegsjugend*. München, 2005 (paperback).

Gelfand, Wladimir, *Deutschland-Tagebuch 1945–1946: Aufzeichnungen eines Rotarmisten (Ausgewählt und kommentiert von Elke Schersjanoi)* (translated from Russian to German by Anja Lutter and Hartmut Schröder). Berlin, 2008 (paperback).

Krockow, Christina von, *The Hour of the Women* (translated by Krishna Winston). London, 1992.

MacInnes, Colin, *To the Victors the Spoils*. London, 1986 (paperback).

Mann, Fritz, *Frühling am Rhein Anno 1945*. Frankfurt, 1965.

Moran, Lord, *Winston Churchill: The Struggle for Survival 1940–1965*. London, 1968.

Nassen, Helmut, *Tagebuch des Helmut Nassen vom 6.3.45 bis 30.4.45*, Dr H. Schnatz, ed. (unpublished typescript, reproduced with permission of Dr Schnatz and Herr Nassen).

Padover, Saul K., *Psychologist in Germany: The Story of an Army Intelligence Officer*. London, 1946.

Reuth, Ralf Georg, Herausg., Goebbels, Josef, *Tagebücher*, Bd 5, *1943–45*. München, 2000.

Salomon, Ernst von, *The Answers of Ernst von Salomon to the 131 Questions in the Allied Military Government 'Fragebogen'* (translated by Constantine Fitzgibbon). London, 1954.

Smith, J. E., ed., *The Papers of General Lucius D. Clay*, vols I & II. Bloomington, Indiana, 1974.

Solzhenitsyn, Alexander, *Prussian Nights* (translated by Robert Conquest). London, 1977.

Welty, Joel Carl, *The Hunger Year: In the French Zone of Divided Germany 1946–1947*. Beloit, Wisconsin, 1993.

Wolff-Mönckeberg, Mathilde, *On the Other Side: Letters to my Children from Germany 1940–46*. London, 2008.

Secondary works

Aly, Götz, *Hitlers Volksstaat: Raub, Rassenkrieg und nationaler Sozialismus*. Frankfurt, 2005.

—— Herausg., *Volkes Stimme: Skepsis und Führervertrauen im Nationalsozialismus*. Frankfurt, 2006 (paperback).

Annan, Noel, *Changing Enemies: The Defeat and Regeneration of Germany*. London, 1995.

Bacque, James, *Other Losses: An Investigation into the Mass Deaths of German Prisoners at the Hands of the French and the Americans After World War II*. Toronto, 1989.

Beevor, Antony, *Berlin: The Downfall 1945*. London, 2002.

Bendersky, Joseph W., *The Jewish Threat: Anti-Semitic Politics of the US Army*. New York, 2000.

Beschloss, Michael, *The Conquerors: Roosevelt, Truman and the Destruction of Hitler's Germany 1941–1945*. New York, 2002 (paperback).

Biddiscombe, Perry, *Werwolf! The History of the National Socialist Guerrilla Movement 1944–1946*, Toronto, 1998.

—— *The Last Nazis: SS Werewolf Guerrilla Resistance in Europe 1944–1947*. Stroud, 2006 (paperback).

—— *The Denazification of Germany: A History 1945–1950*. Stroud, 2007.

Bischof, Günter, and Stephen E. Ambrose, eds, *Eisenhower and the German POWs: Facts against Falsehood*. Baton Rouge, Louisiana., 1992.

Blumenson, Mark, *Patton: The Man Behind the Legend 1885–1945*. New York, 1985.

Boog, Horst, Gerhard Krebs and Detlef Vogel, *Das Deutsche Reich und der Zweite Weltkrieg*, Bd 7, *Das Deutsche Reich in der Defensive*. Stuttgart/München, 2001.

Botting, Douglas, *In the Ruins of the Reich*. London, 2005 (paperback).

Bower, Tom, *The Pledge Betrayed: America and Britain and the Denazification of Post-War Germany*. New York, 1982 (published in the UK as *Blind Eye to Murder*).

Conot, Robert E., *Justice at Nuremberg*. New York, 1993.

Dallas, Gregor, *Poisoned Peace 1945 – The War That Never Ended*. London, 2005.

Davies, Norman, *Europe at War 1939–1945: No Simple Victory*. New York, 2008.

— and Roger Moorhouse, *Microcosm: Portrait of a Central European City*. London, 2002.

de Zayas, Alfred M., *Nemesis at Potsdam: The Anglo-Americans and the Expulsion of the Germans*. London, 1988 (revised edition).

— *A Terrible Revenge: The Ethnic Cleansing of the East European Germans*. New York and Basingstoke, 2006 (paperback).

Denny, Isabel, *The Fall of Hitler's Fortress City: The Battle for Königsberg 1945*. London and St Paul, Minnesota, 2007.

Eckert, Astrid M., *Kampf um die Akten: die Westalliierten und die Rückgabe von deutschem Archivgut nach dem Zweiten Weltkrieg* (Transatlantische Historische Studien 20). Stuttgart, 2005.

Evans, Richard, *The Third Reich at War*. London, 2008.

Fisch, Bernhard, *Nemmersdorf, Oktober 1944: Was in Ostpreußen tatsächlich geschah*. Berlin, 1997.

Frei, Norbert, Herausg., *Hitlers Eliten nach 1945*. München, 2007 (paperback).

Fussell, Paul, *The Boys' Crusade – American GIs in Europe: Chaos and Fear in the Second World War*. London, 2004.

Gaddis, John Lewis, *The Cold War: A New History*. New York, 2005.

Gellately, Robert, *Backing Hitler*. Oxford, 2001.

Gerlach, Christian, *Krieg, Ernährung, Völkermord*. Hamburg, 1998.

Grossmann, Atina, *Jews, Germans and Allies: Close Encounters in Occupied Germany*. Princeton, NJ, 2007.

Guckelhorn, Wolfgang, *Das Ende am Rhein: Kriegsende zwischen Remagen und Andernach*. Aachen, 2005.

Hastings, Max, *Armageddon: The Battle for Germany 1944–45*. London, 2004.

Henke, Klaus-Dietmar, *Die Amerikanische Besetzung Deutschlands* (Quellen und Darstellungen zur Zeitgeschichte, Herausgegeben vom Institut für Zeitgeschichte, Band 27). München, 1995.

Hitchcock, William I., *Liberation: The Bitter Road to Freedom, Europe 1944–1945*. London, 2009.

Höffkes, Karl, *Hitlers politische Generale: Die Gauleiter des Dritten Reiches*. Tübingen, 1986.

Jackson, Kevin, ed., *The Humphrey Jennings Reader*. Manchester, 2004.

Jacobs, Ingeborg, *Freiwild: Das Schicksal deutscher Frauen 1945*. Berlin, 2009.

Jeffreys, Diarmud, *Hell's Cartel: IG Farben and the Making of Hitler's War Machine*. London, 2008.

Judt, Tony, *Postwar: A History of Europe Since 1945*. London, 2005.

Käppner, Joachim, *Die Familie der Generäle: Eine deutsche Geschichte*. Berlin, 2007.

Knopp, Guido, *Die grosse Flucht: Das Schicksal der Vertriebenen*. München, 2002.

Koop, Volker, *Besetzt: Amerikanische Besatzungspolitik in Deutschland*. Berlin, 2006.

— *Besetzt: Britische Besatzungspolitik in Deutschland*. Berlin, 2007.

— *Besetzt: Französische Besatzungspolitik in Deutschland*. Berlin, 2007.

Kossert, Andreas, *Kalte Heimat: Die Geschichte der deutschen Vertriebenen nach 1945*. München, 2008.

Kynaston, David, *Austerity Britain 1945–1951*. London, 2007.

Large, David Clay, *Berlin: A Modern History*. New York, 2000.

Lilly, J. Robert, *Taken by Force: Rape and American GIs in Europe during World War II*. Basingstoke, 2007.

MacDonald, Charles B., *The Siegfried Line Campaign*. Washington, 1961.

Manchester, William, *The Arms of Krupp: The Rise and Fall of the Industrial Dynasty that Armed Germany at War*. New York, 2003 (paperback).

Mawdsley, Evan, *Thunder in the East: The Nazi-Soviet War 1941–45*. London, 2007.

Mazower, Mark, *Hitler's Empire: Nazi Rule in Occupied Europe*. London, 2008.

— *Inside Hitler's Greece: The Experience of Occupation 1941–44*. Cumberland, Rhode Island, 1993.

Middlebrook, Martin, and Chris Everitt, *The Bomber Command War Diaries: An Operational Reference Book 1939–1945*. Leicester, 2000.

Mihan, Hans-Werner, *Die Nacht von Potsdam: Der Luftangriff britischer Bomber vom 14. April 1945, Dokumentation und Erlebnisberichte*. Berg am Starnberger See, 1997.

Milton, Giles, *Paradise Lost: Smyrna 1922. The Destruction of Islam's City of Tolerance*. London, 2008.

Müller, Richard Matthias, ed., *Der Krieg, der nicht Sterben Wollte: Monschau 1945*. München, 2002.

Müller, Rolf-Dieter, ed., *Das Deutsche Reich und der Zweite Weltkrieg – Der Zusammenbruch des Deutschen Reiches 1945, Band 10, Zweiter Halbband: Die Folgen des Zweiten Weltkrieges*. München, 2008.

Muller-Hill, Benno, *Murderous Science: Elimination by Scientific Selection of Jews, Gypsies and Others, Germany 1933–1945* (translated by George R. Fraser). Oxford, 1988.

Naimark, Norman M., *Fires of Hatred: Ethnic Cleansing in Twentieth-Century Europe*. Cambridge, Massachusetts, and London, 2001.

— *The Russians in Germany: A History of the Soviet Zone of Occupation, 1945–1949.* Cambridge, Massachusetts, and London 2001 (paperback).

Olick, Jeffry K., *In the House of the Hangman: The Agonies of German Defeat, 1943–1945.* Chicago, 2005.

Roth, Markus, *Herrenmenschen: Die deutschen Kreishauptleute im besetzten Polen – Karriereweg, Herrschaftspraxis und Nachkriegsgeschichte.* Göttingen, 2009.

Schnatz, Helmut, *Tiefflieger über Dresden: Legende oder Wirklichkeit?.* Köln, 2000.

— *Der Luftangriff auf Swinemünde: Dokumentation einer Tragödie.* München, 2005.

Steege, Paul, *Black Market, Cold War: Everyday Life in Berlin 1946–1949.* New York, 2007.

Taylor, Frederick, *Dresden: Tuesday 13 February 1945.* London, 2005 (paperback).

— *The Berlin Wall, 13 August 1961–9 November 1989.* London, 2009.

Tooze, Adam, *The Wages of Destruction: The Making and Breaking of the Nazi Economy.* London, 2006.

Tusa, Ann, and John Tusa, *The Nuremberg Trial.* London, 1995.

Überschär, Gerd, ed., *Orte des Grauens: Verbrechen im Zweiten Weltkrieg.* Darmstadt, 2003.

Vogt, Timothy R., *Denazification in Soviet-Occupied Germany. Brandenburg 1945–1948.* Cambridge, Massachusetts, and London, 2000.

Waller, Maureen, *London 1945: Life in the Debris of War.* London, 2005 (paperback).

Weitz, John, *Joachim von Ribbentrop: Hitler's Diplomat.* London, 1992.

Whiting, Charles, *SS Werewolf: The Story of the Nazi Resistance Movement.* Barnsley, 1982 (paperback).

Ziemke, Earl F., *The U.S. Army in the Occupation of Germany.* Washington, 1975, and online http://www.history.army.mil/books/wwii/Occ-GY/.

Articles

Augustine, Dolores, 'Wunderwaffen of a Different Kind: Nazi Scientists in East German Industrial Research', in *German Studies Review*, vol. 29, no. 3 (October 2006).

Balfour, Michael, 'Another Look at Unconditionel Surrender', in *International Affairs*, vol. 46, no. 4 (October 1970).

Bauerkämper, Arnd, 'Zwangsmodernisierung und Krisenzyklen, Die Bodenreform und Kollektivierung in Brandenburg 1945–1960/61', in *Geschichte und Gesellschaft*, 25. Jahrg., H. 4, Ostdeutschland unter dem Kommunismus 1945–1990 (October–December. 1999).

Biddiscombe, Perry, 'Dangerous Liaisons: Occupation Zones of Germany and Austria, 1945–1948', in *Journal of Social History*, vol. 34, no. 3 (Spring 2001).

Born, Lester K., 'The Ministerial Collecting Center near Kassel, Germany', in *The American Archivist*, vol. 13, no. 3 (July 1950).

Farquharson, John, '"Emotional but Influential": Victor Gollancz, Richard Stokes and the British Zone of Germany, 1945–9', in *Journal of Contemporary History*, vol. 22, no. 3 (July 1987).

Ferguson, Niall, 'Prisoner Taking and Prisoner Killing in the Age of Total War: Towards a Political Economy of Military Defeat', *War in History*, vol. 11, 2004.

Gimbel, John, 'Byrnes' Stuttgarter Rede und die amerikanische Nachkriegspolitik in Deutschland', in *Vierteljahrshefte für Zeitgeschichte*, 20. Jahrgang, H. 1 (January 1972).

— 'US Policy and German Scientists: The Early Cold War', in *Political Science Quarterly*, vol. 101, no. 3 (1986).

Halder, Winfrid, '"Prüfstein . . . für die politische Lauterkeit der Führenden?" Der Volksentscheid zur "Enteignung der Kriegs- und Naziverbrecher" in Sachsen im Juni 1946', in *Geschichte und Gesellschaft*, 25. Jahrg., H. 4, Ostdeutschland unter dem Kommunismus 1945–1990 (October–December 1999).

Hockett, Jeffrey D., 'Justice Robert H. Jackson, the Supreme Court, and the Nuremberg Trial', in *The Supreme Court Review*, vol. 1990 (1990).

Katz, Barry M., 'The Criticism of Arms: The Frankfurt School Goes to War', in *Journal of Modern History*, vol. 59, no. 3 (September 1987).

Keil, Lars-Broder, 'Vor 75 Jahren wurde in Deutschland die erste Autobahn eingeweiht. Von Adenauer. Und Hitler hatte nichts damit zu tun', in *Die Welt*, 6 August 2007.

Kellerhof, Sven-Felix, 'Brisante Papiere aus dem Müllhaufen', in *Die Welt*, 2.11.2005.

Kudryashov, Sergei, 'Stalin and the Allies: Who Deceived Whom?', in *History Today*, vol. 45, no. 5 (May 1995).

McCreedy, Kenneth O., 'Planning the Peace: Operation Eclipse and the Occupation of Germany', in *Journal of Military History*, vol. 65, no. 3 (July 2001).

Niethammer, Lutz, 'Schule der Anpassung: Die Entnazifizierung in den vier Besatzungszonen', in *Spiegel Special*, 4/1995.

Prowe, Diethelm, 'Economic Democracy in Post-World War II Germany: Corporatist Crisis Response, 1945–1948', in *Journal of Modern History*, vol. 57, no. 3 (September 1985).

Range, Thomas, 'Totaler Krieg, Totaler Profit' at http://www.thomasrange.de/text1/kriegprofit.html (n.d.).

Slatoff, Walter J., 'GI Morals in Germany', in *The New Republic*, 13.5.1946, vol. 114, issue 19.

Wentker, Hermann, ed., *Volksrichter in der SBZ / DDR 1945 bis 1952: Eine Dokumentation* (Schriftenreihe der Vierteljahrshefte für Zeitgeschichte, Bd. 74), 1997.

Wiggers, Richard Dominic, 'The United States and the Refusal to Feed German

Civilians after World War II', in Steven Béla Várdy and T. Hunt Tooly, eds, *Ethnic Cleansing in Twentieth-Century Europe*, New York, 2003.

Willoughby, John, 'The Sexual Behaviour of American GIs during the Early Years of the Occupation of Germany', in *Journal of Military History*, vol. 62 (January 1998).

Young, John, 'The Foreign Office, the French and the Post-War Division of Germany 1945–46', in *Review of International Studies*, vol. 12, no. 3 (July 1986).

Other publications

Der Spiegel
Die Welt
Die Zeit
Frankfurter Allgemeine Zeitung
Hansard
New York Times
The Times (London)
Time magazine
Weekly Information Bulletin of the US Military Government, May 1946–December 1948

Archive sources

National Archives and Records Administration (NARA), College Park, Maryland, USA.*

National Archives (NA) (formerly Public Record Office), Kew, United Kingdom.*

*Individual document codes, references and record groups as specified in footnotes.

Interviews

Herr Götz Bergander, Berlin, Germany, 25 March 2008.
Frau Gisela Fries, Koblenz, Germany, 11 June 2009.
Herr Wolfgang Gückelhorn, Bad Breisig, Germany, 12 June 2009.
Herr Lothar Löwe, Berlin, Germany, 25 March 2008.
Herr Helmut Nassen, Koblenz, Germany, 11 June 2009.
Herr Egon Plönissen, Koblenz, Germany, 12 June 2009.
Herr Helmut Schnatz, Koblenz, Germany, 11 June 2009.
Mr Maurice Smelt, Penzance, United Kingdom, 4 October 2008.
Herr Joachim Trenkner, Berlin, Germany, 24 March 2008.
Frau Marlies Weber, Koblenz, Germany, 12 June 2009.

Index